GCSE
TECHNOLOGY

Trevor Bridges

EDUCATIONAL

Every effort has been made to trace copyright holders and to obtain their permission for the use of copyright material. The authors and publishers will gladly receive information enabling them to rectify any error or omission in subsequent editions.

First published 1995

Letts Educational
Aldine House
Aldine Place
London W12 8AW

Text: © Trevor Bridges 1995

Design and illustrations: © BPP (Letts Educational) Ltd 1994

All our Rights Reserved. No part of this publication may be reproduced, stored in a retrieval system, or transmitted, in any form or by any means, electronic, mechanical, photocopying, recording or otherwise, without the prior permission of Letts Educational.

British Library Cataloguing in Publication Data
A CIP record for this book is available from the British Library.

ISBN 1 85758 238 1

Printed in Great Britain by Ashford Colour Press, Gosport, Hants

Letts Educational is the trading name of BPP (Letts Educational) Ltd

Preface

This book contains examples of the work of many students. Without them and those whom I have taught throughout my career this book would not have been possible. To them this book is dedicated. I am also indebted to Mike Rose for his hard work and encouragement, and to Geoff Westell, who kindly read the manuscript.

Trevor Bridges 1994

Contents

Starting points		vi
Introduction		vi
How to use this book		vi
What is the National Curriculum		vii
Examination group requirements		xi
Design and technology		xi
Technology		xii
Examination groups and addresses		xiii
Coursework and examinations		xiv
Coursework		xiv
Tackling terminal examinations		xix

1	Identifying needs and opportunities	1
1.1	Introduction	1
1.2	Ways of working	1
1.3	Choosing a project	3
1.4	Consider your own qualities	8
1.5	Working with a range of materials	9
1.6	Recording project ideas	10
1.7	Starting your project	14

2	Generating a design and communicating ideas	18
2.1	The design specification	18
2.2	Identifying priorities	19
2.3	First ideas	21
2.4	Communicating ideas	27
2.5	Presenting research information	36
2.6	The design folio	38

3	Planning and making	42
3.1	Introduction	42
3.2	Planning	42
3.3	Making your solution	51

4	Evaluating work in technology	54
4.1	Introduction	54
4.2	Evaluating your own work	54
4.3	Evaluating the work of others	60
4.4	Case study	63

5	Information technology	66
5.1	Introduction	66
5.2	Word-processing (WP)	66
5.3	Databases	66
5.4	Spreadsheets	68
5.5	Integrated software packages	70
5.6	Graphics	71
5.7	Desktop publishing (DTP)	72
5.8	Simulations and models	72
5.9	Computer control	73
5.10	Information technology and society	74

6	Coursework case studies	75
6.1	Introduction	75
6.2	Map holder for skiers	75
6.3	Local history guide	79
6.4	New food from soya	83
6.5	Air-brush	87

7	Core knowledge	92
7.1	Materials	92
7.2	Tools and equipment	108
7.3	Manufacturing processes	115
7.4	Mechanisms	119
7.5	Structures and forces	123
7.6	Energy	126
7.7	Systems and control	129
7.8	Business matters	130
7.9	Technology and society	132

8	Graphic media option	135
8.1	Opportunities for graphic media	135
8.2	Technical drawing	136
8.3	Drawing systems	138
8.4	Pictorial and presentational techniques	139
8.5	Semiology and information graphics	141
8.6	Modelling	143

9	Food technology option	144
9.1	Food groups	144
9.2	Dietary preferences and needs	145
9.3	Characteristics and properties of foods	146
9.4	Factors affecting food properties	147
9.5	Food materials in cooking	147
9.6	The nutrient content of food	148
9.7	Food hygiene and legislation	149
9.8	Preserving food	150
9.9	Measuring food	152
9.10	Food preparation equipment	152
9.11	Preparation of balanced meals	155

10	Textile technology option	156
10.1	Natural fibres	156
10.2	Synthetic fibres	157
10.3	From fibres to yarns	158
10.4	Fabric construction	159
10.5	The properties of fabrics	160
10.6	Surface finishes for fabrics	160
10.7	Tools and equipment	161
10.8	The sewing machine	162
10.9	Seams	163
10.10	Openings and fastenings	163
10.11	Painting fabrics	165
10.12	Printing fabrics	165
10.13	Dyeing fabric	166
10.14	Adding decoration	167
10.15	Designing with textiles	168
10.16	Information technology and textiles	169

11	Data sheets	171
11.1	Measurements of everyday objects	171
11.2	Measurements of recreational items	172
11.3	Anthropometric measurements	172

11.4	Ergonomic factors	174
11.5	Electrical and electronic symbols	175
11.6	Electronic circuits	176
11.7	Basic food recipes	180
12	**Guidance sheets**	**182**
12.1	Undertaking research	182
12.2	Writing a questionnaire	183
12.3	Writing letters	184
12.4	Producing working drawings	185
12.5	Designing product tests	186

13	**Checklists**	**187**
13.1	Specification checklist	187
13.2	Costings checklist	188
13.3	Problems checklist	189
13.4	Details checklist	190
13.5	Planning checklist	191
13.6	Evaluation checklist	192
13.7	Pre-assessment checklist	193
Glossary		**194**
Index		**199**

Starting points

Introduction

How to use this book

This book is intended to help you gain a higher grade in your GCSE technology assessment. Your teacher may have given you a test towards the end of your school year nine (third-year secondary) and you may have some idea of how well you are doing in technology. Your previous years in secondary school have given you a chance to recognise those areas where you need to concentrate your efforts.

The structure of this book

Technology is about doing. It tests your ability to recognise and satisfy needs and opportunities. It is not only about learning specific things. If you are to be awarded a high grade for your efforts then it is important that you know what is expected of you. You must also know how good your work is and how you can improve it. This book will help you to do this in five ways.

1. It will tell you what coursework assessors expect. See Starting Points and Chapters 1–6.
2. It will help you assess your own work. See Starting Points and Chapters 1–6.
3. It will give guidance on what you can do to improve your work. See Starting Points and Chapter 13.
4. It will give you assistance with terminal examinations. See Starting Points and Chapters 7–10.
5. It will give you help with your coursework projects. Look at the examples throughout the book and refer to the data sheets, guidance sheets and checklists in Chapters 11–13.

This book explains the basis on which you will be assessed. There are opportunities for you to look at the work of other candidates and there is an explanation of how your final grade will be worked out. A number of pieces of work are studied and there is guidance from an experienced examiner on how the candidates could have improved their grades. This book will therefore also help you to estimate your own grade.

It is important to realise that this book is not a substitute for the teaching you have had or for the learning that takes place during your technology course. It is quite likely you will not have many 'theory' lessons; you are expected to learn by doing things. Your learning will not be restricted to technology lesson times and you will learn a great deal and gain relevant experience during other subject lessons and at other times. You cannot hope to cover everything and examiners realise this. The questions will allow you to show them what you know and understand and still get high marks even if there are gaps in your knowledge and experience. Use the following hints to help you make the best use of this book.

1. Ask your teacher for the name of the examination group that sets your examination and for the name and number of the syllabus you are following.
2. Refer to the charts on pp. xi – xii to check the requirements for your examination.
3. Check what percentages of the marks available are awarded to the different attainment targets (see pp. ix – x).
4. Since the coursework and projects set by the examination group often carry 60% of the marks you should study carefully the chapters devoted to practical work (Chapters 1–6) so that you can make sure you get your best marks.
5. Whenever you need information refer to the data and guidance sheets in Chapters 11–12.
6. Make sure you use a checklist from Chapter 13 for all stages of each project.

Introduction

7 Study the requirements for your terminal examinations.

8 Use the optional modules (Chapters 8–10) to give you an outline of the work needed for each of these. You will only need to study one option.

What courses are covered?

There is a variety of different GCSE syllabuses provided by the regional examination groups and their requirements are set out on pages xi–xii. The requirements for all GCSE examinations follow a similar pattern and you are unlikely to perform very differently whichever examination group's examination you are entered for.

Your GCSE assessment will depend on which syllabus you are entered for. The possibilities are:

- Technology;
- Design and Technology;
- Information Systems;
- Technology combined with another subject, such as catering or art;
- Design and Technology combined with another subject, such as the performing arts or business studies.

This book provides help with GCSE Technology and GCSE Design and Technology, but it will also be of help to those studying Technology or Design and Technology in combination with another subject. For those courses the technology or design and technology requirements are less demanding.

What is the National Curriculum?

The National Curriculum is a set of ten subjects that schools are obliged by law to teach in state-maintained schools. The National Curriculum is divided into core and foundation subjects. English, mathematics and science are the core subjects. Technology is one of the foundation subjects.

The key stages

You are now at Key Stage 4, which covers the two years taught between the ages of 14 and 16. It is the final key stage of your compulsory education.

- Key Stage 1: ages 5-7
- Key Stage 2: ages 7-11
- Key Stage 3: ages 11-14
- Key Stage 4: ages 14-16

The attainment targets

Each subject has its own set of aims and objectives, called attainment targets (ATs), which describe what you are expected to be able to do when studying a subject. Each attainment target has ten levels and you should aim to progress through the levels as you study.

In technology the attainment targets are as follows.

AT 1: Identifying needs and opportunities
AT 2: Generating a design
AT 3: Planning and making
AT 4: Evaluating
AT 5: Information technology

Just as you have been doing for Key Stage 3, you will be studying things that have been designed, looking for needs, having ideas, proposing solutions, making things, and evaluating your work and ideas and those of others. Throughout your work you should be given opportunities to study and use information technology.

Starting points

Technology or Design and Technology?

The distinction can be rather confusing and it is important that you understand which GCSE subject you are entered for. If you are taking a GCSE examination called Design and Technology you will be assessed on the first four attainment targets. However, if you are taking a GCSE examination called Technology you will be assessed on all five attainment targets.

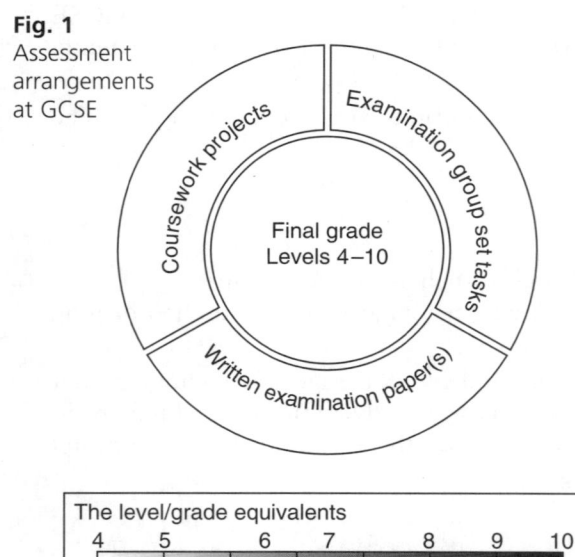

Fig. 1 Assessment arrangements at GCSE

Assessment

Your final assessment will be based on your performance in each of the attainment targets. The projects you do during your course will be assessed and these assessments will be combined with the results of examination papers in order to work out your final grade. Putting this simply, if you were to reach Level 8 in all five attainment targets then your overall level will be 8. On your GCSE certificate your grade will be shown by a letter, ranging from A★ (the highest grade) to G (the lowest grade). Level 8 will be equal to a B grade (see Fig. 1).

It is likely, however, that you will achieve different levels in each attainment target. In fact, the attainment targets are not all of equal worth, so you will need to study carefully the table showing the range of marks awarded to each attainment target by different regional examination groups (see pp. ix–x).

The average distribution of marks in GCSE Design and Technology is as follows.

Attainment target	% assessment
1: Identifying needs and opportunities	15%
2: Generating a design	25%
3: Planning and making	40%
4: Evaluating	20%

However, the average distribution of marks in GCSE Technology is slightly different.

Attainment target	% assessment
1: Identifying needs and opportunities	10%
2: Generating a design	20%
3: Planning and making	30%
4: Evaluating	15%
5: Information technology	25%

If you are taking Design and Technology for GCSE then Information Technology (AT5) will be assessed separately, but probably not by a GCSE examination. You may have lessons specifically for information technology or you may learn about it in the course of your other school subjects.

Although the GCSE syllabuses provided by the regional examination groups are similar the method of arriving at your final grade may differ from group to group. Each syllabus has coursework projects or assignments done in class time, and at least one terminal written paper.

The following diagrams (Figs. 2 and 3) will help you understand the assessment structure in Design and Technology. The assessment method for the London Examinations group is shown separately (Figs. 4 and 5). The percentages are not exact because they vary slightly from one examination group to another, but they give a good idea of the relative importance of each part.

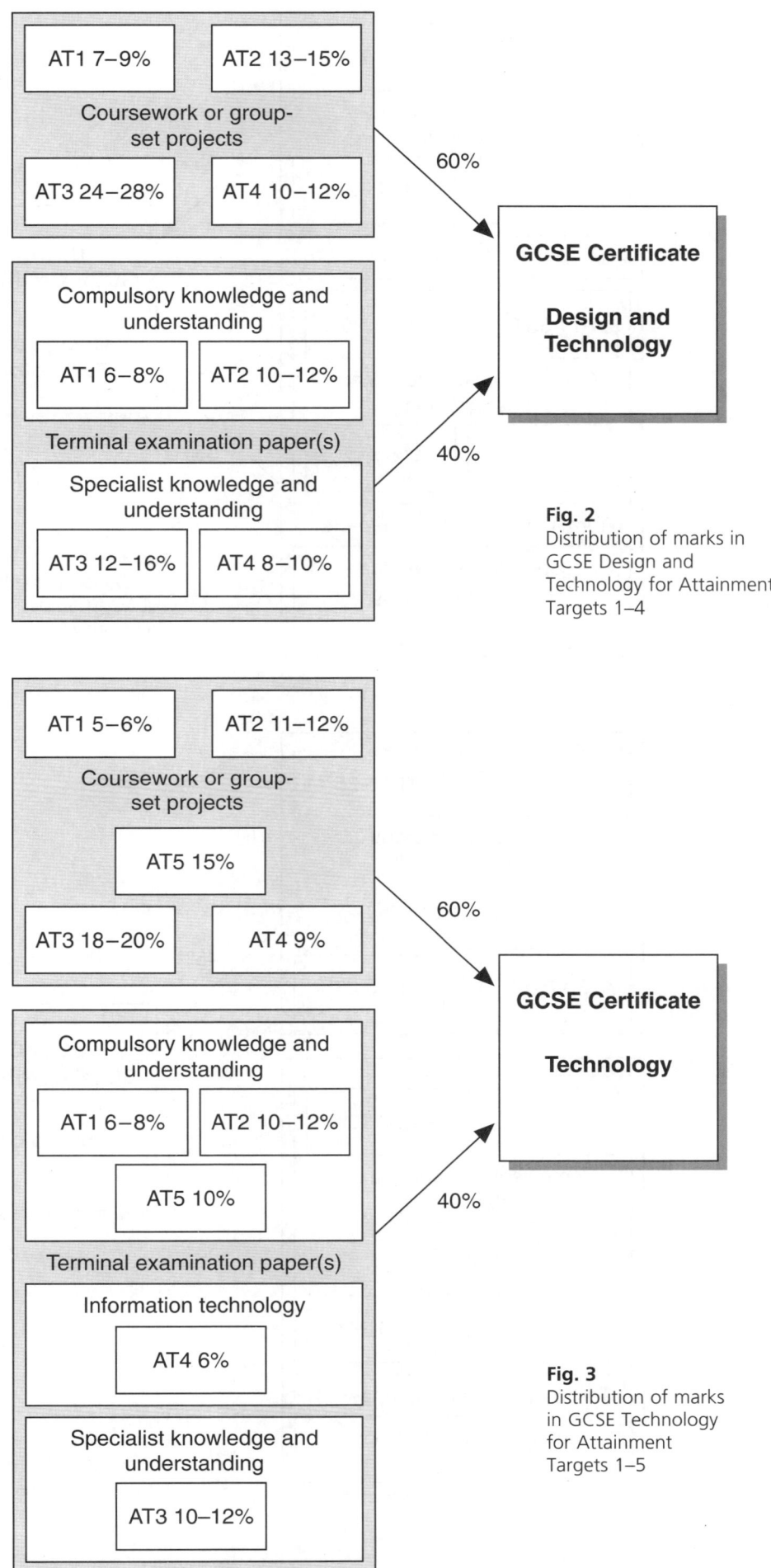

Fig. 2
Distribution of marks in GCSE Design and Technology for Attainment Targets 1–4

Fig. 3
Distribution of marks in GCSE Technology for Attainment Targets 1–5

Starting points

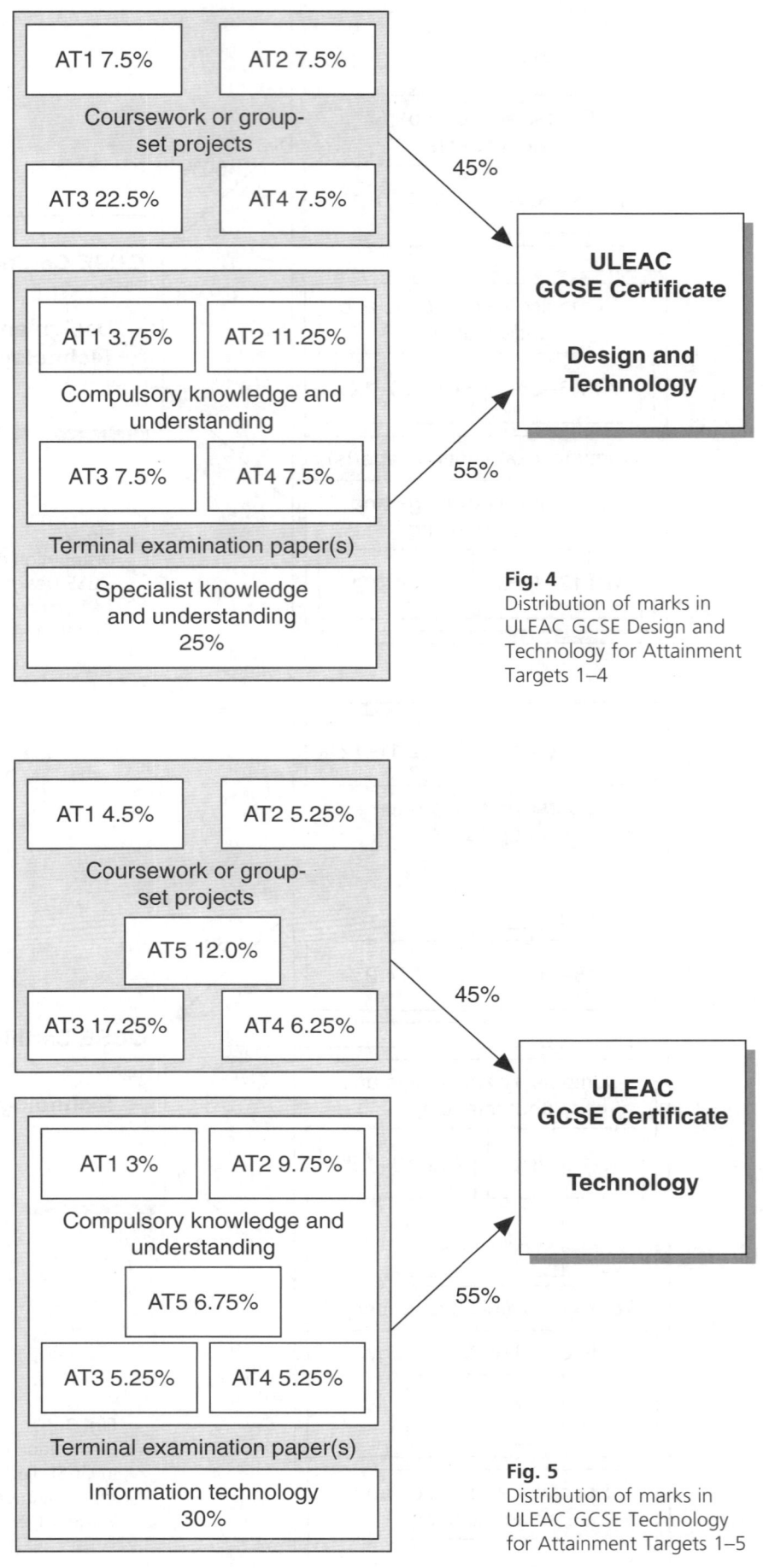

Fig. 4
Distribution of marks in ULEAC GCSE Design and Technology for Attainment Targets 1–4

Fig. 5
Distribution of marks in ULEAC GCSE Technology for Attainment Targets 1–5

Examination group requirements

Design and technology

Exam group and syllabus	Coursework requirements	Approx. time (hrs)	Written examination(s)	Duration (hrs)
WJEC	Task 1. Set by the examination group in advance. 30% Task 2. Set by the school (optional study). 30%		A. A task set by the group. 20% B. Questions on specialist knowledge and understanding. 20%	2 hours
ULEAC	Paper 1. An extended task based on the compulsory core. Paper 2. An extended task using a wider range of materials and techniques. Total 45%	22 hours 22 hours	Paper 3. Section A Structured questions based on the core of knowledge and understanding. 30% Section B Questions based on specialist knowledge and understanding. 25% Total 55%	2 hours
MEG (A)	Two pieces of work: ❐ Constructional materials. 30% ❐ Chosen option. 30%	40–60 hours	A. Structured questions on compulsory knowledge and understanding. 20% B. Structured questions on specialist knowledge and understanding. 20%	2–2.5 hours†
MEG (B)	Capability task 40% Resource task 20% (both tasks set by examination group)	20 hours 10 hours	A. Compulsory knowledge and understanding. 20% B. Specialist knowledge and understanding.* 20%	1.5–2.5 hours†
NEAB	A collection of best work: portfolio 20% project(s) 40%		1. Compulsory knowledge and understanding. 20% 2. Specialist knowledge and understanding. 20%	1.5–2 hours†
SEG 95/57	Assessment of course tasks. ❐ Construction materials. 30% ❐ Optional material. 30%		Section 1 Compulsory questions relating to a theme set by the group. 20% Section 2 Questions on specialist area of study. 20%	2 hours

* MEG Options (Syllabus B) – food, textiles, electrical systems, mechanical systems, structures.

† Depends upon level of entry – Foundation (Basic), Intermediate (Standard) or Higher.

Notes
Core = compulsory knowledge and understanding.
Chosen option = specialist knowledge and understanding (usually selected from graphics, food or textiles).

Starting points

Technology

Exam group and syllabus	Coursework requirements	Approx. time (hrs)	Written examination(s)	Duration (hrs)
WJEC	1. Portfolio of work, including practical work. 20% 2. A prescribed project set by the examination board and based on 'control' or a related topic. 40%		A. Questions based on the prescribed project. 20% B. Questions based on syllabus and including knowledge and understanding of IT. 20%	2 hours
ULEAC	Paper 1. An extended task based on the compulsory core. Paper 2. An extended task using a wider range of materials and techniques. Total 45%	22 hours 22 hours	Paper 3. Section A Structured questions based on the core of knowledge and understanding. 30% Section B Questions based on specialist knowledge and understanding. 25% Total 55%	2 hours
MEG (A)	Two pieces of work: 1. Constructional materials, together with graphics, food or textiles. 30% 2. Constructional materials with a little IT and chosen option. 30%	40–60 hours	A. Structured questions on compulsory knowledge and understanding. 20% B. Structured questions on specialist knowledge and understanding. 20%	1.5–2.5 hours[†]
MEG (B)	Capability task 40% Resource task 20% (both tasks set by examination group)	20 hours 10 hours	A. Compulsory knowledge and understanding. 20% B. Specialist knowledge and understanding, including relevant IT. 20%	2.5 hours[†]
NEAB	A collection of best work: portfolio 20% project(s) 40%		1. Compulsory knowledge and understanding, including IT. 20% 2. Control systems and IT. 20%	1.5–2 hours[†]
SEG 95/57	Assessment of course tasks. ❑ Construction materials. 30% ❑ Optional material. 30%		Section 1 Compulsory questions relating to a theme set by the group. Section 2 Questions on specialist area of study. Section 3 IT questions. 40%	2 hours

* MEG Options (Syllabus A) – mechanisms, structures, pneumatics, food, textiles.

[†] Depends upon level of entry – Foundation (Basic), Intermediate (Standard) or Higher.

Examination groups and addresses

MEG   **Midland Examining Group**
1 Hills Road
Cambridge
CB1 2EU
Tel: 0223 553311

NEAB   **Northern Examinations and Assessment Board**
Devas Street
Manchester
M15 6EX
Tel: 061 953 1180

RSA   **RSA Examinations Board**
Westwood Way
Coventry
CV4 8HS
Tel: 0203 470033

SEB   **Scottish Examination Board**
Ironmills Road
Dalkeith
Midlothian
EH22 1LE
Tel: 031 663 6601

SEG   **Southern Examining Group**
Stag Hill House
Guildford
GU2 5XJ
Tel: 0483 506506

ULEAC   **University of London Examinations and Assessment Council**
Stewart House
32 Russell Square
London
WC1B 5DN
Tel: 071 331 4000

WJEC   **Welsh Joint Education Committee**
245 Western Avenue
Cardiff
CF5 2YX
Tel: 0222 561231

Coursework and examinations

Coursework

During your course you will be expected to do a number of different tasks. These can be divided into two groups, resource tasks and capability tasks.

Resource tasks

These are likely to be short projects intended to help you learn and increase your practical skills. These tasks are likely to be closely directed by your teacher so that you gain the knowledge you are required to have.

Capability tasks

These are likely to be longer in duration and may be used for your final assessment. These tasks allow you to apply the knowledge, skills and understanding you have gained from the resource tasks.

Capability tasks will be designing exercises. The National Curriculum expects you to have some experience of designing three types of things:

1 **Artefacts** – objects or things, such as a packed lunch or a garden table.
2 **Systems** – groups of objects that together perform a function, such as a board game, telephone switchboard or a computer database that helps keep track of the dietary requirements of the residents of an old people's home.
3 **Environments** – places in which people work, live or play, such as an office or the interior of a car.

Sometimes a design can belong to two or even three of the groups. An aircraft, for example, is an artefact but it is made up of other objects, so it is therefore a system. Equally, it is also an environment in which people work and relax.

Contexts for tasks

The National Curriculum requires you to produce your designs and make solutions within a range of contexts. These contexts are:
- home;
- school;
- recreation;
- community;
- business and industry.

A chart similar to Table 1 may help you to see if your work shows a balance of experience across the five contexts. This balance should illustrate a range of:
- types of products;
- contexts;
- materials and techniques.

Coursework and examinations

	Type of project		
Context	Artefact	System	Environment
Home	KS1 Card calendar	KS2 Card/clay Easter egg	KS3
School		KS3 Electronic weather station	
Recreation	KS2 Plastic case for radio	KS1 Card/paper ball game	KS4 Fabric/metal low-cost tent
Community	KS4 Metal/plastic street signs	KS4 IT database	
Business and industry	KS4 Fun food mini-enterprise		KS4 Corporate image designs

Table 1
Sample chart showing how coursework tasks may be organised across Key Stages 1–4

You are expected to undertake projects that result in a range of outcomes suited to different situations. A chart like Table 1 will help you see where you need to concentrate your effort. The abbreviations KS1, KS2, etc. (Key Stage 1, Key Stage 2, etc.) have been used to indicate at what stage each project might have been undertaken.

Getting the highest marks for your coursework

Here are a few useful tips if you want to get the highest possible marks for your coursework.

1 **Know the rules.**

    If you know the rules assessors follow, you will be able to do what the assessors expect and avoid unnecessary work for which you may gain no extra credit. The following are important points.
    - The quality of your work counts more than the quantity.
    - You don't need to reach the same level in each attainment target for each project.
    - You must have done all the work for the lower levels in order to gain an award at a higher level.
    - You must show evidence of all your work. If the actual work is not available a photograph, video or other evidence must be provided.
    - Your projects do not need to be long, complex or take hundreds of hours to complete.
    - The attainment targets are not all worth the same (see pp. ix–x).

2 **Look at the levels of attainment.**

    Compare your work with the attainment levels for each attainment target. The examination syllabus describes what you have to do to satisfy each attainment target. By careful study of what is expected you will be able to estimate the level you have reached in each attainment target. The marks awarded for each level can be assessed in three stages.
    Stage 1: 'I have just started work at this level.' This is likely to earn the minimum marks for the level, for example, 8–9 marks in AT2 Level 5.
    Stage 2: 'I have produced good evidence of work at this level.' In AT2 at Level 5 this would earn about 10–11 marks.
    Stage 3: 'I have completed all the work for this level but not started work on the next level.' This might produce the maximum marks for the level, for example 12–13 marks in AT2 at Level 5.

3 **Work out your own grade.**

    Using the mark scheme provided by the examination group you can estimate the mark you are likely to get for each project. Remember that for each level there may

Starting points

be a range of marks available. For example, in London Examinations – Design and Technology, the marks for Attainment Target 1 at Level 6 range from 16–18.

If you are unsure whether you have reached a level compare your work with the descriptions for a lower level and if you have reached that level completely see if you have done any work of a higher standard. If you have, then your work may justify marks from a higher level.

4 Make sure you have submitted all of your work.

Check that you have not missed out any work. It's too easy to think that the early rough sketches are not worth credit. Maybe you made an initial mock-up or perhaps you have some photographs showing other parts of your work. Maybe you talked to someone but you didn't think their advice was helpful. If you did something appropriate you deserve credit. Even if the advice was not positive it may have influenced your ideas. List everything you do related to the project, and even if you have no other evidence submit the list for assessment. However, don't be tempted to make things up as you may be interviewed about them! When awarding marks your teacher and the assessor will be looking for *evidence* of what you have done.

5 Decide in which attainment targets you can most easily improve your performance.

You must think carefully which attainment target you will try to improve. Perhaps you have nearly reached a higher level in one of them already.

Table 2
Range of marks available at Levels 4–10 in each attainment target

		Level 4	Level 5	Level 6	Level 7	Level 8	Level 9	Level 10
Attainment target	1	2	3–4	5–6	7–8	9–10	11–12	13–14
	2	2–7	8–13	14–19	20–25	26–31	32–37	38–42
	3	2–14	15–28	29–42	43–56	57–70	71–84	85–98
	4	2	3–4	5–6	7–8	9–10	11–12	13–14

Reproduced from MEG (Syllabus A)

Look at Table 2 to find the proportion of marks awarded to each attainment target. AT3 is worth 40% of the total marks for a Design and Technology project. You can see that an improvement of one level in AT3 will improve your overall score by the largest number of marks. AT1 is only worth 15% of the total marks for a Design and Technology project, which means that an improvement of one level in AT1 will increase your overall score by fewer marks.

Look again at the marks in the table above. At Level 7 the range of marks available for AT1 is 7–8, a range of only 2, whereas the range of marks available for AT3 is 43–56, a range of 14. You may feel that you can more easily increase your overall mark by an improvement in AT3. Indeed, if you improved your performance in AT1 from Level 6 all the way up to Level 10 you would still get fewer extra marks than by improving in AT3 by less than one level!

6 Do some extra work.

If you have some time to spare after you have assessed your work and there is no other work you have failed to include in your assessment folder, then do some extra work on your project. Your grading is based on the evidence that you present; if you do the work you get the credit! Be careful not to repeat things; you cannot get the marks twice and it is better to concentrate on the things that will earn extra marks.

Use Table 2 to help you decide what to do.

- See what is missing from your project for you to reach a higher level in a particular attainment target. For example, you may not have shown expanded detail and modifications in your final design and hence may not be able to reach Level 8 in AT2. All that may be necessary are a few sketches of some of the changes you have made after thinking about your ideas.

- Make a list of the extra work necessary and alongside write the number of extra marks you will get if you do the work.
- Decide if you have done the work already. It is quite possible you have done the work but it's on a rough scrap of paper. No matter, include the scrap of paper anyway.
- Do things that can be done easily and quickly.
- Decide which of the remaining things will earn you the most marks. Generally, it is easier to gain marks at the lower levels.
- Do the work.

		Level 4	Level 5	Level 6	Level 7	Level 8	Level 9	Level 10
Attainment target	1				8			
	2			19				
	3			42				
	4		3					

A student has used this chart to estimate the marks for her own work. It may be quite easy to improve in AT4, since it is quite low, and improving from lower levels is easier than increasing from higher ones. However, it is worth remembering that increasing performance in AT4 by one level can only gain a maximum of three marks, but improving in AT3 could gain up to 18 marks.

Displaying your work for assessment

Examination groups do not insist that you put on an exhibition of your work, but some do require the work to be available for a visiting assessor or moderator. If you can make sure that it is carefully displayed when it is presented for assessment, with the best pieces on view, you will have a good chance of impressing the assessor.

Fig. 6 shows a display of work for a student's project on mechanical toys.

Fig. 6 A well presented display of project work

Starting points

Put yourself in the position of an examiner. What impression do you think the display gives? Make sure an assessor can see all the good things you have done so that he or she can give you the credit.

The self-check chart below may help you to decide how you can improve your coursework marks.

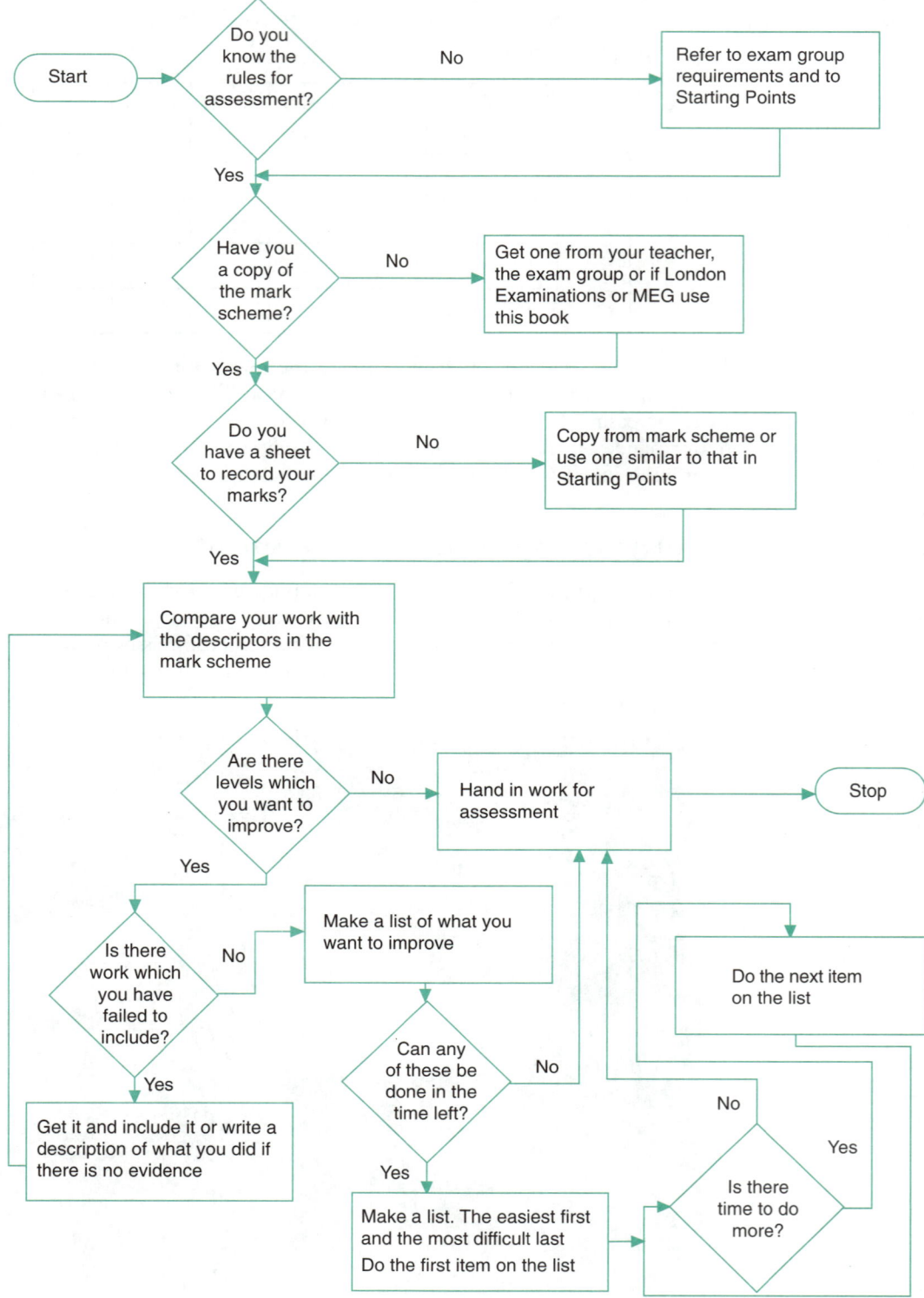

Fig. 7 Self-check list for improving coursework marks

Tackling terminal examinations

All examination groups:
- set at least one terminal exam (Northern Examinations set two);
- test a core of knowledge and understanding;
- test optional modules, either in Section B or, in the case of Northern Examinations, Paper 2;
- test using a range of question types, including:
  - multiple choice questions (London Examinations only);
  - short-answer questions;
  - structured-answer questions;
  - open-ended questions.

Tiered papers

All examination groups will set a range of papers, called tiered papers, aimed at different levels of ability. You should ask your teacher which tier you are entered for. Each paper allows you access to a limited range of grades. If you do particularly badly you will not be awarded a grade lower than the lowest grade available in that tier, in other words, you will not get nothing! However, if you do particularly well you cannot be awarded a grade higher than the top grade for the paper for which you are entered. It is important that you are entered for the tier to which you are best suited. Table 3 shows the range of grades available for each paper.

	NEAB	SEG	MEG(A)	MEG(B)	ULEAC	WJEC
Basic (Foundation)	G–C	G–C	G–C	G–C	G–C	G–C
Intermediate (Standard)	G–A	F–A	G–A	F–A	G–A	G–A
Advanced (Higher)	E–*A	D–*A	E–*A	E–*A	E–*A	D–*A

Table 3 Range of grades available for tiered examination papers

The focus of a written examination is on the experience you have had and what you have learned throughout your course. A written examination paper does not, of course, test in the same way as coursework. In particular, it is impossible for written examinations to test your 'making' ability. You will, however, be expected to show your ability to plan things. The level you are entered for will determine the difficulty of the questions and how much detail and depth is needed in the answer.

Starting points

The following example illustrates the differences between questions set at different levels (tiers). As you read through the question you can see that:
- as the tier increases the examiner expects more detail in your answers;
- at the basic level the examiner may allow you more freedom in your answer, whereas the detail in a question at the highest level gives a more precise requirement to the answer;
- at the basic level you are more likely to be faced with questions relating to a topic with which you are familiar, for example, 'fresh food'. At the higher level, in the example shown below, the subject is 'lawnmowers', with which you are less likely to be familiar;
- there may be easier questions at the basic level, which do not exist on the higher level papers, that is, the easiest questions on a higher paper may be more difficult than the easiest questions on a lower paper;
- the early parts of questions can be easy but get harder as you progress.

Basic level

Question. You are employed by a market research company. One of your customers, a supplier of fresh foods, wants to know whether there is a need for a new product to complement their range.

a) How would you find out where the supermarket gets its fresh food from?

b) What sources of information would you use to find out if there is a need for a new fresh product?

Intermediate level

Question. You are employed by a market research company. One of your customers, a supplier of fresh foods, wants to know whether there is a need for a new product to complement their range.

Devise a strategy to investigate this situation.

Higher level

Question. You are employed by a market research company. One of your customers, a supplier of lawnmowers, wants to know whether there is an opportunity to extend its product range.

a) Devise a strategy for investigating and reporting on the situation.

   You should:
   i) identify each of the key stages of your strategy;
   ii) order these in the form of a flow chart;
   iii) explain each of the stages you have identified.

b) Clearly state how you would implement your strategy, referring to each of the identified stages.

Now read the questions again and try to work out suitable answers. Before looking at the suggested answers given below, write out your answers on a sheet of paper. Remember, at the highest level the examiner will require a fairly comprehensive and detailed answer.

The following answers would be sufficient to gain all of the available marks.

Basic level

Question. You are employed by a market research company. One of your customers, a supplier of fresh foods, wants to know whether there is a need for a new product to complement their range.

a) How would you find out where the supermarket gets its fresh food from?

   Answer. Ask questions at the supermarket. Go to a library to find out where different foods come from.

b) What sources of information would you use to find out if there is a need for a new fresh product?

Answer. Produce questionnaires that ask customers if there is a need for a new fresh food. Ask customers about their eating habits. Produce prototype foods and use customers to evaluate them.

This answer is appropriate to Levels 4 and 5.

Intermediate level

Question. You are employed by a market research company. One of your customers, a supplier of fresh foods, wants to know whether there is a need for a new product to complement their range.

Devise a strategy to investigate this situation.

Answer.

Method – Find out criteria for new product, about money available, time scale, production costs, profit margin and at which group in society is the product aimed?

Research – Initial survey of potential customers, use question-and-answer techniques, identify social groupings.

Analyse research – From research discover whether there is a need for a new product. Produce report for client, outlining the advantages and disadvantages of producing the new product.

Manufacture prototype foods – Arrange testing of prototype food and packaging.

Analyse research – Brief client on final results.

This answer allows Level 8 to be reached.

Higher level

Question. You are employed by a market research company. One of your customers, a supplier of lawnmowers, wants to know whether there is an opportunity to extend its product range.

a) Devise a strategy for investigating and reporting on the situation.

   You should:
   i) identify each of the key stages of your strategy;
   ii) order these in the form of a flow chart;
   iii) explain each of the stages you have identified.

b) Clearly state how you would implement your strategy, referring to each of the identified stages.

Starting points

Answer.

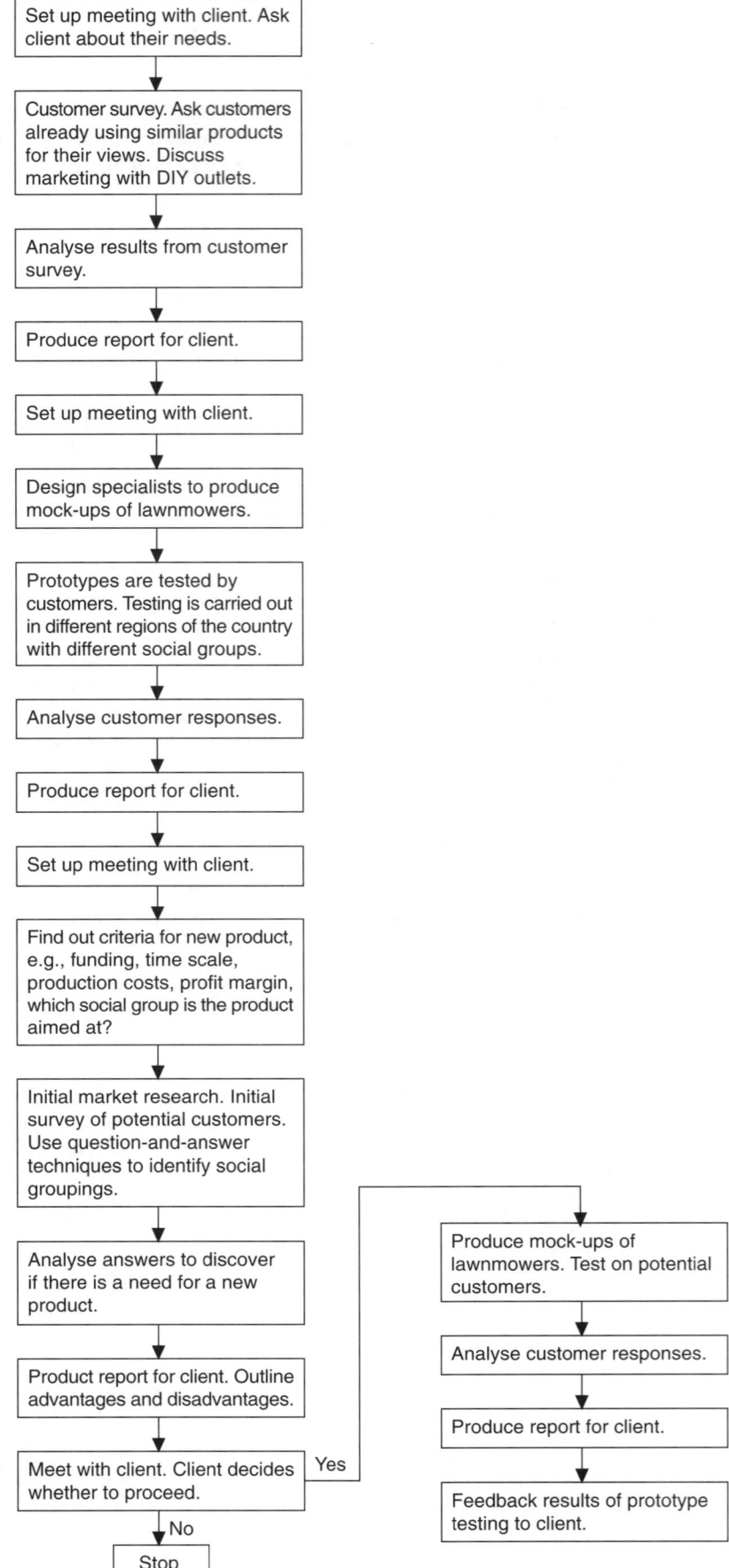

Notice that in the above answer both parts of the question have been answered together by including notes within the flowchart boxes. This answer allows Levels 8, 9 and 10 to be reached.

Although much of this examination requires written answers, any drawings should be done in pencil so they can be corrected easily if you make a mistake. There are frequently no right or wrong answers, only good and poor ones. The worst thing you can do is to leave a blank. If you really think you have no idea make a sensible guess. The examiner is there to give you marks and not to take them away, but do not be tempted to put down silly answers.

Although some short-answer questions will only require understanding from one area of knowledge or experience, longer-answer questions will require understanding from a range. Questions are set to test your ability in applying knowledge and understanding in several situations, such as selecting the most appropriate resources for a particular purpose.

You may find the following advice helpful as you approach your written examinations.

- Check that you know how many questions you will need to answer.
- Make sure you know which questions are compulsory and which are optional.
- Read through all the questions marking in pencil the ones you think you can answer best. (Only read the section or option for which you are entered.)
- Alongside each question it will say how many marks it is worth. If there are few marks then a simple answer is all that is needed.
- Some candidates find it easier to tackle any compulsory questions first. You are sure to find you can answer some of them without much hesitation. The rest may require more thinking.
- Ensure that you balance your time carefully between the sections.
- The early parts of most longer questions are easy, so don't be fooled into starting a question only to find that you can't answer the parts with the largest number of marks.
- Make sure that you write your answers clearly. If the examiner cannot read your answers you cannot be awarded the marks you might otherwise deserve.
- Plan your time carefully and don't spend too long on those questions that don't have many marks.
- If you have time left at the end go over the paper and make sure you have not made any silly mistakes. Remember, a few marks can make a big difference to the grade you get.

Hints

Multiple-choice questions

1. These will only be used by London Examinations for the lowest tier paper. There will probably be four choices. One will be unlikely to be correct. You should, therefore, only have to choose one from the other three.

Short-answer questions

2. Identify the key points in each question and make sure you answer them.
3. Be specific, e.g.,
    - Junior hacksaw, not just saw;
    - micro-switch, not just switch;
    - self-raising flour, not just flour;
    - muslin, not just cotton.
4. The space provided gives a clue to how much information is needed.
5. There are frequently a number of suitable answers.
6. Attempt all compulsory questions and parts of questions.
7. Use words and drawings, if possible.

Structured-answer questions

8. Structured-answer questions are based on a theme, e.g., a question concerned with transport. They usually get harder as they progress and later parts frequently draw upon information in earlier parts of the question.
9. Identify the key points in each question, underline them and ensure you answer those points.

Starting points

10. Answer all the parts of each question.
11. Only answer the required number of questions.

Open-ended questions

12. London Examinations may set questions where you are asked to give an extended answer. Such questions will only be set for the highest tier of entry. You are advised to proceed as follows:
    - look at the mark scheme (the marks are alongside the questions) and calculate how long you should spend on each part of the question;
    - underline the key points of the question;
    - decide upon the relative importance of each part;
    - note down quickly all the points you want to include in your answer;
    - answer the question while keeping a careful watch on the time;
    - illustrate your answer with diagrams, wherever possible;
    - check that you have answered all of the key points of the question.

Chapter 1   Identifying needs and opportunities

1.1 Introduction

'Pupils should be able to identify and state clearly needs and opportunities for technological activities through investigation of the contexts of home, school, recreation, community, business and industry' – National Curriculum statement.

You are likely to score better and gain a higher assessment if you identify a need and can show why you have selected your project. However, your teacher or the examination group may ask you to work within a specific theme.

Choose carefully

Choose your projects carefully so that you can do your best work, develop your understanding and, most importantly, reach the highest possible level of attainment.

Tackle a balanced range of projects

All examination groups require you to tackle a balanced range of projects constructed from a range of materials. It will not be sufficient for you simply to design and make a wardrobe of clothing for yourself, for example, or manufacture a collection of ornamental objects from ceramic materials.

Identify the needs yourself

You will gain most credit if you identify and solve your own problems. In other words, if you always ask your teacher what to do then you are not likely to reach the highest levels of attainment.

Ask the advice of others

You are expected to consult other people. Asking others for their advice is not 'cheating'. Your teacher will probably be the first one you ask for advice and guidance, but remember, your teacher is not an expert on everything. Your school friends may know a great deal about some things, if they have a special interest or hobby. Your teacher can help you avoid many pitfalls, such as tackling a project for which it will be impossible to find the resources or which will take too long. He or she will encourage you to identify problems, needs, opportunities and tasks yourself.

Identify opportunities

The world is full of technological opportunities waiting to be satisfied. Try to be broadminded. Satisfying those opportunities can be the easy part. Recognising they are there is the difficult bit.

1.2 Ways of working

There are a variety of ways in which you can work on your project.

Individual projects

You might be lucky enough to come up with a completely new idea. For example, you may do a job for which you need a special piece of equipment. If the equipment isn't available the only thing to do is to design and make it yourself. Very probably it will only be a simple device, but if it has not been thought of before and there is a widespread need for it, you could make your fortune!

Identifying needs and opportunities

About thirty years ago a person invented a portable folding bench. He had difficulty persuading any manufacturer to take the idea seriously since no-one had ever seen anything like it before. A leading manufacturer of workshop tools eventually took on the idea and since then several million have been sold.

Fig. 1.1 This portable folding bench has revolutionised home maintenance

Group projects

Some students find it helpful to work as a member of a group, which has the advantage of allowing you to tackle a bigger project. Group projects also allow each individual to contribute their own skills, while at the same time benefiting from those of others. National Curriculum work encourages group projects; the higher levels of attainment cannot be reached unless you work with others. If you are thinking of working in a group, you will have to consider the following.

- Can the project be divided into sufficient parts or tasks to enable each member of the team to be responsible for one task, or group of tasks?
- Can the project be planned so that all members of the group will be employed throughout the project?
- Are you all sure that you want to undertake the project?
- Are all of you willing to make an equal contribution of effort?
- Have you carefully thought through the problems you may have?
- What will you do if one member of the group loses interest, leaves the school or stops studying the subject?
- How will you record the contributions made by each member so that the work can be assessed?
- Who will own the completed project?
- How will project decisions be made?

Which of the following are good ideas for a group manufacturing project?
1. Toys for a children's play group.
2. Garden seating.
3. A computer workstation.
4. A puppet theatre.
5. Airline menus.
6. Protective clothing to be worn in a school science laboratory.

Give reasons for your choice.

Co-operative projects

These are similar to group projects but usually involve producing a range of different parts or products, which link together. On page 7 you can see details of an air-brush designed by a student.

> 1. What other pieces of equipment could be designed to go with the air-brush?
> 2. What advantages are there in working on a co-operative project rather than on a group or individual project?
> 3. Which of the following projects would lend themselves to co-operative working?
>   - badges and buttons;
>   - personalised pencil cases;
>   - shopping bags.

1.3 Choosing a project

Enterprise projects

However you choose to work, you could get involved in a product with commercial potential. A group from one school recorded some music. They designed the sleeve and the packaging for the audiotape, organised the publicity and sold the tapes, donating the profit they made to charity.

Fig. 1.2 Packaging for an enterprise project

Helping the community

Many students give up their spare time to work with community groups. The students may help in a local hospital, give assistance at a children's nursery, visit elderly people living alone, or raise money for a local charity by running sponsored events or helping with door-to-door collections.

One student helped in a home for elderly people where her aunt was a member of staff. She noticed that some of the residents were having difficulty lifting themselves out of their armchairs. The difficulty was that the residents did not have the strength to push themselves up on the arms of their chairs. They had been offered a 'grab' rail, to be fixed

Identifying needs and opportunities

above the seat and suspended from the ceiling, but this would have meant that the chairs couldn't be moved. Also, the student's aunt felt that such 'grab' rails would make the lounge look too much like a hospital. This situation provided a starting point for a project. The student tackled the problem with enthusiasm and some of her design work is shown below. It consists of a rising wooden seat operated by compressed air from an inexpensive compressor.

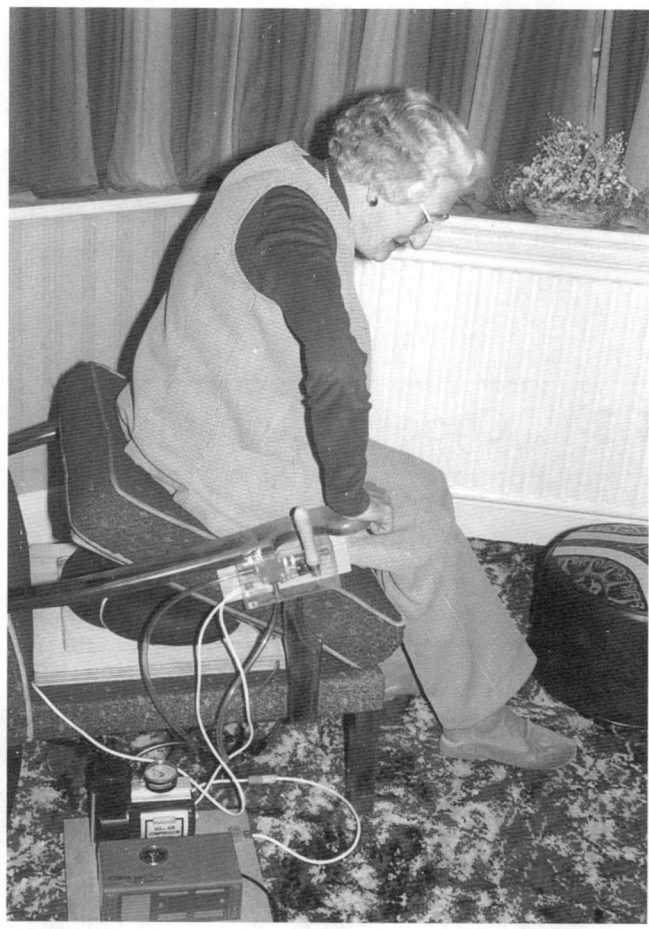

Fig. 1.3 Community project to aid elderly people

Design competitions

Design competitions are run on both a local and a national basis. You may see details advertised on school notice boards, in public libraries or your school may be sent them. If you want to enter one you can usually submit your entry as part of your technology coursework. You may already be working on a project that would be suitable, without alteration, for entry into the competition. It can do no harm to enter: you may do well and bring credit to yourself and to your school.

Choose something which interests you

To help you find a topic for a project, list your interests or illustrate them in a chart like fig. 1.4:

1.3 Choosing a project

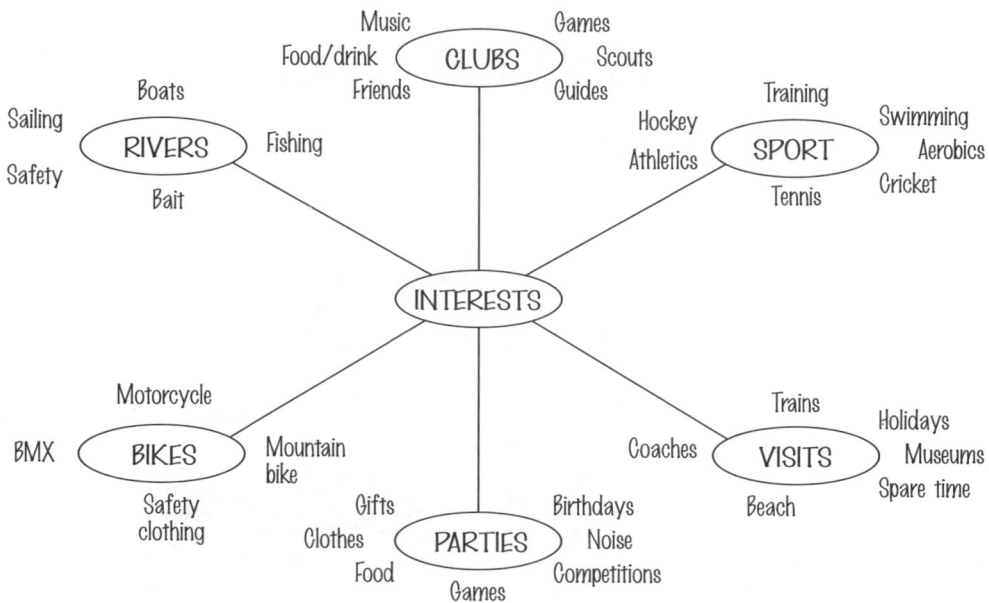

Fig. 1.4 Bubblechart based on the topic of 'interests'

One student developed the idea of personal interests further by considering the topic of games and sports. Different sports were listed under a number of headings. For example, athletics was identified as a sports category and within that the long jump. The student remembered the difficulty faced when deciding if a jump was a 'foul'. The design of a simple 'foul-jump indicator' was the result. It was placed at the edge of the take-off board and had a pressure-sensitive strip that switched on a light if the athlete's foot went over the front of the board.

Fig. 1.5 Foul-jump indicator

The world around you

You will often see things that are not being done as well as they might be. The following list may give you ideas for starting points:

- something that might be made easier to do or use;
- an article for sale, which might sell better if you made changes to it;
- people using too much energy;
- materials being wasted;
- operations that are not as safe as they might be;
- rubbish being blown around the streets;
- things being left in an untidy state.

Identifying needs and opportunities

? Look for ways in which this environment could be improved. Make a copy of the chart below and list some of the other dangers and difficulties you might find in a typical workplace.

Fig. 1.6 A hazardous environment

Food hygiene problems	Dangers with heat	Dangers with chemicals
1 _____	1 _____	1 _____
2 _____	2 _____	2 _____
3 _____	3 _____	3 _____
4 _____	4 _____	4 _____
5 _____	5 _____	5 _____
Organisational problems	Dangers with sharp tools	Electrical risks
1 _____	1 _____	1 _____
2 _____	2 _____	2 _____
3 _____	3 _____	3 _____
4 _____	4 _____	4 _____
5 _____	5 _____	5 _____

Evaluate and improve existing products

Whenever you use any product, ask yourself 'is this doing the job as well as it should?' If the answer is 'no', make a note of your discovery in your technology notebook. In this way you will gather a number of possible starting points for projects in the future. One student noticed that air-brushes were difficult to clean and that the only solution was a commercially made brush that used an expensive felt marker as the source of ink. The student designed an air-brush that could use any size of felt pen.

1.3 Choosing a project

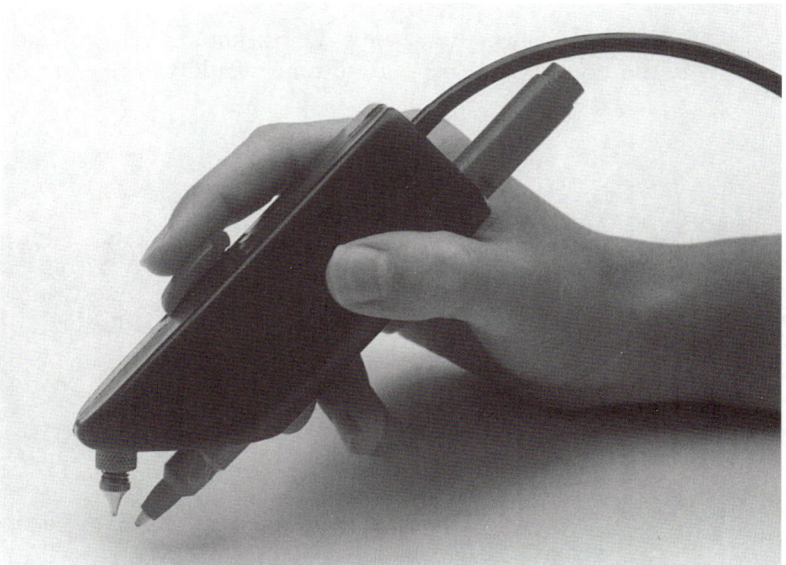

Fig. 1.7 Student's improved air-brush

? Can you see ways of improving these items or making them suitable for a wider range of users?

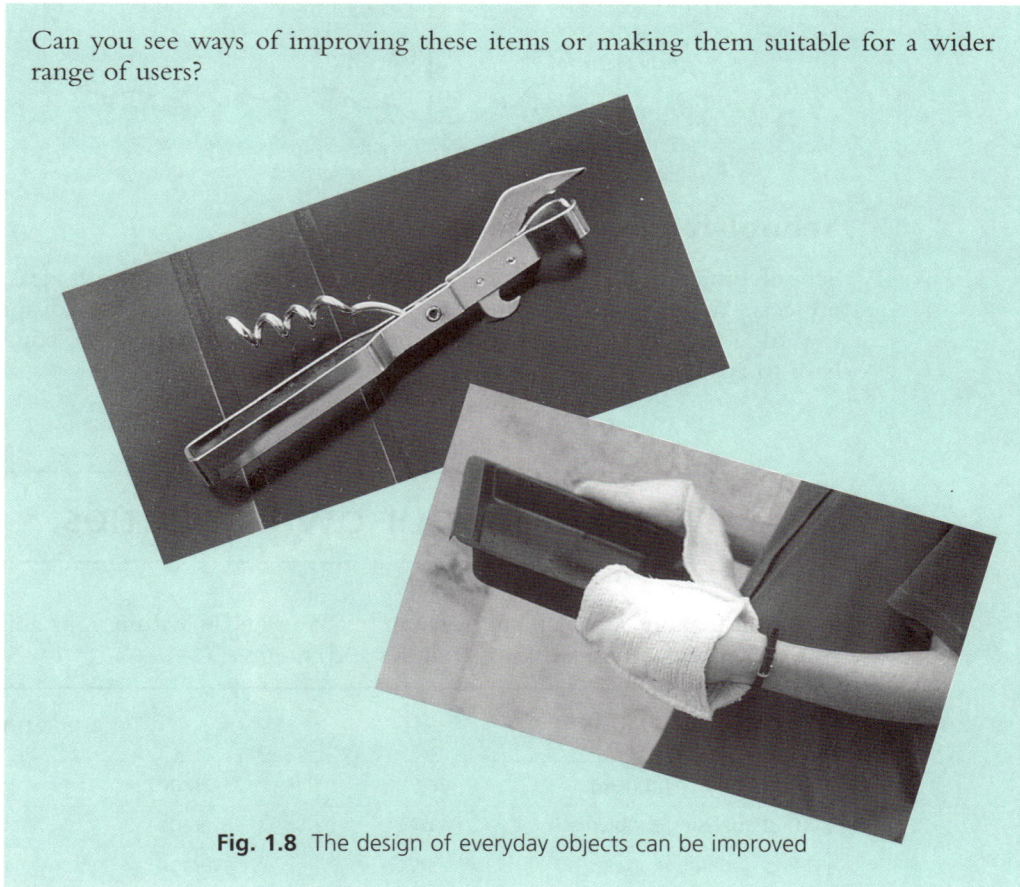

Fig. 1.8 The design of everyday objects can be improved

Analyse a situation

Analysing existing products and situations not only provides a start for projects, it also develops your evaluation skills. This is precisely what you are expected to do for Attainment Target 4.

Identifying needs and opportunities

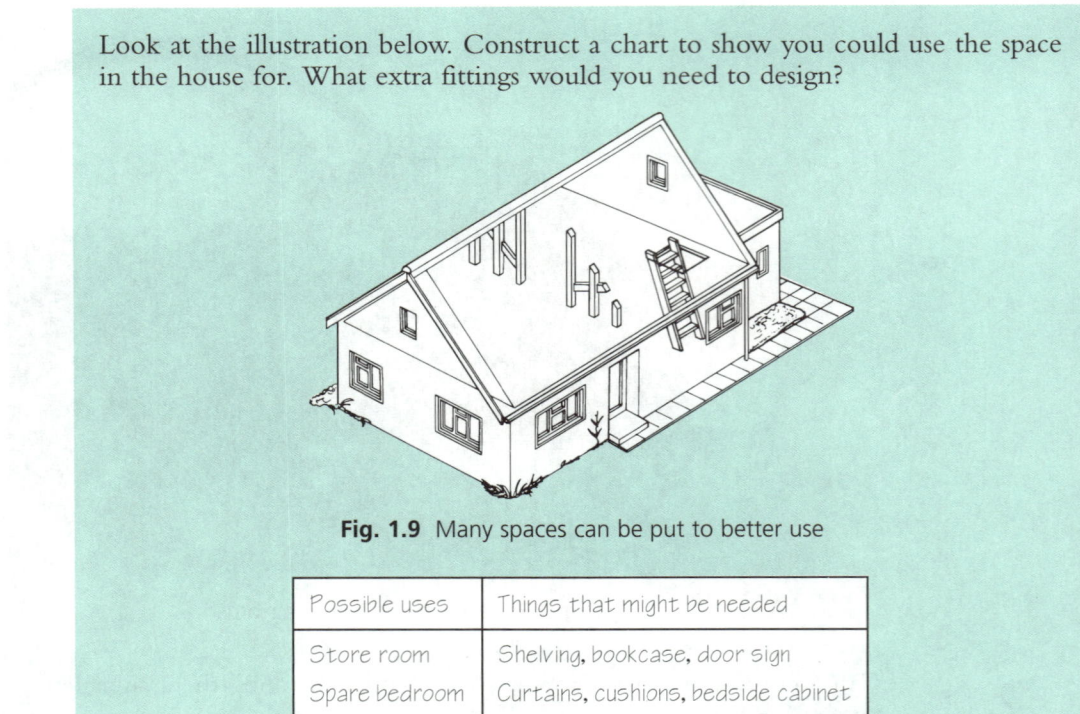

? Look at the illustration below. Construct a chart to show you could use the space in the house for. What extra fittings would you need to design?

Fig. 1.9 Many spaces can be put to better use

Possible uses	Things that might be needed
Store room	Shelving, bookcase, door sign
Spare bedroom	Curtains, cushions, bedside cabinet

School-focused projects

School projects, such as plays and concerts, can be sources of ideas for technology projects. When you work on such a project you will have the advantage of working towards a real goal. There will be time and money restrictions, of course, and you will have to co-operate with others.

1.4 Consider your own qualities

A way of making sure your project interests you and is within your ability is to remind yourself of your personal skills, qualities and interests.

Technology skills						Tick the appropriate boxes (✓)	
I find researching needs:	easy	☐	average	☐	difficult	☐
I find analysing problems:	easy	☐	average	☐	difficult	☐
I find generating ideas:	easy	☐	average	☐	difficult	☐
My graphic skills are:	very good	☐	good	☐	poor	☐
My models are:	very good	☐	good	☐	poor	☐
I find planning:	easy	☐	average	☐	difficult	☐
I find I need:	hardly any help	☐	average help	☐	constant help	☐
The quality of my practical work is:	very high	☐	high	☐	poor	☐
I find evaluating and testing my work:	easy and enjoyable	☐	average	☐	difficult	☐

Table 1.1 What technology skills do you have?

Personal qualities, interests and experience					Tick the appropriate boxes (✓)	
I can use:	most hand tools	☐	tools for one material only	☐	only a few tools	☐
I can use:	a range of machine tools	☐	machinery for one material only	☐	only one or two machines	☐
I have worked:	in a range of materials	☐	mainly in one material	☐	only in one material	☐
In my projects I have included:	information technology	☐	a little information technology	☐	no information technology	☐
I prefer to work on:	artistic projects	☐	technology projects	☐	a mixture of the two	☐
I like working:	alone	☐	with a partner	☐	as a team member	☐
I like making:	large projects	☐	average-size projects	☐	small projects	☐
I like making things that:	work	☐	have working parts	☐	have no working parts	☐
I like to learn:	new processes	☐	new processes when necessary	☐	prefer to stick with what I already know	☐
I prefer to do my work	at home	☐	at lunchtime	☐	in lessons	☐

Table 1.2 What are your qualities, interests and experience?

After completing these charts you will find it helpful to discuss them with your teacher.

1.5 Working with a range of materials

It is important to have experience in a range of materials. As your course progresses you could find that your experience has been limited to one main material or a small range of techniques. You should ensure that you widen your experience and that different materials are incorporated into your projects. You will often be advised not to consider materials until the problem is clearly identified, analysed, and a design brief and specification written. This is good advice but if you find yourself in the position of having to work in a different material, there are a few things you can do to help identify a suitable need.

Timber

Certain types of project lend themselves to solutions made in timber. You could look at your home for inspiration. In particular, you could identify areas where things need to be tidier or better organised. This may lead to the design of some form of container or small piece of furniture.

Plastics

Since plastics are easily cleaned and not easily affected by hot water they have many uses in the bathroom or kitchen.

Metals

By their nature, metals are usually strong and durable. They are best used in situations where objects are subject to bangs and knocks. If you have a motor-cycle or if you help with repairs to the family car, you may find that specialist tools or simple jigs, clamps or

Identifying needs and opportunities

attachments are needed. Alternatively, if you are aesthetically inclined you could tackle a jewellery project in metal, which of course can be combined with other materials.

Textiles

Consider the different uses of fabrics. Think about how, say, hats have changed over the ages or how and why they differ in various countries and cultures. Consider how you could use fabrics to made a new version of an old idea. What about folding furniture for use on picnics? Not only chairs but tables and other objects use fabrics for surfaces that might otherwise be made from rigid materials. One student designed lightweight scenery for a play when his drama group was invited to travel abroad and he needed to keep the weight of the luggage low. Consider the special properties of fabrics. For example, fabrics are usually light, flexible and available in large pieces.

Food

Find out why certain foods are eaten at certain times. You could consider seasons, religious festivals, celebrations and different locations. What about trying to present food in different ways so as to make it attractive to a wider market? What about investigating kosher foods and trying to promote them to others? Study what is available in different supermarkets and how and why it has changed over the years. Conduct a survey on 'value for money' in restaurants. Find out why people eat out and why some don't.

Ceramics

Ask yourself what special properties ceramic materials have. Could these special properties enable them to be used for a new purpose? Have you considered an enterprise project using ceramics? Have you tried digging your own clay and firing it in a kiln you designed yourself? Try visiting the library to find out how ceramics are fired in other countries. How are building bricks made hard?

Graphic media

Try designing some packaging for an old product to give it a new image. What about gaining valuable information technology experience by exploring the possibilities of graphics software? Graphics projects can often be done at home, although you will be expected to show some evidence that it is your own work. What about designing the packaging for some product you have already designed? How about a multilingual instruction booklet?

Since many of your projects are based on a general theme, it is likely that you will need to incorporate a range of materials. Be realistic. A project should not only be done because it satisfies the requirements of the examination. Tackling a realistic and meaningful project will be much more enjoyable; you are likely to perform better and reach a higher level of attainment.

1.6 Recording project ideas

Brainstorming

Arrange for a group of friends or classmates to sit around a large table, clear the table of distractions and appoint one person as scribe. Their task will be to write down everyone's ideas. It is important that the scribe does not contribute ideas or they may miss something suggested by the others. Begin with a topic, problem or theme and allow all members of the group to call out ideas. The scribe writes them down as quickly as

1.6 Recording project ideas

possible. After a few minutes there may be as many as twenty or thirty ideas. Some may not seem directly connected to the theme but they will certainly give you ideas to think about. One group, asked to brainstorm the theme of 'security', came up with this list.

> Alarm — lock — insurance — key — bank — money — safe — paper — combination — burglary — robber — man — woman — child — birth — embryo — social — abortion — death — weapons — guns — war — ammunition — President Bush — Nato — Star Wars — Warsaw pact — Gadaffi — Rushdie — Moslem — faith — belief — hiding place — The Hobbit — Tolkien — books.

Fig. 1.10 Brainstorming ideas on the subject of 'security'

At this point the session was stopped, as the topics had moved quite a long way from 'security'. It is interesting to see, however, that topics you certainly would not have expected were mentioned: Moslem, abortion, books. One student was motivated to develop a project about locks and another to design a personal alarm. Another student thought it would be interesting to develop this session further and the group brainstormed the topic of 'babies'. It resulted in the development of a set of kitchen scales!

> Babies — birth — embryo — reproduction — life — contraception — clinic — NHS — BUPA — flowers — fertilisation — in-vitro fertilisation — hospitals — doctors — nurses — surgeons — midwife — family — post-natal — clinic — baby care — child weight — scales — health visitor.

Fig. 1.11 Brainstorming ideas on the subject of 'babies'

Brainstorm some of these topics. You may be surprised at the results.
1. Animals
2. Open spaces
3. Spare time
4. Recycling rubbish
5. Packaging
6. School holidays
7. Birthdays
8. Music
9. Things I hate
10. The weather
11. Love stories
12. Fashion

Bubblecharts and spidergrams

Another approach that can help is to write down a list of all the important points in a topic. You can show this in the form of a bubblechart or spidergram and then add subtopics to each topic. This will help you think generally about the problem. When considering the theme of children's learning toys, one student made a list of the important points (as the student saw them) and presented them in the chart below. It shows how thoughts were developing, one thought triggering off another.

Identifying needs and opportunities

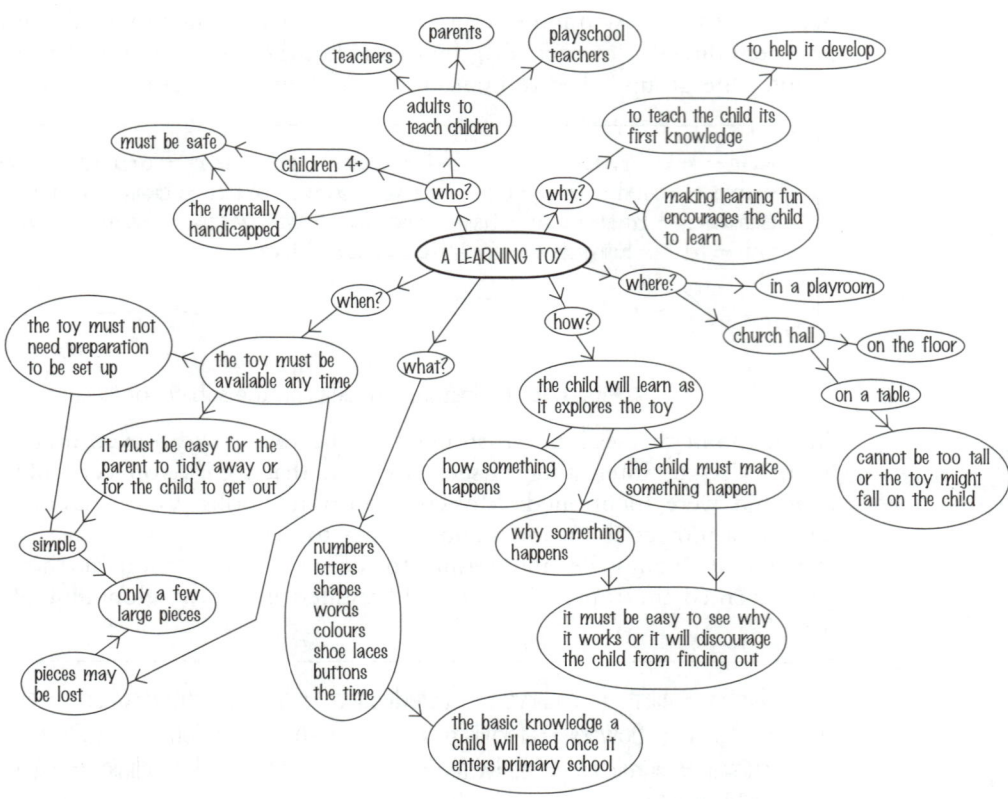

Fig 1.12 Bubblechart of ideas generated by considering 'A Learning Toy'

The student could equally have drawn a chart, which could have included a number of columns, like this one:

CHILDREN	LEARNING	PLACES	SAFETY	EASE OF USE	FUN
Hand-size	Alphabet	Playschool	Non-toxic	Simple	Colourful
Strength	Numbers	Home	Rounded	Sizes	Movement
Handicap	Shapes	Table	No corners	Number of pieces	Noise
Teachers	Words	Church hall	Not heavy		Activity
	Shoelaces	Playroom	No loose bits	Simple rules	Not boring
	Time				

Fig. 1.13 Chart describing ideas generated by considering 'A Learning Toy'

> **?** Consider the topic of storing food. Spend about five minutes putting down your thoughts in either a bubblechart similar to this one, or in columns. 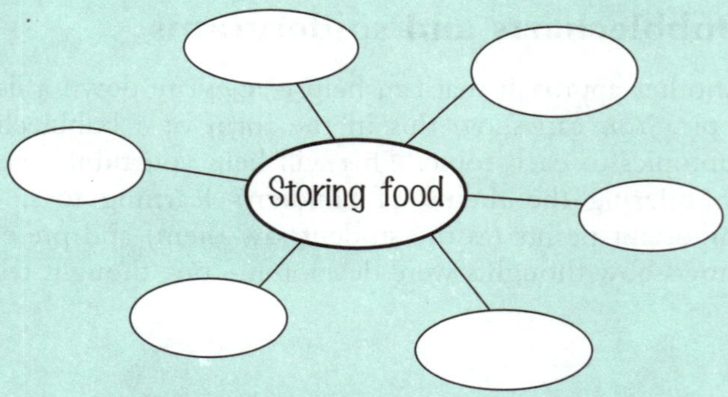
>
> **Fig. 1.14** 'Storing food' bubblechart

1.6 Recording project ideas

This bubblechart shows what you might have included.

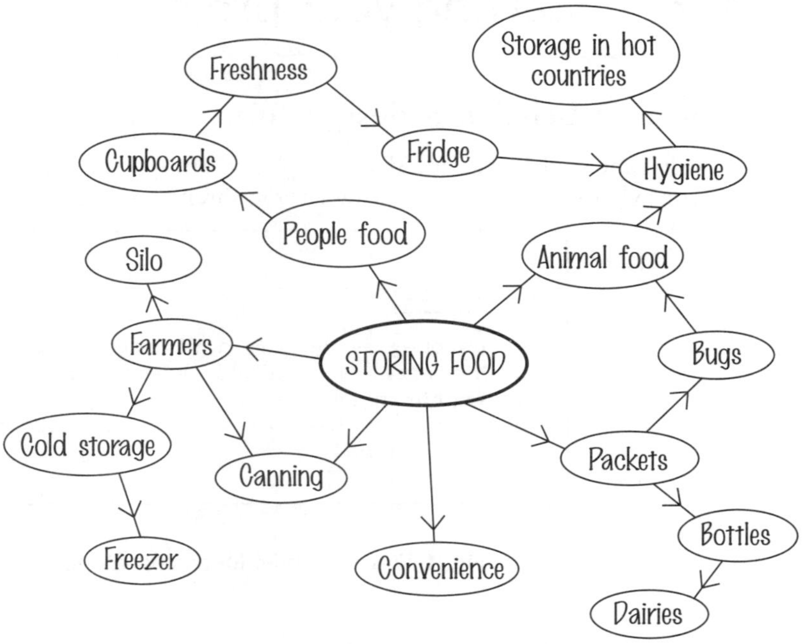

Fig. 1.15 Possible ideas for 'Storing food' bubblechart

You may have missed some of the points. Ask yourself why you missed the points. Did you get stuck in a rut? Did you only think of human food? You may have restricted yourself to food in the home. You must try to think widely. Different foods from different countries should be considered. If you think you are getting into a rut, stop, remind yourself of the starting point and you might be able to continue in a different direction. Of course, you may have included other relevant points.

Index cards

Use index cards or photocopied chart templates to record your thoughts. You may not need the idea today, but tomorrow you will have forgotten it.

Fig. 1.16 shows how you could organise information on your index card or chart.

Subject	Apples	Date	20/10/9X

Detail of idea
     A device to pick apples from high in a tree
 Where did the idea come from?
     When on holiday in Kent			

Possible uses of idea   Could use myself or sell idea to manufacturer
 Good points   Lots of apple trees
                 Dangerous to climb
 Weak points   Maybe other products exist
                  Customer may prefer to use a stick			

Possible improvements Identify unique selling points to make it more attractive			

Fig. 1.16 Index cards can be used to record project ideas

Identifying needs and opportunities

1.7 Starting your project

Stating a brief in a design folio

A well-expressed brief should be simple, to the point and expressed neatly. It should explain what the problem is and what you intend to do about it.

```
Design brief

A customer is having difficulty turning
on her bath taps because she has lost the
strength in her hands. Devise a method
that will enable her to turn on and off
the bath taps.
```

Fig. 1.17 Design brief for a new bath-tap design

Hints for writing a design brief

1. Make it short and to the point.
2. Include only relevant details.
3. Don't give a hint of a solution.
4. Use broad terms such as 'container' or 'system' rather than 'box' or 'filing cabinet'.
5. Highlight KEY words.

Analysing the need

Analysing a need means dividing it into key parts, asking questions and providing answers. Begin by listing everything you want to find out and where you might go for the answers. You should go to the place that most easily gives you the answers to your questions. Here are some of the questions a student posed in a project on bathroom design for the disabled, with suggested answers. You may have other ideas.

Question	Where to go for answer
1. Does the customer have the same problem with both taps?	Telephone or visit customer.
2. What are the dimensions of the taps?	Customer's home.
3. How much room is there next to the bath?	Customer's home.
4. Would differently shaped taps help?	Plumbers' merchant and customer's home.
5. Can the plumbing be modified?	Discuss with plumber.

Fig. 1.18 Analysing a need by question-and-answer

Hints for analysis of the problem
1. Break down the problem into key parts.
2. Ask questions that need researching.
3. Search for answers from the most appropriate source.
4. Record findings in your design folder.

Research

When you have analysed your problem, you will need to collect information to help you design a solution. This research should be presented in your design folder. Research is not intended to pad out your folio and, if irrelevant, will not impress the assessor. The golden rule is: if you don't need the information to help solve the problem or satisfy the need, don't waste time looking for it. Use your time sensibly. You could get information by asking an expert, by reading a book, or by cutting out sections from newspapers and magazines. Because you will be using the work of someone else this is called secondary research. Undertaking a survey or doing experiments to find out things that cannot be obtained from secondary research is called primary research.

You may need to find out information by experiment. You could, for example, find out what finish will look best on a small table by applying a variety of finishes and then asking other people's opinions. Or you may wish to undertake a trial tasting of some foodstuff you are 'designing'. You might want to find out what shapes children like or what colour is best for a kitchen appliance. You should record your findings and, where appropriate, take photographs.

Primary research can take a long time, so before spending time on it check that the information you need is not available from secondary sources.

What kind of information do you need?

Sometimes it can be very frustrating to have to wait for a reply to a letter. Would it have been better to have telephoned in the first place? Do you know precisely what you want to find out? Simply asking for information about materials may not be enough. On page 184 you will see how to write a letter asking for information.

The kind of information you will need is likely to be one or more of the following:
- ideas;
- background information;
- evidence to back up a theory or an idea;
- information about gaps in the market;
- guidance with an idea;
- technical information;
- other sources of information.

The chart on page 182 tells you some of the places to go for information. It could save you a lot of wasted time. Make sure that the following information is included in your project folder:
- what you did;
- where you went;
- who you spoke to;
- what questions you asked;
- what you found out;
- the importance of the information you obtained.

Here is the research material produced by a student who wanted to design educational toys for young children.

Identifying needs and opportunities

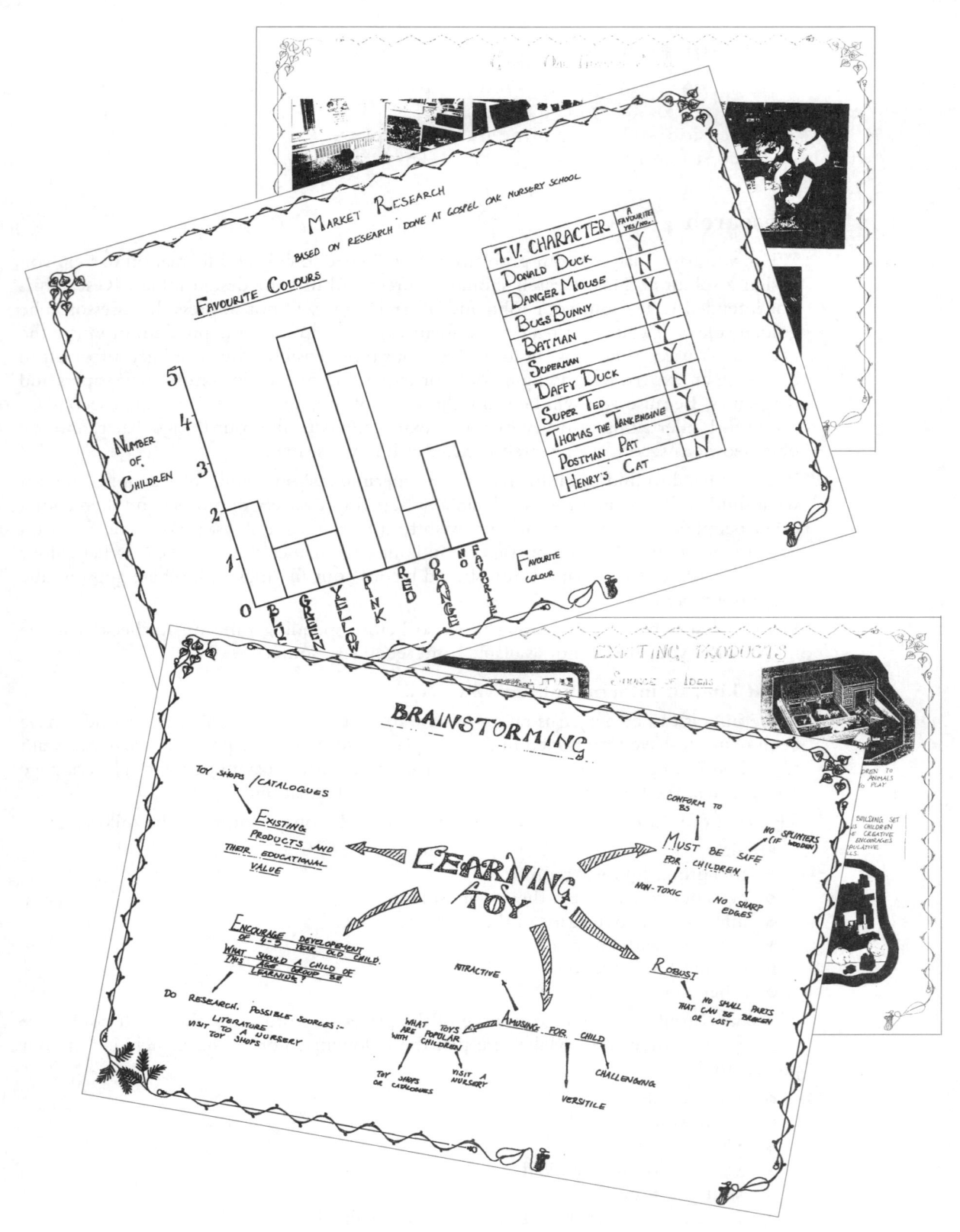

Fig. 1.19 Market research on children's toys

The research work has been clearly presented and shows that the student has observed children in a school with which he may not be familiar. He has asked questions to establish the likes and dislikes of the children (primary research). Existing toys have been studied and their particular features noted (secondary research). The student has presented his work well but he could have gone further in his investigations. The brainstorming has probably helped him gain ideas from other people.

In addition, the following might have been possible:
- toys from other countries and those used in earlier times could have been studied, e.g., by visiting museums;

- the children could have been interviewed and a tape-recording presented, together with a summary;
- the opinions of teachers and parents could have been sought;
- it may have been useful to find out which kinds of learning toys sell best;
- the student could have studied advertising material and packaging in order to improve them.

Hints for good research

1. Know what aspects or areas you want to find out about.
2. Go to the most appropriate source of information.
3. Record all your findings – not just the most helpful, but also any information that contradicts what you believe.
4. Choose an effective way to present the research in your design folio.

Checklist

Do you know what kind of project is expected of you?
Have you any original ideas?
Do you want to work as part of a group or co-operative?
Can you do something to benefit others?
Are you interested in what you are planning?
Have you considered your previous experience?
Have you discussed your ideas with others?
Have you observed and identified a real need?
Have you written a design brief?
Have you analysed the need and decided what to find out?
Have you done all the necessary research?
Do you still think your idea has a good chance of success?

Chapter 2 Generating a design and communicating ideas

2.1 The design specification

Once you have prepared a design brief you need to produce a design specification. This is a set of targets that you want to achieve. It will outline the restrictions placed upon you by the problem. It needs to be as open as possible and allow a wide range of solutions, but it must contain considerably more detail than the brief. The specification must also describe those factors over which you have no control, such as maximum size allowed or time deadlines.

Suppose you have been asked to design a first-aid kit for a hiker. Your specification might look something like this:

> The first aid kit must:
> 1. Contain all the necessary medical kit.
>   (LIST THE CONTENTS)
> 2. Be small enough to be carried in the outside pocket of a day rucksack.
> 3. Be waterproof.
> 4. Have no sharp edges or corners.
> 5. Have separate compartments for the corners.
> 6. Be able to be made with the school facilities.
> 7. Be able to be made by me.
> 8. Be able to be made in the time available.
>   (STATE HOW LONG IT MIGHT TAKE IN HOURS)
> 9. Be able to be tested so that an evaluation can be made at the end.

Fig. 2.1 Design specification for a hiker's first-aid kit

Points 6, 7, 8 and 9 are common to most projects but you should include them for completeness. If you are required to write a specification you will get most of your marks for the points that are specific to the given situation. The points listed must relate to the task in hand. There is little point is including general or vague comments, such as 'not too expensive' or 'use the correct materials'.

Here is a student's specification for a range of quick meals for diabetics. The points are concisely written and relevant to the need.

High-starch carbohydrate quick meals

1. The product must be a balanced range of meals that must be suitable for diabetic consumption.

2. Each meal must be packaged to allow easy transport, storage, display and microwave reheating.

3. The product must be commercially appealing both on the supermarket shelf and after re-heating.

4. The selling price must not be greater than £1.85.

5. The products must be developed and trial tastings completed within four months.

Fig. 2.2 Specification for a diabetic range of quick meals

A candidate drew up this specification for a solution to the 'bath tap problem', described in Chapter 1. The notes at the side indicate mistakes that have been made.

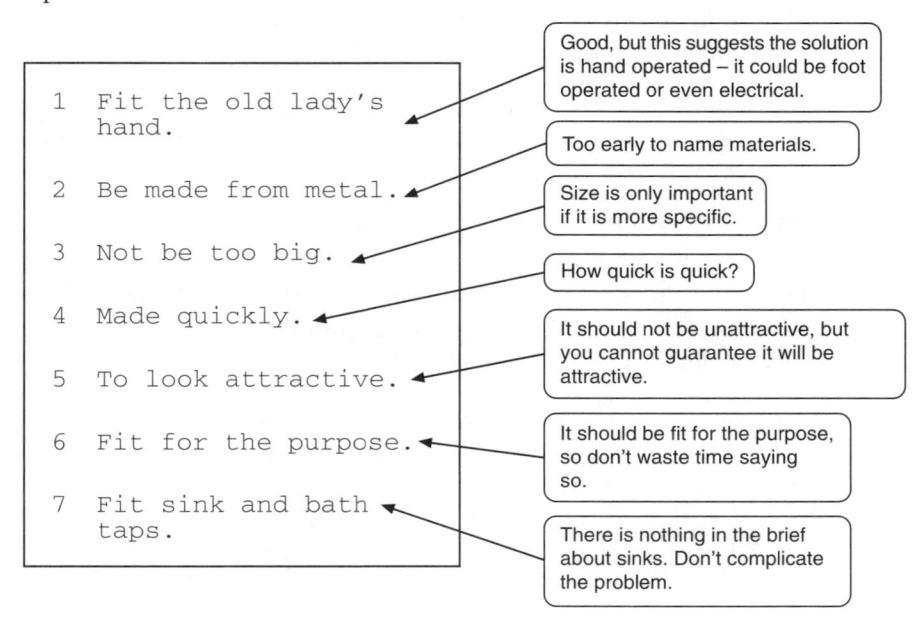

```
1  Fit the old lady's
   hand.
2  Be made from metal.
3  Not be too big.
4  Made quickly.
5  To look attractive.
6  Fit for the purpose.
7  Fit sink and bath
   taps.
```

- Good, but this suggests the solution is hand operated – it could be foot operated or even electrical.
- Too early to name materials.
- Size is only important if it is more specific.
- How quick is quick?
- It should not be unattractive, but you cannot guarantee it will be attractive.
- It should be fit for the purpose, so don't waste time saying so.
- There is nothing in the brief about sinks. Don't complicate the problem.

Fig. 2.3 Commentary on a student's design spedification

Although it is well presented the specification is badly expressed and will not help to produce a good solution. It is unrealistic and far too limiting. It does not allow for a wide range of solutions.

2.2 Identifying priorities

Whenever you draw up a design specification ensure it is realistic. When you carry out your project you will try to meet all the points in the specification, but some will be more important than others. You should consider the following points.

- Most designing is for people.
- People will be happier if they can use things safely and in comfort.
- Well-designed things work properly.
- Designs need to be pleasant to look at and to live with.
- Consider cost carefully – people like value for money.

In particular, the following aspects are important.

Reliability. Will the solution work or is it likely to need frequent maintenance?

This need will vary. You may be designing something that has to be left unattended for long periods, such as a remote weather station, or the item may be designed for one-time use, such as a simple label for sale goods.

Safety. Is the solution safe?

You must make sure that your designs are safe. When making toys, for example, you must avoid sharp edges and painting with lead-based (poisonous) paints. Remember, the elderly and the young are particularly at risk. Be careful when preparing food, since hygiene is particularly important.

Performance. How well does it work?

Put simply, designs only have to be as good as they need to be. Think about doing things in different ways to find the best method. Consider the bath tap problem described in Chapter 1. You could, of course, design an attachment for the tap, which would be easier to grip or to hold. But it might be even easier for the customer to use the tap if you were able to connect the attachment to levers so she could operate it with her foot. An electrically operated solenoid valve (like those inside automatic washing machines) could also be fitted. However, there are no prizes for making things more complicated (and more expensive) than they need to be.

Cost. How affordable is the solution?

All designing will be constrained by a budget or by what the market will be prepared to pay.

Appearance. Will the solution be attractive?

Appearance is the way things look. Everything has an appearance but not everything is pleasing to look at, and what is pleasing to one person may seem ugly to another.

An awareness of good proportions is important and you may find the so-called 'golden ratio' helpful.

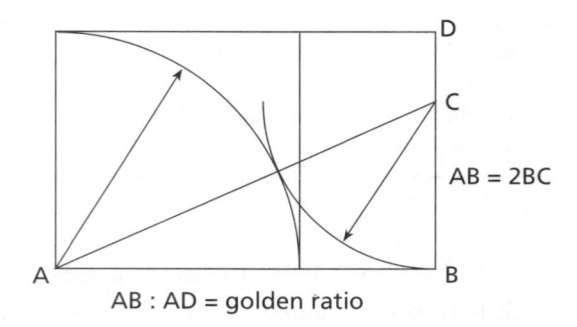

Fig. 2.4 The 'golden ratio'

Objects with proportions similar to AB:AD tend to be pleasant to look at.

Simple shapes without too many decorative bits are usually best, although there may be times when you want to make your designs 'outrageous'.

Colours and patterns that fit in with the proposed surroundings and appropriate textures will help to make your solution more effective.

Comfort

Seats must be the right shape and size to be comfortable. If you have ever sat cramped in the back of a small car you will know what it can be like not to have enough legroom. You will also realise how uncomfortable it can be to work at a table that is too high or too low for your chair. If you were designing leisure clothing you would need to pay particular attention to comfort. You should also consider the following.

- **ergonomics**

  This concerns making sure objects, systems and environments are designed so that people can use them easily, for example, with the minimum of effort. Care is taken to design the dashboard of a car so that everything is easy to reach and the steering wheel is at the most appropriate angle. There is a useful chart in the data section of this book, which you can use as a checklist of ergonomic factors.

- **anthropometrics**

  This science is the measurement of the dimensions and limits of the human body. The chart on page 173 will gives you of some of the more important anthropometric information. In the design of a car anthropometric information is used to ensure that the seats fit and support the human body. Car seats are usually adjustable so that they can be made to fit different-sized people.

- **environment**

  This refers to the situation in which the solution will be located or used. It is important to match the design to the location.

Hints for drawing up a design specification

1. Your specification must be a set of targets.
2. You must be able to use your specification to test and evaluate your product.
3. Make your targets realistic.
4. Ensure your targets don't contradict each other.
5. Make your targets specific, e.g., minimum and maximum sizes.
6. Don't try to achieve more than is asked for in the brief.
7. Make sure your list is in a realistic order of priority.

?

The following chart shows a list of priorities for the design of a compact-disc player.

Priorities for design of compact-disc player (in order of importance):
1. Safety
   It's electrical so it must be made safe.
2. Reliability
   It must not need frequent repair.
3. Performance
   It must play CDs but ergonomics are not important.
4. Cost
   It needs to be economically priced so people will buy it.
5. Environment
   It will be used anywhere.

What do you think about this list of priorities? Do you agree that ergonomics is not important? Will a CD player be used anywhere?

Now list the priorities for TWO of the following products:

- a mousetrap;
- a teenage magazine;
- an evening dinner for two;
- a pair of heavy-duty work shoes;
- a school bag;
- a holiday in the Sun.

2.3 First ideas

As soon as you have ideas get them down on paper. Don't waste time trying to perfect them. To begin with it doesn't matter what your ideas look like as long as you can understand them. It you wait or waste time the idea will be lost.

Add explanatory notes (but not long essays) from the start. They will help to clarify your own thinking, make your drawings clearer and help an assessor to know what you were thinking. This will help you reach higher levels of achievement. Try to name materials as you think of them. Be as specific as you can, although you may have to ask for advice or consult a reference book. For example, if you know the material needs to rot-resistant, specifying 'cloth' is not very helpful – 'artificial fibre' is better and specifying 'Nylon' would be best of all. Check that you can get hold of the material you choose. Look at this candidate's ideas for a piece of sculpture.

Generating a design and communicating ideas

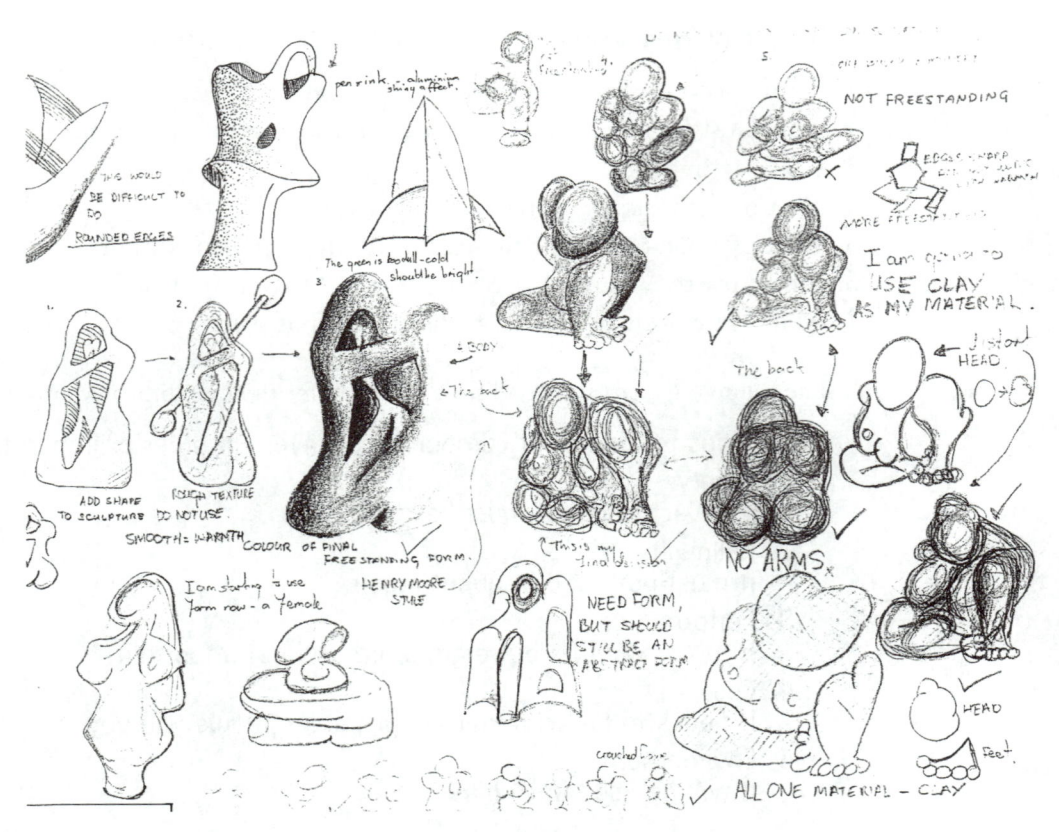

Fig. 2.5 First ideas for a piece of sculpture

Notice that there is a range of ideas with some explanatory notes and a certain amount of detail even at this early stage. Here, on the other hand, are one candidate's ideas for a 'fuse tester'.

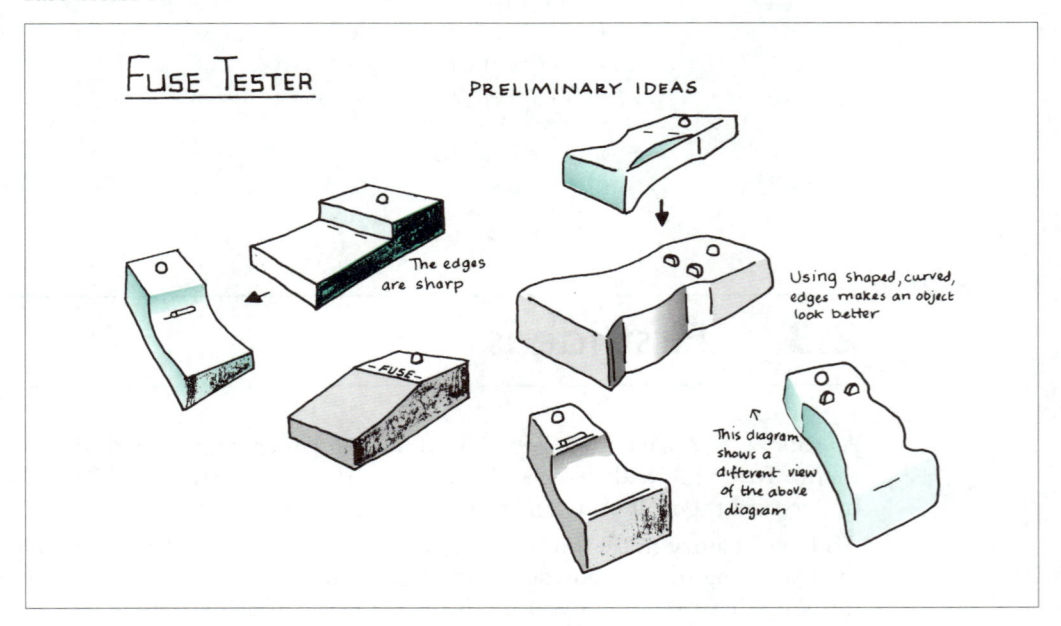

Fig. 2.6 Preliminary ideas for a fuse tester

These ideas are really only variations on a theme and the drawings show little depth of thinking, imagination or creativity. They are clearly drawn and probably took quite a long time. Little information is given about materials, function or construction. It would have been better if the candidate had either drawn a wider range of ideas (but in less detail at this stage) or taken one idea and shown how it could be improved.

2.3 First ideas

The following illustration shows some early ideas for a jacket. Alongside are the final drawings used to communicate the proposal to others. When Attainment Target 2 is being assessed your drawings and models will be essential evidence of achievement.

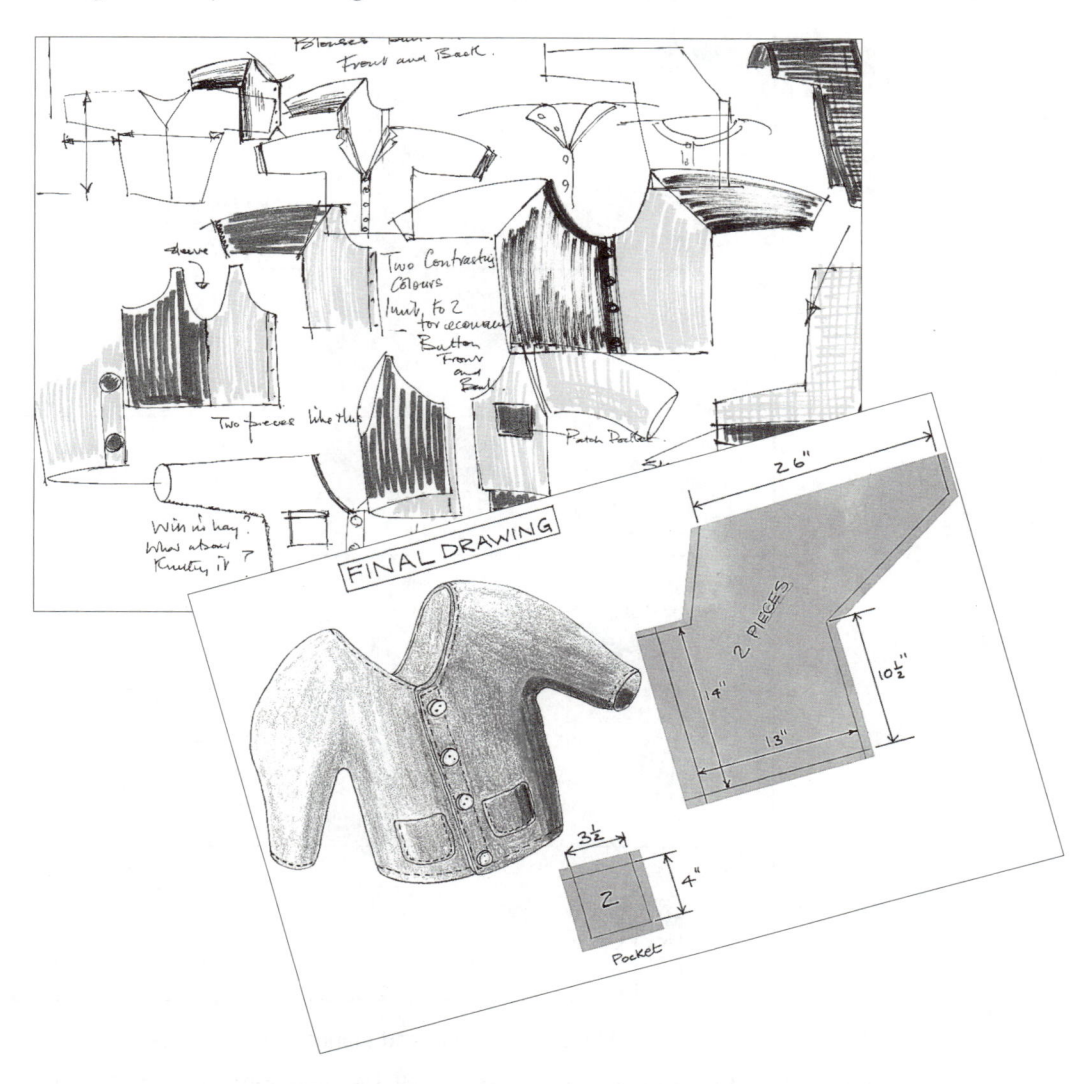

Fig. 2.7 Development of ideas for the design of a jacket

Hints for presenting first ideas

1. Show ideas that indicate different ways of solving a problem, e.g., the bath tap problem in Chapter 1.
2. Showing ideas that are simple variations on a theme, e.g., six different shapes for bath tap extensions, is less valuable than showing completely different ways of tackling the problem.
3. Add notes to your ideas to indicate their good and weak points. Keep checking back to your design brief and specification. It isn't important to make your early ideas fantastic works of art.
4. Draw later ideas accurately in two and three dimensions, and add colour or shading to make your ideas clearer.
5. Add details of materials, construction, sizes, likely problems, better methods, etc.

Selecting materials and manufacturing processes

Having ideas about the appearance of designs may not be too difficult; choosing suitable materials and deciding how they should be worked is more difficult. The following chart may help you select suitable materials and manufacturing processes.

Generating a design and communicating ideas

Desired shape	Possible materials	Manufacturing processes
Circular hollow shapes 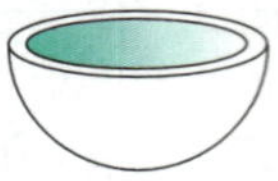	Rigid polystyrene, acrylic, copper, aluminium, shortcrust pastry	Blow moulding. Beaten to shape with mallet; pressed into mould
Circular solid shapes 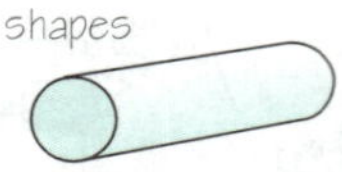	Timber, mild steel, acrylic, sponge cake	Turned on lathe. Cut from pieces of cake or glued together with jam
Straight lines. Corners or rigid angles 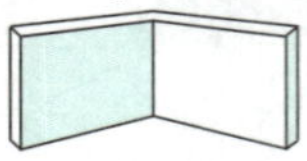	Timber Acrylic Brass	Corners can be glued, jointed, soldered or sewn
Smooth curves 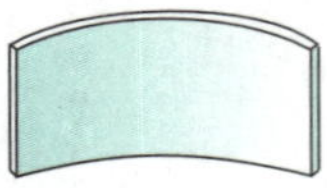	Sheet aluminium, steel, acrylic, fabrics, icing	Bend around a former. Fabrics can be either stiffened or bent around a frame
Hollow and lightweight 	Polystyrene, felt	Vacuum formed or plug and yoke formed. Felt can be "blocked"
Awkward shapes 	Aluminium, sponge cake, jelly, fabrics	Casting. Cooked in shaped tins or poured into moulds. Complex twists etc can be made in fabrics
Very strong structures 	Mild steel	Beaten to shape "hot" on an anvil

Fig. 2.8 Materials and manufacturing processes

The important point to note here is that the shape and function of a component will determine the properties of the materials from which it is made, and hence its method of manufacture.

Estimating the cost of an idea

Throughout the design process, be conscious of cost. To help you comment on cost when you are presenting your ideas, remember the following:

- materials;
- labour;
- heating and lighting;
- wear and tear on equipment;
- energy to run machines;
- time.

You can find out the cost of materials and components from catalogues. One student even produced a database of prices for commonly used materials and ingredients. It is also possible to use computer software, such as a spreadsheet program, when making decisions about costings (see Chapter 5).

Choosing the best idea

You may think that all or most of your ideas are good ones, after all, if they are not good ideas why did you bother to draw them? Your problem is to decide which idea you are

2.3 First ideas

going to select and develop further. You will need to consider a whole range of factors and the result will be a compromise. Remember the list of priorities in the design specification? Look though your ideas and identify positive and weak points. Add brief notes, like those in Fig. 2.9.

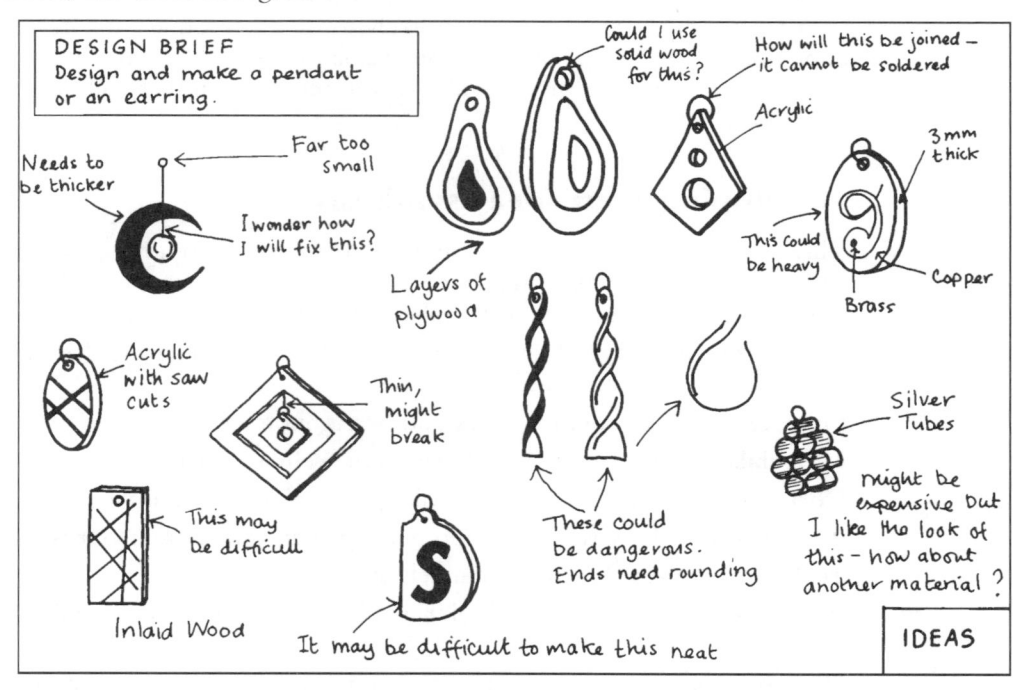

Fig. 2.9 Make comments on your design ideas

Remember that you have produced or been given a design specification. It is very important that you compare your ideas with it. If your idea does not match the specification then the idea does not achieve what you set out to do. Choose solutions that match the specification or make changes to ones that are close to it. If none of your ideas can be ruled out at the start, then drawing a chart similar to Fig. 2.10 may help.

	IDEA 1	IDEA 2	IDEA 3
EASE OF USE	1	3	5
COST	3	1	2
SIZE	4	5	2
EASE OF MAKING	3	3	3
RELIABILITY	2	4	3
SURVEY OF POSSIBLE USES	1	3	2
BEST AT SOLVING PROBLEMS	1	2	3
TOTAL	15	21 (Best idea)	20

Fig. 2.10 This chart will help you choose the best idea

1. List the most important points about the problem you are solving and write them down the left-hand side of a chart.
2. Draw a column for each idea or solution you have thought of and award a mark out of five to show how well each solution satisfies each point:

   0 = hopeless, 5 = excellent.
3. Enter the marks on the chart and add up the numbers in each column.
4. From the totals, choose the solution with the highest overall mark as the possible best idea.

If two solutions have almost the same score then you might like to consider which point is the most important. You must decide on the priorities, but explain why you have made the decision.

Don't forget to ask the opinion of others and you may also need to carry out a survey of your friends or those who are most likely to use the product you are designing. Record your findings and show them in the evaluation section of your project folder. Asking others or conducting a survey will give you information that will help you make design decisions.

Developing your idea (synthesis)

This is an opportunity to perfect and improve your chosen idea. You may, for example, have selected an idea that basically is an existing solution to a similar problem or need. You will now be able to alter it so that it fits exactly the specification for your solution.

During this next stage of development you should consider the details of your solution. These details should include:

Function: will the solution work and be ergonomic?

Materials: will they do the job? Have you accurately named them?

Costs: are there cheaper ways of making the solution just as well?

Construction: how is the solution put together? Are there better ways?

Technical details: are they accurately shown?

Aesthetics: does the solution look right for its task, for its surroundings, for you and for others?

Dimensions: are the sizes appropriate for the task? Are you planning to use standard sizes and standard forms of materials?

Safety: will the solution be safe for the user and for others?

Do you have the necessary skills, knowledge and know-how to manufacture the solution?

Have you checked everything against the specification?

Hints for developing ideas

1. Make changes that you believe are improvements.
2. Do not change too much at once.
3. Check that materials and facilities are available.
4. Is the time available sufficient to make what you are proposing?

Producing a working drawing (or production drawing)

It is not always necessary to produce a three-view working drawing. Indeed, only one view will sometimes be necessary and sometimes a single three-dimensional drawing may be better. For some projects, in textiles, for example, you will need to produce patterns while, for food technology projects, it may be appropriate to produce working drawings of moulds or cutters. The important thing is that a working drawing should contain all the details that could enable someone else to make your design. Whatever form of working drawing you do, you should include the following details:

- the dimensions;
- a list of parts, components or ingredients, using their specific names;
- the method of joining the parts together;
- the fittings (hinges, handles, catches, zip fasteners, etc.) or decorations to be used;
- the type of finish to be applied.

The drawing below is of exceptional quality and its standard far exceeds that which assessors normally expect, although it does illustrate what some candidates can achieve.

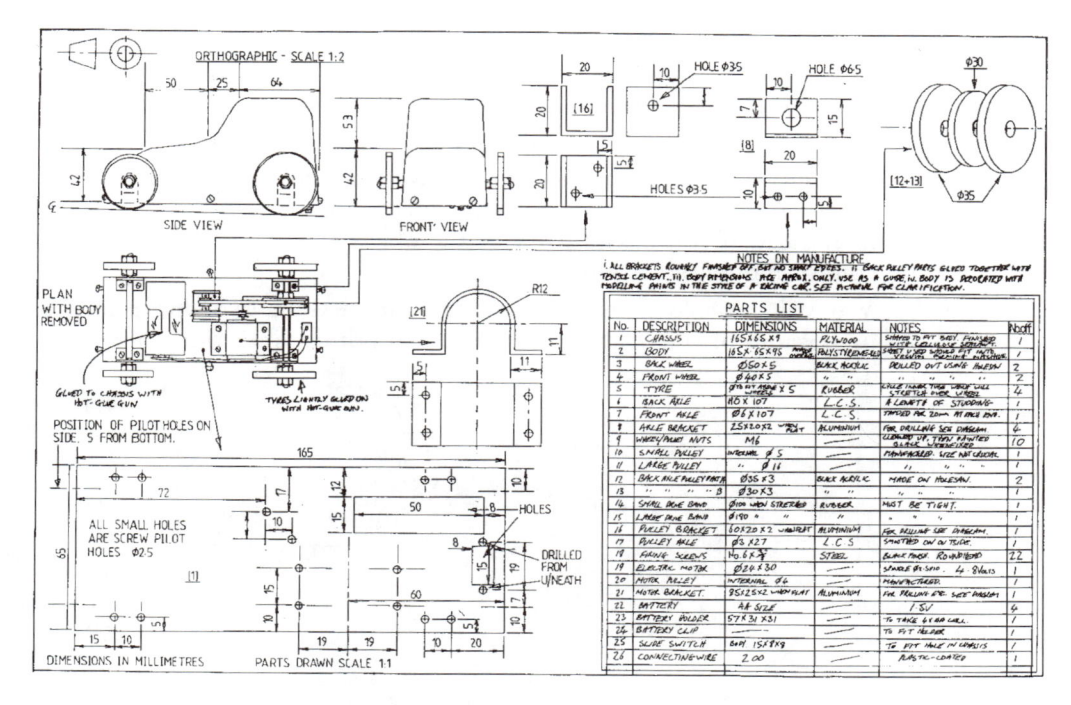

Fig. 2.11 A student's working drawing for a racing car design

Hints for producing working drawings

1. Select a suitable way of showing clearly all the information.
2. Other students should be able to work from your drawings.
3. Drawings may need to be modified after you start construction.
4. Space the drawings out a little so that the sheet does not look cluttered.
5. Use colour only where it is needed to make the drawing clearer.
6. Orthographic drawings can be done according to the appropriate British Standard.
7. List all parts, components or ingredients.

2.4 Communicating ideas

Throughout your course your teacher will want you to communicate your ideas as clearly as possible. This could simply be explaining your thoughts to your teacher or friends, or it could involve the making of models and mock-ups. Most commonly, however, it will mean drawing your ideas on paper. Expressing your ideas clearly is a very important part of developing a design solution. No matter how many good or even great ideas you have you will not do well in technology if you cannot communicate them to others. In addition, recording your ideas on paper and as models will help you decide which are good ideas and which are less good.

Freehand drawing

You can draw straight lines by using a ruler or set and T-squares, but it is worth practising freehand, otherwise you will find that you cannot put your ideas down quickly enough for a timed examination. It's surprising how easy it can be once you've mastered the basics.

Generating a design and communicating ideas

Remember these points.
- Think simple to begin with and draw straightforward objects correctly before you go on to more complicated ones.
- Use a soft (2B) pencil and work faintly until you are sure the lines are in the correct place.
- When you are sure the lines are correct go over them to make them darker.
- Do not work in ink until you are confident with pencil.

To begin with make sure you can draw vertical and horizontal lines. Sloping lines are less common and curves are often only a matter of rounding the edges where two straight lines meet. If you intend to make the object then you may find it easier to shape if it consists mostly of straight lines and simple curves.

You will be able to draw many of your ideas in two dimensions but to give true impressions of your ideas you must draw in three dimensions.

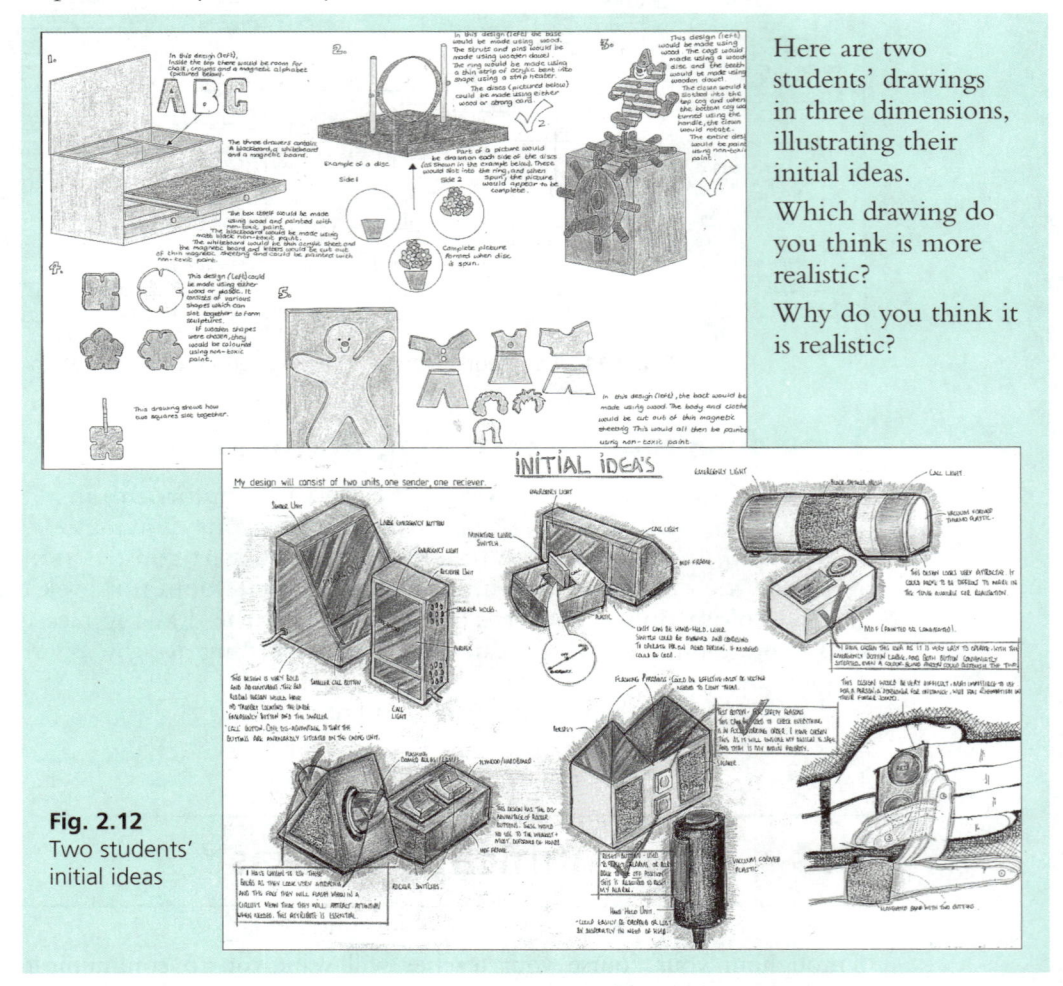

?

Here are two students' drawings in three dimensions, illustrating their initial ideas.

Which drawing do you think is more realistic?

Why do you think it is realistic?

Fig. 2.12 Two students' initial ideas

You may have learned something about perspective. A grasp of perspective will make your drawings even more realistic.

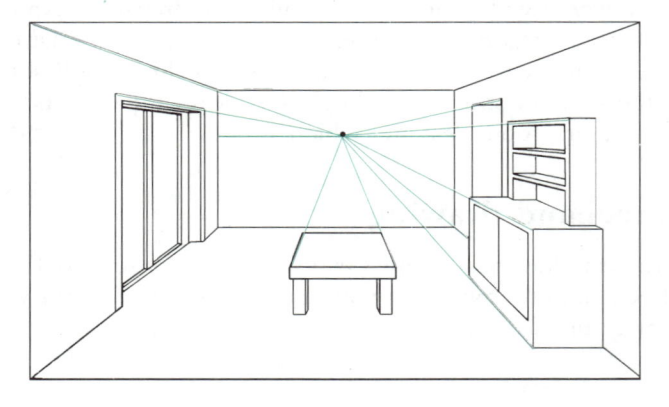

Fig. 2.13 Single-point perspective can show the inside of things

2.4 Communicating ideas

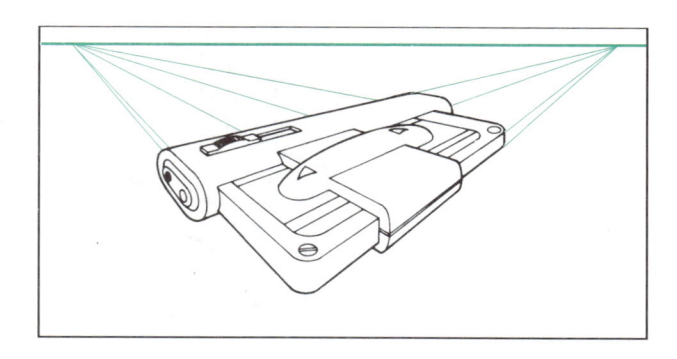

Fig. 2.14 Two-point perspective can show the outside of things

Making ideas flow

Try to make your ideas flow naturally from one idea to the next. When you are developing an idea change details gradually so that you can judge if your new idea is an improvement. Let the assessor see how your ideas have developed by linking them together. Using arrows can help. This student has communicated the way an idea developed.

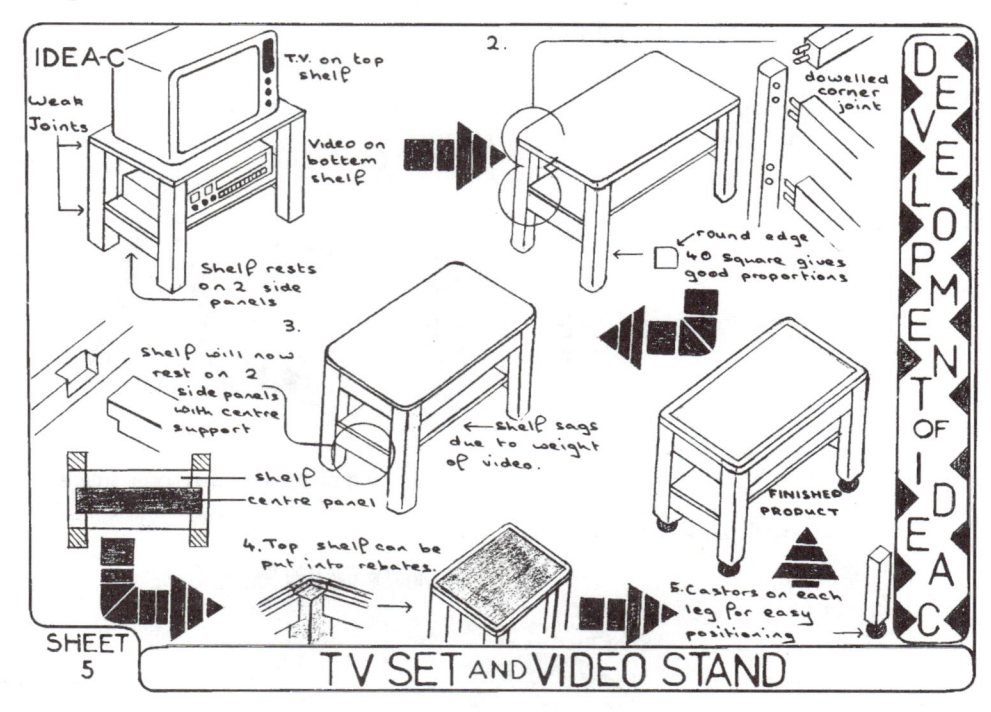

Fig. 2.15 Using arrows to show how ideas developed

Making drawings stand out

If you are particularly pleased with a drawing or you think it is your best idea you will want to make it stand out. The following techniques allow you to highlight ideas on a page and draw the observer's attention to one of particular interest. Of course, if you apply these techniques to all your drawings, the effect will be lost.

- **thick and thin lines**

    This simple technique is frequently used for book illustrations. A line represents the edge where two surfaces meet. If you can see both surfaces draw a thin line. It you can only see one of the surfaces draw a thick one. It is most effective when done either with a 2H pencil (thin line) and 2B pencil (thick line) or with fine fibre, felt-tip or drawing pens.

Generating a design and communicating ideas

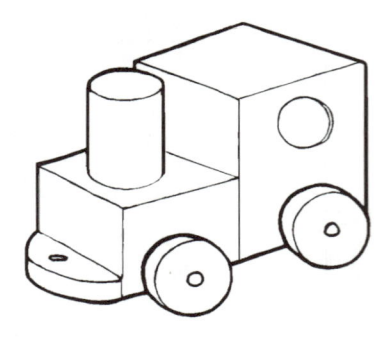

Fig. 2.16 Using thick and thin lines to emphasise a drawing

- **colour shading**

    In this technique, you imagine that light is shining over one shoulder, say your left, onto the object you're drawing. These are the main points of the technique.

    1 Leave the top surface white.
    2 Shade left-hand verticals lightly and right-hand verticals slightly heavier.
    3 Shade sloping surfaces somewhere in-between. Notice how curves are done. Note the position of the highlight.
    4 If you decide to colour try to make the colour you use represent the colour you intend the finished object to be.
    5 You can also shade using ordinary pencils.

    If you are drawing in ink then you may use vertical lines of different spacing to give an illusion of shade.

Fig. 2.17 Pencil shading of three-dimensional shapes

- **outlining with felt marker**

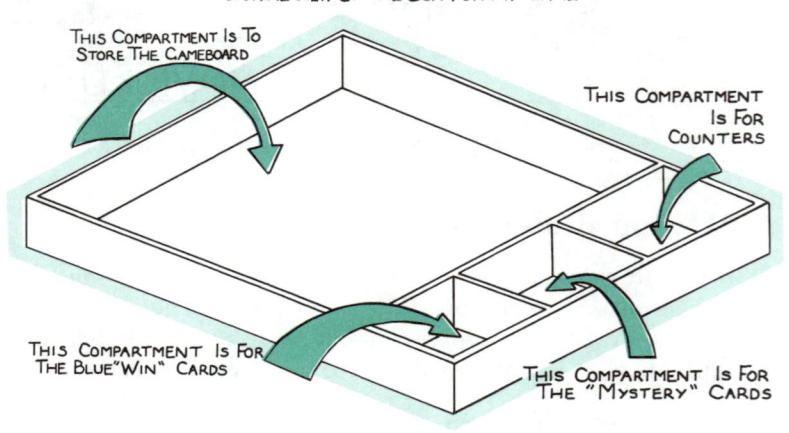

Fig. 2.18 Using felt marker to emphasise an idea

The effect of outlining is to make your designs appear as if they are drawn against a coloured background. Use a broad felt marker and not fine-tipped pens. A similar effect can be achieved by double mounting on a sheet of contrasting-coloured paper. This second technique may take a little longer but it will look neater. Make your drawings full-size whenever possible; it will make it easier for you to take measurements for modelling. If you cannot draw full-size, however, always give some idea of scale.

Students often ask how many drawings there should be on each sheet. It's impossible to give a precise answer since drawings will be of different sizes, will be drawn for different purposes and contain different amounts of detail. As a guide consider the following points.

1. Make sure each drawing is large enough to communicate or record what you intend but not so large as to waste space.
2. Arrange your drawings on the paper so that there is a little space between them and the sheet does not look cluttered.
3. Don't waste paper by putting a single drawing in the centre with lots of space all around it.

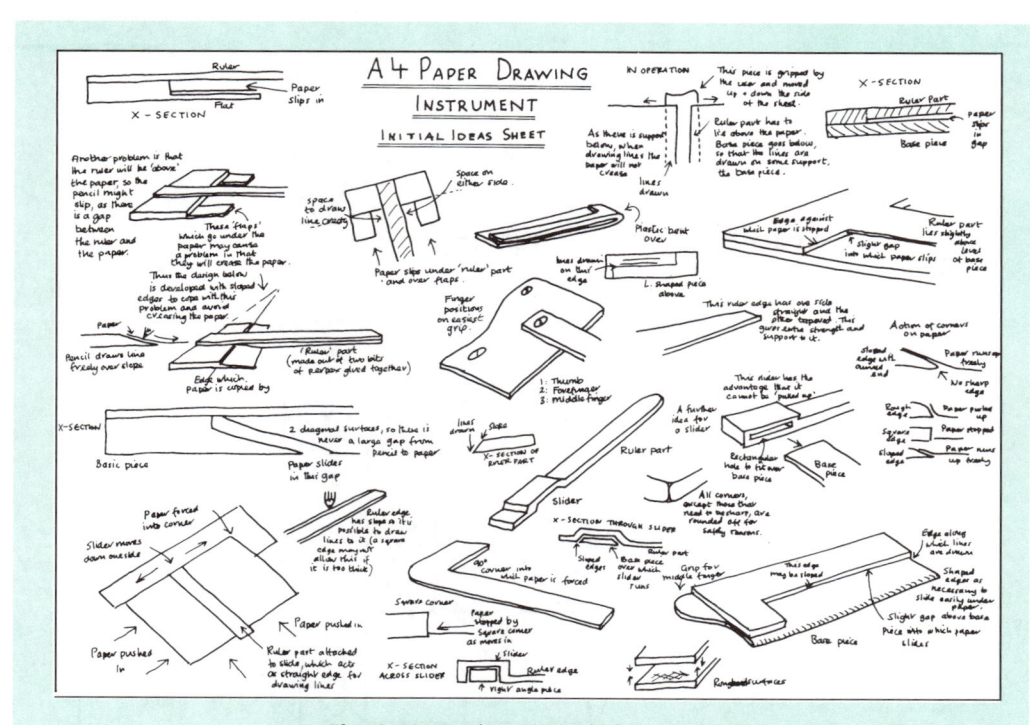

Fig. 2.19 Student's initial ideas sheet

Do you think the student has made sensible use of the paper?

Lettering and writing

Adding notes to ideas is essential but it can present difficulties if your handwriting is not very good. To improve this:

- make sure the written lines are horizontal;
- write small and keep your writing to a minimum;
- make your notes brief;
- add lettering by hand or use stencils;
- use commercially produced rub-down letters for your final presentation and working drawings;
- produce headings and section titles ('Need', 'Design Brief', 'Analysis', etc.) on a computer and paste them onto your work. These can look very effective if mounted on coloured backgrounds (double mounting);
- photocopy several times words, such as the project title or your name, that appear repeatedly and paste the copied words onto each sheet.

Generating a design and communicating ideas

D E V E L O P M E N T

Analysis

designs

IDEAS

CAPITAL

Not capital

PLAYGROUND

Specification:

MATERIALS

DESIGN BRIEF

Fig. 2.20 A variety of project headings and titles

Computer-aided drawing

The increasing use of computers and the availability of graphics software now make it possible to produce a wide variety of drawings, graphs, charts and diagrams by using a computer.

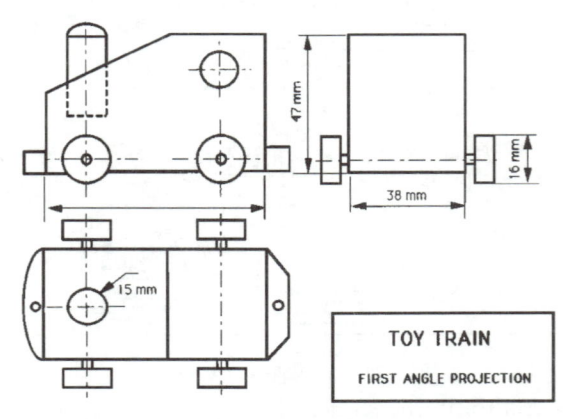

Fig. 2.21 Computer-aided design of a toy train

Computer-generated drawings are usually unsuitable for first ideas because they can take a long time to do. If you do intend producing your final drawings by computer then it will probably save time if you sketch them with a pencil first.

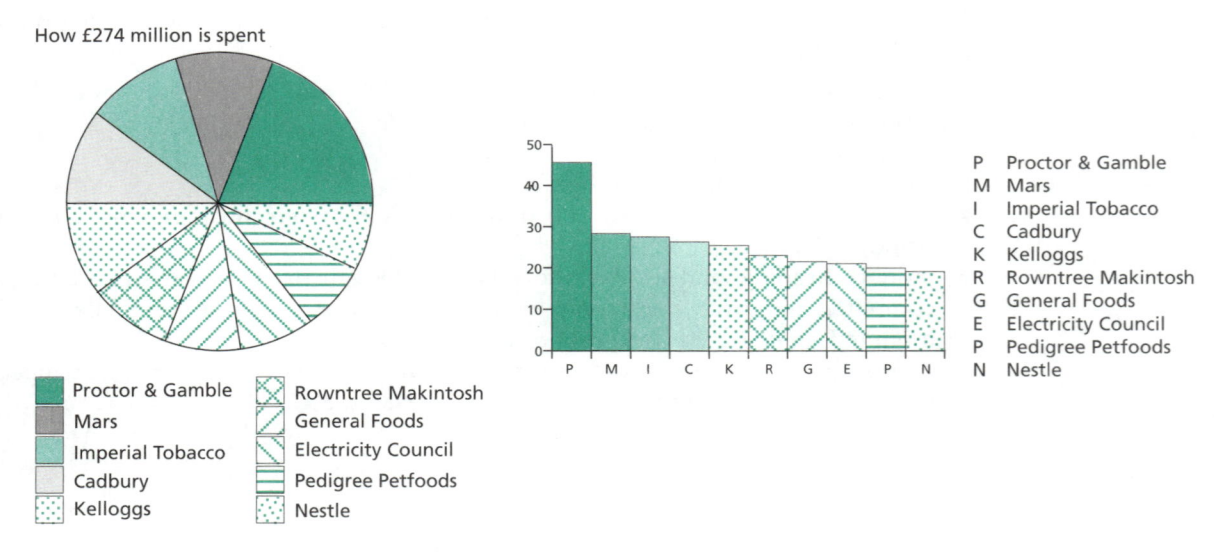

How £274 million is spent

- Proctor & Gamble
- Mars
- Imperial Tobacco
- Cadbury
- Kelloggs
- Rowntree Makintosh
- General Foods
- Electricity Council
- Pedigree Petfoods
- Nestle

P Proctor & Gamble
M Mars
I Imperial Tobacco
C Cadbury
K Kelloggs
R Rowntree Makintosh
G General Foods
E Electricity Council
P Pedigree Petfoods
N Nestle

Fig 2.22 Computers can be used to present information graphically

2.4 Communicating ideas

Isometric grids

Isometric grid paper can be used to produce three-dimensional drawings. Sometimes you can get a better looking result by putting the grid onto a light-box or even a light-coloured surface, placing plain white paper on top and using the grid as a guide. If you haven't got a light-box then hold the drawings against a window. The following example shows how a student has used isometric grid paper to good effect.

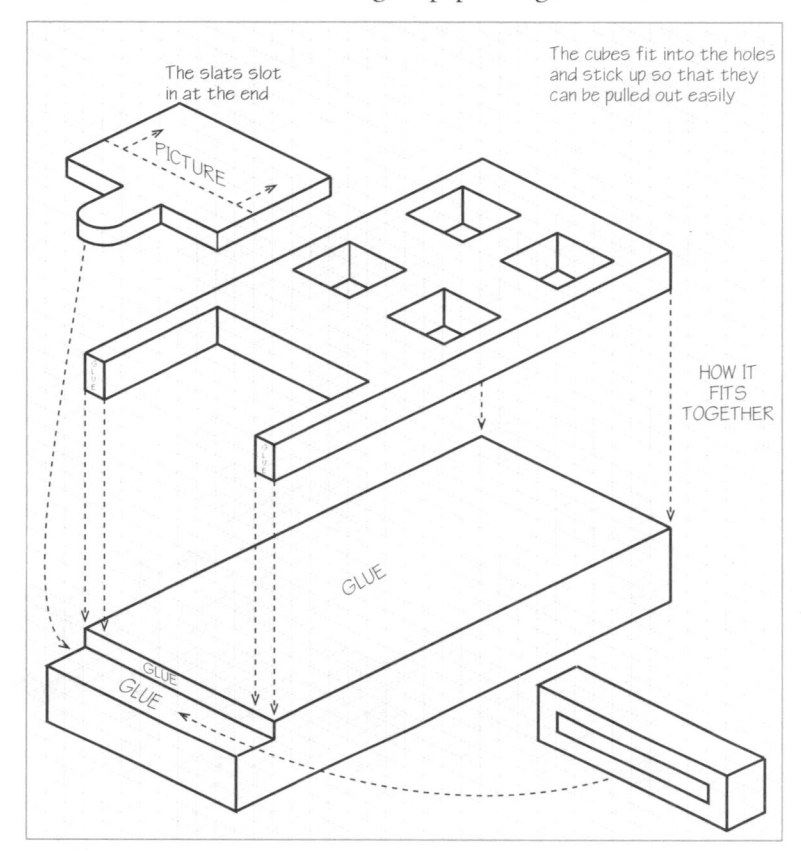

Fig. 2.23 Using isometric grid paper to produce a three-dimensional drawing

Exploded drawings

An exploded drawing can be an excellent way of showing how a product is assembled. You may find that using isometric grid paper will also help.

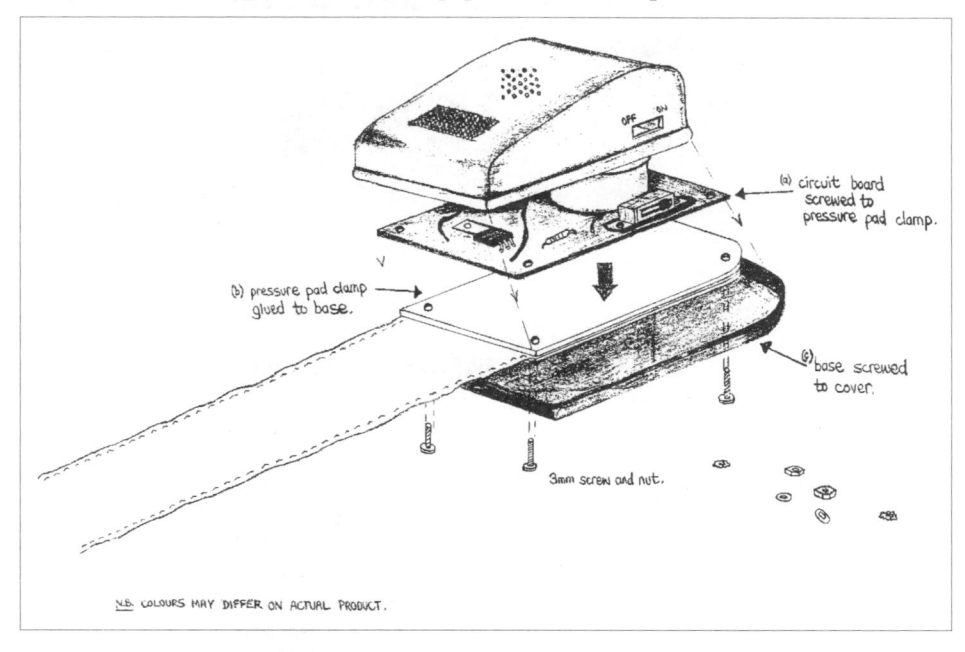

Fig. 2.24 Exploded drawing of an electronic project

Generating a design and communicating ideas

Models and mock-ups

Models are made for different reasons:
- to communicate an idea that can be done more easily with a model than with a drawing, e.g., a free or organic shape, such as a carving or a piece of pottery, jewellery or confectionery;
- to illustrate how a moving system works, e.g., using card linkages or a model made from a construction kit;
- where it is necessary to explore how two or more parts fit together, such as when designing clothing;
- when investigating the layout of parts of a project, in particular, when making ergonomic considerations;
- where full-size would be impractical.

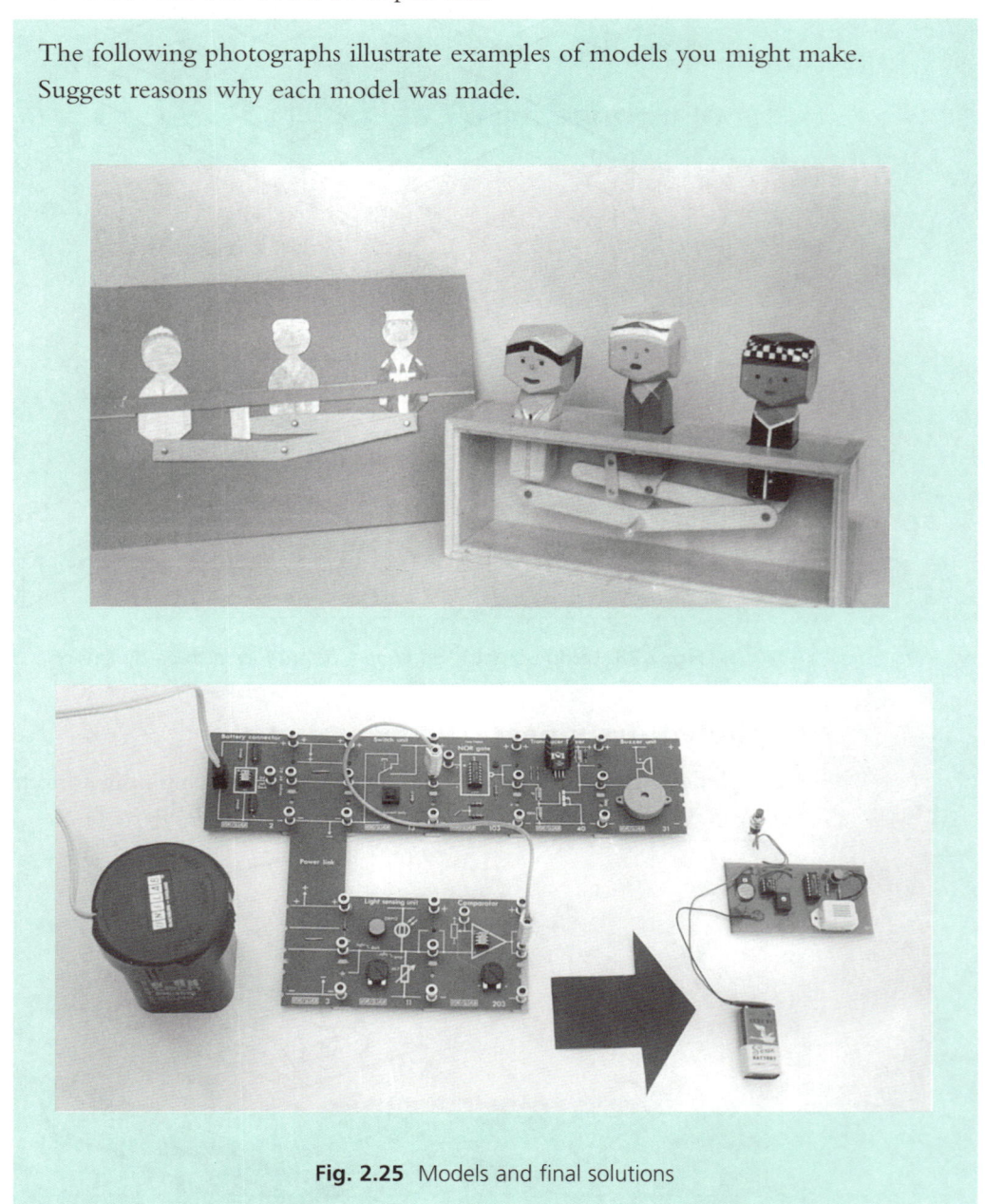

? The following photographs illustrate examples of models you might make. Suggest reasons why each model was made.

Fig. 2.25 Models and final solutions

Photographs

Photographs can be very effective in showing your work as it progresses as well as the finished product. They can be particularly valuable if your work has to be sent away for assessment or if the product is perishable. Models and mock-ups sometimes cannot be kept because other students may need to use the materials, such as a construction kit.

Photographs can be a useful way of communicating the positive aspects of a project, such as parts that are particularly well made, if you follow a few simple rules.

- Make sure the photograph is big enough to show the important details. Use a close-up lens if necessary.
- Make sure relevant details are in focus.
- Make sure there is enough light so that only a small aperture is needed.
- Take photographs from different angles but only put the best pictures in your design folio.
- Try to arrange a plain background for your photographs. A large piece of paper, a bed sheet or a large piece of felt can be effective.
- Include in the photograph an object, e.g., a coin, a ruler, or a hand to give an idea of scale.
- Take photographs out-of-doors, if possible, to obtain the best results.

Aids to drawing

- Place tracing paper over your initial ideas and draw changes on the overlay.
- Trace ideas from books and use tracing paper to show changes.
- Photograph objects.
- Use a video camera and trace the image directly from the TV screen.
- Photocopy ideas, cut-and-paste then photocopy again.
- Photocopy onto heatproof acetate sheet and use an overhead projector to project the drawing. Trace the enlarged image off the projector screen.
- Use an optical scanner connected to a computer to convert diagrams or photographs into electronic form. Change the shape and proportions of the image, add details and print it.

Hints for communicating ideas on paper

1. Think simple to begin with.
2. Don't overdo shading and highlighting techniques. Use these techniques to draw attention to one or two drawings on a sheet.
3. If possible, keep ideas on one topic or theme on the same sheet.
4. Computer-aided drawing (CAD) is effective for some production drawings but you will waste a lot of time if it isn't necessary.
5. Isometric grid paper can help for some drawings, but for best effects use the grid as a guide and draw on plain white paper, using a light-box or a window as a source of illumination.
6. Leave a little space between your drawings so that sheets don't appear cluttered, but don't make the spaces too large or it might look as though you are trying to fill up the paper.
7. Make your ideas flow around the paper so that the assessor can see how your idea developed.
8. Don't draw in ink or felt-tip pen unless you are experienced. It's better to use an ordinary pencil and then add colour using pencils.
9. Leave a little space around the edges of each sheet to act as a border. Alternatively, draw a border about 10 mm wide – a little wider at the side where the folder is to be bound.

Hints for making models

1. Make models only when they are needed.
2. Don't make models more complicated than they need to be.
3. Keep models or take photographs of them if they have to be dismantled.

2.5 Presenting research information

You should clearly present your research in a folio so that the assessor can see how much effort you have made.

Primary research (experiments, tests, questionnaires, interviews or surveys)

The results of experiments, tests and surveys can be presented as:
- tables;
- graphs, pie charts and bar charts;
- photographs of experiments.

The answers to interviews, questionnaires and surveys can be presented as:
- tables;
- photographs of interviews or situations;
- videos and tape-recordings.

Conclusions drawn from questionnaires can be presented as:
- tables and graphs;
- a summary in prose.

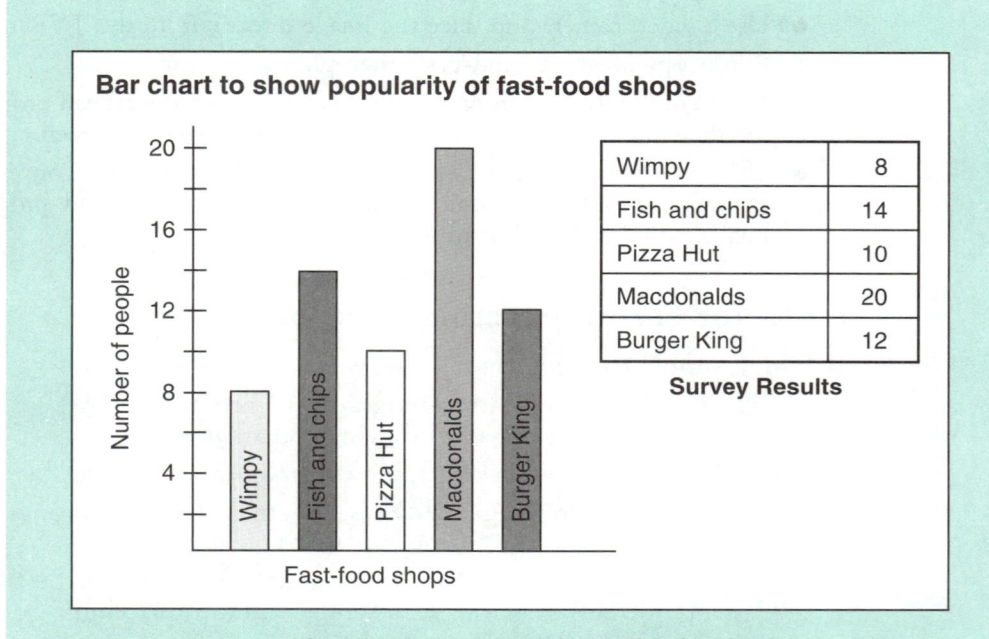

Bar chart to show popularity of fast-food shops

Wimpy	8
Fish and chips	14
Pizza Hut	10
Macdonalds	20
Burger King	12

Survey Results

Fig. 2.26 Primary research into 'fast food'

What conclusions can you draw from this research material?

Secondary research

Press cuttings and photocopies can be presented by:
- pasting-in or double mounting;
- adding notes and comments;
- acknowledging the source of the information.

Replies to letters can be presented by:
- pasting-in;
- highlighting the relevant information;
- adding comments on the value of the information.

2.5 Presenting research information

Technical data from books and charts can be presented by:
- pasting-in photocopies;
- highlighting the parts that relate to the project;
- acknowledging the source of the information.

Photographs and photocopies can be presented by:
- pasting-in;
- acknowledging the source and giving reasons for inclusion in the project.

Using catalogue illustrations

Cuttings from catalogues (mail order, brochures, etc.) should be used with caution. They should not be used merely to fill a project folder. Catalogue cuttings do have value when surveying and evaluating existing products.

Any catalogue cutting must be accompanied by a written commentary indicating:
- the source of the illustrations;
- the strengths and weaknesses of the ideas;
- possible ideas for improvements.

Fig. 2.27 Catalogue illustrations used in a survey of existing products

Using photocopiers

Copyright laws prohibit you from making photocopies of published material unless you have previously obtained permission from the author or publisher. You school will very probably have a licence to photocopy, but even then you are not permitted to make copies of large sections of a publication.

Photocopiers can help you present your ideas if you wish to:
- make copies of an original drawing and experiment with different colours;
- enlarge or reduce drawings;
- cut up drawings and experiment with different arrangements on the page;
- copy photographs and illustrations before colouring them with markers;
- produce copies of logos or headings.

Generating a design and communicating ideas

2.6 The design folio

A design folio or folder is evidence of the work you have done. During the project, you may keep the work you do and the results of your research loose in a pocket folder or separately. Before submitting your work for assessment, however, you should gather together the material for each project into a folio and present it in an organised way. If you have magazine cuttings, for example, paste them onto sheets of paper and add appropriate notes.

Your folio doesn't need to be elaborate but it should be neat and secure. It isn't very important what size you choose but A3 has proved a suitable size and some examination groups specify that the work must be on A3 sheets. It is helpful to an assessor if your folio is divided into separate sections and clearly labelled, and it will also help if assessors can find quickly where each section begins. One examination group suggests that about sixteen sheets should be sufficient for a single project.

Fig. 2.28 gives an indication of how your folder can be organised.

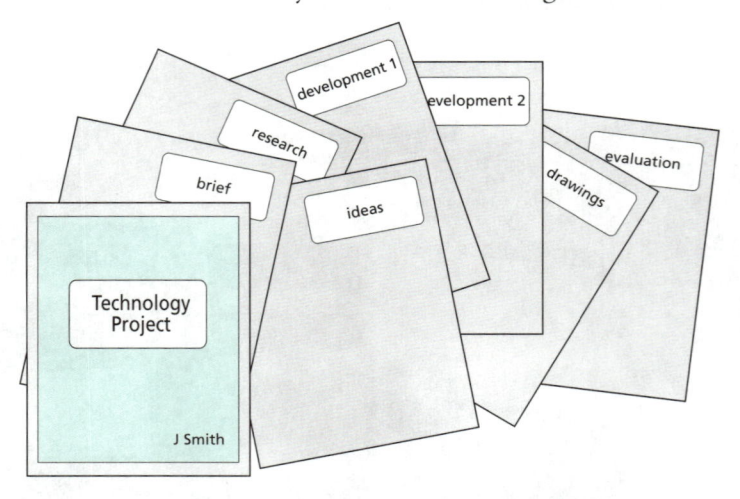

Fig. 2.28 Possible headings for sections in a design folio

Sections of a design folio

Each of the following areas needs to be covered.

1 **Statement of need, problem or opportunity**. Explain why you chose this project.
2 **Analysis, research, investigation, design brief and specification**. Explain what you did, present your findings clearly, state the brief and give a detailed specification.
3 **Possible solutions**. Show a range of different ideas and show alternative ways of satisfying the brief and the specification. Demonstrate that you have considered existing solutions to similar problems. Indicate how your ideas compare with your specification.
4 **Development of the proposed solution**. Give evidence for selecting your chosen idea and develop it as fully as possible. The idea may begin as a simple outline drawing and you should modify, perfect and change the idea until it is as good as you can make it.
5 **Details of the final solution**. This section should include presentation drawings and working drawings, where appropriate. It might also include patterns or templates.
6 **Testing and evaluation**. Make sure you evaluate your work as you go along and show this in your folder. At all stages, undertake appropriate tests and record the results. After you have completed manufacture, test your project to see if it satisfies the need, problem or opportunity. Don't forget to consult other people. Report all your test results, including the negative ones; you will gain marks, not lose them.

2.6 The design folio

7 **Planning**. Show how you organised the manufacture of your work. You can use any suitable method, including those described in Chapter 3. Planning must show both what you intended to do and what you actually did, and why it was necessary to make changes. Some candidates think they should write a description of the manufacture after the project is finished. This is not what the assessor is looking for and it will not gain you as much credit as evidence that you carefully planned, in advance, what you intended to do.

In addition, assessors will judge how well you communicate your ideas. They will look for drawings in two and three dimensions, notes, graphs, charts, models and photographs. The assessor will also judge presentation, organisation and layout.

Sometimes your work will be such that it cannot easily be arranged in a logical order. The assessor will want to give you as much credit as possible, so you can help yourself by looking at your own work and identifying where there is evidence of reaching the highest levels of attainment in each of the attainment targets. You can then draw attention to this by adding labels to your sheets. This candidate has added stickers to the design sheets in order to help the assessor understand how the work was done.

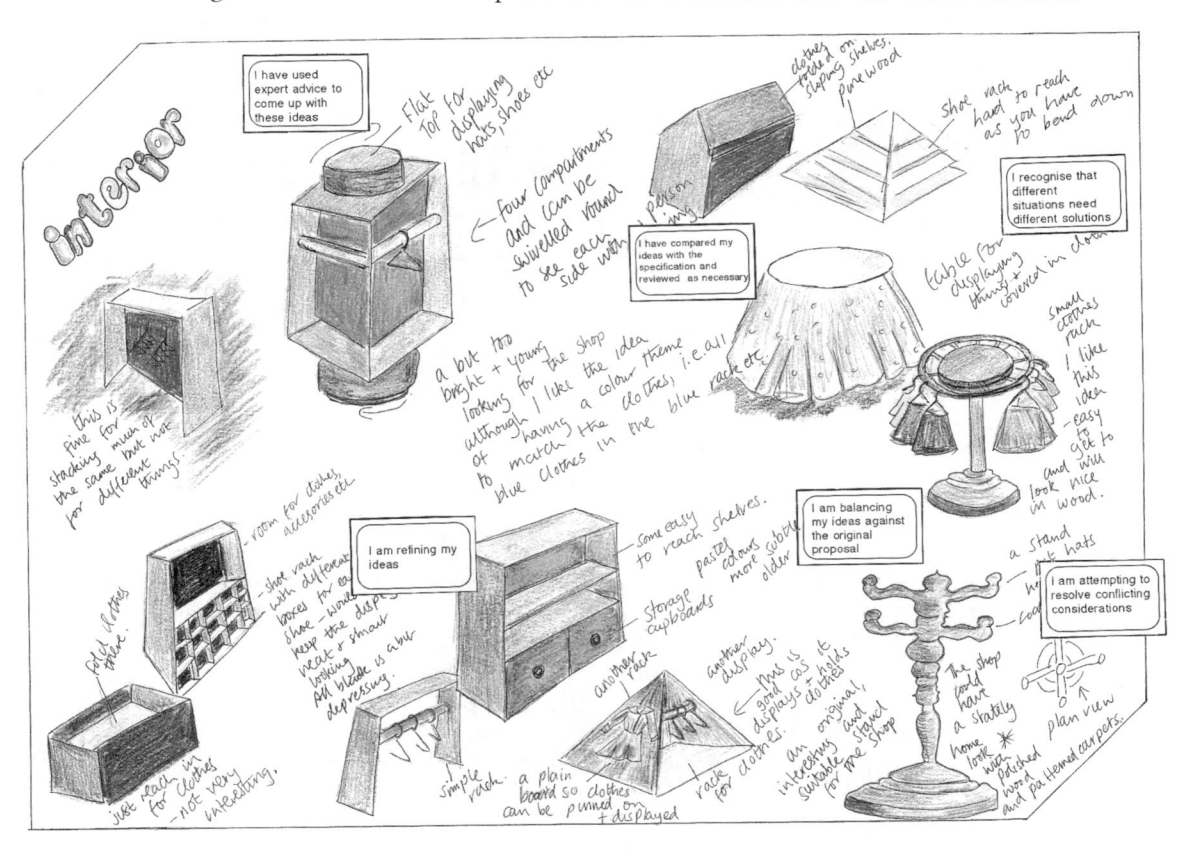

Fig. 2.29 Using stickers to highlight comments on design ideas

Personalising your work

Your work will impress the assessor if it has individual touches, for example:
- adopt a personal colour scheme;
- make sure each project folio has a contents page produced in a consistent style;
- use a personal logo, possibly produced on the computer and photocopied, which could be added to all your drawing sheets, say, at the bottom right-hand corner;
- ensure all labels are produced in the same style.

Mistakes

You are likely to make mistakes in your design folio. The following suggestions may help you avoid or remedy most errors.
- Redraw corrected diagrams on a separate piece of paper and paste them over the previous versions.

Generating a design and communicating ideas

- Double mount your work by pasting the corrected material onto a piece of paper of a different colour and then pasting this over the previous version.
- Avoid crossing out and use of correction fluid, as it looks very untidy.
- Draw with faint lines until your drawing looks correct and then 'line in' with a heavier pencil.

Gaining more space on the paper

This can be achieved by the use of fold-out flaps, pockets and by folding illustrations.

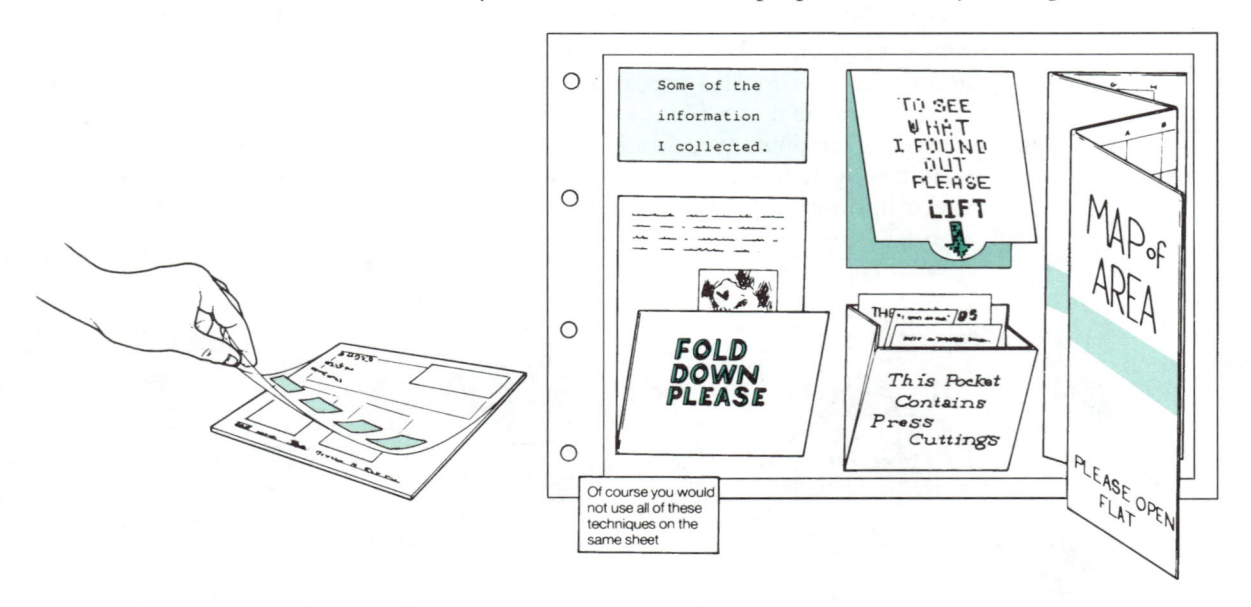

Fig. 2.30 Devices to gain extra display space

This can be useful when you want to keep together on one sheet information on one topic or when you want to display your work.

Checklist

Is your design specification a list of specific targets?
Have you put the priorities in the best order?
Have you looked for ideas from a range of sources?
Have you a range of ideas?
Have you put down your early ideas?
Have you taken care over selecting materials, components and constructional techniques?
Have you developed ideas carefully and gradually?
Have you communicated in the most appropriate way?
Have you shown all your research material ?
Have you used every resource available to make your ideas possible or easier to manufacture?
Have you presented your work carefully in a project folder?

Chapter 3 — Planning and making

3.1 Introduction

This chapter will help you understand what is required by Attainment Target 3 and will also help you reach your highest possible level of achievement. You will already have considerable experience in planning and making, so you will realise that projects do not always work out the way you intend. Making your project can be the most enjoyable part of the process and it is likely that most of the time available for a project will be spent making it. You must make the most of that time to produce your best work.

3.2 Planning

Benefits of organising your time

Whenever you set out on a technology project you will have a deadline to work to and your teacher will insist that the work is handed in on time. If you waste time you will not complete your project and you will not fully demonstrate your skills. Experience shows that if you leave things until the last minute, you may end up rushing and then something is likely to go wrong. All the subjects you study at school matter and careful planning of your time will enable you to do your best in every subject. Being organised can make you feel better about your work and the very act of planning your time will gain you credit in your technology assessment.

Work out what you need to do well in advance. Arriving at a technology lesson and saying to your teacher, 'What shall I do today?' is not a positive approach. Your teacher will want to help, but waiting your turn while someone else's problems are sorted out is not a good use of your time. It is better to plan in advance what you intend to do and then you need only ask permission to do something. If you are working with a partner or as a member of a group it is important that each member of the team knows in advance what the others will be doing.

In whatever way you plan your work, you should:

- know in advance what you intend to do;
- record what you actually do;
- check that what you have done is what you intended to do;
- decide what changes, if any, you now need to make;
- modify your plans for the future.

Everyone finds it difficult to estimate how long things will take and there are often unforeseen difficulties. Assessors realise this and will reward you for the efforts you make in overcoming problems. However impossible the task may seem you must adjust your plans to make it possible. You can, for example, simplify the construction or produce fewer drawings. Remember: although you will do your best, you cannot achieve perfection! Completing the project is often more important than spending time planning to make it perfect.

Planning your work

When planning your work think about:

- the whole project and not just one part at a time;
- the best order for the operations;
- alternative tasks, in case equipment, materials or facilities are not available;
- things that may go wrong and need repeating or changing;
- any processes that require to be left, e.g., paint drying (arrange to do it before the weekend or at the end of the day);
- how long tasks will realistically take;
- parts or materials that need to be ordered in advance.

Planning and making

Find out when each project has to be completed. Some projects may be done in a few lessons, others could last months. However long a project is supposed to take, do not underestimate the importance of completing it on time. Begin by dividing your project into smaller units of time. The two major parts may be designing and making. Each is of equal importance, although making usually takes longer than designing.

A student was given twelve weeks in which to design and make a protective cover for a garden table.

Here is the plan for her designing time:

- Identify need and write design brief — 1 week
- Analyse and research requirements; write design specification — 2 weeks
- Develop ideas — 1 week
- Make final drawings and patterns — 1 week

For making the cover, she divided seven weeks like this:

- Prepare and buy materials — 1 week
- Mark out and cut out pieces — 1 week
- Sew together — 4 weeks
- Trim and finish — 1 week

At the end of the project she wrote the following report:

```
1. The project began well and by the end of the first week a
   brief had been written, although I wasn't quite sure what
   potential customers really wanted because I hadn't had time
   to discuss it.

2. In the second week, I discovered that garden tables can be
   different sizes but this didn't present too much of a
   problem, except I realised that I would need to produce a
   range of sizes of cover, so the economy of making them all
   the same was lost and I thought the finished selling price
   might have to be increased.

3. I tried to find out what kinds of material were available
   by writing letters and looking up information at the local
   library. I didn't get replies to some of my letters and the
   two who did reply were kind and wished me well but did not
   give me much advice or help. I must try next time to make
   my requests more specific.

4. The librarian was super but I couldn't get any idea of how
   much suitable materials would cost. My dad helped by
   phoning two companies and they sent me samples and prices.
   (In fact one sample turned out to be big enough for me to
   make my cover out of it!) All this took longer than I had
   expected but I was able to get some ideas down on paper by
   the end of week 4.

5. I discussed my ideas with my teacher and a friend but it
   wasn't until the end of week 5 that I was able to start
   finalising my ideas.

6. I produced patterns and then ordered some plastic and the
   trimming materials (I hadn't realised at that stage that
   the sample was big enough) It was two-and-a-half weeks
   before the materials arrived. I couldn't do anything. I was
   so excited to get the parcel but unfortunately they had not
   sent exactly what I expected. I had made a mistake in the
   order and they asked for clarification.

7. My mum suggested I use the sample material. I got on with
   it very quickly and because my mum has a sewing machine at
   home I was able to finish everything within a week.
```

? What do you think the student could have done while waiting for her materials? How do you think she might have better planned the use of her making time?

Planning schedules

Another method of setting out your planning is shown in Fig. 3.1. This project was undertaken for a two-term period, although it is likely that your projects will be for shorter periods of time. The chart shows that time has been allowed for each stage of the project. The grey blocks show the amount of time the candidate expected each task to take and when he expected to do it. The blocks shaded green show what actually happened.

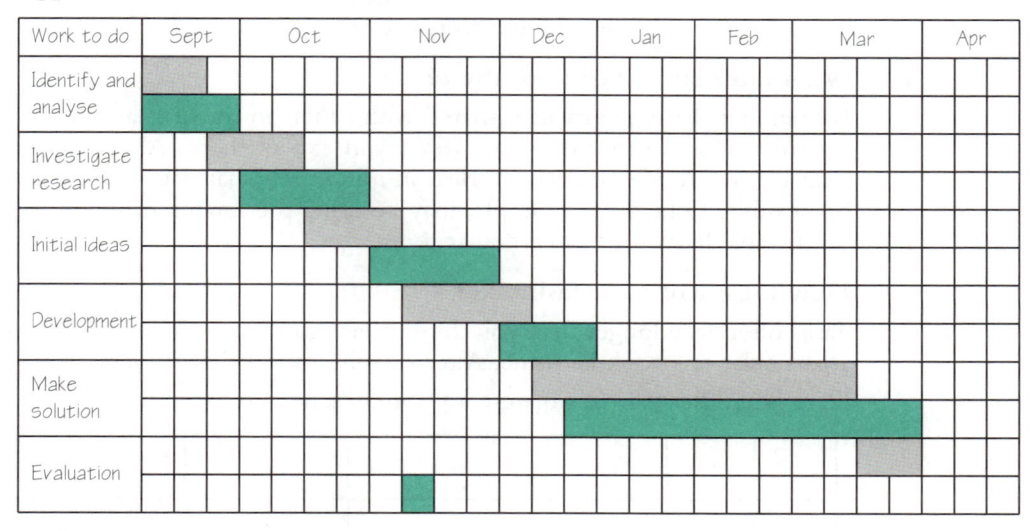

Work to do	Sept	Oct	Nov	Dec	Jan	Feb	Mar	Apr
Identify and analyse								
Investigate research								
Initial ideas								
Development								
Make solution								
Evaluation								

Fig. 3.1 Organising a planning schedule

?
1. Why do you think the student has shaded a green block for evaluation during early November?
2. The project deadline was set for the end of April. Why do you think the candidate shows nothing planned to be done in April?

Keeping a diary

To be really effective a technology diary needs to:
- allow you to plan well ahead (not just the next event);
- keep a record of what you did;
- avoid wasted time.

?

A student made this entry in her technology diary.

Monday 23rd November

Made the lid today. I don't know what to do tomorrow because the hinges haven't arrived.

Suggest two things the student could do while she's waiting for the hinges.

Producing a planning schedule

You will need to decide:
- the tasks you are going to perform;
- the best order in which they should be done;
- alternative tasks, should equipment and resources not be available;
- how long each task will take.

43

What tasks are you going to perform?

This will differ with each project, but the tasks referred to in Fig. 3.1 will be included in most projects. If you aren't sure what tasks are involved ask your teacher for help or discuss your ideas with a friend.

In what order will you perform the tasks?

The tasks will broadly follow those given, but you may need to change the order if, for example, you find you need more information or an idea requires more refinement before you can decide whether to reject or accept it.

What alternative tasks are there?

Remember that equipment is shared with others in the class and materials may need to be ordered, and may not arrive when you expect them. Always have alternative tasks available in advance of a lesson. Bear in mind that what you would like to do might not be possible. Others, for example, may be using the sewing machine or the teacher may not be able let you use a particular room.

How long will each task take?

Tasks often take longer than you think. Keep good records and you will know how long a particular task took last time. Alternatively, ask another student.

Here is another way to organise a planning schedule.

WEEK	DATE	STAGE	PREPARATION	COMPLETION DATE	ACTUAL DATE COMPLETED	COMMENTS
20	26 Feb	Materials	Check availability	2 Feb		Start marking if time
19	2 Feb	Marking out		9 Feb		
18						
17						
16						
2						
1	23 Apr	Finish		30 Apr		

Fig. 3.2 Week-by-week planning schedule

The 'week' column indicates the number of weeks left for the completion of the project. The 'date' column indicates either the date of the last day of the school week or when you have your final technology lesson in that week. The 'stage' column may be repeated where that stage is to be spread over several weeks. In the 'preparation' column you should indicate short-term plans, such as checking that equipment will be available. Alternative activities can be entered into the 'comments' column.

A slippage chart

A student prepared this time plan to help him organise his project.

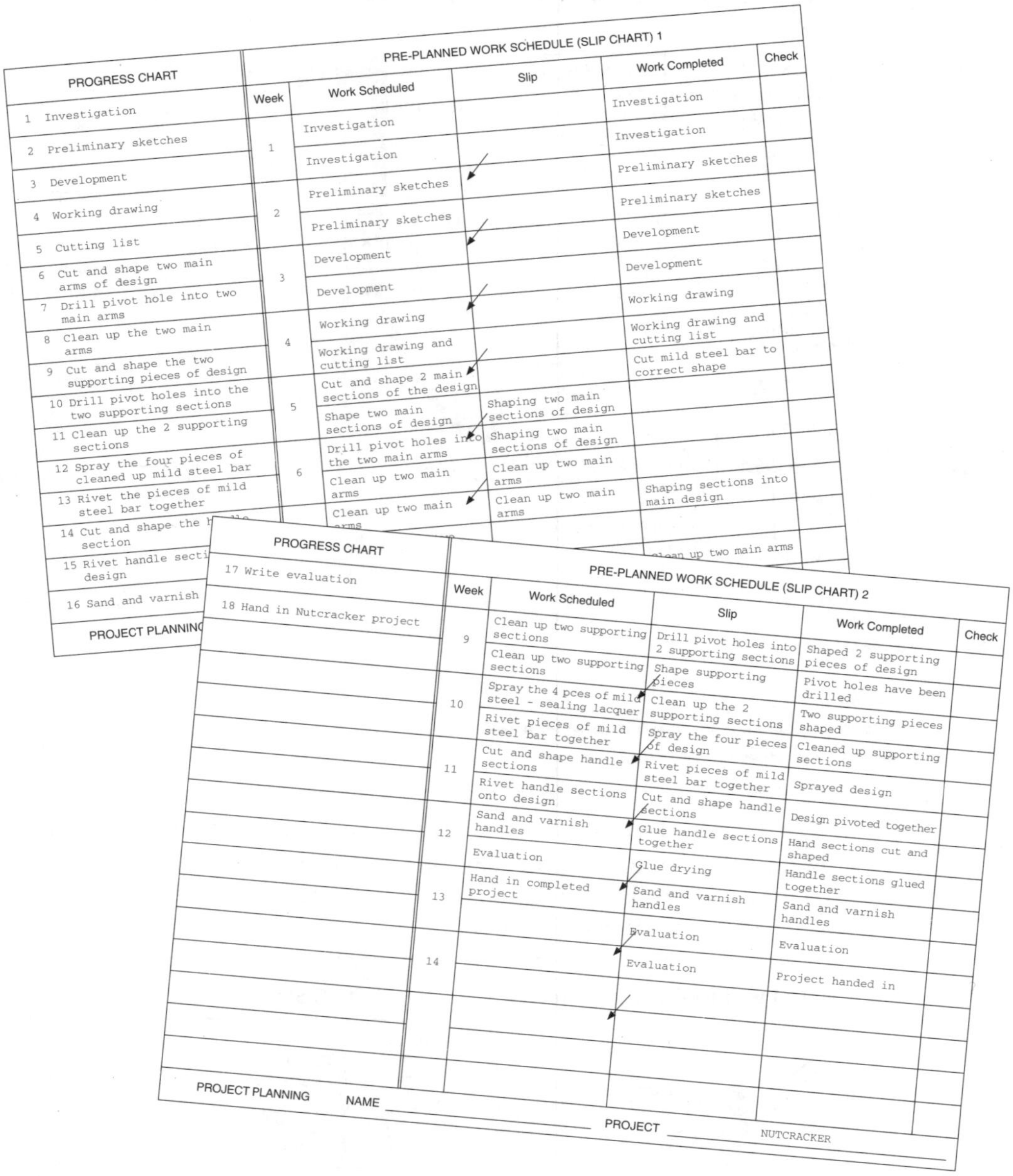

Fig. 3.3 A slippage chart shows where time has been lost

The 'slippage' column is for tasks that you failed to do in the time allowed. This slippage then becomes part of the tasks for the next work period. Because a chart like this highlights 'slippage' it is known as a slippage chart. The use of such a chart can help you avoid getting too far behind.

Describing the sequence of operations

Sometimes it is helpful to show the sequence of operations. This can be done using a flow chart similar to the one in Fig. 3.4. Such a chart can be particularly valuable when you are working as team and you need to plan the work of several people.

Planning and making

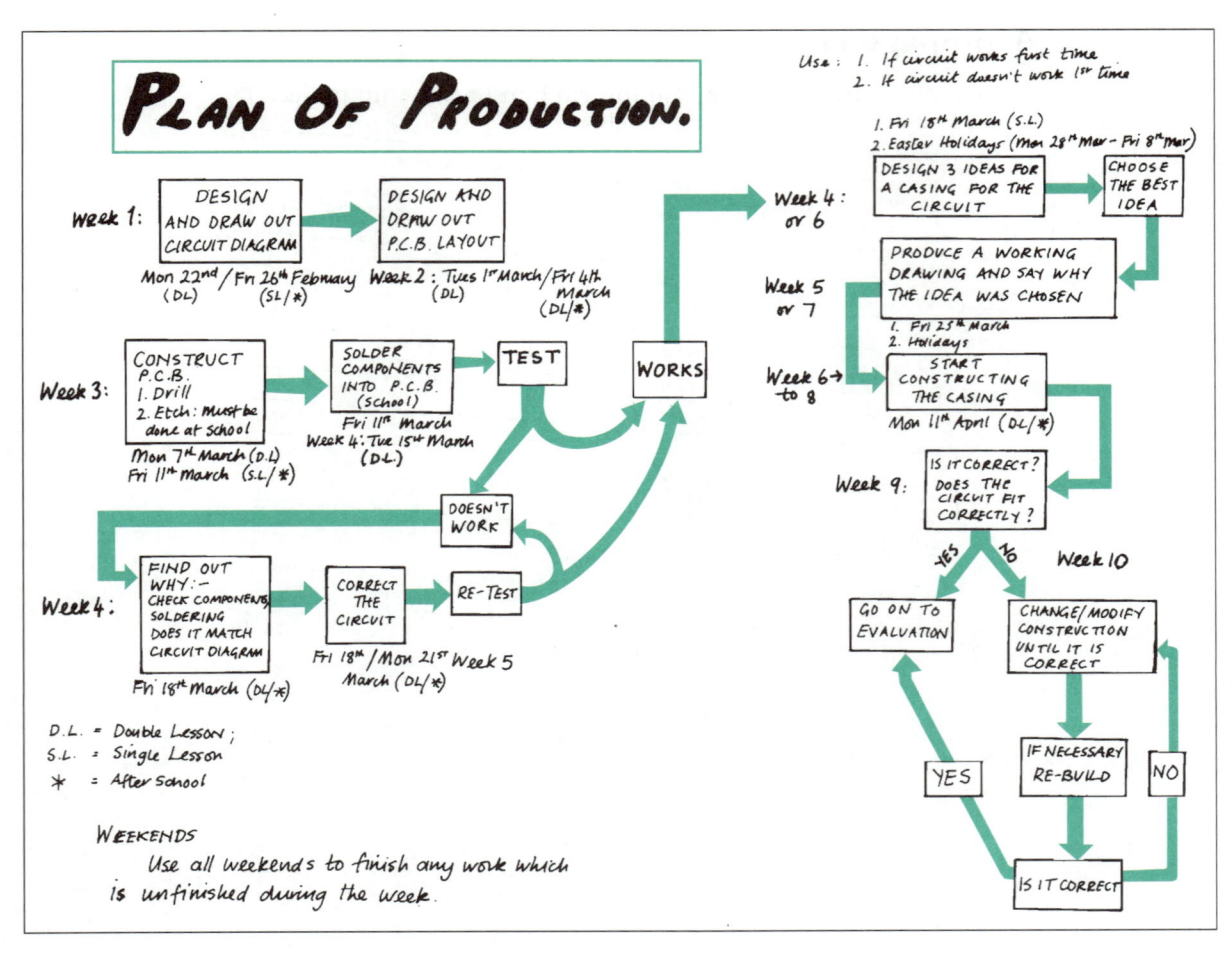

Fig. 3.4 Production plan to show steps in an electronics project

On the other hand, some students prefer to show their planning by a series of annotated sketches, rather like a story board. Fig. 3.5 was produced by a student intending to manufacture some special sweets.

Fig. 3.5 Production flowchart for making sweets

3.2 Planning

Planning for food projects

Food products often need to be manufactured on a very short time scale. The following planning sheets may be of use in such situations, as well as for other projects.

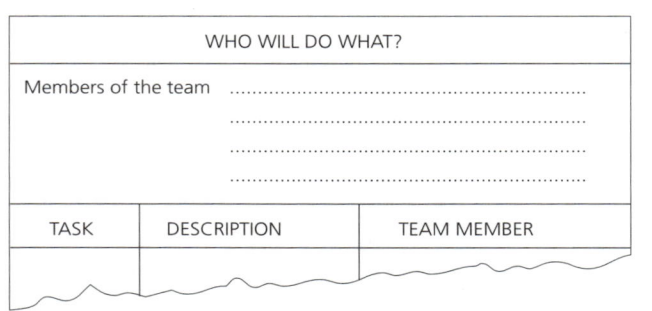

SHOPPING LIST			
I will buy my ingredients/materials from...			
ITEM	QUANTITY	UNIT COST	TOTAL COST

WHO WILL DO WHAT?		
Members of the team		
TASK	DESCRIPTION	TEAM MEMBER

EQUIPMENT NEEDED		
Project title.....................................Date........................		
ITEM	SIZE/TYPE	QUANTITY

TIME PLAN			
Project title.....................................Date........................			
Time	Task	Member responsible	Notes

Fig. 3.6 Project planning charts

Can it be made?

Designers often claim that making something complicated is easy, but producing a simple solution is difficult. How often have you heard it said that something is 'obvious', when what was meant was, it's 'simple'. Simple is seldom obvious. You are bound to make simple mistakes that you don't notice, and which others will say are obvious. It's all too easy to design things incapable of being made. This may sound ridiculous but it is often true.

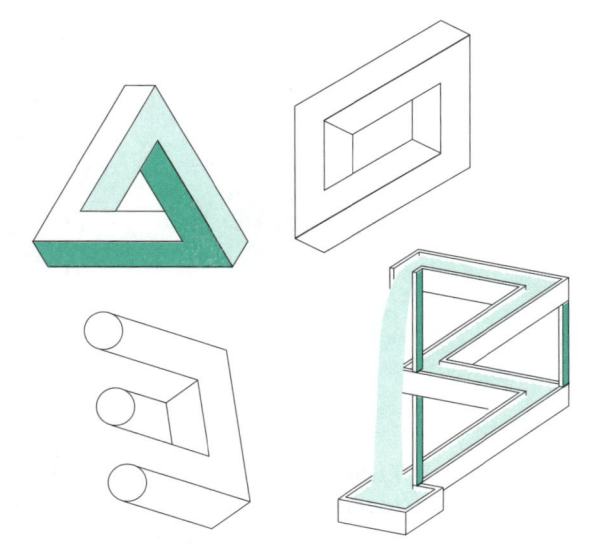

Fig. 3.7 Optical illusions. Can they be made?

These shapes are optical illusions and you will realise that it would be impossible to make them.

Planning and making

? What about the drawing of this table? Can you foresee any problems in constructing the table shown in this diagram?

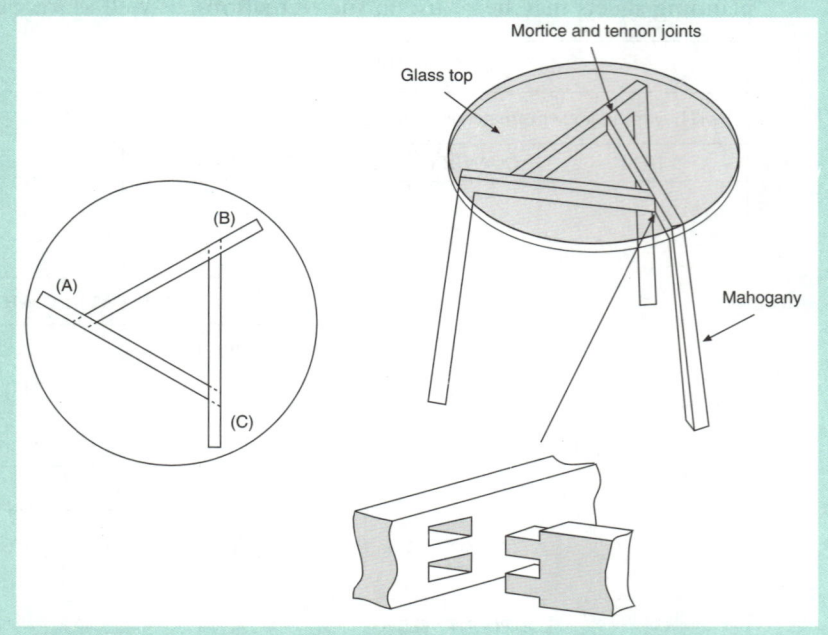

Fig 3.8 Can this table be made?

On the face of it, it seems perfectly feasible. Each of the rails is jointed into the legs, but the rails are jointed into each other, and that's the problem. All the joints can be cut and fitted together individually but if you try to assemble it, although (A) will fit into (C) and (C) might fit into (B), you'll never get (B) into part (A).

? What problems will the candidate encounter in constructing this folding chair?

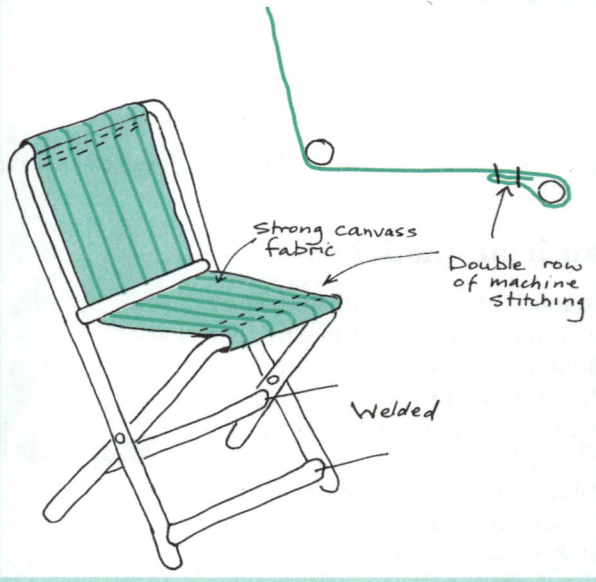

Fig 3.9 Another construction problem

Look at the idea for the seat cover. The student has decided to machine the pieces together, but it will be impossible to get the cover under the sewing machine foot after the material is wrapped around the frame.

Hint

Work out the order in which you will assemble a solution before you start to make it.

3.2 Planning

Choosing materials

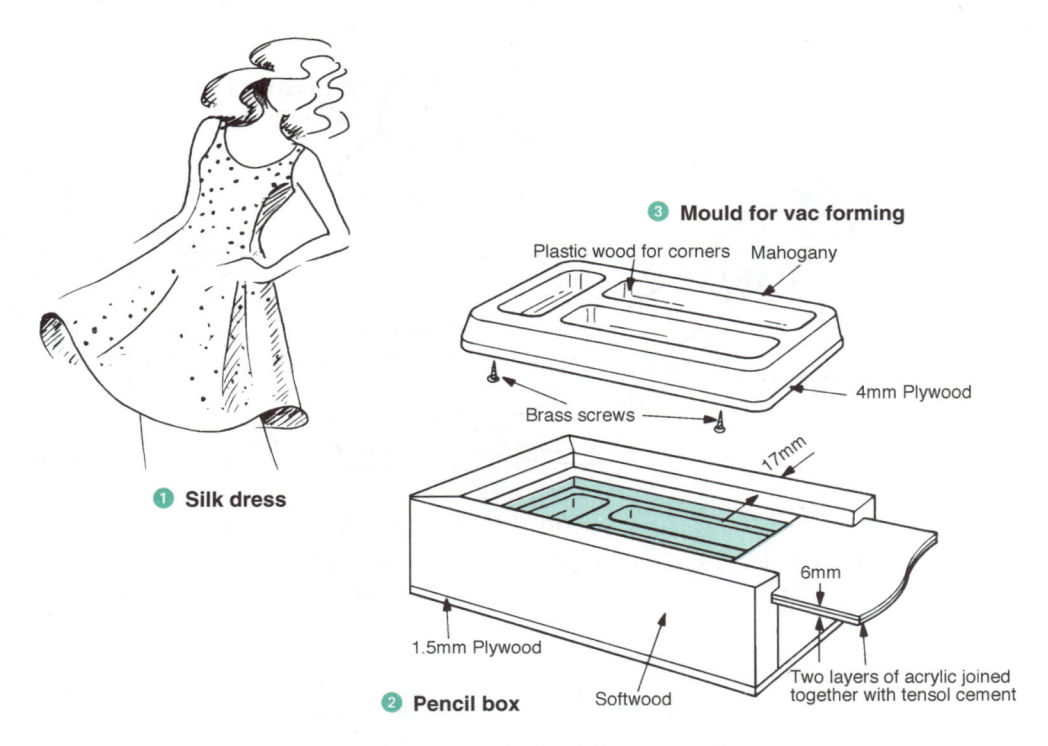

Fig. 3.10 Materials should be appropriate

It's not so easy to see what's wrong here but many of the materials will be difficult or impossible to obtain.

❶ The student has chosen to make the dress from silk, but I wonder if he or she is aware just how expensive it might be and how difficult it can be to work with? It might have been better to choose polyester, which is both cheaper and easier to work with.

❷ The pencil box is made from non-standard size timber. Use 12 or 15 mm wood, which is standard size and cheaper. Plywood 1.5 mm thick is too thin for the base – 4 mm is suitable and is, in fact, cheaper. The lid could be made from one piece of 6 mm acrylic and so save the cost of the glue. Better still, use a single piece of 3 mm acrylic; it will be strong enough.

❸ The plywood used for the base of the mould inside the pencil box could be changed for cheaper hardboard, which would be equally good. Mahogany is far too expensive for the mould; softwood or MDF could be used. Why are the pieces fixed with brass screws when gluing alone would do? Plastic wood filler is expensive, why not use polyfilla?

At all stages refer back to your specification and you will be reminded what you are trying to achieve.

Hint

Design using readily available materials. Use stock sizes, quantities, colours, etc. Try to avoid wastage. With food, it is the 'left-overs' from standard packaging that adds to the overall cost.

Save money and natural materials by substituting cheaper ones. Ask yourself, do I really need the properties of the more expensive material I have chosen?

Difficult or impossible processes

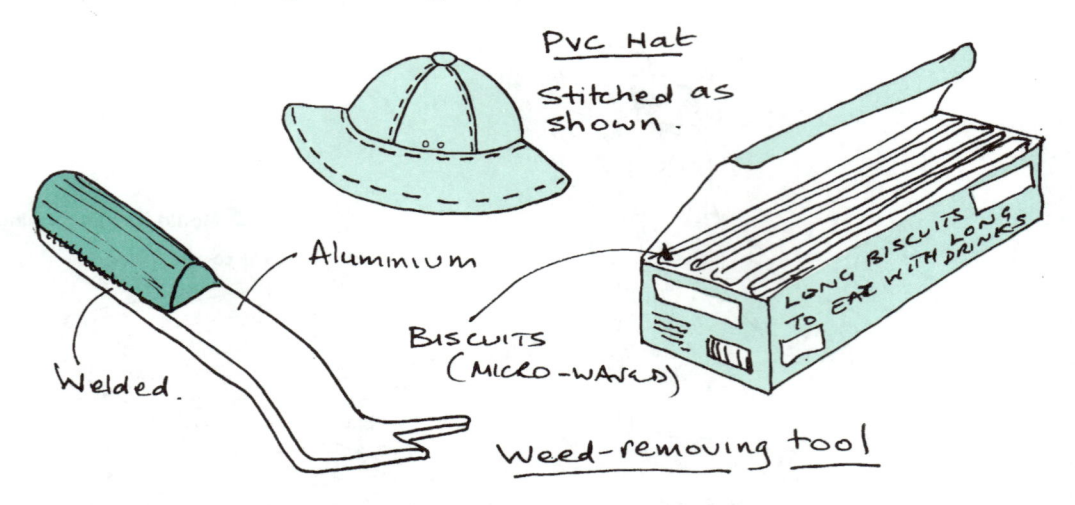

Fig. 3.11 Processes should be appropriate

① The PVC hat is going to be stitched by hand, but unless the PVC is reinforced it will split, so it might be better to find a method of gluing (or welding) it.

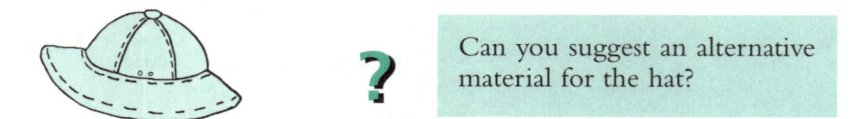

> ? Can you suggest an alternative material for the hat?

② If the biscuits are going to be packed as shown they will have to be handled very carefully. Cooking them in the microwave oven may be fine but remember, the colour won't change.

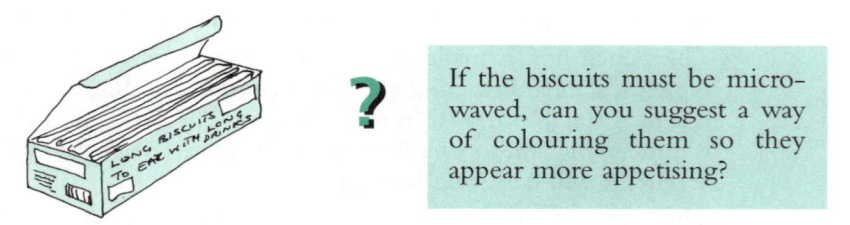

> ? If the biscuits must be microwaved, can you suggest a way of colouring them so they appear more appetising?

③ Consider the garden tool. Soldering the aluminium is going to be very difficult and will aluminium be strong enough anyway?

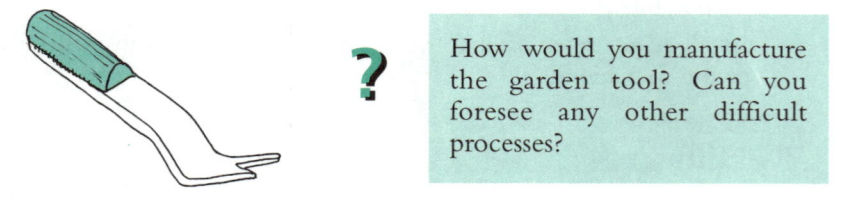

> ? How would you manufacture the garden tool? Can you foresee any other difficult processes?

Hints to avoid difficult or impossible processes

1. Check you can put the solution together logically. Draw up a list of steps or model it.
2. Specify materials that are readily available. Make sure you are specifying standard forms or standard quantities.
3. Make sure that the materials you choose can be fixed together.

Frequently students are unaware of what can or cannot be done. It is not unusual for processes to be selected that are incapable of being performed. The following chart will remind you of some processes that should be avoided.

PROCESSES TO AVOID

Adhesives

1. Glue gun is not a permanent method.
2. Glue gun gels quickly, so warm surfaces first.
3. Some PVA glues stain wood and should be washed off before they set.
4. It is almost impossible to glue many plastics, especially nylon.
5. Two-part adhesives, such as epoxy often set quickly, but still need thorough mixing to work properly.
6. Wood glues such as PVA cannot be used for plastics and metals.

Joining processes

1. Aluminium cannot be soldered using most school equipment.
2. Self-tapping screws shatter acrylic.
3. Round nails split wood. Drill a pilot hole first.
4. Wood screws do not hold well in end grain. Use a plastic (wall-fixing) plug.
5. Soft soldering large items cannot be done with a soldering iron. Use a bunsen burner or a blow lamp.
6. It is dangerous to weld galvanized steel, due to the production of poisonous fumes.

Making processes

1. You cannot drill holes in carbon or high-speed steel (files or hacksaw blades).
2. Riveting needs access to at least one side for the pop rivet tool or a hammer.
3. Through joints are stronger but need to be more accurate, and hence take more skill and care.
4. Acrylic requires lubricant when sawing on an electric saw or it may weld itself back together.
5. 'Joints' cannot easily be cut in plywood and other manufactured boards.
6. You are unlikely to have facilities to cast metals other than aluminium.

Finishing processes

1. Oily and dirty surfaces cannot be painted.
2. Gloss painting with brushes can be difficult. Consider using spray cans or dyes and varnish.
3. Avoid scratches by sanding or using emery cloth in **one** direction only.
4. Plastic dip coating is a good protection for steel, but is difficult for large objects.
5. The polishing buff can easily damage acrylic. Consider polishing by hand using liquid metal (or acrylic) polish.
6. It takes a lot longer to remove scratches from the surface of plastics than to avoid making them in the first place. Cover surfaces with paper.

Fig. 3.12 Manufacturing processes that you should avoid

3.3 Making your solution

The following advice will help you make your project.

Clean and tidy the area where you are going to work.
Make sure you have all the equipment and materials you need for each work session.
Wear the correct protective clothing.
Adopt all safety precautions.
Work logically, thinking ahead to the next stage.
Put away equipment when you are not using it.
Don't guess how to do something. If you are not sure, ask your teacher.
Practice new skills before applying them to your project.
Use jigs and templates to help you make several identical items.
Be prepared to make changes to your plans.

Coping with problems

During the making of your project things are likely to go wrong. Part of being a good technologist is learning to cope with difficulties. If things go wrong you will not be penalised. An important part of your assessment is how you react. If you always get angry or dispirited you are unlikely to make much progress and your assessment is likely to suffer. Whenever you have a problem make sure you make a note of it in your technology diary describing what happened and what you did about it. So what kinds of things can go wrong?

Not enough time

Probably the biggest problem you will have is not having enough time. Of course, you should estimate how long a job will take and if you think you don't have enough time then modify the task. The following may help you avoid tackling too much.

- Tasks, particularly practical tasks, will often take longer than you expect.
- Keep a record of previous projects so that you will have some idea how long things take.
- If you are getting hopelessly behind it is possible that you are aiming for perfection!
- Ask your teacher or the technician for advice.
- Talk to students who have tackled the same task before.

Cost too high

If you find that a project is going to cost too much but you still think it is worth doing, you can try the following.

- Make a model.
- Make part of the project.
- Go into partnership with someone else.
- Try to get sponsorship, e.g., from local business, another department in the school, bank, etc.
- Simplify your idea.
- Construct a prototype from cheaper materials.

Materials not available

Although you should try to design using readily available materials, sometimes what you thought was available turns out to have been used up. Try the following suggestions.

- Persuade someone to give you theirs.
- Change the material.
- Use second-hand materials.

Others not co-operating

From time to time there will be disagreements between members of your group. If you are working on a group project then overcoming such problems is part of life and also part of GCSE Technology. The following may help.

- Try to agree in advance what you will do if there is a disagreement.
- Decide who is going to be responsible for which decisions.
- Don't lose your temper. Try to talk through the problems.

Teacher absent or workroom not available

If you are excited about your work it can be very disappointing not to be able to get on with it. Think about the following.

- Have alternative tasks available.
- Evaluate your work so far (see Chapter 4).
- Plan your work for the next session.
- Start designing other things.
- Start preparing how you might present your work to others.

3.3 Checklist

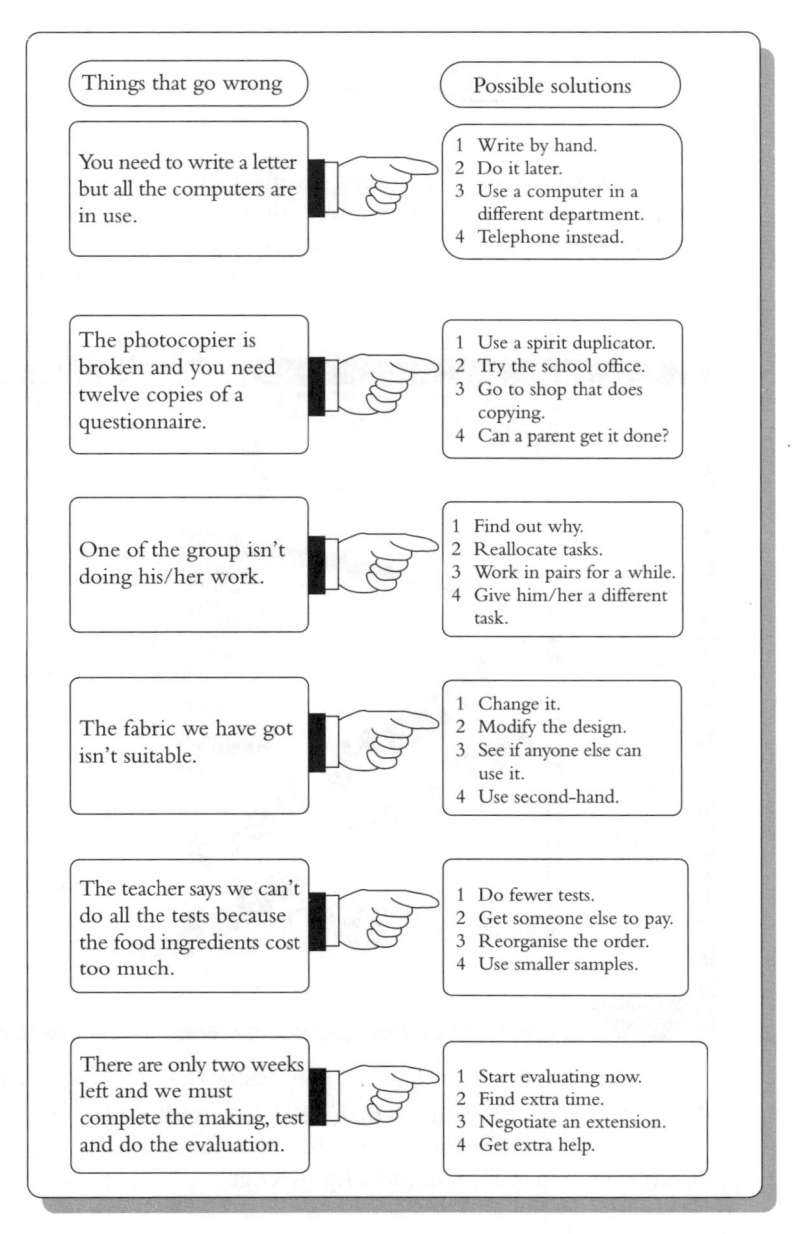

Things that go wrong	Possible solutions
You need to write a letter but all the computers are in use.	1 Write by hand. 2 Do it later. 3 Use a computer in a different department. 4 Telephone instead.
The photocopier is broken and you need twelve copies of a questionnaire.	1 Use a spirit duplicator. 2 Try the school office. 3 Go to shop that does copying. 4 Can a parent get it done?
One of the group isn't doing his/her work.	1 Find out why. 2 Reallocate tasks. 3 Work in pairs for a while. 4 Give him/her a different task.
The fabric we have got isn't suitable.	1 Change it. 2 Modify the design. 3 See if anyone else can use it. 4 Use second-hand.
The teacher says we can't do all the tests because the food ingredients cost too much.	1 Do fewer tests. 2 Get someone else to pay. 3 Reorganise the order. 4 Use smaller samples.
There are only two weeks left and we must complete the making, test and do the evaluation.	1 Start evaluating now. 2 Find extra time. 3 Negotiate an extension. 4 Get extra help.

Fig. 3.13 Quick-reference guide to some problems and their solutions

Checklist

Plan well ahead.
Use charts or diagrams to show your planning.
Organise things in a logical way.
Always have alternative tasks.
Keep a record of what you do.
Make sure there are no features in your design which will make manufacture difficult or impossible.
Select economical materials.
Be aware that things may go wrong and be prepared to be flexible.
Work in a tidy, well-organised environment.

Chapter 4   Evaluating work in technology

4.1 Introduction

Product evaluation is an expanding business and there is a wealth of information available to the consumer on a wide range of topics. In Which? magazine the Consumer Association produces a monthly analysis of products and services. The Association also publishes advice on specific topics in magazines such as Holiday Which, Which Car? and What Video?

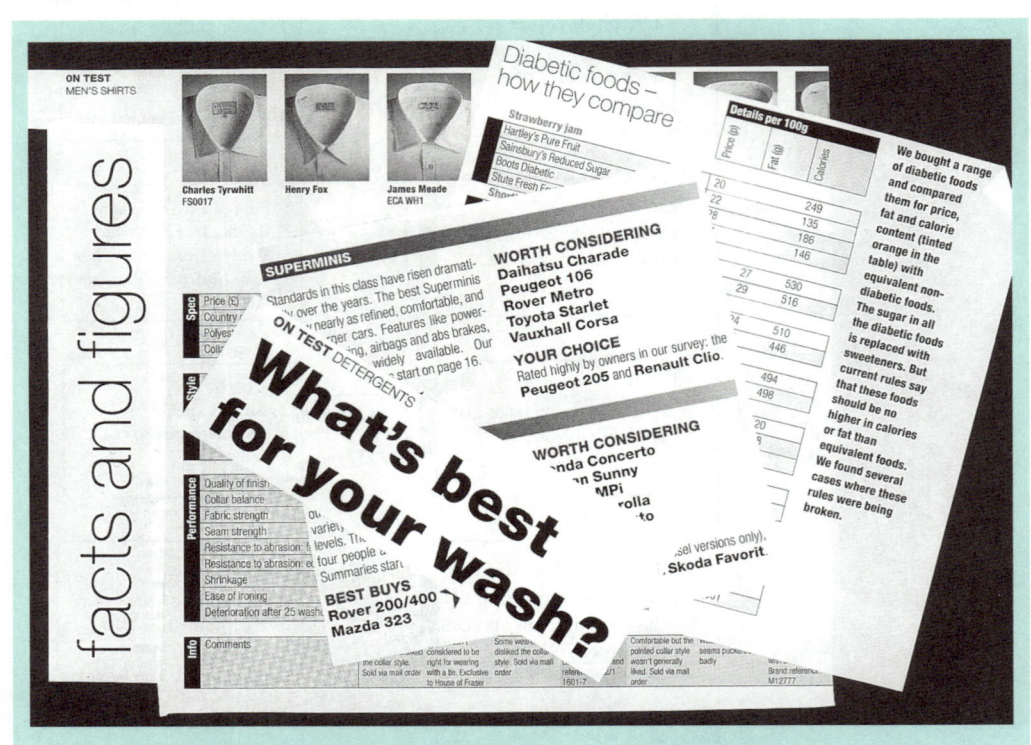

Fig. 4.1 Product evaluation depends on the clear presentation of information

Look at a copy of Which? magazine (you will find it in most public libraries). In what ways is information presented in order to make advice clear to readers who do not have specific technical knowledge?

At GCSE level you are expected to evaluate your own work and to have experience of evaluating the work of others. If you make a mistake (and everyone does), be honest about it and say what you should have done instead. Although your finished products may not satisfy the specification perfectly, a careful and critical analysis will improve your marks. It may also help you avoid making the same errors with your next project.

4.2 Evaluating your own work

Some students think evaluation is a task to be left until the project is completed. In fact, it is a continuous process that will help you produce the best possible final soution. Throughout the design process you will need to evaluate your work, make decisions and make changes as a result of those decisions. Make sure the assessor knows what you and others think of your work by adding notes to your drawings when, for example, you are choosing the best idea or the most suitable materials. Such comments not only help with making design decisions, they also show the assessor what you were thinking and why you made your decisions.

4.2 Evaluating your own work

? Here is an example of how a student has annotated sketches with appropriate evaluative comments.

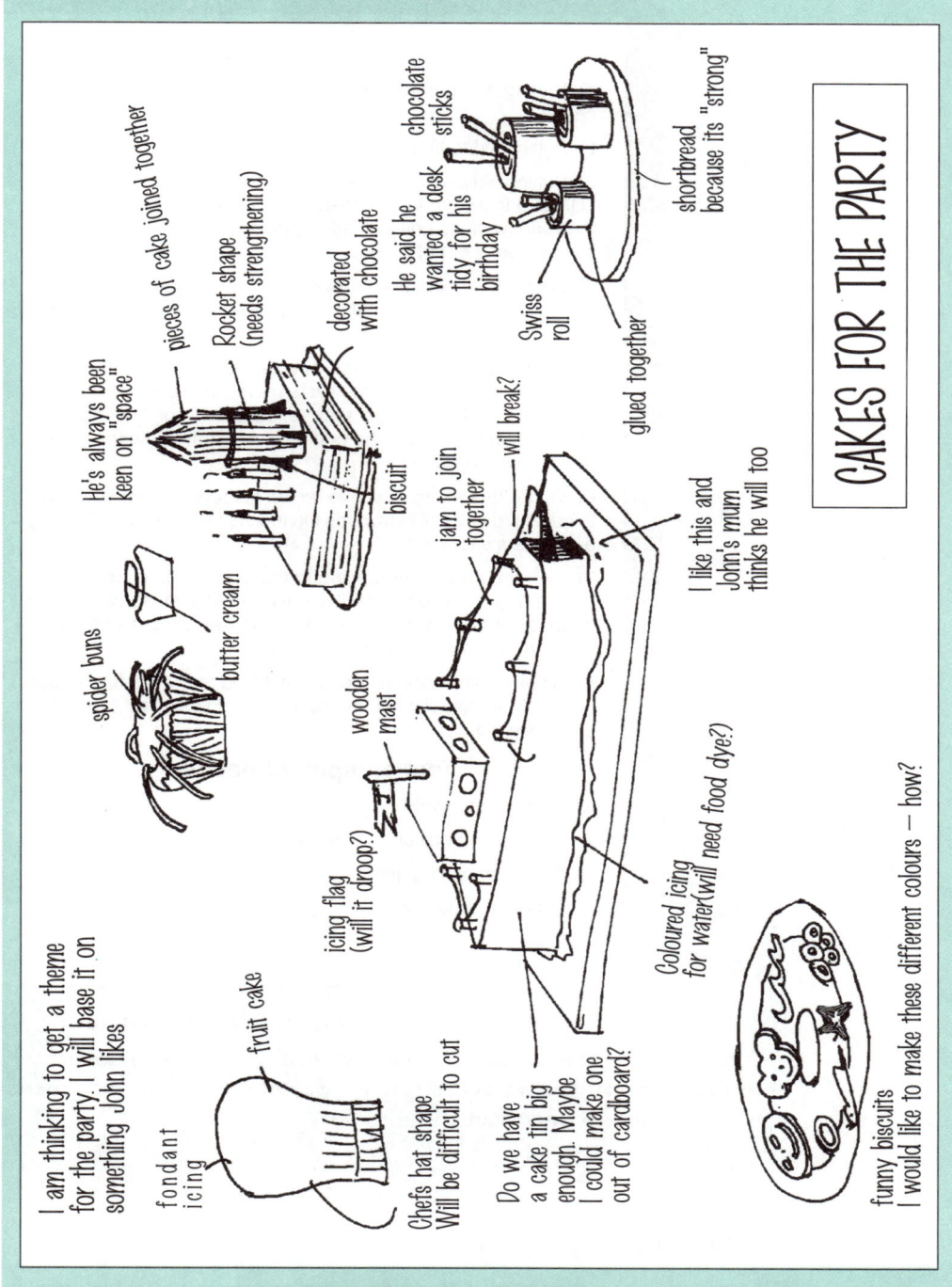

Fig. 4.2 Cakes for John's party

Look at what the student has said. What else might this student have done? What do you think she means by 'gluing together' the Swiss roll and the shortbread?

Testing

At all stages you will need to test your project. Begin by deciding what you want to find out and write it down. You will now need to produce a test schedule, which is an ordered list of what you intend to do.

Evaluating work in technology

? Here is a test schedule produced by a student designing a putting aid for golfers.

Test specification

1) Putting aid to be tested inside, on a carpet, not a thick pile carpet.

2) Putting aid to be tested outside on a putting green.

3) Putting aid's sensitivity is to be tested, i.e. whether or not the LDR and therefore the mechanism is triggered by dim light, or if the shadow of the golf ball, as it approaches the LDR, if it covers it will trigger it or not.

4) When the mechanism inside the system is subjected to an inclination uphill or downhill is it rendered more or less efficient as a result of the slope?

5) When the system is used outside or inside is the golf ball always guided in towards the system's mechanism? i.e. does the golf ball sometimes not get returned as a result of it not reaching the mechanism – does the golf ball just hit the guiders and roll back down the slope?

6) With reference to 5) above do the guiders that are supposed to guide the golf ball in towards the mechanism work as efficiently as they are supposed to?

7) If a putt is struck properly and firmly on the line for the LDR does the golf ball, because it is travelling so fast, sometimes hit the back of the system and return of its own accord without the mechanism playing any part in its return?

8) What do other golfers feel about it? Do they think it is a good idea? Would they like one themselves would they find it useful as a practice aid.

Test equipment needed

1) My golf putting aid.
2) A flat, long piece of non-thick-pile carpet.
3) A practice putting green.
4) Different slopes on 5)

Fig. 4.3 Test schedule for golfers' putting aid

Although the student has stated clearly what he intends to do and what he is trying to find out, can you suggest a simpler way of setting out the schedule in order to make it easier to understand?

Testing food products

When testing foods you may need to use a tasting panel. Here is a list of factors you should consider when setting up a tasting panel.

- Decide what you are trying to find out and design a suitable chart on which to record answers.
- Choose a selection of people who represent those most likely to purchase your product.
- Try to arrange for members of the panel to test in private so that they don't influence each other.
- Allow testers to clean their mouth with a drink of water between each test.
- Make sure the foods with the strongest flavours are tasted last.
- Present you findings in a way that clearly shows the results, e.g., pie charts.
- Indicate what conclusions you have drawn.
- Show how these conclusions will influence your design decisions.

Here is a chart design you may like to use when conducting food tests.

4.2 Evaluating your own work

Food Test

Appearance
Tick the box that best describes what you think ✓

☐ Like very much ☐ Like moderately ☐ Dislike ☐ Dislike a lot

Smell
Smell the product and tick the box of your choice

☐ Like very much ☐ Like moderately ☐ Dislike ☐ Dislike a lot

Taste
Taste the product and tick the box of your choice

☐ Like very much ☐ Like moderately ☐ Dislike ☐ Dislike a lot

Texture
Taste the product and decide how much you like the texture

☐ Like very much ☐ Like moderately ☐ Dislike ☐ Dislike a lot

Fig. 4.4 Food testing questionnaire

Following a holiday in Russia, a group of students decided to undertake a project on Russian food. They had liked the food in Moscow and wanted to discover the opinions of others. The students set up a taste panel to survey classmates' opinions of some Russian biscuits the group had brought back.

The Biscuit Test

We asked a tasting panel of twenty people what they thought of our special Russian biscuits – 'Korzhiki'.

On a scale of one to five, they were asked to judge colour, flavour, texture, appearance and originality. They were also invited to make suggestions if they felt that there could have been some changes.

On the whole, our biscuits were successful – as the following average marks out of five show:

Flavour	3
Colour	3.2
Texture	3.3
Originality	3.3
Appearance	4.15

Almost half our panel would not have changed the recipe. Those who did make sensible comments felt that the biscuits could have been more moist. One boy wanted to include chocolate but as we weren't making chocolate biscuits, this doesn't really seem relevant! Another thought that our biscuits were "dry, tasteless, burnt and similar to cream crackers – but quite good".

So, dismissing lunatics, we can confidently recommend our Khorzhiki!

Fig. 4.5 Results of the biscuit taste survey

It is clear that tasters liked the biscuits' appearance, which will be important if the students want to produce and sell them.

1. How do you think the tasters' opinions of flavour will affect sales?
2. Would you do anything to change the flavour?

Evaluating the process

Throughout the project you will be making changes both to the design and to how you will use your time. Your changes should be recorded in some way, such as on paper, by photography, or on video or cassette tape. When the making is completed you should evaluate the process. It may be useful to ask these three questions.

- Did I use my time effectively?
- What difficulties did I have with this project and how did I overcome them?
- How would I do the project differently next time?

Evaluating the product

When you have completed your project you must evaluate the result and record your results in your project folder. One way of evaluating your work is to ask yourself the following four questions.

- Does my solution satisfy the design brief and specification?
- What are the strengths and successes of my solution?
- What are the weaknesses and failures of my solution?
- How can my design be further improved?

Comparison with the specification

List the points of your specification but rephrase them as questions, with the answers to the questions alongside. This example looks at the first-aid kit for hikers, referred to in Chapter 2.

1. Does the kit contain all necessary medical items?	1. Almost, but there wasn't enough room for everything. I decided to put the aspirins in a smaller jar.
2. Is the kit small enough to be carried in the outside pocket of a rucksack?	2. Yes. It fits inside all the rucksacks I have tested.
3. Is the kit waterproof?	3. I have tested it with a hosepipe and the contents didn't get wet. I also submerged it in a bath of water and the items still stayed dry.
4. Does the kit have any sharp edges or corners?	4. It hasn't any sharp edges or corners but the catch sometimes gets caught on my rucksack.
5. Are there separate compartments in the kit for the contents?	5. I decided they would not be necessary. To make separate compartments would be fiddly. I did, however, find it was difficult to get small items out without emptying everything onto the ground. Next time I will produce sections for the most used items, scissors, safety pins and tweezers.

Fig. 4.6 Product evalutation against the design specification

In addition the student could have proposed other solutions to the difficulties, e.g.,

> Catch – I have considered a plastic catch with smoother edges so that it doesn't get caught. Alternatively, I have an idea for a case made from canvas which, as well as being lighter, will not have any hard or sharp edges or corners.

Finally, the student should have produced drawings of any ideas for further improvements.

4.2 Evaluating your own work

Final testing

You must test your finished project and present the test results as tables or graphs. Fig. 4.7 shows some evaluation sheets produced by a student who designed an electronic device to measure angles between surfaces, such as walls. He was particularly careful to have the device tested in use on a building site.

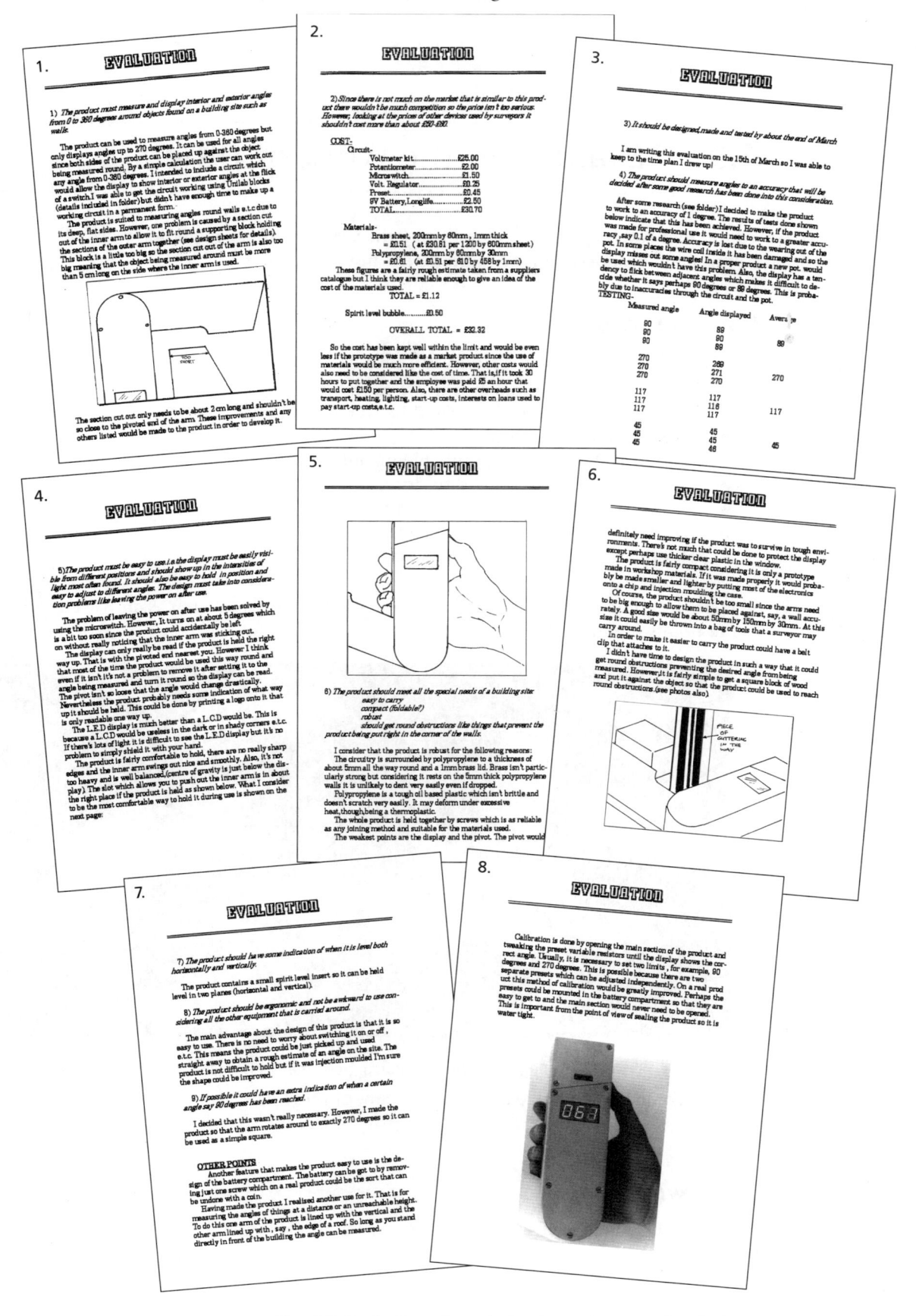

Fig. 4.7 Evaluation of an electronic angle-measuring device

Evaluating work in technology

The student has begun his evaluation of the finished product by comparing it carefully with the original specification. The details are covered in depth and he summarises the good and bad points, giving an explanation of why things are not as good as they should be and suggesting improvements.

? What other things do you think this student might have done?

4.3 Evaluating the work of others

You should have experience of evaluating the work of others, including work of different cultures and products designed in different historical times.

Looking at products

A useful start to evaluating the work of others is to:
- find out what the product is made from;
- find out if other materials would be suitable;
- find out how it was made;
- find out if there are other suitable manufacturing processes;
- find out what it is supposed to do;
- ask others how well it performs its task;
- suggest improvements to its design;
- ask others to suggest improvements.

? Here are some photographs of hats from around the world. For each hat consider the points mentioned above.

Fig. 4.8 Some products have many purposes
How could you improve the design of any of these hats?

Who will gain?

Deciding who will gain from a design can be another useful way to start analysing a product. Often a design will benefit some people but disadvantage others. You can set out a chart like the one in Fig. 4.9 to help you see who will be affected by a design.

4.3 Evaluating the work of others

① List in the middle column all who will be affected by the design.
② List in the left-hand column only those who will be *directly* affected.
③ List in the right-hand column only those who will be *indirectly* affected.
④ Now highlight (underline, colour, etc) all who will benefit from the idea.

The others will lose as a result of the design.

Consider this example of inexpensive imported clothing. As you can see not everyone benefits.

Who will be affected?		
Product Inexpensive imported clothing		
Directly affected	**All affected**	**Indirectly affected**
General public	General public	
Workers in UK factories	Workers in UK factories	
	UK factory owners	UK factory owners
	Clothing shops	Clothing shops
Clothing designers	Clothing designers	
Textile manufacturers	Textile manufacturers	
Overseas workers	Overseas workers	
Transport companies	Transport companies	
	Advertising agents	Advertising agents
	Market traders	Market traders
UK spending abroad	UK spending abroad	
	Exporters	Exporters
	UK farmers	UK farmers

Fig, 4.9 Evaluating a product's effects

Product analysis

An excellent way to find out information about an existing product is to examine its performance against a set of criteria. You might like to use a chart similar to Fig. 4.10.

Score / Criterion	Poor 1	Bad 2	Average 3	Good 4	Very good 5	Score
Function						
Aesthetics						
Ergonomics						
Economics						
Safety						
					Total Score	

Fig. 4.10 Evaluation of a product against performance criteria

In addition you could draw a sketch of the product and add comments.

Top – you can be burned by steam if this is removed when water is hot

Sometimes steam escapes from here, which can be dangerous

Spout – pours well

Switch – conveniently placed

Aesthetics – quite elegantly shaped: well co-ordinated neutral colours

Handle not shaped – difficult to hold when the kettle is full

Shows level of water inside. After a time the "hardness" in the water causes the surface to go cloudy

Economics – reasonably priced

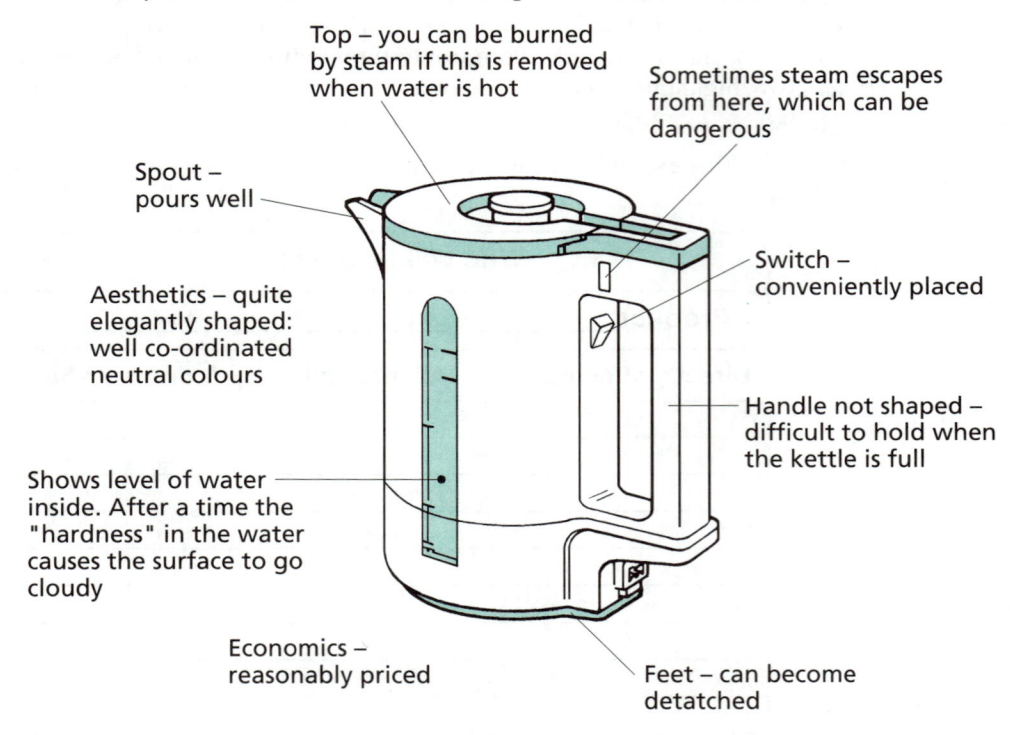

Feet – can become detatched

Fig. 4.11 Evaluation of an existing product

Presenting your findings

A group of students undertook a survey to find out what people thought about a range of low-calorie chocolate drinks. The students investigated the following factors.

1 **Cost**
   They calculated an average of three drink prices, each taken from a different shop.
2 **Quantity**
   They noted the mass (in grams) of each portion of drink.
3 **Energy content**
   They noted the energy content (in kilojoules) of each portion.
4 **Protein content**
   They noted the protein content (in grams) of each portion.
5 **Carbohydrate content**
   They noted the carbohydrate content (in grams) of each portion.
6 **Colour**
   Four people judged each drink for colour and each tester gave a mark out of ten. An average mark was then calculated for each portion.
7 **Smell**
   Four people judged each drink for smell and each tester gave a mark out of ten. An average mark was then calculated for each portion.
8 **Taste**
   Four people judged each drink for taste and each tester gave a mark out of twenty. An average mark was then calculated for each portion.

Fig. 4.12 presents the results of the survey.

4.4 Case study

Product	Cost	Amount	Energy	Protein	Carbohydrate	Fat	Colour	Smell	Taste	Overall
Cadbury's Chocolate Break	110	36	1850	13.4	52	34.7	4	5	6	BAD / 5 / BUY
Ovaltine Options: Choc n' Toffee	99	28	1612	14	45.5	23.3	6	9	8	GOOD / 8 / BUY
Ovaltine Options: Choc n' Banana	99	28	1612	14	45.5	23.3	6	9	10	BEST / 10 / BUY
Cadbury's High-Lights	105	32	1459	13.4	40.3	22.9	3	5	2	TOTAL / 4 / FAILURE
Instant Ovaltine Light	99	28	1343	14	45	25	3	6	4	AVERAGE / 6 / BUY

(Scale: ○○○○○ Worst ← → Best)

Fig 4.12 Findings from chocolate-drink survey

?
1. Why do you think the group scored taste out of twenty but smell and colour out of only ten?
2. What do you think was the purpose of listing the energy, protein and carbohydrate content of each drink?
3. The group judged Cadbury's Options (Choc n' Banana) to be the 'best buy'. From the results of the survey, do you agree with them?

4.4 Case study

A student produced the following design brief for a bird table that would also function as a nesting-box.

> **Design brief**
> I can see a lot of birds from the balcony of our flat. I will design a bird table and nesting-box to attract them.

Fig. 4.13 shows the student's working drawings and a simple planning sheet, together with a solution to the design problem.

Evaluating work in technology

WEEK	HOW I PLANNED MY TIME	
	TASK	SLIPPAGE
1	Get materials	Some materials missing
2	Mark out	Only just started
3	Cut to shape	Cut top only
4	Finish shaping	Cut rest of pieces
5	Drill holes Sand	Drilled wrong holes, must make pieces again
6	Assemble	Still some parts to make
7	Varnish	Assemble next week
8	Evaluate	Won't varnish - don't want it pretty!

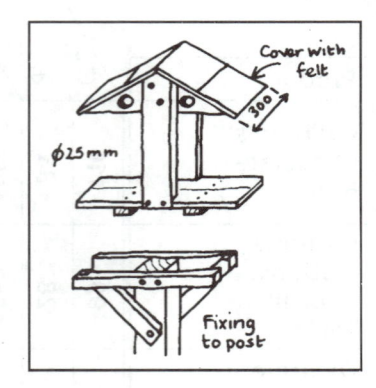

Fig. 4.13 Stages in production of a bird table and nesting-box

> Look carefully at the photograph of the finished product and decide how well it satisfies the brief. Compare it with the working drawings and try to answer the following questions.
> 1. How well does the solution satisfy the brief?
> 2. Are there any obvious problems with the manufacture of the solution?
> 3. What recommendations for improvements or changes in the manufacturing process would you suggest?

Here are an assessor's answers to those questions.

1 How well does the solution satisfy the brief?

It is impossible to say if the product works as a bird nesting-box, but the table seems large enough. Had the project been better researched the student would have discovered that birds will not normally nest in a nesting/feeding unit due to overcrowding of the table at feeding times. The solution has all the requirements to attract birds (table, nesting-box, perches), and above the ground the birds will be protected from cats, but the holes appear too large, and certainly bigger than on the drawing. It is unlikely to meet the requirements of the brief if it is intended for a balcony; the post cannot be driven into the ground and it might be better to consider fixing the unit to the wall.

2 Are there any obvious problems with the manufacture of the solution?

The finished product looks like the working drawing but differs in a few details, e.g., addition of perches and slight enlargement of the nesting-box and access holes. The planning schedule shows that time was well allocated to the different tasks, but a problem arose with fixing the box to the post. Holes for the perches were drilled too large and this meant the uprights had to be replaced. Having lost time, there was little chance to catch up and so the product appears to have been rushed at the end. More time should have been allowed for making and some time might have been left free in case things went wrong.

3 What recommendations for improvements or changes in the manufacturing process would you suggest?

If the drawing had been changed when the design was altered materials may not have been wasted. More research should have revealed that the table cannot be combined with a nesting-box. The nesting area is quite large and might be better if it were smaller. It was a serious oversight to make the solution with a post that needed to be fixed into the ground. Even a post with a stand might take up too much room on the balcony. A design where the box and table would hang from the edge of the balcony could be considered. It would not take up balcony space and the birds would not need to come too close to the flat. There would also be less mess on the balcony. It was a mistake not to varnish the box; varnishing not only improves the appearance but protects the timber from bad weather.

Further comments

1. In a complete evaluation the student should have compared the finished design with the details of the specification.
2. The student should have tested the design, for example, by mounting the nesting-box/bird table on the balcony, and over a month or so recording which types of birds were attracted to it.
3. Over a longer period, the student could have recorded which types of birds took up residence in the nesting-box.
4. If the student had wanted to restrict the box to smaller birds, such as tits, the access hole needs to be very small.
5. It is possible that mice might be attracted to the nesting-box, too!

Checklist

Evaluating includes testing.
Evaluate as you go along.
Be honest and not self-congratulatory.
Choose a testing panel from those who are most likely to be your customers.
Study the ways in which professionals have designed and manufactured similar products.
Present your findings in a way that helps you draw conclusions.
Draw conclusions and suggest improvements.

Chapter 5 — Information technology

5.1 Introduction

Although you will probably learn about and use information technology (IT) in a number of your school subjects, it is particularly likely that you will use it in English, mathematics, science, humanities and modern languages. You may also use IT as part of your technology projects. In this book you will find examples of the use of information technology, but if you are studying for a GCSE in Information Systems (Attainment Target 5) or Technology (Attainment Targets 1–5) then you should consult a specialised textbook.

This chapter will introduce you to the software (programs) with which you are likely to become familiar. If you have access to a computer at home you will be able to work away from the distractions of school.

5.2 Word-processing (WP)

For some years students have used word-processors in project work and, apart from games, it is likely that word-processing was your first experience of a computer. This chapter does not attempt to teach you how to word-process, but here are some suggestions for uses to which word-processing software can be put:

- writing reports, letters, etc.;
- summarising interviews;
- creating questionnaires;
- writing evaluations and recording the results of tests.

The advantages are:

- your work will be neater and tidier than handwriting;
- it gives work a professional appearance;
- your letters, reports, etc., can be changed quickly or adapted for a different situation;
- your spelling (and sometimes your grammar) can be checked automatically.

The disadvantages are:

- WP can be slower than writing by hand, at first;
- there is a tendency to use a word-processor when a hand-written note will do;
- your spelling can suffer.

5.3 Databases

A database is a store of information. Databases come in many forms – not all are computerised. Examples include:

- books and encyclopaedias;
- filing cabinets;
- card indices;
- databases available on disk, such as Quest or Archive;
- databases available on CD-ROM;
- databases accessible through telephone lines, such as NERIS, Campus 2000 and Prestel;
- teletext (the BBC have called their service Ceefax, on ITV it is called Oracle).

Some of these databases can provide you with valuable sources of information and others will allow you to store your own information. Some, such as teletext, are free to use, others can work out to be quite expensive since, as well as paying a monthly subscription you also have to pay for the time you are on the telephone. There are no charges for using a CD-ROM or your own computer, but the initial cost of the equipment can be high.

Computerised databases

A computerised database will allow you to:
- store information;
- find information;
- provide information for others;
- reorganise information.

When to use a database

1. Decide what you want to find out.
2. Decide if a database is the most appropriate source for the information.
3. Check how much it will cost to use.
4. Ask if there is a cheaper way to obtain the information.

As part of a project on nutrition and diet, two students used a database on an Apple Macintosh computer. Fig. 5.1 shows three pictures of the screen display.

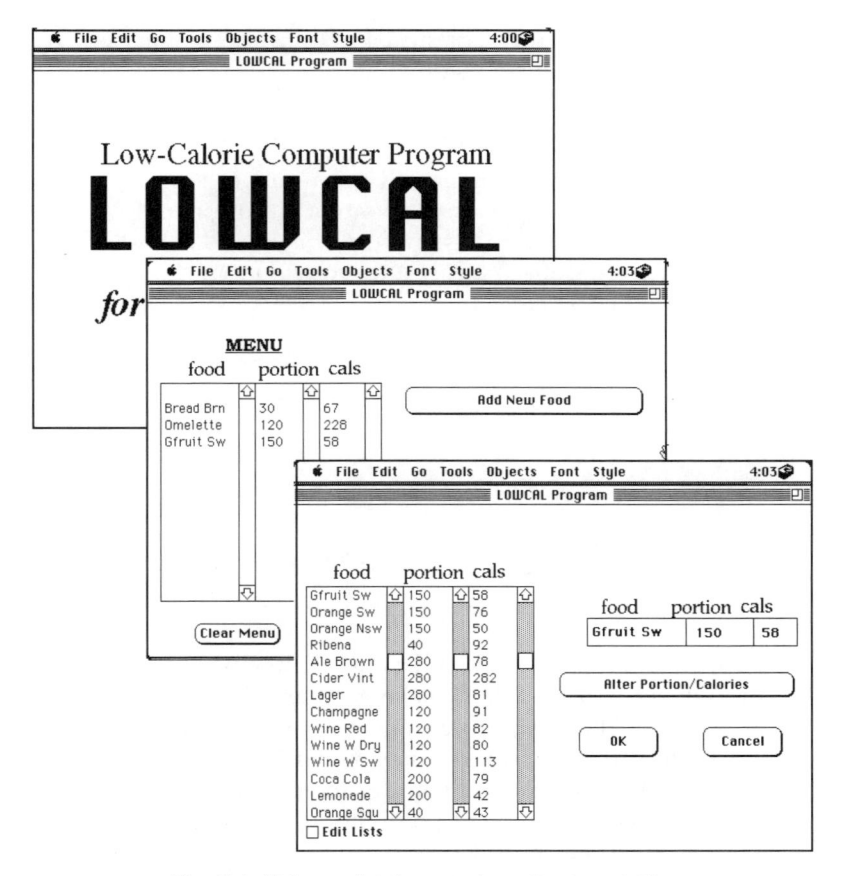

Fig. 5.1 Using a database to investigate nutrition

In addition, the students produced a manual to use with the database.

Information technology

Fig. 5.2 Manual and disk for the nutrition database

Hints for constructing a computerised database

Begin by asking yourself these questions.
  1 Will a card index or similar system be adequate?
  2 Have I suitable software?
  3 Can I write the software?

Then make these decisions and act upon them.
  4 Decide what information you want to store.
  5 Decide how you want to view the information.
  6 On paper, design a structure for your database.
  7 Enter the information into your database.

Now test what you have produced.
  8 Try it out yourself.
  9 Get someone else to use it.
 10 Modify it if necessary.

5.4 Spreadsheets

A spreadsheet is a quick and convenient way of performing calculations, such as you would need to do when making design decisions or when setting up a business. A spreadsheet allows you to change one or more of the pieces of information and then it will automatically change others, rather like a programmed calculator. The spreadsheet re-calculates instantly and you can see the outcome immediately. For example, a group of students considered the possibility of setting up a business to provide food for office parties, functions, birthdays, etc.

They decided they wanted to provide a range of menus.
- Basic – a cold buffet.
- Executive – a hot buffet.
- De luxe – hot food served by waiting staff.

They worked out what expenses each menu would incur.

Fixed costs (or overheads – those costs not directly related to sales)
  administration   £25.00 per function

Variable costs (costs directly related to sales)
  transport   £25.00 (for an average function)
  breakages   20p per cover (a cover is a person to be fed)
  waiting staff   1 per 10 covers (basic and executive)
                          1 per 5 covers (de luxe)
  wages for waiting staff £20.00 per session

Food preparation
  basic meal   £2.50
  executive meal   £5.00
  de luxe meal   £8.00

The students realised they could use a spreadsheet to calculate the overall cost of providing their services for any particular function.

Fig. 5.3 is a picture of the computer screen observed while the spreadsheet program was running. It shows the cost of a function for 100 covers.

Buffet Costings (SS)

	A	B	C	D
1		Basic	Executive	De Luxe
2				
3	No of covers	100	100	100
4	Fixed costs per function	25	25	25
5	Transport per function	20	20	20
6	Breakages	20	20	20
7	Waitresses	200	200	400
8	Food cost per head	2.5	5	8
9	Total food cost	250	500	800
10				
11				
12	Total cost	515	765	1265
13				
14	Cost per head	5.15	7.65	12.65
15				
16	No of waitresses needed	10	10	20

Fig. 5.3 Spreadsheet to calculate costs of three menus

Now look at Fig. 5.4, showing the same spreadsheet with the same information. Notice that some of the rectangles, known as cells, now contain equations.

Buffet Costings (SS)

	A	B	C	D
1		Basic	Executive	De Luxe
2				
3	No of covers	100	=B3	=C3
4	Fixed costs per function	25	=B4	=C4
5	Transport per function	20	=B5	=C5
6	Breakages	=B3*0.2	=C3*0.2	=D3*0.2
7	Waitresses	=B3/10*20	=C3/10*20	=D3/5*20
8	Food cost per head	2.5	5	8
9	Total food cost	=B3*B8	=C3*C8	=D3*D8
10				
11				
12	Total cost	=B4+B5+B6+B7+B9	=C4+C5+C6+C7+C9	=D4+D5+D6+D7+D9
13				
14	Cost per head	=B12/B3	=C12/C3	=D12/D3
15				
16	No of waitresses needed	=B3/10	=C3/10	=D3/5

Fig. 5.4 Spreadsheet cells contain formulae used to calculate menu costs

For example, cell B9 contains the equation: '= B3*B8'. This means that cell B9, the total cost of the food, contains whatever is in cell B3, the number of covers, multiplied by whatever is in cell B8, the food cost per head.

Information technology

?

1. Explain in words the equation in cell B7.

   Hint:

   The number of waiting staff needed to serve the basic menu (B)
   = number of covers/10
   = B3/10

   Remember: for the basic menu, the students decided on a ratio of 1 member of staff for every 10 covers.

2. The project group realised that by changing the value in just one cell they could quickly work out the cost of a function for 50 covers. Fig. 5.5 shows the printout they obtained.

	A	B	C	D
	Buffet Costings (SS)			
1		Menu A	Menu B	Menu C
2				
3	No of covers	50	50	50
4	Fixed costs per function	25	25	25
5	Transport per function	20	20	20
6	Breakages	10	10	10
7	Waitresses	100	100	200
8	Food cost per head	2.5	5	8
9	Total food cost	125	250	400
10				
11				
12	Total cost	280	405	655
13				
14	Cost per head	5.6	8.1	13.1
15				
16	No of waitresses needed	5	5	10

   Fig. 5.5 Menu costs for 50 covers

   Construct a spreadsheet to show the numbers in each column for 30 covers.

3. After starting their business the students discovered that breakages were lower than expected (only 10p per cover) and transport worked out at only £10.00. Work out a price per cover (assuming 50 covers), using this new information.

Hints for writing a spreadsheet

1. Decide if you really need one.
2. Obtain suitable software, the simpler the better.
3. Write down the headings for your columns.
4. Write down the titles for your rows.
5. Enter the appropriate figures.
6. Enter the formulae.
7. Check with the spreadsheet manual to find out how to make changes.
8. Try changing some of the figures to check that the formulae work.
9. Modify the spreadsheet as necessary.

5.5 Integrated software packages

It is sometimes necessary, particularly for business purposes, to combine information from a database directly into a spreadsheet, e.g., in a letter or a report. Integrated software packages are designed to make such a procedure easier. It is unlikely that you will use an integrated package in school, although the word-processing, database and spreadsheet programs in some packages can be used separately – a useful means of getting all three programs for little more than the price of one. A simple version of an integrated package (Mini Office) is produced for Acorn computers. Integrated packages often contain the necessary software to allow you to communicate with other computers.

5.6 Graphics

Throughout this book there are examples of graphics produced on computer. There are a number of ways that you can use graphics. You can:

- produce illustrations or drawings;
- produce logos;
- write titles for videos or films (although you will need special equipment if you want to add them directly to your video);
- modify drawings, diagrams or photographs, e.g., by scanning a picture and then changing its shape or proportions;
- experiment with shapes;
- experiment with colours;
- explore three-dimensional ideas;
- produce animation;
- display information from a database as a graph, chart or diagram (see the information on fast food, page 36).

> Think about your current or most recent project. How can it or could it have been improved by the use of computer graphics?

Graphics from spreadsheet programs

You can often print out the information from a spreadsheet program, in the form of bar charts, line graphs and pie charts. Similarly, charts and graphs can be produced directly from a database. Fig. 5.6 includes an example of a spreadsheet being used to predict worldwide sales of a product, together with two charts displaying data from the spreadsheet.

	A	B	C	D	E	F
1	Region	June	July	August	Total	Percent
2						
3	Africa/Asia	£ 90	£ 98	£ 107	£ 295	12.14%
4	Australasia	£ 100	£ 109	£ 119	£ 328	13.50%
5	North Europe	£ 99	£ 108	£ 118	£ 325	13.38%
6	Central Europe	£ 110	£ 120	£ 131	£ 361	14.86%
7	South Europe	£ 140	£ 153	£ 168	£ 461	18.98%
8	North America	£ 95	£ 104	£ 114	£ 313	12.89%
9	South America	£ 105	£ 115	£ 126	£ 346	14.24%
10						
11	Total	£ 739	£ 807	£ 883	£ 2,429	100.00%

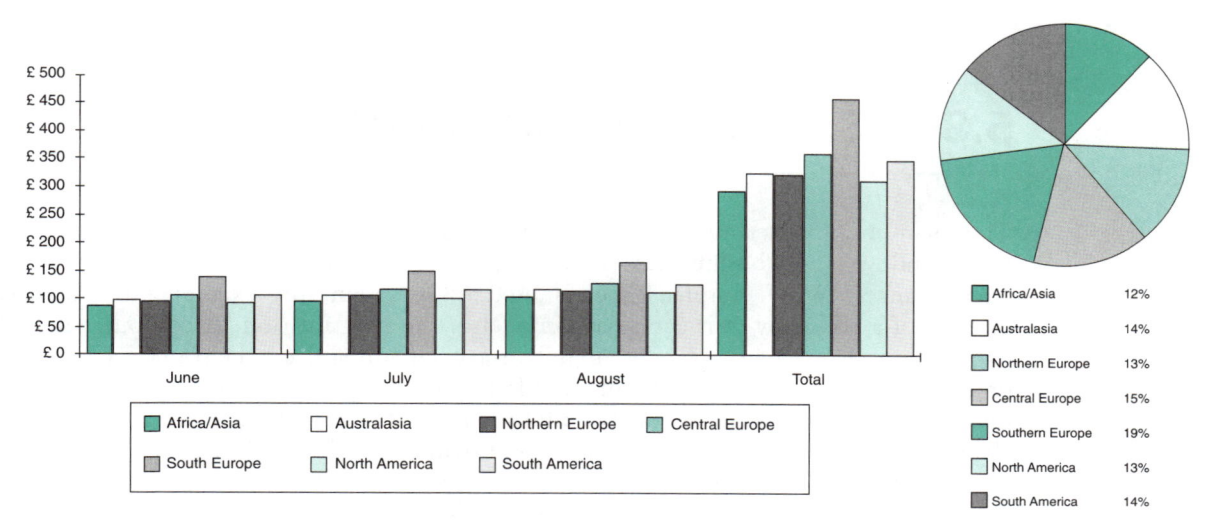

Fig. 5.6 Graphical representation of data from a spreadsheet

5.7 Desktop publishing (DTP)

Desktop publishing is a sophisticated way of handling text and illustrations electronically. DTP programs allow you to move sections of text and pictures around the screen and produce very professional-looking documents. The original text for this book, for example, was produced using the Pagemaker™ desktop publishing software.

Many students have used DTP technology to produce school magazines, brochures and instruction books for their projects. In the following example, Pagemaker™ has been used to produce a catalogue for a range of South American woollen goods.

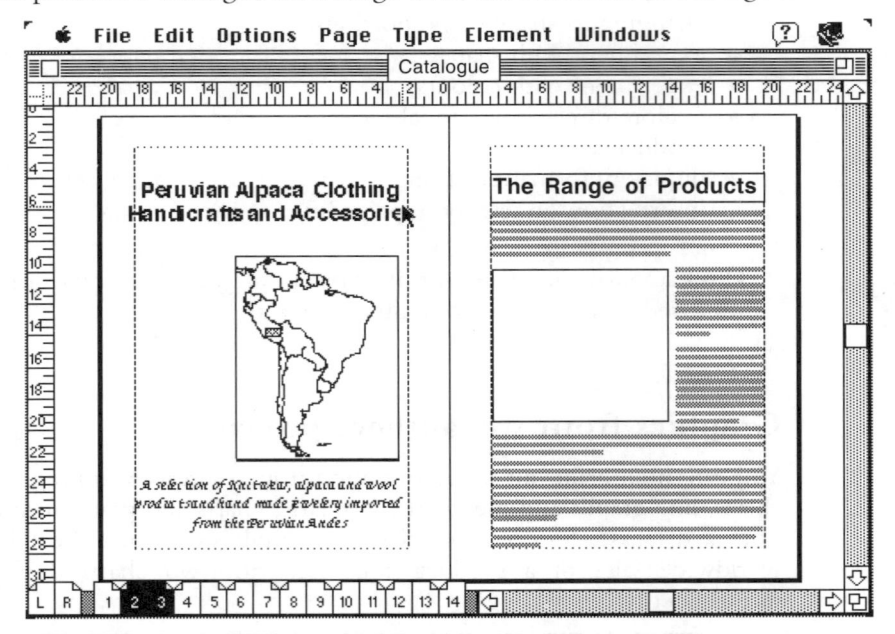

Fig. 5.7 Catalogues and leaflets can be produced using desktop publishing software

The following features of the display are typical of DTP programs.

1. The text was prepared using a word-processor and 'placed' into the document.
2. The map came from a database of world maps.
3. The empty box on the right-hand page represents a photograph. The box was produced using graphics tools within the software package. The photograph will be scanned electronically and inserted later.
4. The text 'flows' around the picture. The photograph can be reduced in size if it is larger than the space allowed for it, parts of the picture can be 'cropped' or the text can be shortened to make more space available.

5.8 Simulations and models

The form of computer model with which you are probably most familiar is a computer game. Industry and business use models to predict what will happen under various circumstances. When a spreadsheet is used to represent, for example, the financial forecast of a company, it is acting as a model of the real situation. A computer model, like a physical one (e.g. a model aircraft in a wind tunnel), can help predict how real objects or situations will change, but at a fraction of the cost of constructing the whole thing full-size. Although computer models have the advantage that details can be changed quickly, they are, perhaps, less good than physical models, because it is easy to miss things out when designing a computer model. Simulations, such as virtual reality games or flight simulators, enable you to experience situations as if they were real.

5.9 Computer control

Many students have used computers and micro-electronics to control their projects. You may be aware of CNC (Computer Numerical Control) machinery, and many schools have CNC lathes, milling and sewing machines. You may even be lucky enough to have a computer-controlled embroidery machine in your school. Many electric and microwave cookers, and food processors are now controlled by microprocessors, and even some modern electric kettles are IT-controlled.

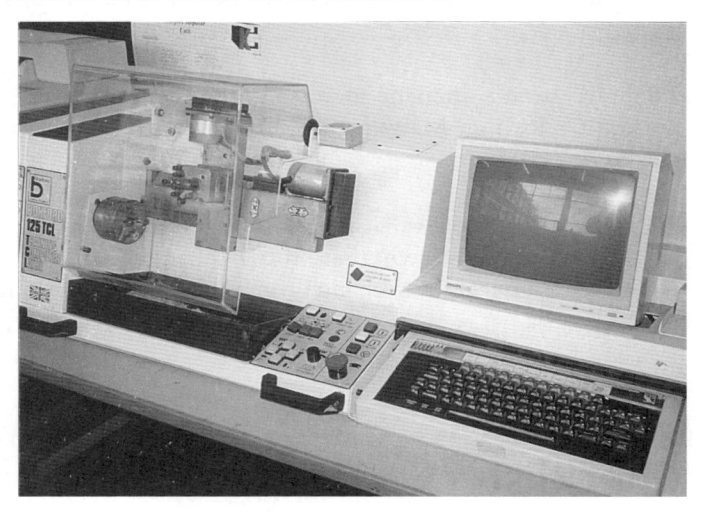

Fig 5.8 CNC lathe

Some students have designed computer-controlled equipment. Below, a student has designed an ergonomic input device to enable a blind person to dial telephone numbers. The system is linked into the telephone system via a computer and phone numbers are entered using a Braille-type keyboard. The computer acknowledges a number by using a voice synthesiser, and then dials the number and keeps a record of the call. This allows the user to have a permanent record of all calls and costs, and at any time the information can be printed out or spoken to the user.

Fig 5.9 Computer-controlled tlephone dialler

In science classes computers can be used to gather information. Sensors can detect temperature, humidity, wind speed, etc., and these variables can be input automatically into a computer database. The database can then be used to provide information on an experiment. This is particularly useful when it is difficult or impossible to take the readings yourself, at night, for example.

Programming in a control language

One of your earliest introductions to control technology may have been the use of Logo, or a similar control language. In these languages, short program routines are built up and stored separately. They can then be linked to make a single complex movement. On an industrial scale, robots and computer-controlled work stations operate on the same basis.

5.10 Information technology and society

There has been a dramatic increase in the use of IT over recent years and the rate shows no sign of slowing. Many people are concerned about the impact of IT on the lives of citizens everywhere.

> 1. List four changes that IT has brought about or may bring about in the future.
> 2. Comment on whether those changes are advantages or disadvantages. Remember, in any change some may gain while others lose.

Checklist

Use IT in your projects only when appropriate.
IT can improve the presentation of your work.
IT can give you access to information that might otherwise be more difficult to obtain.
Information technology has changed and is changing our world in positive and in negative ways.

Chapter 6

Coursework case studies

6.1 Introduction

This chapter describes examples of candidates work. Although you should not try to copy these projects you are sure to get useful ideas. The projects have been selected to show a range of products. They have also been chosen to illustrate a variety of approaches and a range of presentational techniques. These projects are not accompanied by comprehensive assessor's comments since, without seeing the whole projects it would be impossible to do them justice. There is, however, an indication of the approximate level of attainment that each is likely to achieve.

Although there is no perfect way to do a project, each major project or set task will involve the processes of designing and making. Not all students do the work in the same order, but in assessing a project an examiner will look for evidence that you have done everything in this list:

- identified a need;
- undertaken necessary and relevant research;
- produced a detailed specification;
- generated original ideas;
- developed your ideas into a final proposal;
- planned what you intend to do;
- manufactured your final proposal;
- shown evidence of evaluation and testing of your work.

If your final project is not available to the assessor you must provide suitable photographs. In the following examples, you can decide if the photographs explain fully what the final result looked like and how well it has been made.

6.2 Map holder for skiers

The following sheets show some of the work done by a student after she recognised the need for a suitable holder for a map, whilst on holiday in Italy. When cross-country skiing, her map soon became damaged by water and by handling. She was unable to buy anything that adequately protected the map whilst also holding it securely. As you will see, she produced one idea before recognising several areas for improvement. The student went on to manufacture a second version of the map holder and then to test it.

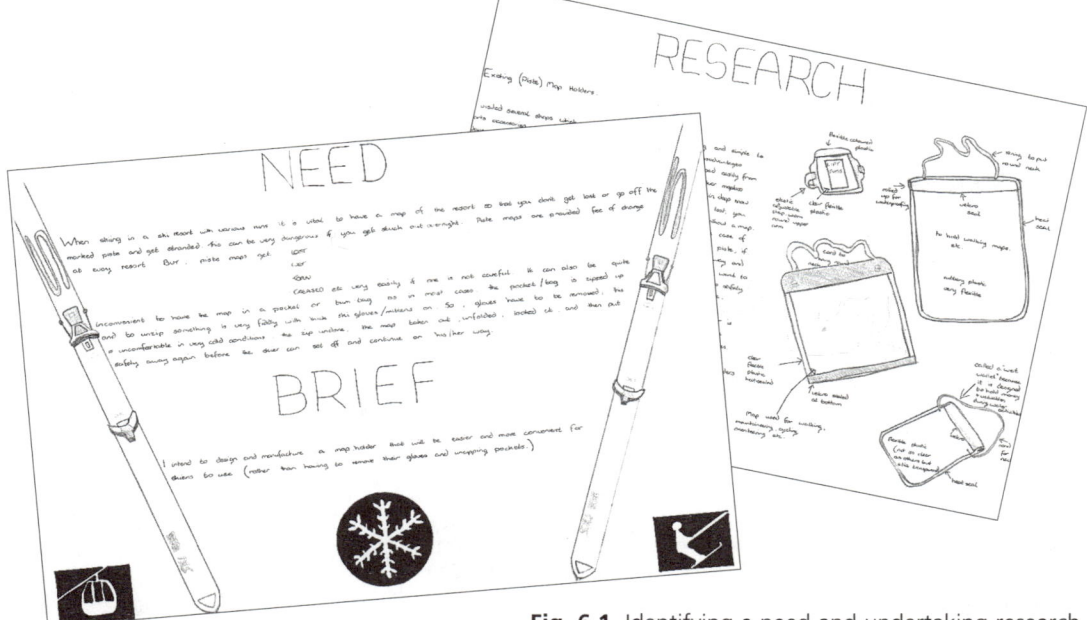

Fig. 6.1 Identifying a need and undertaking research

Coursework case studies

The student has used logos and illustrations to liven up the page, but it might have been better to spend the time researching the problem more extensively. She could, for example, have discussed her proposals with more than one friend and tried to discover if there were any commercial needs for such a holder.

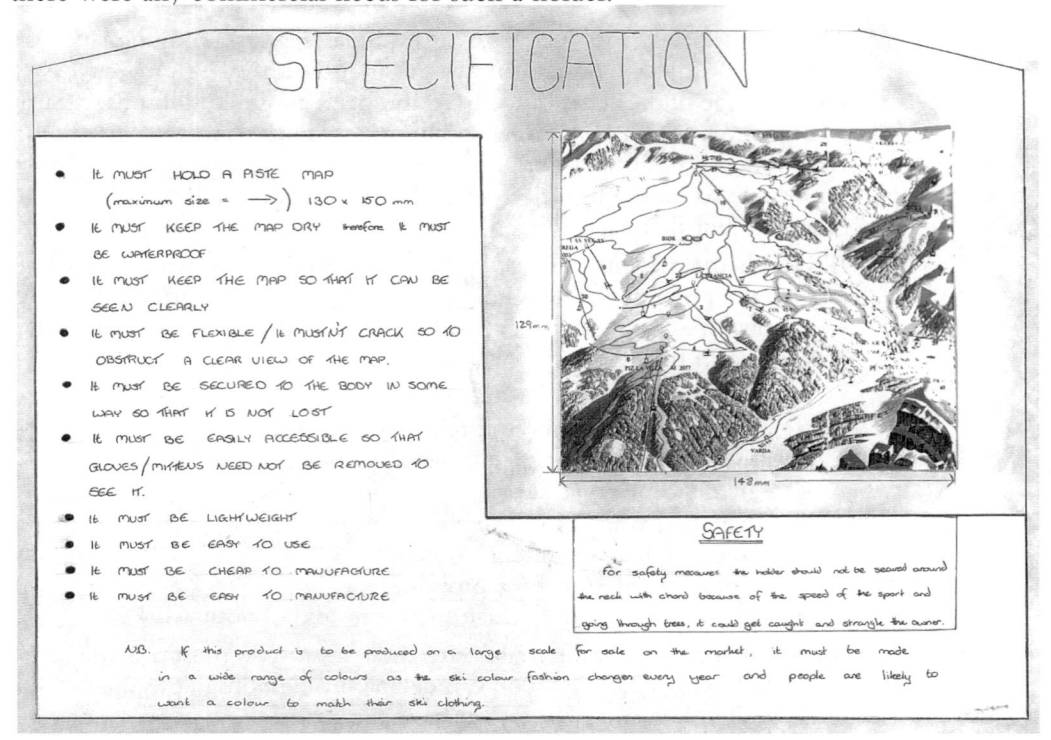

Fig. 6.2
Producing a detailed specification

The specification was useful and allowed the finished product to be tested. The student began by exploring a range of solutions.

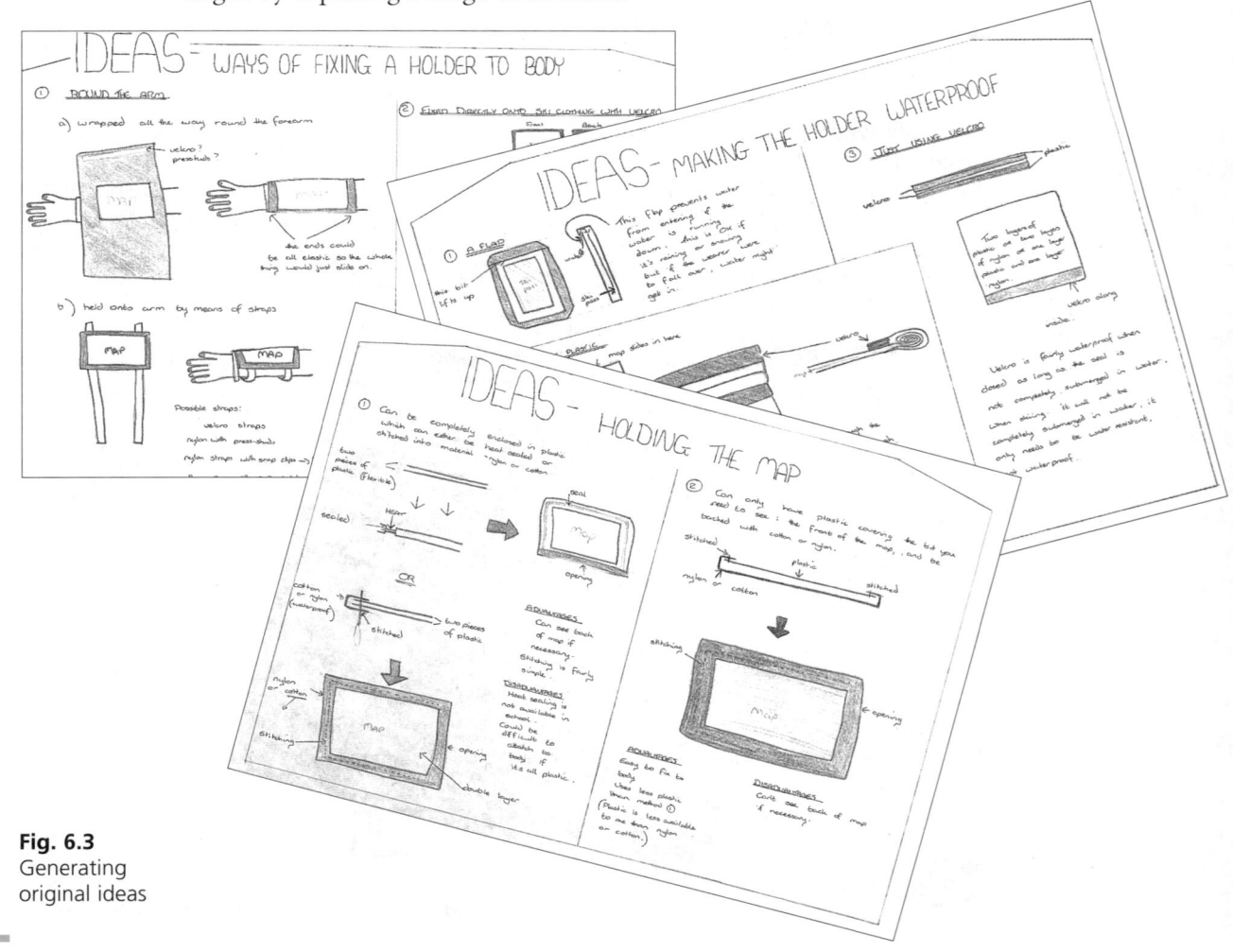

Fig. 6.3
Generating original ideas

6.2 Map holder for skiers

She quickly recognised the need for the map holder to be waterproof. She collected what she considered to be suitable materials and tested them. This stage is important and allowed her to proceed with the development of ideas.

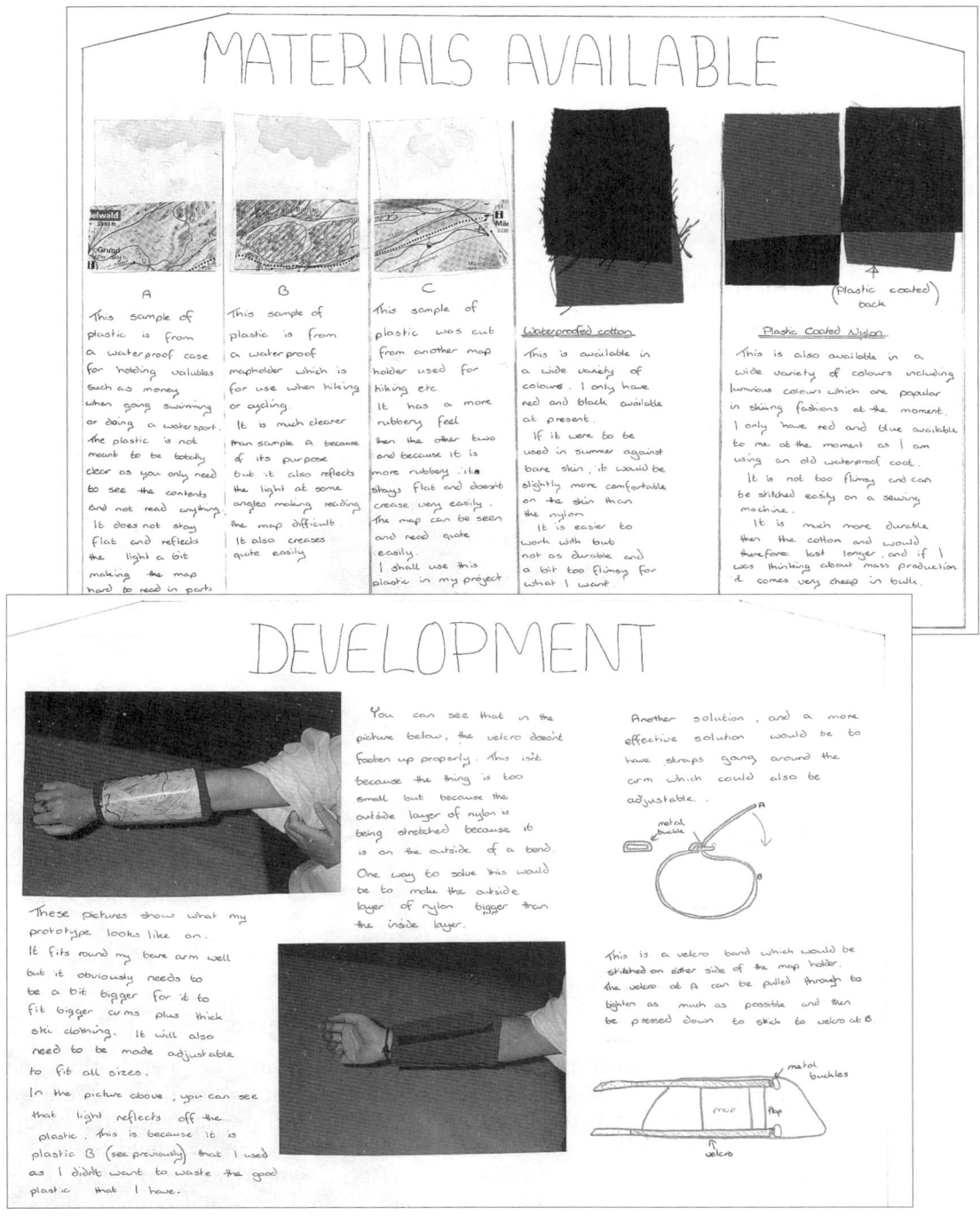

Fig. 6.4 Developing ideas into a final proposal

The student proceeded with her ideas and photographed an early prototype model in which she glued everything that, in the final version, she would expect to be sewn.

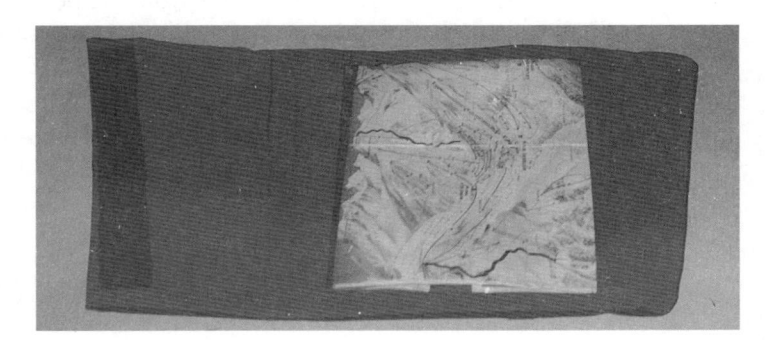

Fig. 6.5
Model of map holder

The prototype has now been made up and is in position. The candidate realised that there are problems with the design and continued to make improvements before producing a final design. At this stage it would have been useful to see more details of the construction, together with patterns for cutting out the fabric.

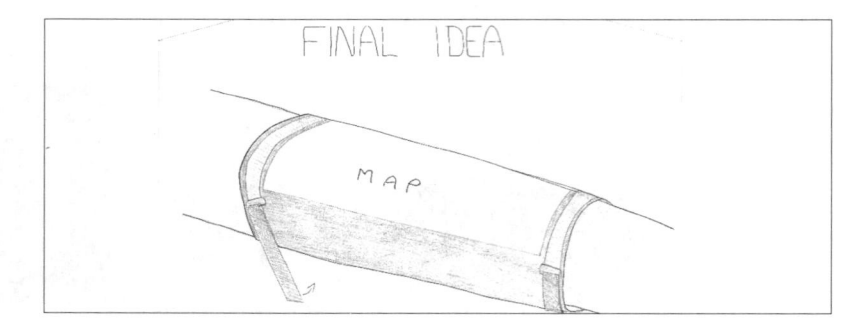

Fig. 6.6 Final proposal

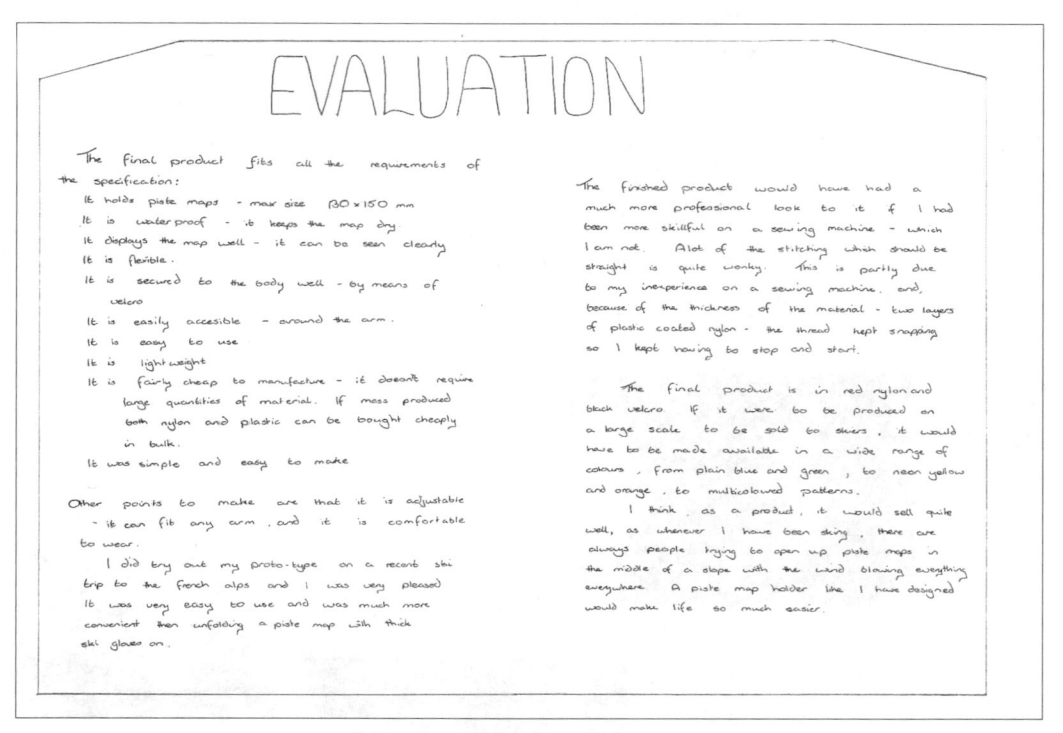

Fig. 6.7 Evaluation of final product

The evaluation sheet compares the final result with the specification and she has commented on the process. She has tested her solution but there is little evidence of either consultation with others or of the product being compared with anything commercially available. She does acknowledge that changes would be necessary if the product was to be manufactured commercially. It would have been better to see evidence that she had discussed this with companies who might manufacture the map holder.

Final comment

Most of the stages that an examiner would expect to see are evident. The quality of the final result is better than average, although the simplicity of construction could have allowed opportunities for further development.

This is a competent project produced by a student of above average ability. If all her work is of this standard she can expect to gain a grade C or better.

6.3 Local history guide

A group of students was asked by their teacher to identify ways of assisting visitors to the local town. Two students decided that a local history guide was needed. Another student decided to produce a brochure/audio-tape package that could be hired by visitors. A third student designed an interactive notice-board for the town centre.

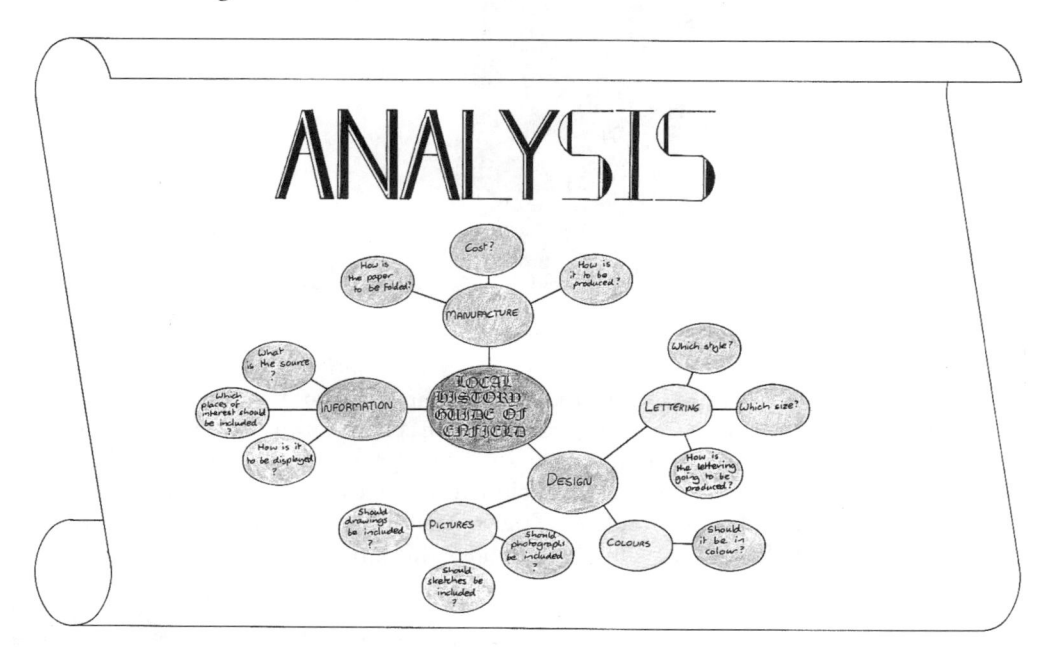

Fig. 6.8 Analysing the problem

The cover sheet is clear and says all that is required. The student has attempted to analyse the problem but seems more concerned with colourful, neat presentation than with in-depth analysis. As well as identifying problems he should have attempted to provide solutions.

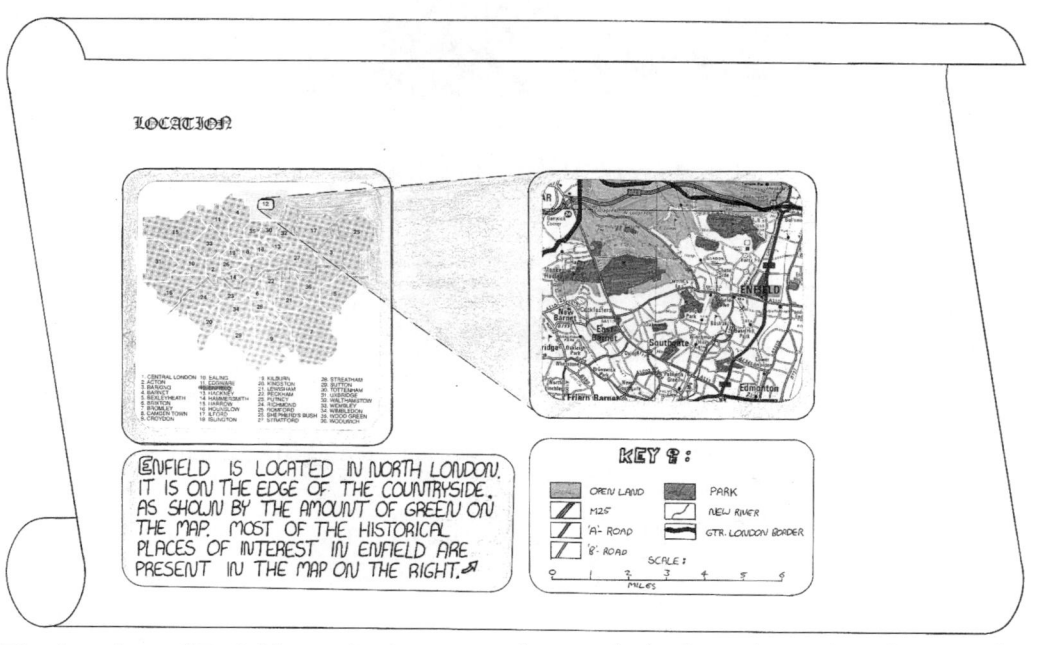

Fig. 6.9 Researching the area

The location of Enfield may be important, but a whole sheet devoted to showing the town's whereabouts seems lavish. Although it is important to research how other brochures are made, it would have been more useful if the student had commented on the value of each method.

Coursework case studies

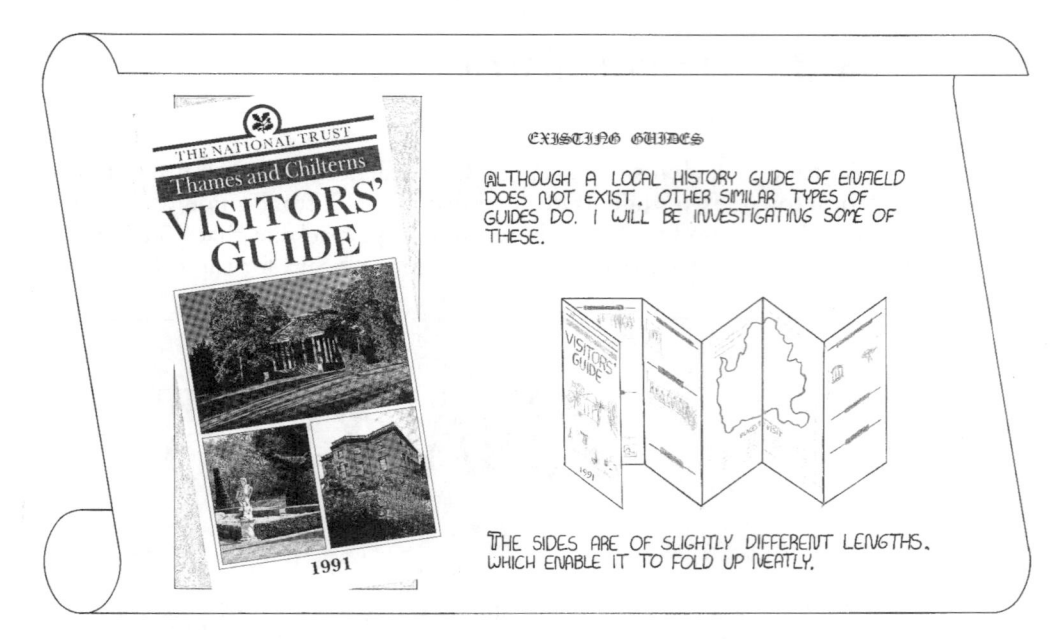

Fig. 6.10
Look at existing products

EXISTING GUIDES

ALTHOUGH A LOCAL HISTORY GUIDE OF ENFIELD DOES NOT EXIST, OTHER SIMILAR TYPES OF GUIDES DO. I WILL BE INVESTIGATING SOME OF THESE.

THE SIDES ARE OF SLIGHTLY DIFFERENT LENGTHS, WHICH ENABLE IT TO FOLD UP NEATLY.

The study of existing brochures is important and the drawing is very good, but again, the student seems preoccupied with presentation at the expense of analysis. Before showing places of historical interest, it would have been useful to show what other people thought should be included. It is clear already that the project is moving towards a very traditional solution. This in itself is not bad, but at this stage of the design it would be helpful to see examples of wider thinking.

Fig. 6.11
Use eye-catching graphics

A RUMOUR CONNECTS WHITE WEBBS HOUSE WITH THE GUNPOWDER PLOT OF 1605. IT WOULD APPEAR THAT THE HOUSE WAS AN 'ACCESSORY AFTER THE FACT', AND THAT GUY FAWKES STAYED THERE FOR 5 DAYS, FROM THE 5TH TO THE 9TH OF NOVEMBER.

WHITE WEBBS HOUSE, FRONT AND BACK

Good quality photographs will be needed and the student is obviously taking care with his photography.

6.3 Local history guide

Fig. 6.12 Deciding on presentation

7 - FRONT PAGE

The front page is the most important page as it grabs peoples attention or gets ignored. Therefore, it must be eye-catching and attractive. It must also be immediately obvious that it is a history guide of Enfield.

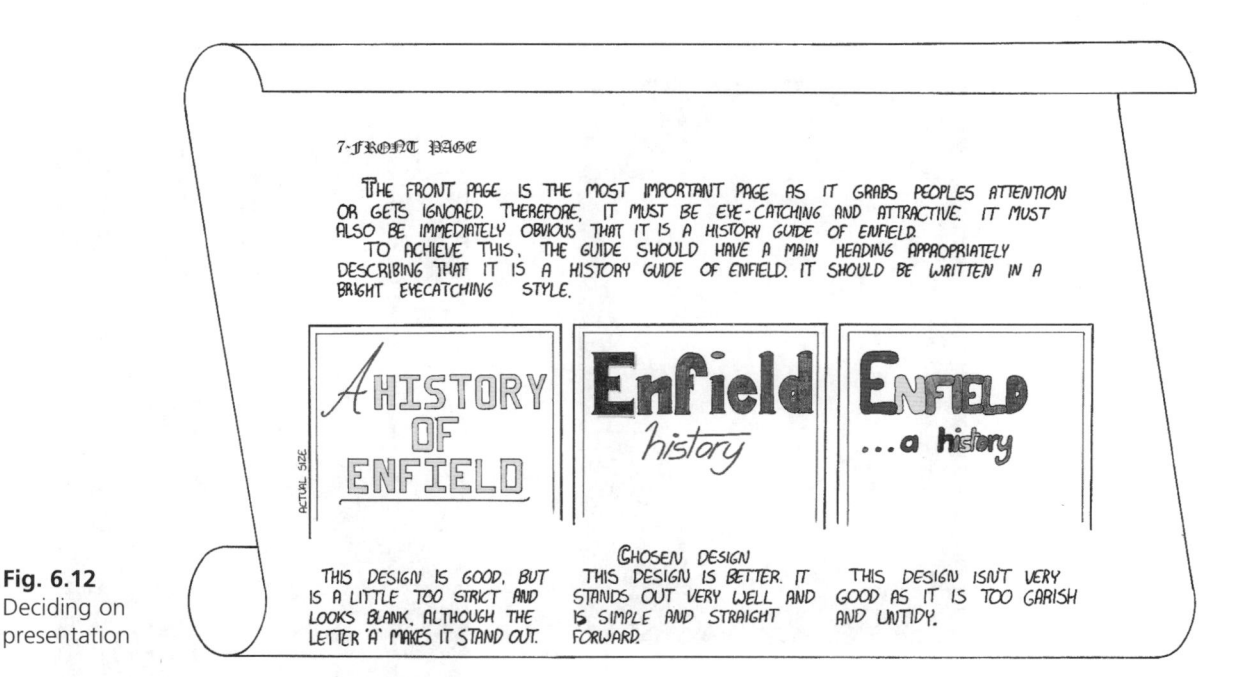

To achieve this, the guide should have a main heading appropriately describing that it is a history guide of Enfield. It should be written in a bright eyecatching style.

A HISTORY OF ENFIELD — ACTUAL SIZE
This design is good, but is a little too strict and looks blank. Although the letter 'A' makes it stand out.

Enfield history — CHOSEN DESIGN
This design is better. It stands out very well and is simple and straight forward.

ENFIELD ...a history
This design isn't very good as it is too garish and untidy.

Once more, you can see a pleasant presentation of materials, which could have been shown in a much smaller space. It is possible, however, to see reasons for some of the student's decisions. The three ideas for the front cover recognise the importance of first impressions, but there is still no evidence of consultation with others.

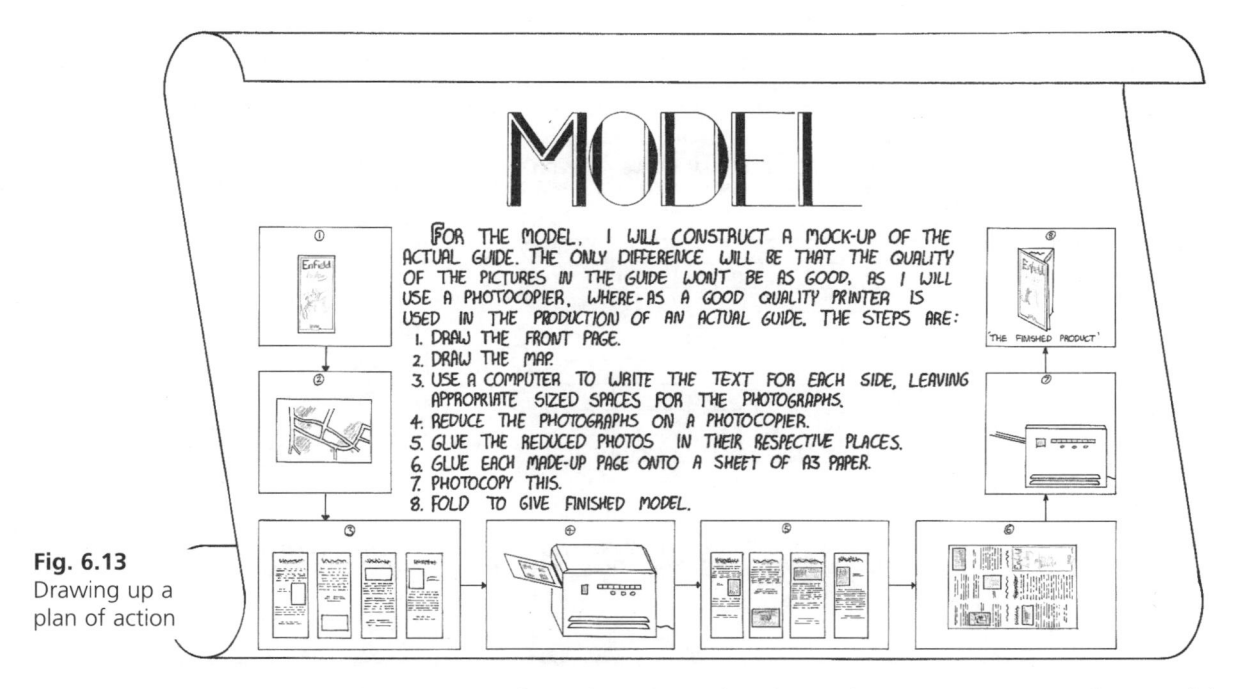

Fig. 6.13 Drawing up a plan of action

MODEL

For the model, I will construct a mock-up of the actual guide. The only difference will be that the quality of the pictures in the guide won't be as good, as I will use a photocopier, where-as a good quality printer is used in the production of an actual guide. The steps are:
1. Draw the front page.
2. Draw the map.
3. Use a computer to write the text for each side, leaving appropriate sized spaces for the photographs.
4. Reduce the photographs on a photocopier.
5. Glue the reduced photos in their respective places.
6. Glue each made-up page onto a sheet of A3 paper.
7. Photocopy this.
8. Fold to give finished model.

The layout sheet and the flow chart show that the student is nearing completion of the design stage of the project. It is unfortunate that there are no alternative layout proposals and there is no indication that the student anticipated problems with manufacturing.

Coursework case studies

Fig. 6.14
The final solution is made and tested

These photographs of the final solution show that great care has been taken to produce a very professional result.

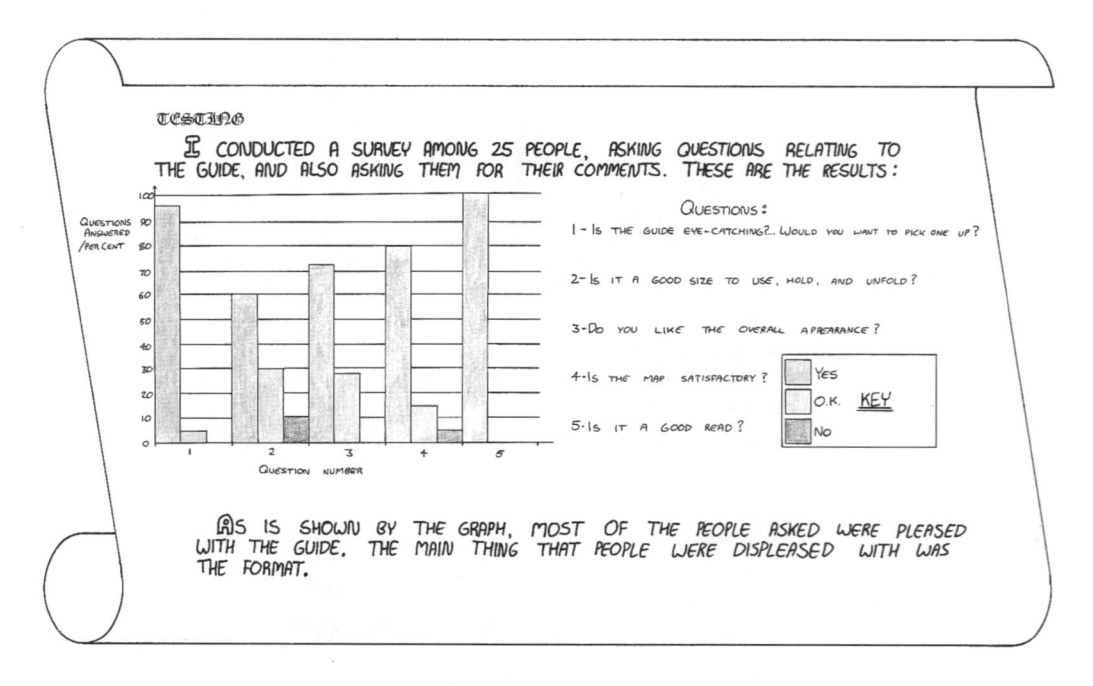

Fig. 6.15 Surveying user opinions

The sheet that illustrates testing indicates that other people have now been consulted. Why were people unhappy with the format? How does the student know users were pleased with the guide? It isn't clear what they wanted in the first place!

Final comment

The quality of presentation of this graphics-based project is high, although there is a lack of depth in the research and in the development of ideas. It would have been valuable to have seen alternative designs for the guide. On balance, this project would also earn grade C.

6.4 New food from soya

Students were asked to identify gaps in the convenience food market. One student identified the need for healthy foods and proceeded to design and develop a healthy product based on soya protein. He began by considering healthy foods in general before narrowing his choice to soya products. He was careful to survey the marketplace.

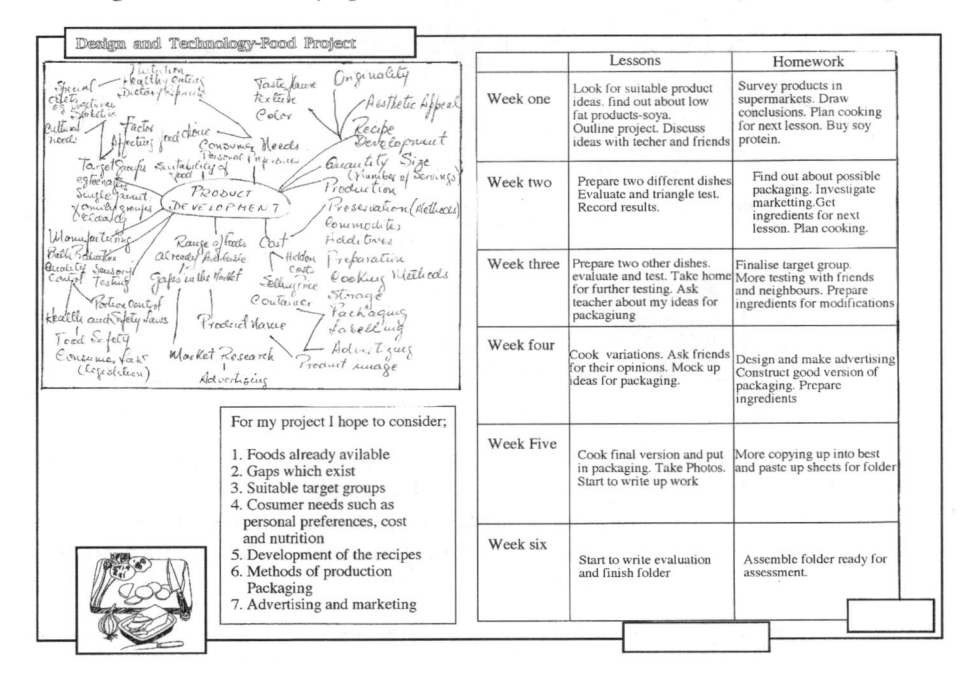

Fig. 6.16 Brainstorming and project planning

After looking generally at the idea, he formalised what he wanted to achieve. The student had only six weeks for this project, but he went well beyond what could be expected in that time. The manner in which he has recorded the planning stage suggests, however, that this may have been done at the end of the project!

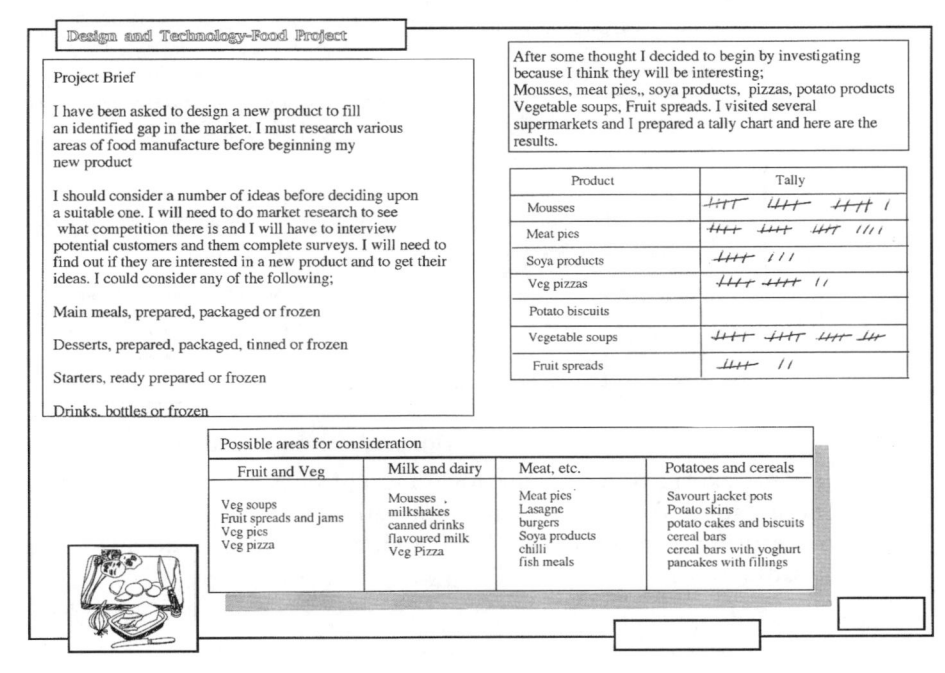

Fig. 6.17 Project brief and research

The candidate investigated a range of existing food products and wisely chose to study those he found interesting. He recorded his findings on a tally chart and the layout of these two sheets is neat and well presented.

Coursework case studies

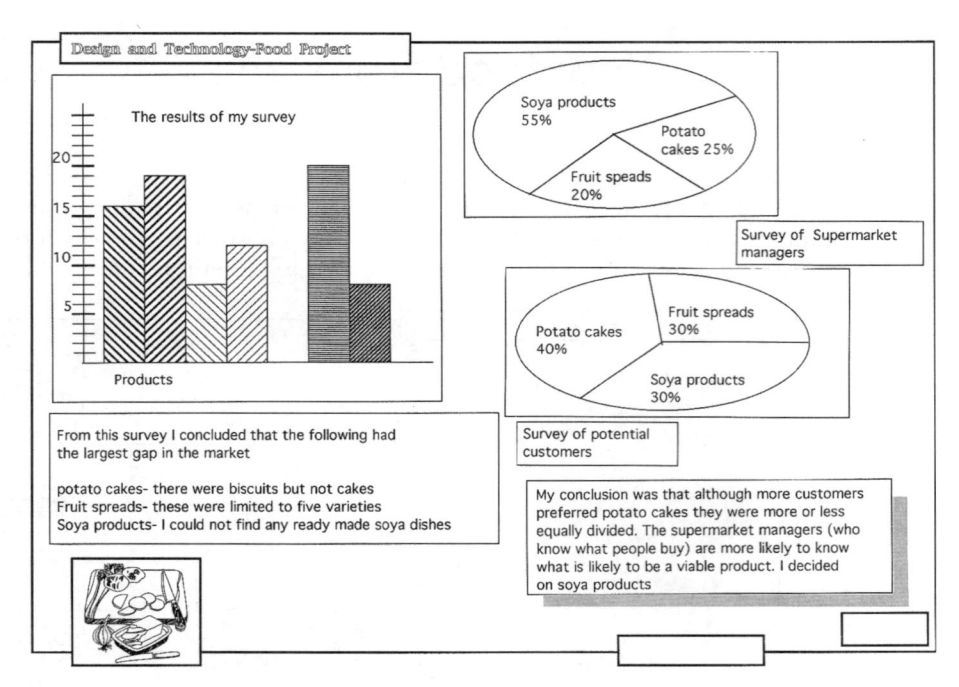

Fig. 6.18 Presenting research findings

The conclusions from the previous survey have been expressed in a bar chart, but it is a little confusing since he has not labelled it fully. It is also evident that two other surveys have taken place and the student has provided copies of the questionnaires used (not shown here). The conclusion demonstrates the student's ability to compromise between otherwise conflicting information.

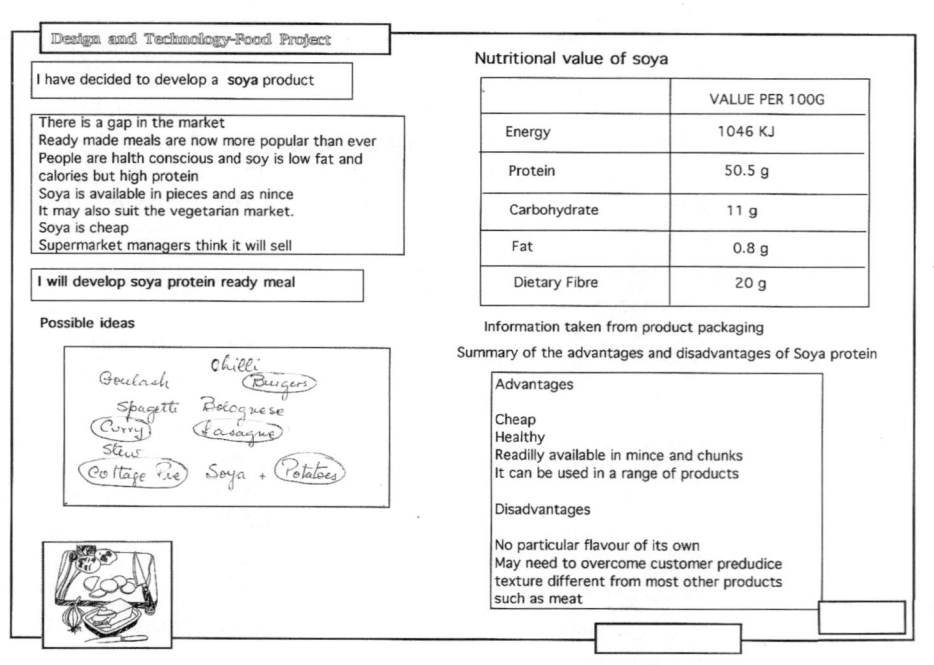

Fig. 6.19 Developing ideas

He has explained his reasons for wanting to develop a soya product and he has provided information about soya. This information would be useful later when marketing and advertising the product. The student has also described some advantages and disadvantages of soya.

6.4 New food from soya

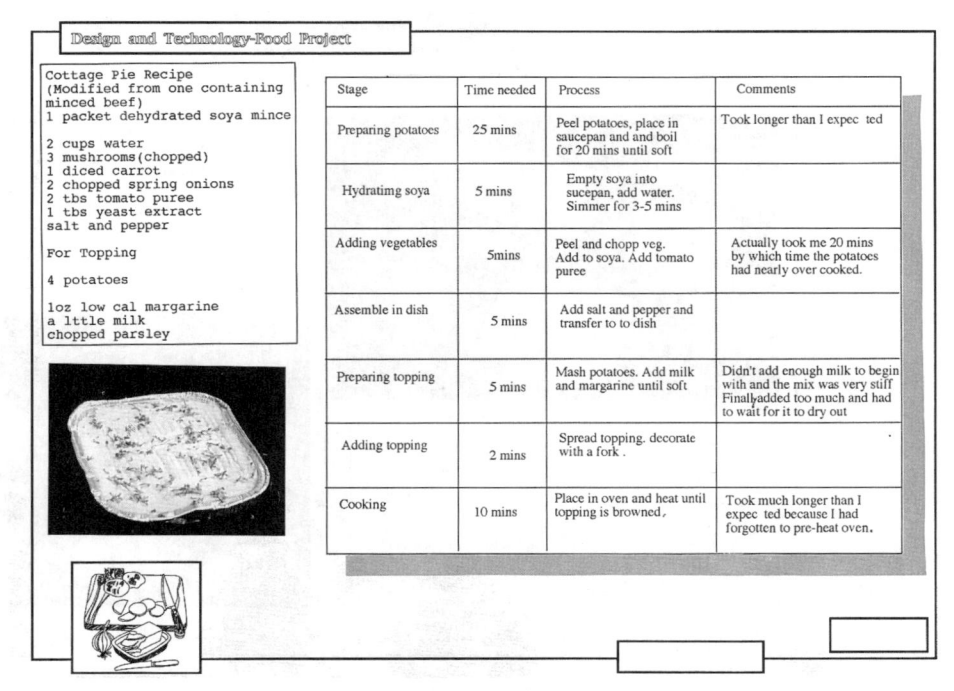

Fig. 6.20 Product testing

This sheet is one of four, one for each product prepared by the student. At an earlier point in the project he said he would produce three food samples, but now he has decided to increase this to four. He has not, however, given a reason for this change of plan. The sheet is nicely set out and shows clearly what he intended to do and summarises what went wrong.

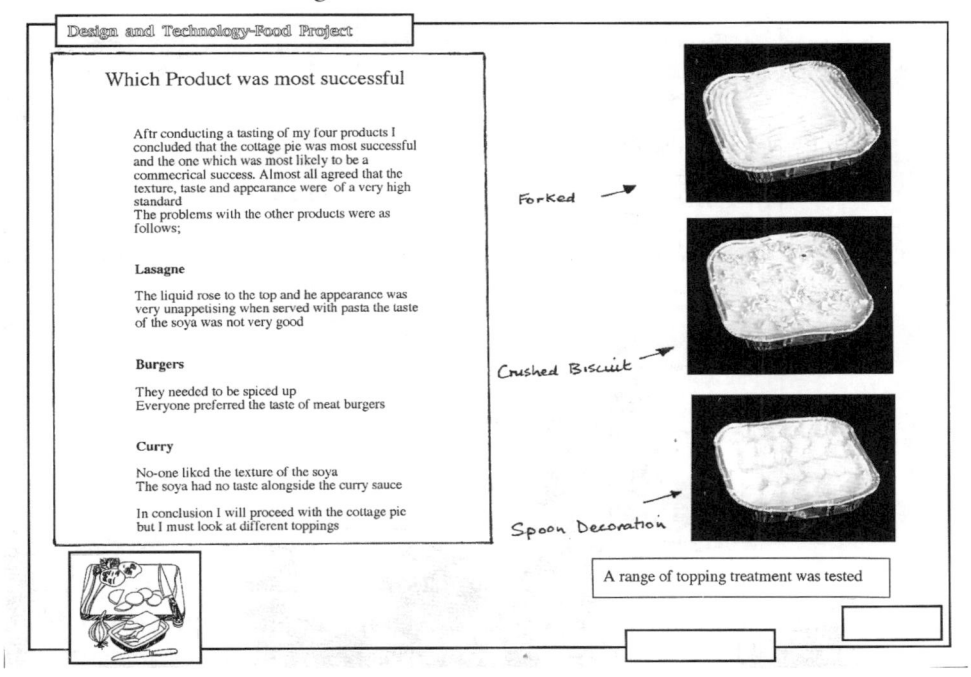

Fig. 6.21 Evaluating product tests

The student has given details (not shown here) of the food testing procedure; it was carefully organised but, as he admitted later, he used too few people. Here, he has summarised his findings and has begun to develop his product further. It is clear he realised the need for regular testing and revision of ideas.

Further sheets of the project (not shown here) document experiments with various toppings and the shape of the soya-based pie, before moving on to consider packaging and marketing. The student conducted another survey to establish a name for the product, but it is clear he was running out of time and so only touched on this aspect.

Coursework case studies

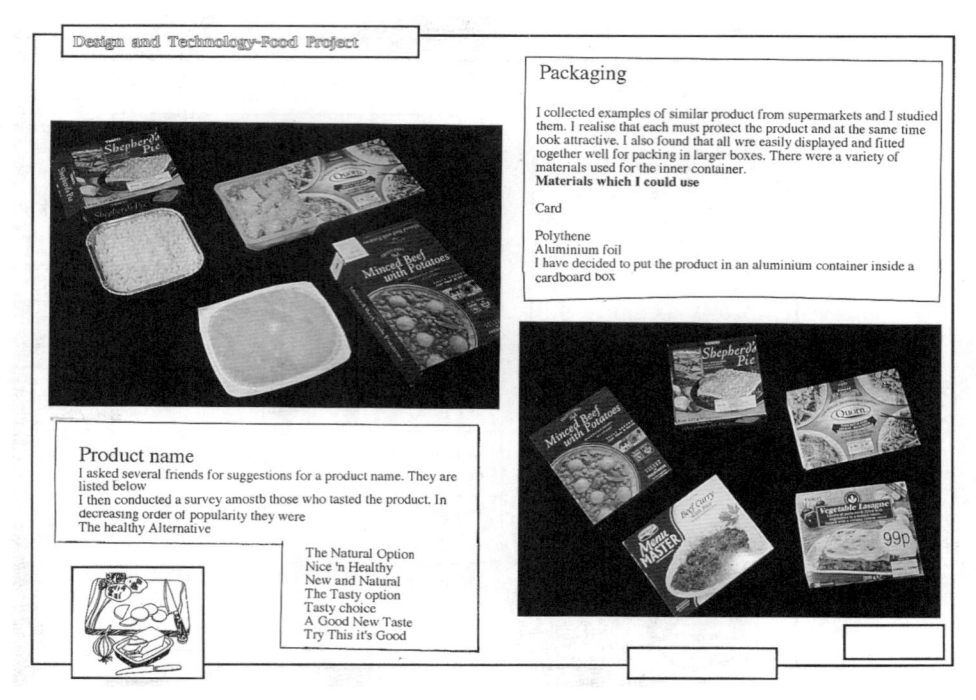

Fig. 6.22 Considering appropriate packaging

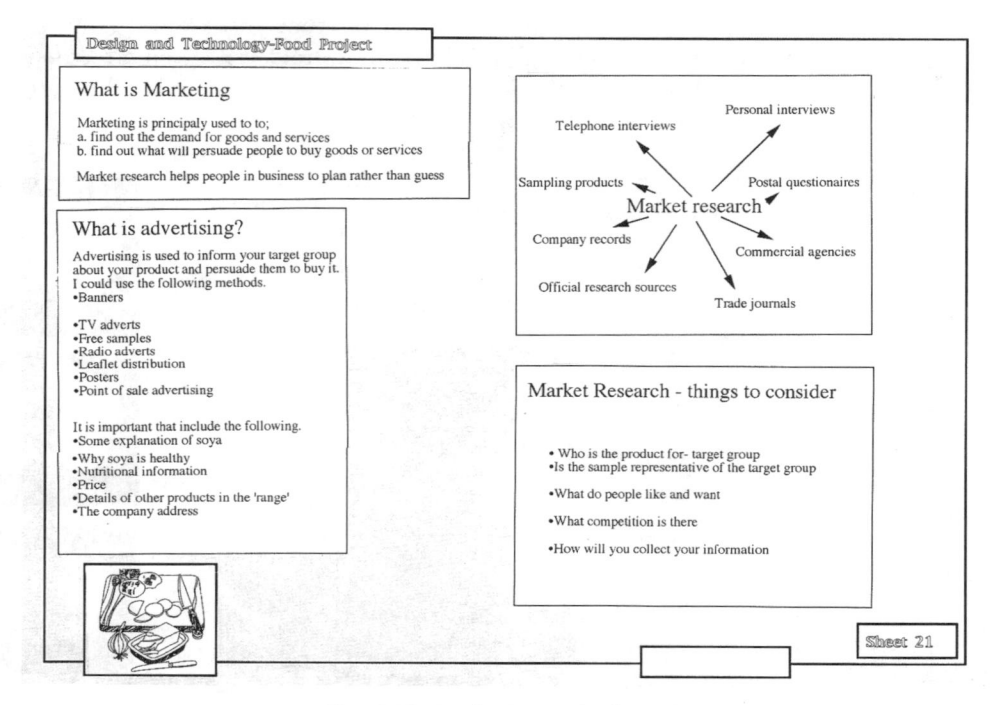

Fig. 6.23 Marketing and advertising

Marketing and advertising have been treated in a rather academic manner and are not well related to the product. However, he has shown an understanding of the concepts and if there had been more time available, he would have gone further.

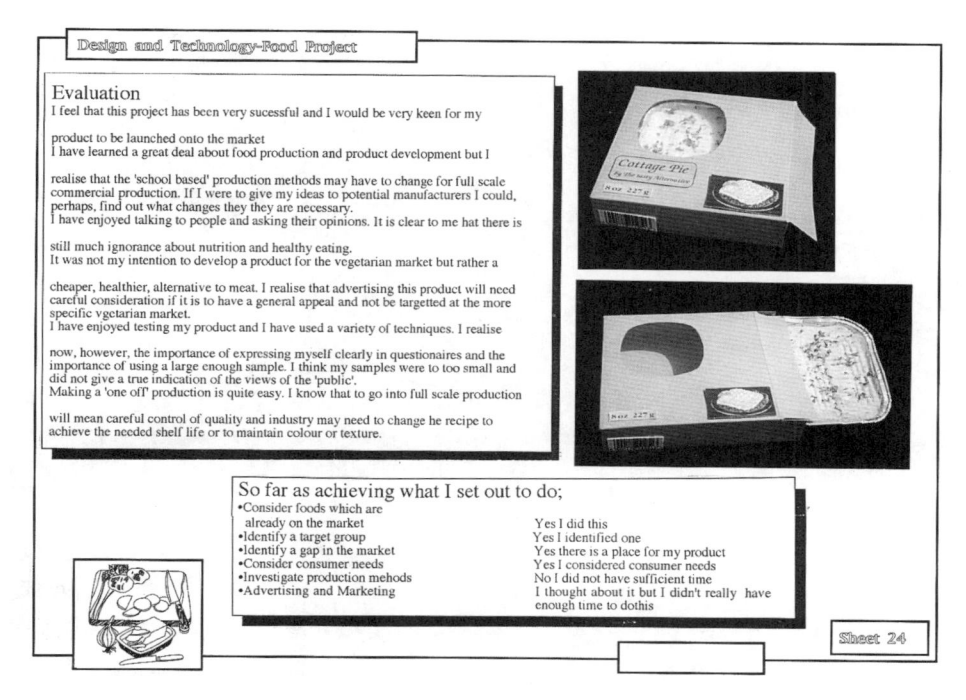

Fig. 6.24 Evaluating against the original specification

The evaluation is rather vague and very brief. It may well be another symptom of running out of time. Most of the conclusions are based on his own opinions and, although he has attempted to compare what he has achieved with the original specification, because that specification itself was unclear, he has found this stage difficult.

Final comment

This is a very well-executed project, which has engaged the candidate in a good deal of detailed work. He has achieved most of what he intended and, for a six-week project, it is highly commendable. The student has shown a mature approach to the project, which is very well presented and easy to understand. The use of a word-processor is to be commended, but this student may have spent rather too much time on presentation at the expense of detail and analysis. In view of the importance of good spelling, punctuation and grammar, it is a pity he did not check his written work more thoroughly. Despite these shortcomings, the candidate deserves a high grade for the thoroughness of this project. He would be likely to score a B-grade or better.

6.5 Air-brush

A student interested in graphics and aware of the high price of good air-brushes decided to produce one that was both inexpensive and easy to use.

Coursework case studies

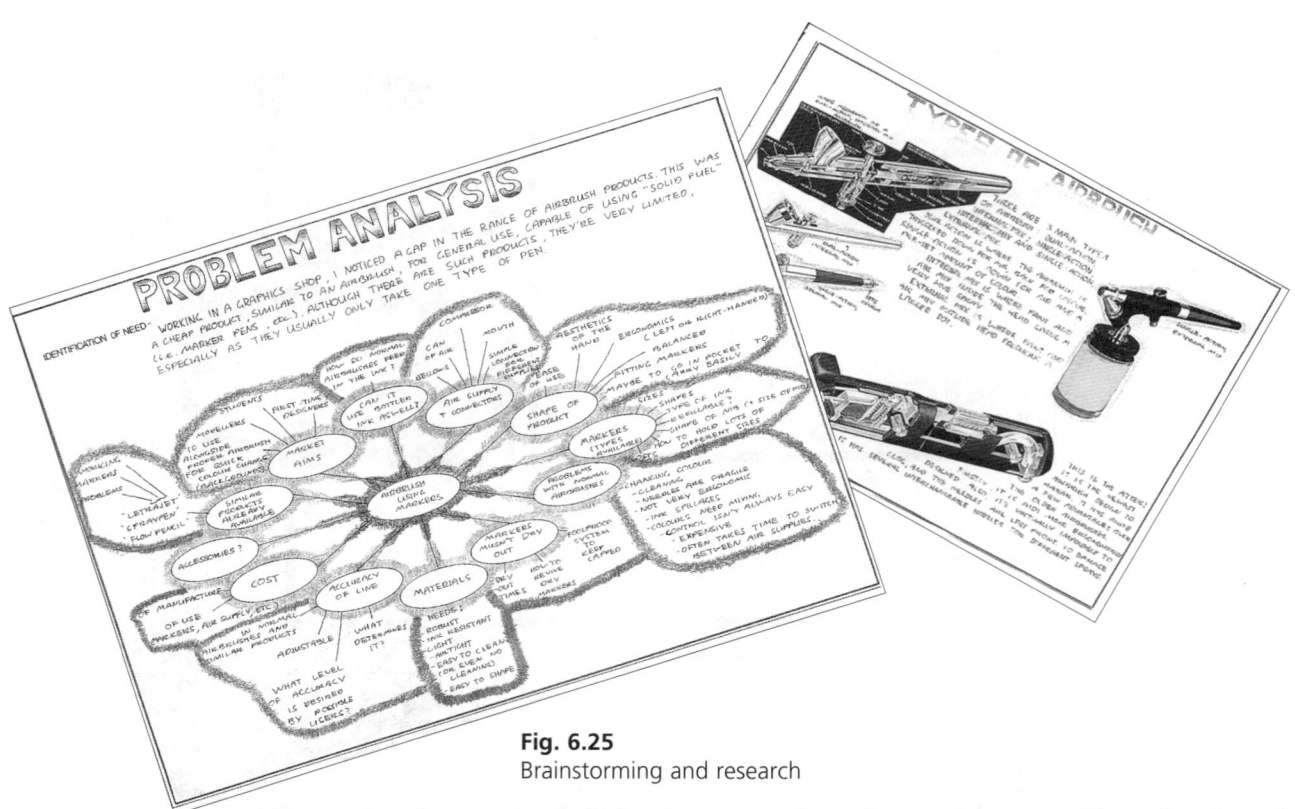

Fig. 6.25
Brainstorming and research

The student has used a bubble chart to analyse the requirements. There is a lot of information here and many questions are posed, but she has not attempted to solve the problems at this stage. The second sheet shows details of commercial air-brushes and she has attempted to explain the illustrations cut out from catalogues.

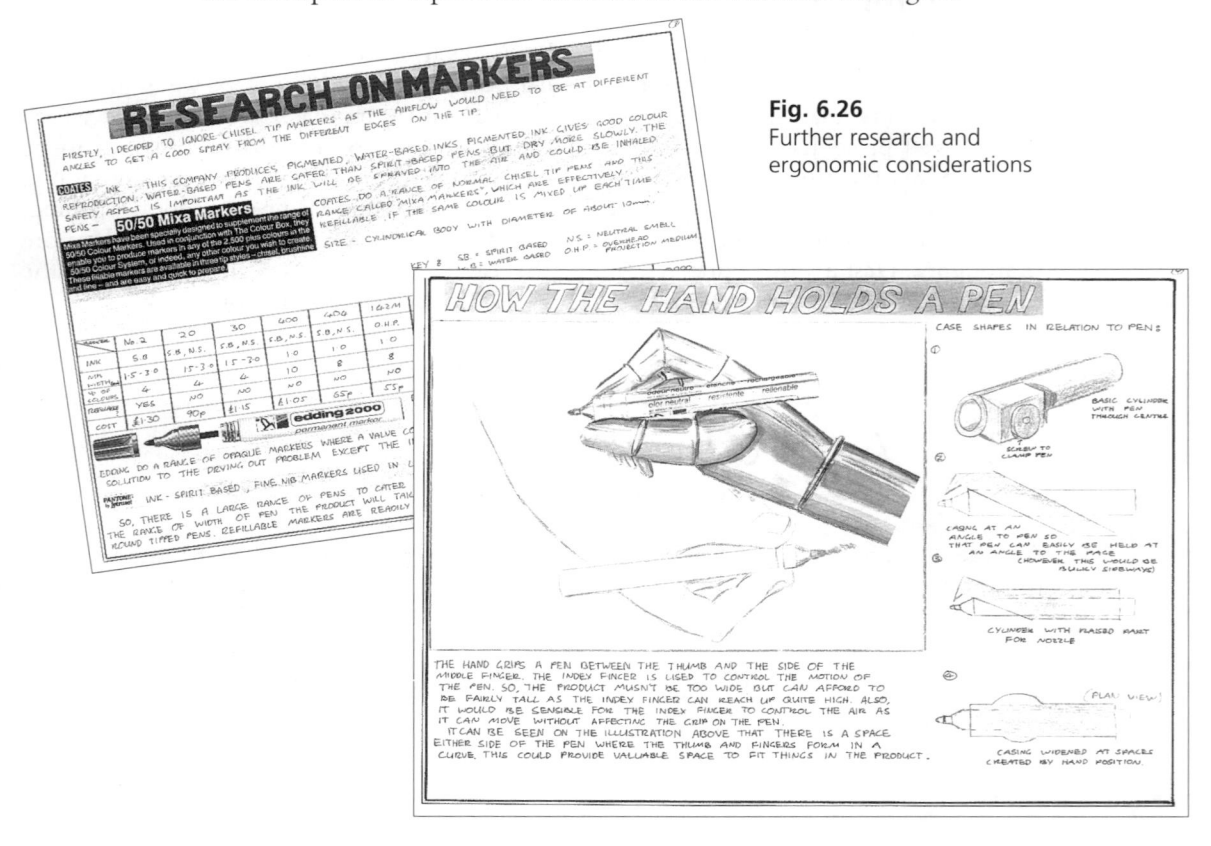

Fig. 6.26
Further research and ergonomic considerations

The candidate has analysed existing products. She has also looked at the ergonomics of holding a pen and has attempted to design an air-brush to be held in a similar way.

Fig. 6.27
Statement of problems

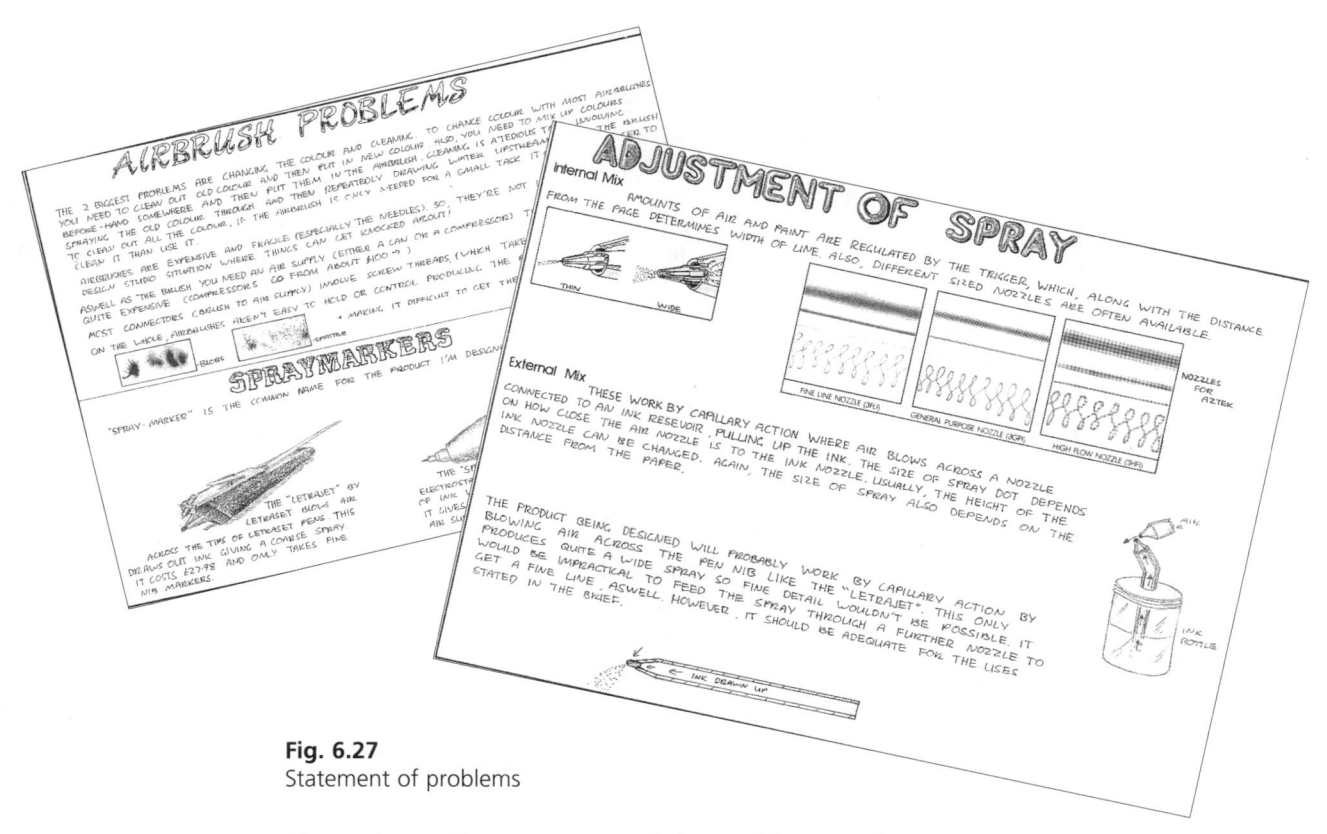

These sheets illustrate some of the problems to be overcome. It is evident that she decided at an early stage to produce an air-brush that uses a felt pen as a source of ink. The student has not explained why she made this decision and if others have advised her.

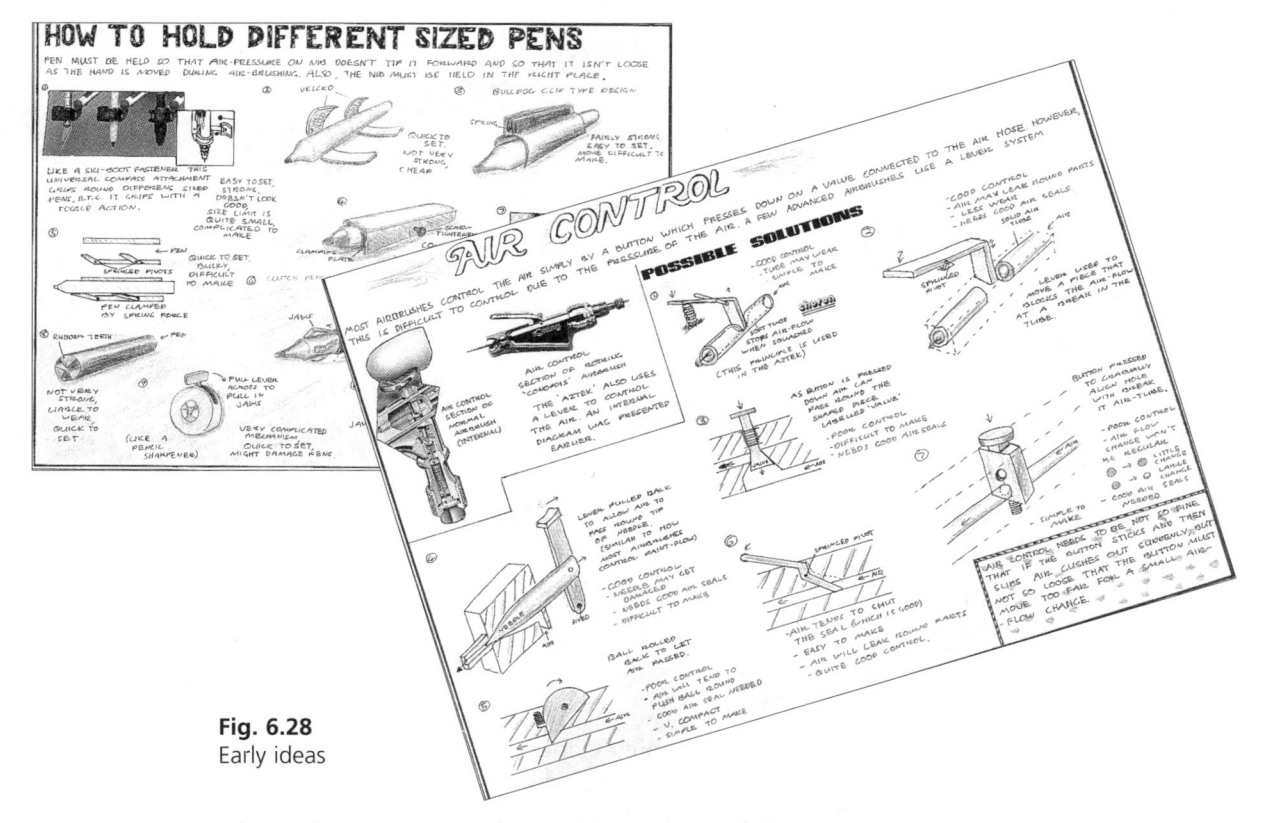

Fig. 6.28
Early ideas

These drawings are clear and very carefully done. The student has combined photographs of existing solutions with her own refinements and she has provided evaluative comments throughout.

Coursework case studies

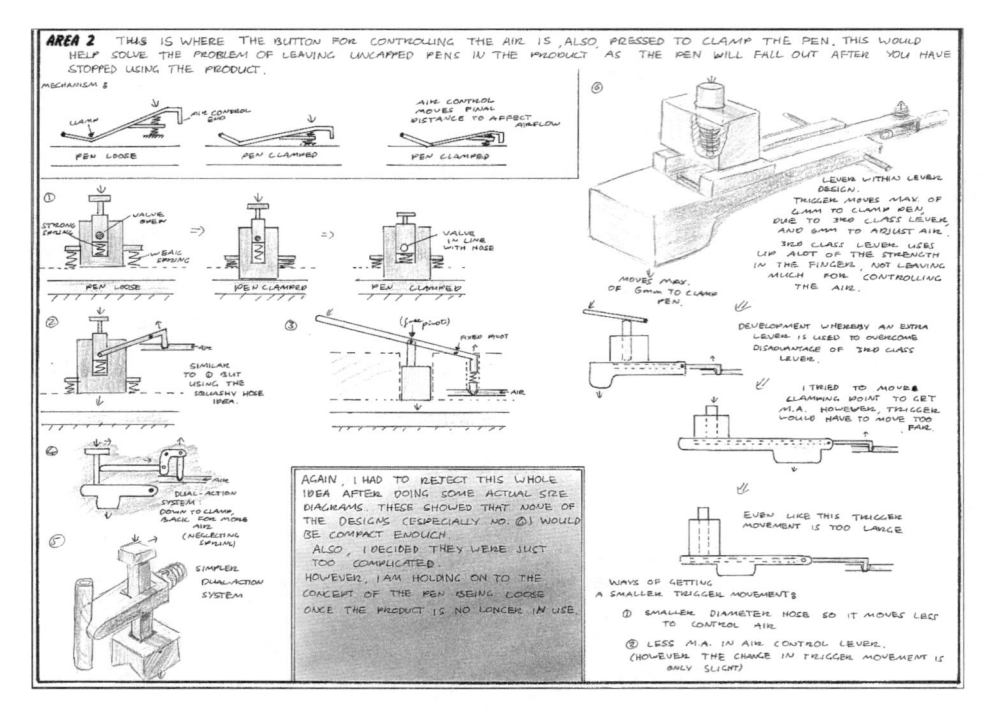

Fig. 6.29 Other early ideas

She has continued with her ideas and concluded that she will have to abandon this design, since it will not be compact enough. Consequently, she has proceeded with a simpler solution.

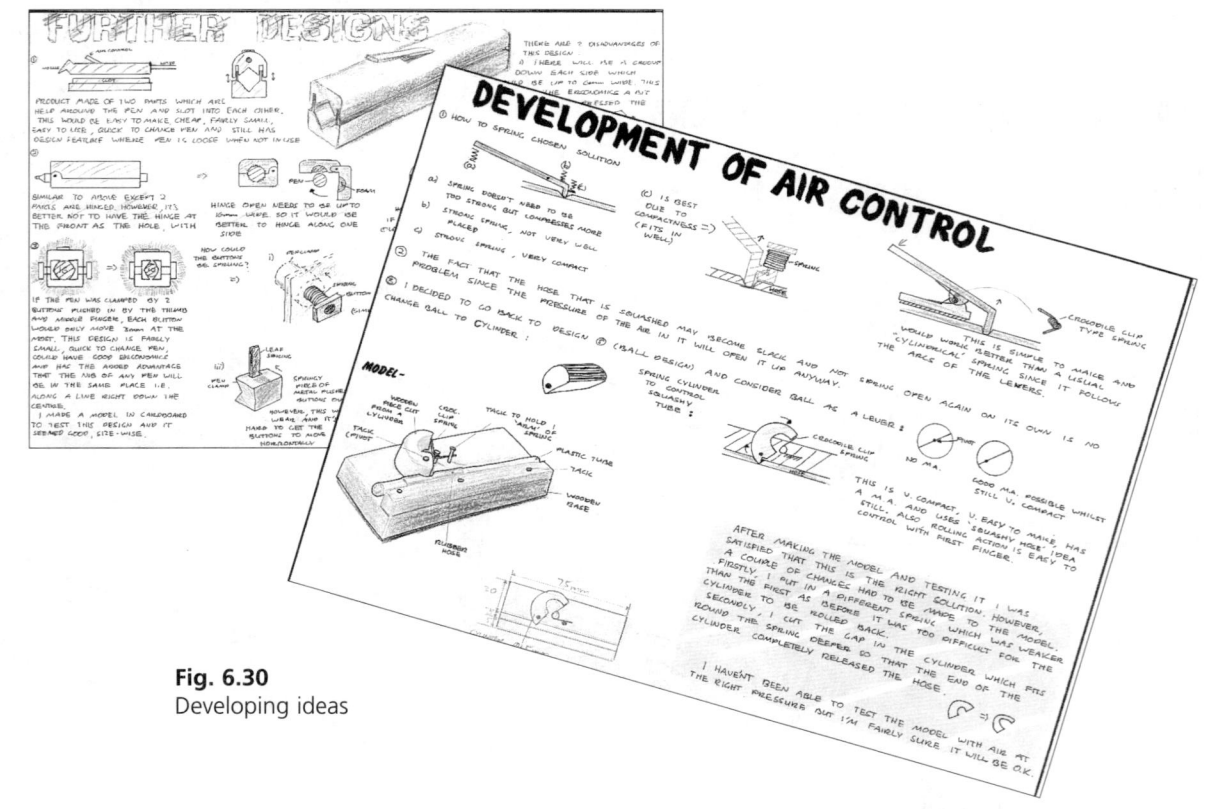

Fig. 6.30 Developing ideas

The simplicity of this idea is becoming evident. However, before proceeding further she has made a model and tested it. She has admitted that her testing was incomplete but thinks things will be alright in the end.

6.5 Air-brush

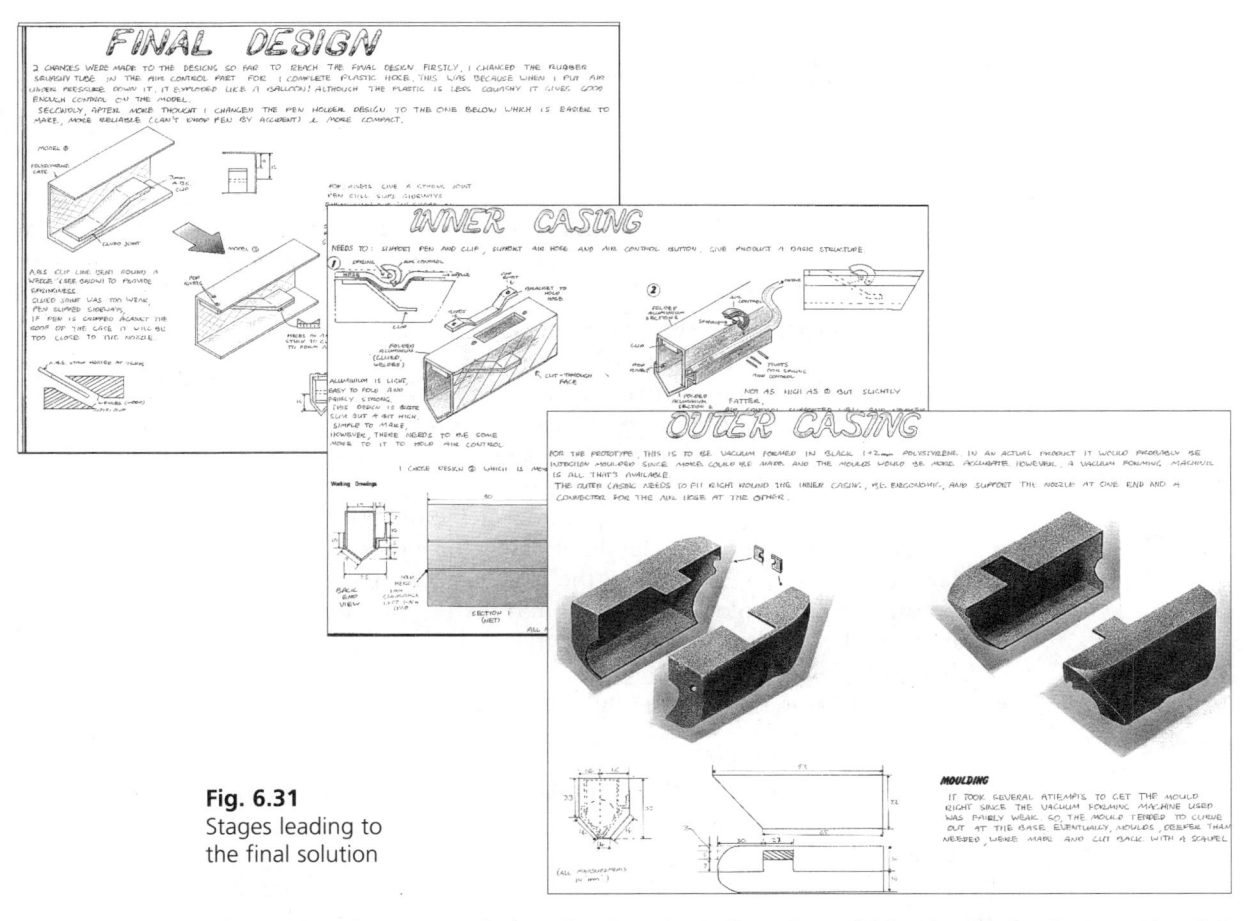

Fig. 6.31 Stages leading to the final solution

The student has proceeded with what she believed would be the final solution. She did not select her first idea immediately, but was prepared to develop it thoroughly.

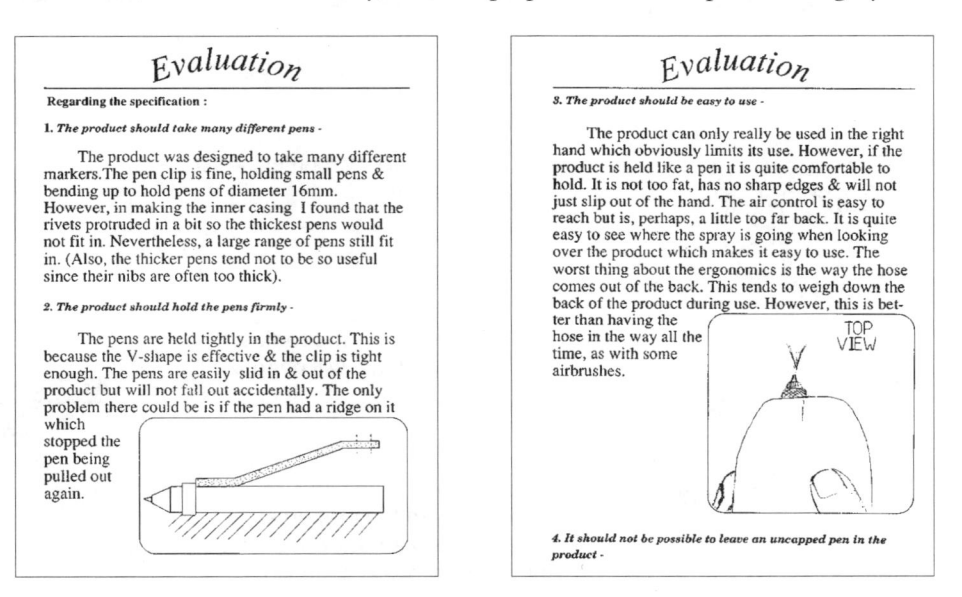

Fig. 6.32 Evaluation of the project

The final solution for the casing was illustrated using the student's own air-brush, so demonstrating that it works. The evaluation sheets shown are two of several. They reflect the care and detail that have characterised the project.

Final comment

A thoroughly comprehensive project. Depth and care are evident throughout. The quality of presentation is excellent. The candidate will certainly gain a very high mark for this piece of work and, if it fairly represents her ability, it would be reasonable to expect an A-grade or better.

Chapter 7 — Core knowledge

7.1 Materials

Properties of materials

All materials have a range of properties, only some of which will be suitable for a particular solution. It is important to match the properties of the materials available to the needs of the solutions. These properties include:

- thermal properties – how well the material conducts heat;
- stiffness – how well the material retains its shape;
- toughness – how well the material resists impact;
- strength – how well the material resists an applied force;
- hardness – how easily the material is scratched or marked;
- resistance to corrosion – how easily the material becomes oxidised;
- density – a measure of the compactness of the material;
- optical properties – how easily light passes through the material;
- electrical properties – how well the material conducts electricity;
- appearance – the colour, brightness and texture of the material;
- ability to be worked – how easily the shape of the material can be physically changed;
- ability to be joined – how easily the material can be joined to others.

Selecting the best material

The following flow chart will help you select the best material for your idea.

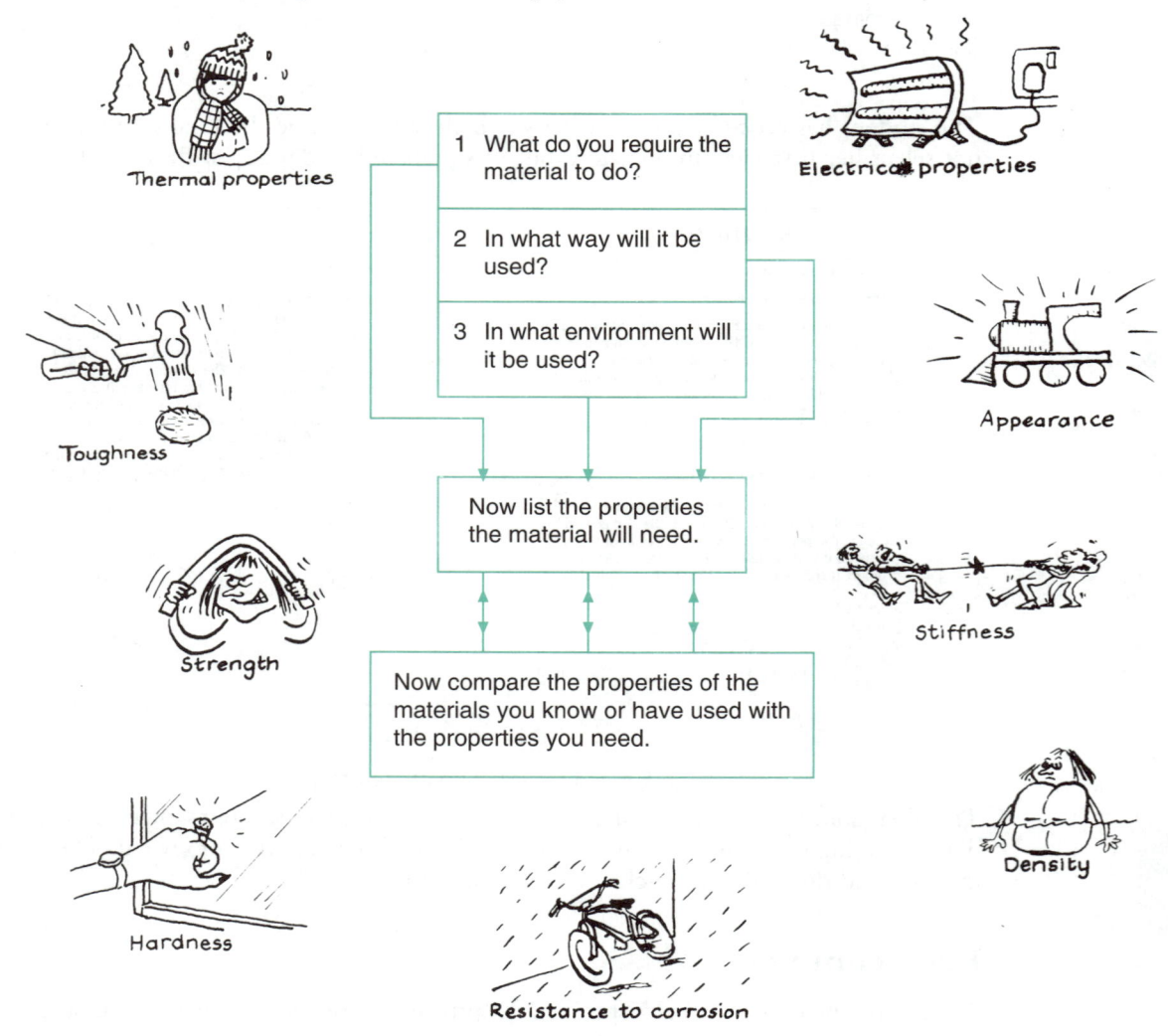

Fig. 7.1 Selecting the best material

Metals

Ferrous metals. These contain iron and are almost all magnetic, for example cast iron and steel.

Material	Uses	Notes
Cast iron	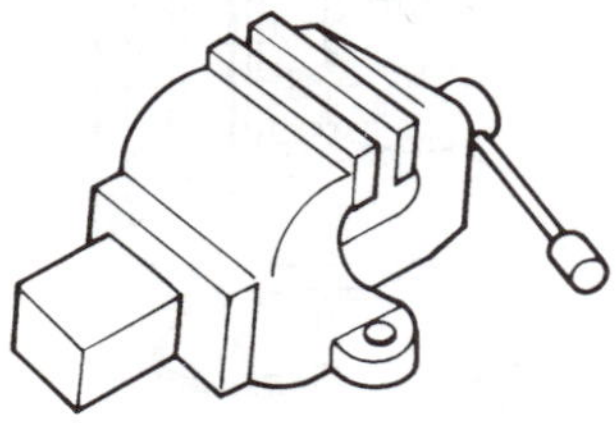	Hard skin. Strong under compression. Cannot be bent or forged.
Mild steel	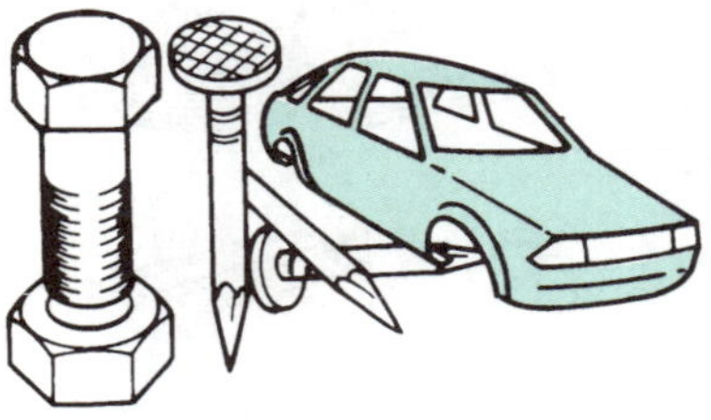	Tough, ductile and malleable. Easily joined but with poor resistance to corrosion. Cannot be hardened or tempered.
High-carbon steel	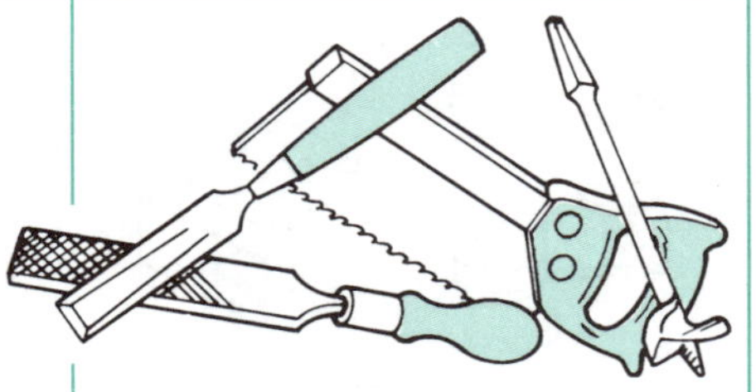	Very hard but less ductile, tough and malleable. Difficult to cut. Can be hardened and tempered.
Stainless steel (alloy)		Hard and tough. Resists wear and corrosion. Quite difficult to cut or file.
High-speed steel (alloy)	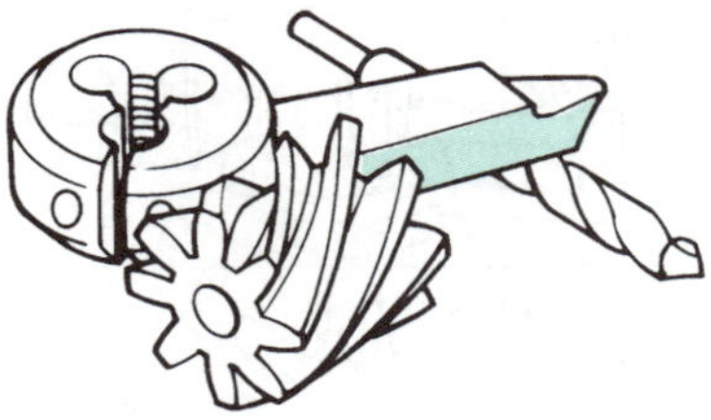	Very hard. Can be used as a cutting tool even when red hot. Can only be shaped by grinding.

Fig. 7.2 Ferrous metals

Core knowledge

Non-ferrous metals. These do not contain iron, for example copper, tin and lead. They are frequently more expensive than ferrous metals.

Material	Uses	Notes
Aluminium		High strength/weight ratio. Difficult to join. Good conductor of heat and electricity. Corrosion resistant. Polishes well.
Copper	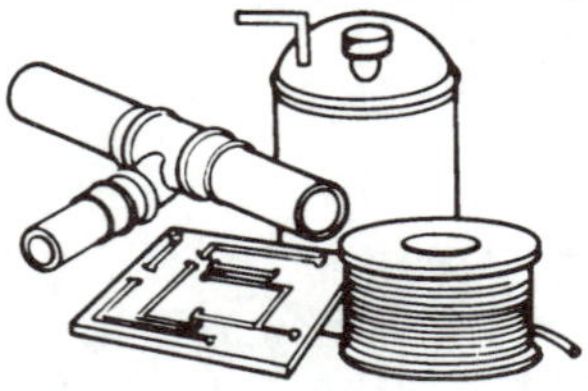	Malleable and ductile. Good conductor of heat and electricity. Easily joined. Polishes well. Expensive.
Lead	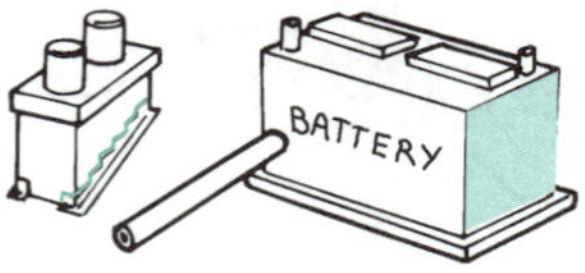	Very heavy, soft, malleable and ductile. Corrosion resistant. Low melting point. Difficult to work and expensive.
Tin (tin plate)		Soft and weak. Ductile and malleable. High corrosion resistance. Low melting point. Used to coat steel to produce 'tin plate'.

Fig. 7.3 Non-ferrous metals

Alloys. These are mixtures of two or more metals or other elements. Alloys have different properties to their constituents, for example, a lower melting temperature.

Material	Uses	Notes
Brass (alloy of copper and zinc)		Corrosion resistant. Harder than copper. Good conductor of heat and electricity. Polishes well. Cheaper than copper.
Bronze (alloy of copper and tin)		Strong and tough. Corrosion resistant. Resistant to wearing.
Duralumin (alloy of several metals and a non-metal)		Nearly as strong as mild steel, but much lighter. Hardens with age. Machines well after annealing.

Fig. 7.4 Alloys

Timber

The words softwood and hardwood are often used to describe different families of timber. These words do not, however, describe the properties of the materials, but the types of trees from which they come.

Hardwoods. These come from deciduous trees, which have flowers and broad leaves. Balsa, a lightweight wood often used for model making is, in fact, a hardwood.

Fixing	Appearance	Uses
Mahogany		Easy to work. Fairly strong. Durable. Prone to warping.
Beech	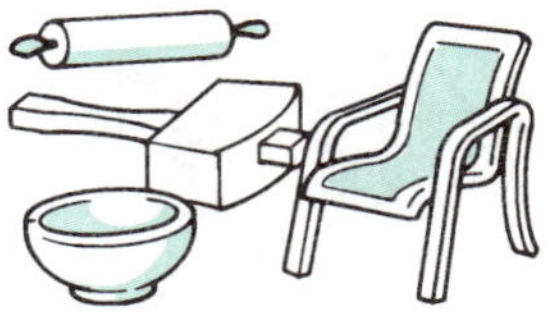	Close-grained, hard, tough and strong. Works and finishes well. Prone to warping.
Ash		Open-grained, tough and flexible. Good elastic qualities. Works well.
Oak		Very strong, heavy and durable. Hard and tough. Open-grained. Contains tannic acid, which corrodes iron and steel.
Teak		Hard, very strong and very durable. Very resistant to acids and alkalis. Contains grit, which blunts tools easily. Very expensive.
Jelutong	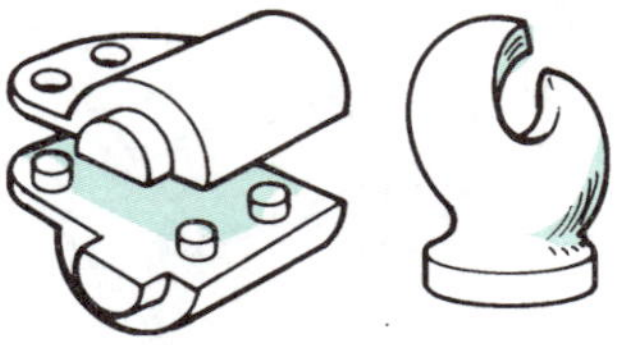	Pale cream in colour. Uniform grain. Shapes easily. Very few knots.
Balsa		Very soft and light. Ideal for models. Quite expensive.

Fig. 7.5 Hardwoods

Core knowledge

Softwoods. These come from cone-bearing (coniferous) trees, which have needle-like leaves. In some cases, yew for example, the timber is much harder than many hardwoods.

Material	Uses	Notes
Scots pine	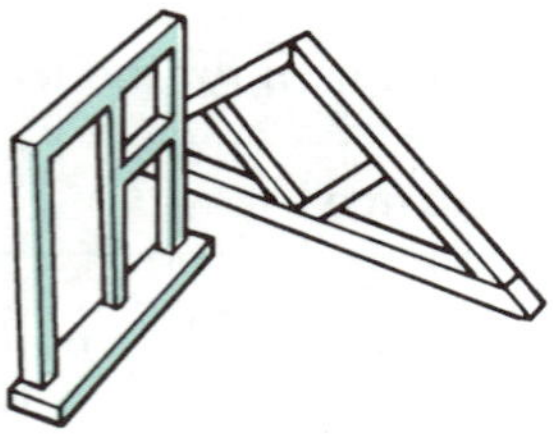	Straight-grained but knotty. Fairly strong, easy to work and cheap. Readily available.
Spruce	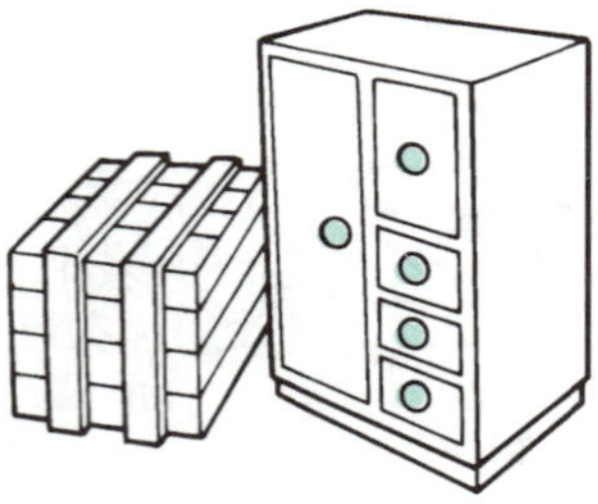	Fairly strong. Small hard knots. Resistant to splitting. Not durable.
Douglas fir		Dark red/brown. Fairly durable and quite dense.
Western red cedar		Lightweight, knot-free, soft, straight silky grain. Durable against weather, insects and rotting. Easy to work but expensive.
Parana pine	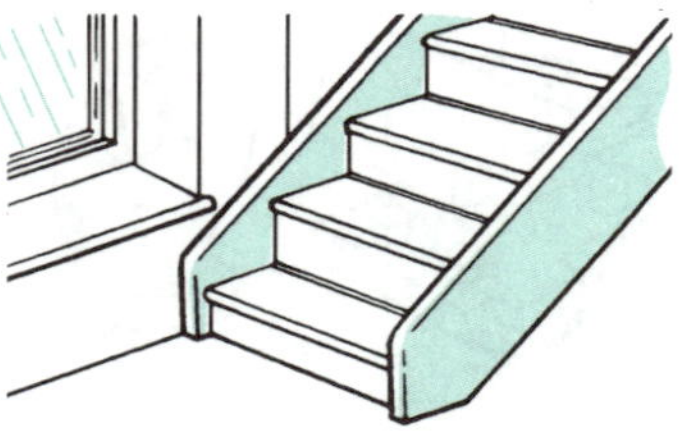	Hard, straight-grained. Almost knot-free. Strong and durable. Tends to warp. Expensive for a softwood. Used for internal joinery.

Fig. 7.6 Softwoods

7.1 Materials

Manufactured boards. These are sheet materials made from natural timber, but they often have properties superior to natural timber. Manufactured boards include plywood, chipboard and insulation board.

Material	Thickness available	Uses	Notes
Hardboard	3.2 mm 6 mm	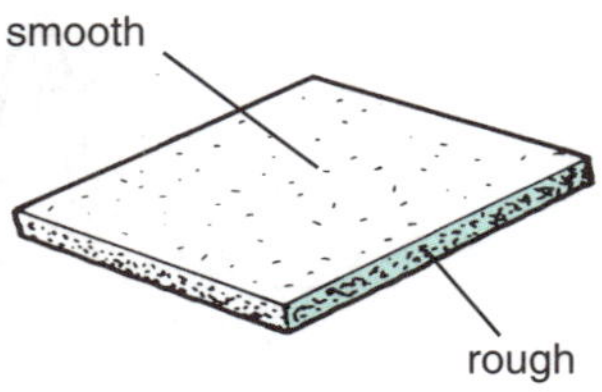	Cheap and fairly light. Used as a substitute for plywood. No grain. Equally strong in all directions. Standard hardboard absorbs moisture and must not be used outdoors. Usually smooth on one side only.
Veneers	1 mm 2 mm 3 mm	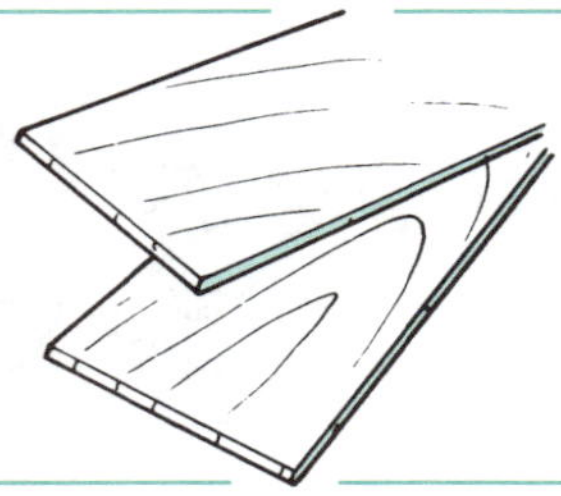	Thin layers of wood. Used for making plywood or laminating. A very economical use of timber, since very little of the tree is wasted.
Plywood	3 mm, 4 mm 6 mm, 8 mm 10 mm, 12 mm 15 mm, 18 mm	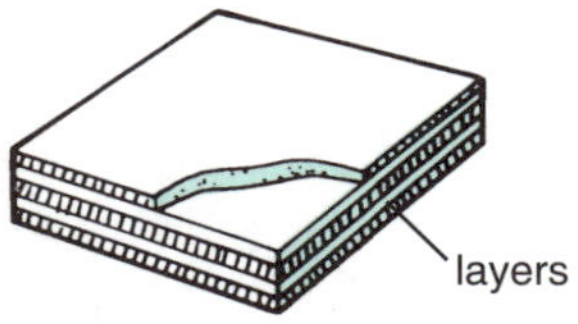	Made from veneers of birch, alder, meranti or gaboon. Odd number of layers. Fairly cheap. Much stronger than hardboard. Some forms of plywood resistant to moisture.
Blockboard and laminboard	12 mm 15 mm 18 mm	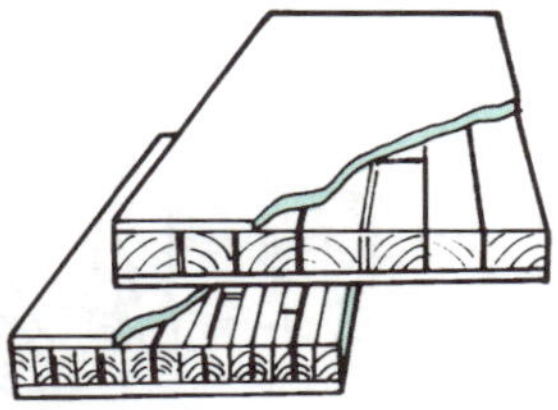	Cheaper to make, thickness-for-thickness, than plywood, although not the same uniform strength.
Chipboard	12 mm 15 mm 18 mm	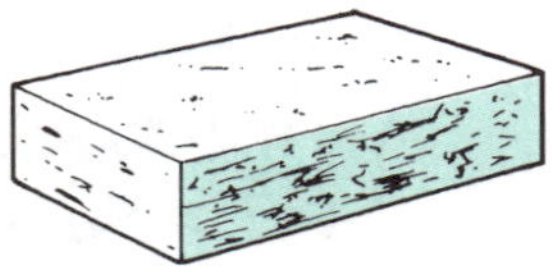	Chips of variety of timbers are bonded using synthetic glue. Available veneered with timber or plastic and used for cheaper, often 'flat pack', furniture.
Medium density fibreboard (MDF)	6 mm 12 mm 15 mm 18 mm	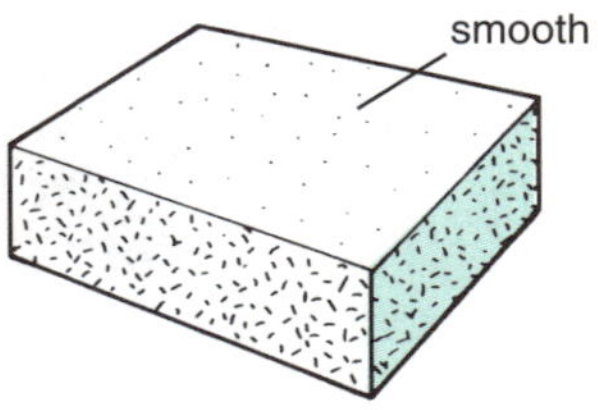	A sort of thicker, smoother, better quality hardboard. Has smooth faces and takes paint well.

Fig. 7.7 Manufactured boards

Core knowledge

Plastics

Thermoplastics. These soften when heated and can therefore be formed into shapes. You will almost certainly have used or seen acrylic, sometimes referred to as Perspex (ICI tradename) or PMMA. Most plastic items are made from thermoplastics.

Material	Uses	Notes
Acrylic (PMMA)		Stiff, hard and uniform strength. Scratches easily. Clear; has good optical properties. Non-toxic. Good insulator, easily machined and polishes well.
Rigid polystyrene (PS)		Light, hard, stiff, often transparent. Brittle with low impact strength. Water resistant. The toughened type can be coloured.
Expanded polystyrene (PS)		Buoyant, lightweight. A good sound and heat insulator.
Polyamide (nylon)		Usually creamy in colour. Hard, tough and resistant to wear. Low friction. Machines well, but very difficult to join.
Polyethylene (polythene, PE)		Tough, very popular. Quite cheap. Available in a wide range of colours. Fairly low melting point.
Acrylonitrile butadienestyrene (ABS)		High impact strength. Tough and scratch resistant. Resistant to chemicals.
Polyvinyl chloride (PVC)		Chemical and weather resistant. Wide range of colours. Needs a stabiliser for outdoor use. Good electrical insulator.
Polyethylene terephthalate (PET)		Used extensively for mineral water bottles. Clear and very tough.

Fig. 7.8 Thermoplastics

Thermosets. These behave differently from thermoplastics. Once a thermoset has hardened heating will not soften it. Thermosets solidify by a chemical reaction, which is usually speeded up by heat, hence 'heat sets' – thermosets. You will probably have seen polyester resin (GRP), or possibly have used an epoxy adhesive such as Araldite.

Material	Uses	Notes
Polyester resin (GRP)		Stiff, hard and brittle. Used for casting and, when reinforced by glass fibres, produces GRP. Easy to colour. Excellent for outdoor uses.
Urea formaldehyde (UF)		Stiff, hard and brittle. Excellent electrical insulator. Used as an adhesive.
Epoxy resin	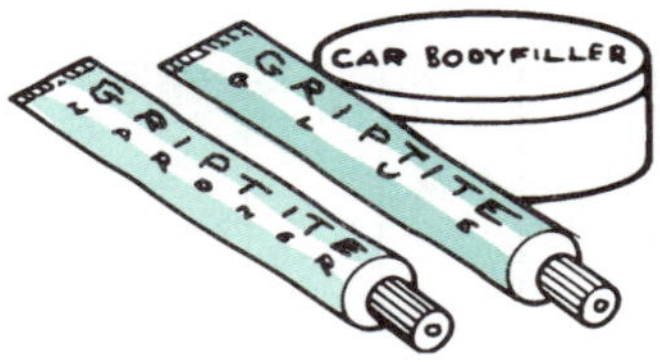	Very strong, especially when reinforced by glass or carbon fibres. Used as an adhesive for unlike materials.
Melamine formaldehyde (MF)		Stiff, hard and strong. Scratch resistant. Low water absorption. Stain resistant. No odour. Available in a wide range of colours.

Fig. 7.9 Thermosets

Core knowledge

Market forms

Timber, metals and plastics can be bought in standard sizes and forms, called market forms.

Timber. Strips, squares and dowel are sold by length, e.g., 1.8 m. Boards and planks are often sold per square metre, e.g., one plank 6.3 m × 300 mm = 1.89 sq. m.

SHEETS	PLANKS	BOARDS	STRIPS	SQUARES	DOWEL
Up to 1220 mm × 2440 mm. Plywood, hardboard, etc.	Up to 375 mm × 50+ mm	100 – 375 mm × up to 50 mm	Under 100 mm × up to 50 mm	Up to 100 mm × 100 mm	Ø 3 mm – Ø 50 mm

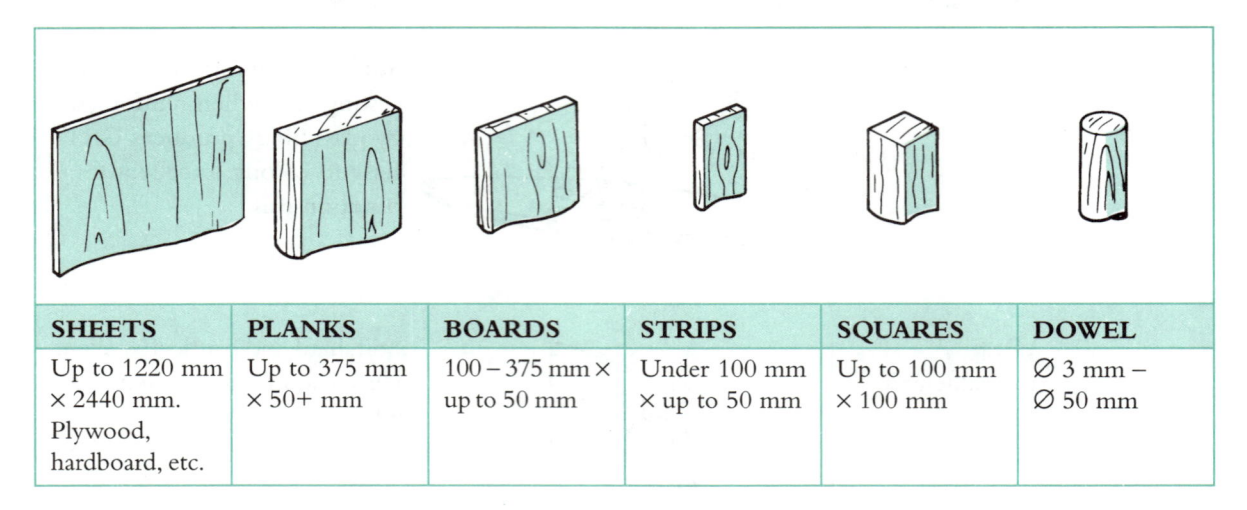

Metals

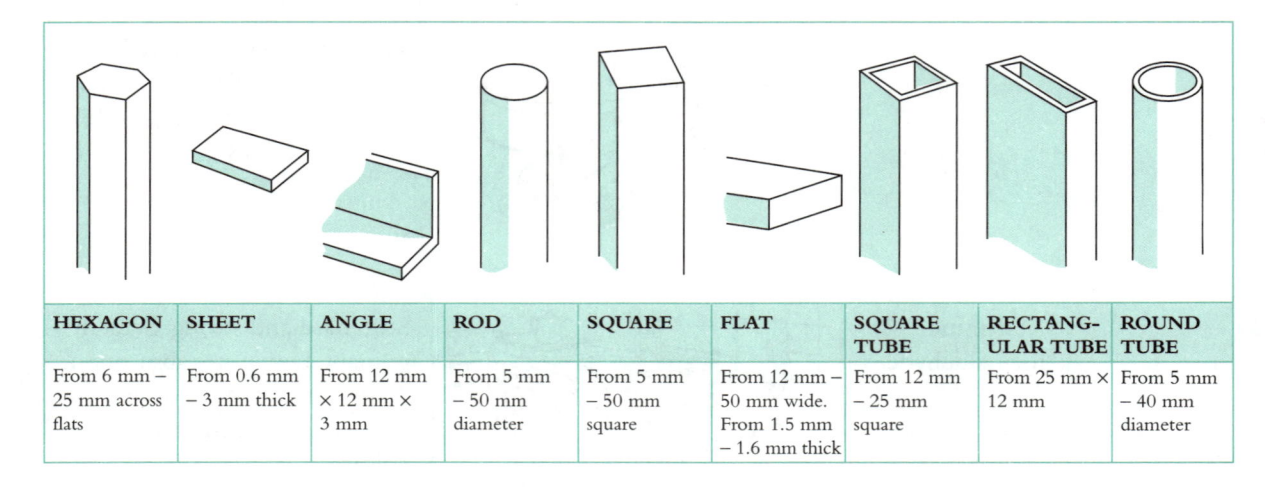

HEXAGON	SHEET	ANGLE	ROD	SQUARE	FLAT	SQUARE TUBE	RECTANG-ULAR TUBE	ROUND TUBE
From 6 mm – 25 mm across flats	From 0.6 mm – 3 mm thick	From 12 mm × 12 mm × 3 mm	From 5 mm – 50 mm diameter	From 5 mm – 50 mm square	From 12 mm – 50 mm wide. From 1.5 mm – 1.6 mm thick	From 12 mm – 25 mm square	From 25 mm × 12 mm	From 5 mm – 40 mm diameter

Plastics

	POWDER	GRANULES	FOAM	FILM	SHEET	BLOCK	HEXAGONAL BAR	RODS	TUBES	RESINS AND PASTES
Polyethylene (PE)	✓	✓	✗	✓	✗	✗	✗	✗	✓	✗
Acrylic (PMMA)	✗	✓	✗	✗	✓	✓	✗	✓	✓	✓
Nylon	✓	✓	✗	✗	✗	✓	✓	✓	✗	✗
PVC	✓	✓	✗	✗	✓	✗	✗	✗	✓	✗
Polystyrene (PS)	✓	✓	✓	✗	✓	✓	✗	✗	✗	✗
Polyester	✗	✗	✓	✗	✗	✗	✗	✗	✗	✓
Epoxy	✗	✗	✗	✗	✗	✗	✗	✗	✗	✓

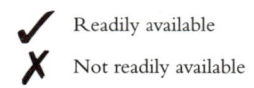

✓ Readily available
✗ Not readily available

Fig. 7.10 Market forms

Adhesives

Gluing hints

1 Make sure the gluing surfaces are clean, and do not apply onto paint, polish, etc.
2 Assemble 'dry' before applying any glue. Have the cramps ready before you start.
3 Make sure you use the correct adhesive for the job.
4 If you haven't used the adhesive before then read the manufacturer's instructions.

Adhesive	Uses		Hints on use	
Polyvinyl acetate (PVA)	Used mainly for timber and paper products.	Long setting time (several hours)	Not always waterproof. Wipe off excess before it dries.	Sustained pressure is needed
Evostik resin W				
Synthetic resin	Stronger than PVA and also waterproof.		Chemically active. Needs mixing with water. Will fill small gaps in a joint.	
Cascamite Aerolite 306				
Acrylic cement	Used only for acrylic. It does not work with other plastics or other materials.		Ensure good ventilation. Replace cap when not in use.	
Tensol 12				
Epoxy resin	Expensive but versatile. Will bond almost any clean material.		Resin and hardener need to be mixed. It hardens quite quickly but does not reach full strength for two to three days.	
Araldite				
Contact adhesive	Used mainly for gluing sheet material, such as melamine to work surfaces.	Short setting time (less than one hour)	Apply thin layers to each side. Allow to dry. Adhesion occurs on contact. The vapours are harmful and ventilation is essential.	Usually only hand pressure is needed
Evostik Contact Thixofix (Dunlop)				
Latex adhesive	Suitable for fabrics, paper and upholstery.		Non-toxic and safe for young children to use.	
Copydex				
Polystyrene cement	Used only on rigid polystyrene (expanded polystyrene will melt).		Ensure good ventilation.	
Airfix cement				
Rubber solution	Used only for rubber, especially in bicycle puncture repairs.		Read the manufacturer's instructions carefully.	
Bostik				
Glue gun	Used for rapid gluing of small pieces.		Take care, as the glue is used hot and can burn the skin badly.	

Table 7.1 Adhesives

Core knowledge

Soldering and welding

Adhesives are not the most usual materials for joining metals. They are recommended in situations where heat processes cannot be used and where mechanical fixings might weaken the structure, e.g., in modern aircraft construction. They are, however, often used for joining fabrics. Heat processes, such as soldering and welding, are used in situations where a fixing is to be permanent.

Soldering. You will probably have soldered electronic components using a soldering iron and you may have seen high-temperature soldering, called brazing, which makes use of a gas-and-air blowtorch. In all soldering, the surface of the metal has to be clean. A chemical flux has to be applied to keep it clean and the metals are bonded together by melting a separate metal onto the heated joint.

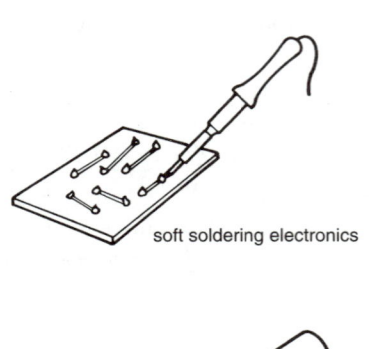

Soft soldering uses a solder made from lead and tin, and takes place at relatively low temperaturs, using an iron or a 'soft' gas flame.

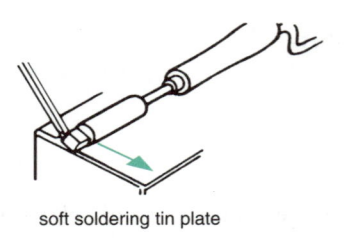

Fig. 7.11 Soldering techniques

Hard soldering is done at higher temperatures, using a gas/air flame with a solder that is a higher-temperature alloy made from brass or silver.

Welding. In welding the process may seem similar, but the difference is that you use an oxygen/acetylene gas torch at a much higher temperature and the actual metals to be fixed are melted together. Any gaps are filled with a filler rod of the same material as that being welded. Fixing plastics can present special difficulties. Heat welding is used for bonding polythene; you can see this in the manufacture of plastic food bags.

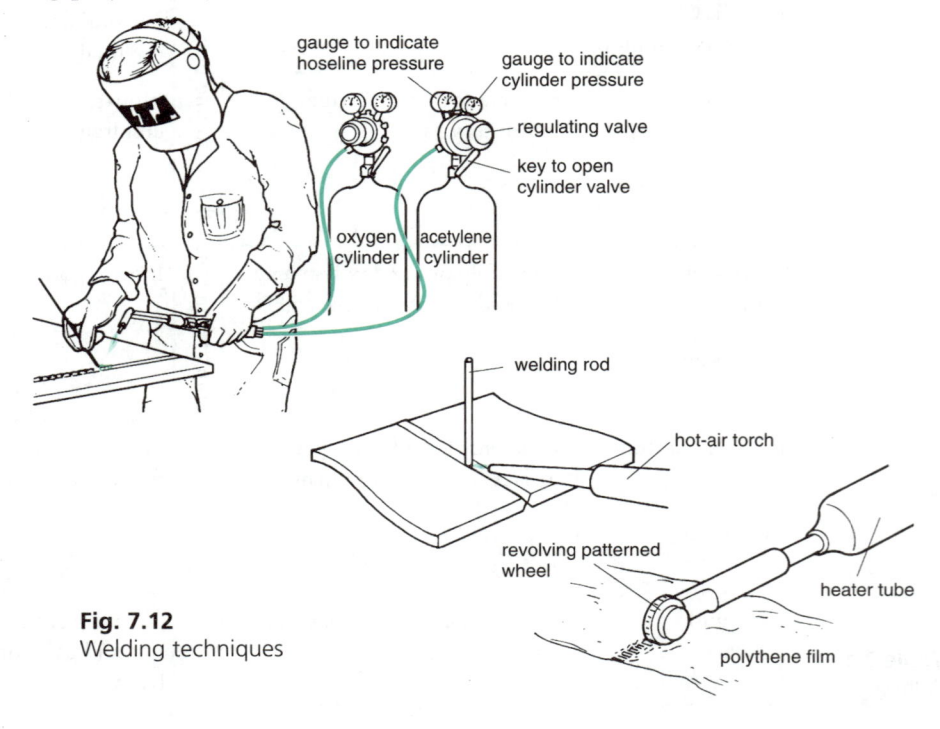

Fig. 7.12 Welding techniques

Mechanical fixings

Mechanical fixings are normally used when the joint is either temporary or semi-permanent. Some mechanical fixings, such as hinges, will allow joints to be adjustable. Mechanical fixings are very useful in joining metals if you wish to avoid heat processes. They are also useful when joining dissimilar materials, such as metal to timber.

Fixing	Appearance	Uses
Round wire nail	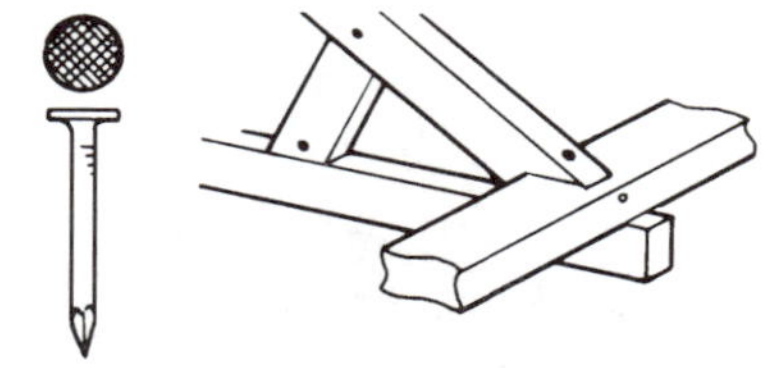	General purpose nail. Do not use near end of timber or timber will split.
Oval wire nail	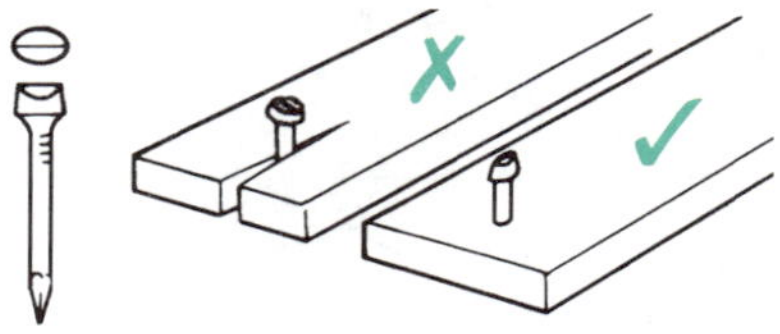	Similar use to round wire nail, but less likely to split wood if used correctly. More likely to bend.
Hardboard nail	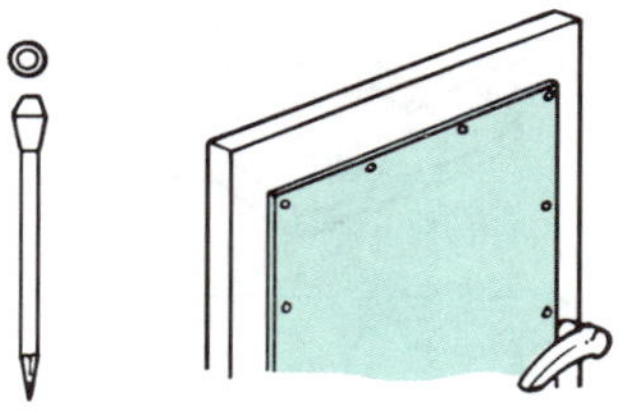	Designed to fix panels of hardboard. The head is shaped so that it sinks into the surface.
Masonry nail		Useful for quick (and sometimes crude) fixing to brick, concrete and block walls.
Countersunk woodscrew	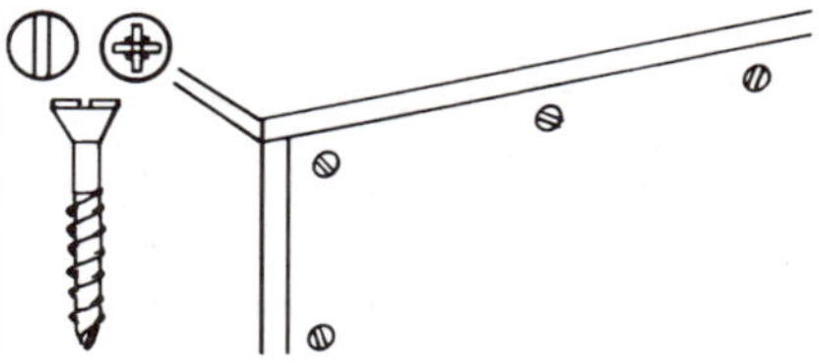	Usually with a slotted or cross-point head. Used to fix two pieces together. Make sure the piece nearest to the head has a clearance-size hole drilled.
Round-head woodscrew	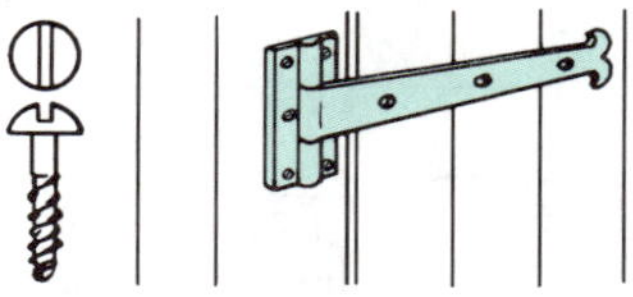	For holding panels of thin material or where it is not possible to make a countersink.
Clout nail		For holding roof felt. Galvanized for outdoor use.

Fig. 7.13 Mechanical fixings

Core knowledge

Fixing	Appearance	Uses
Nut and bolt	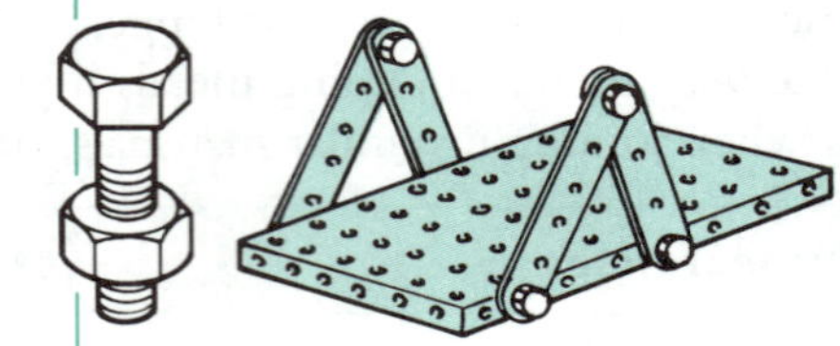	General purpose. Tightened with spanners. Can be very strong.
Self-tapping screw	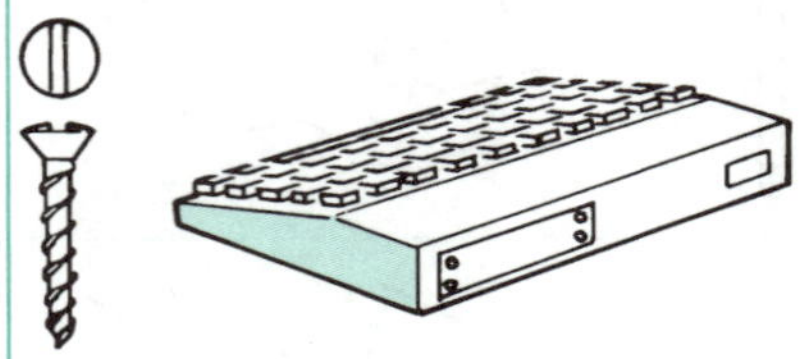	Used to cut a thread in sheet metal and soft plastics. A small pilot hole is needed.
Rivets	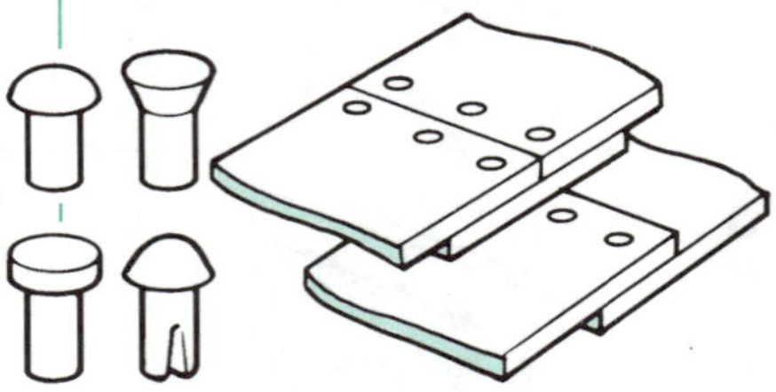	Available in a range of materials, but frequently with countersunk or snap heads (as shown). Used to fix metal components together.
Pop rivet	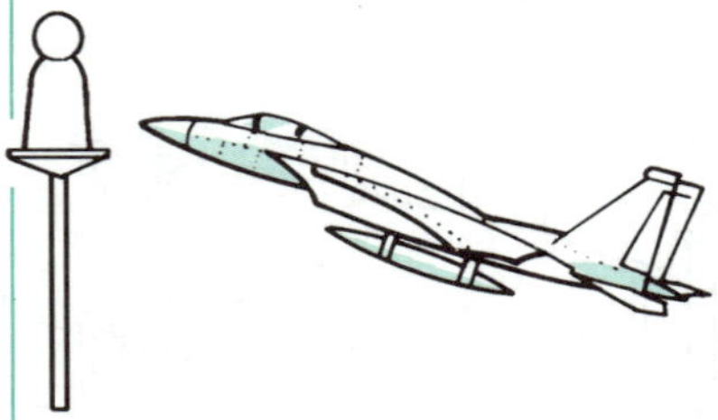	Used in sheet metal and fixed with a special tool. Used when it is impossible to reach both sides of the metal.
Butt hinge	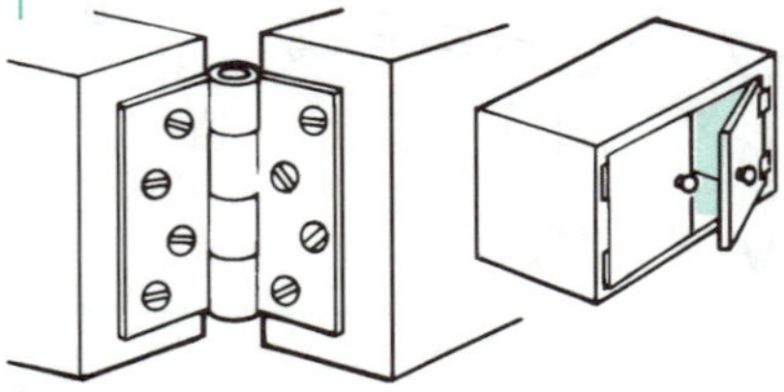	A general purpose hinge used to allow movement on doors, for example.
Kitchen cabinet hinge		Used for modern kitchen fittings. Hinge is invisible from outside.

Fig. 7.13 Mechanical fixings (continued)

7.1 Materials

Knockdown fittings

The increase in the manufacture of materials such as chipboard and medium-density fibreboard (MDF) has led to the growth of the 'flat pack' industry. You can buy a piece of furniture ready for self-assembly. A whole range of special, easy-to-use fittings, known as knockdown fittings, has been produced, some of which are shown here.

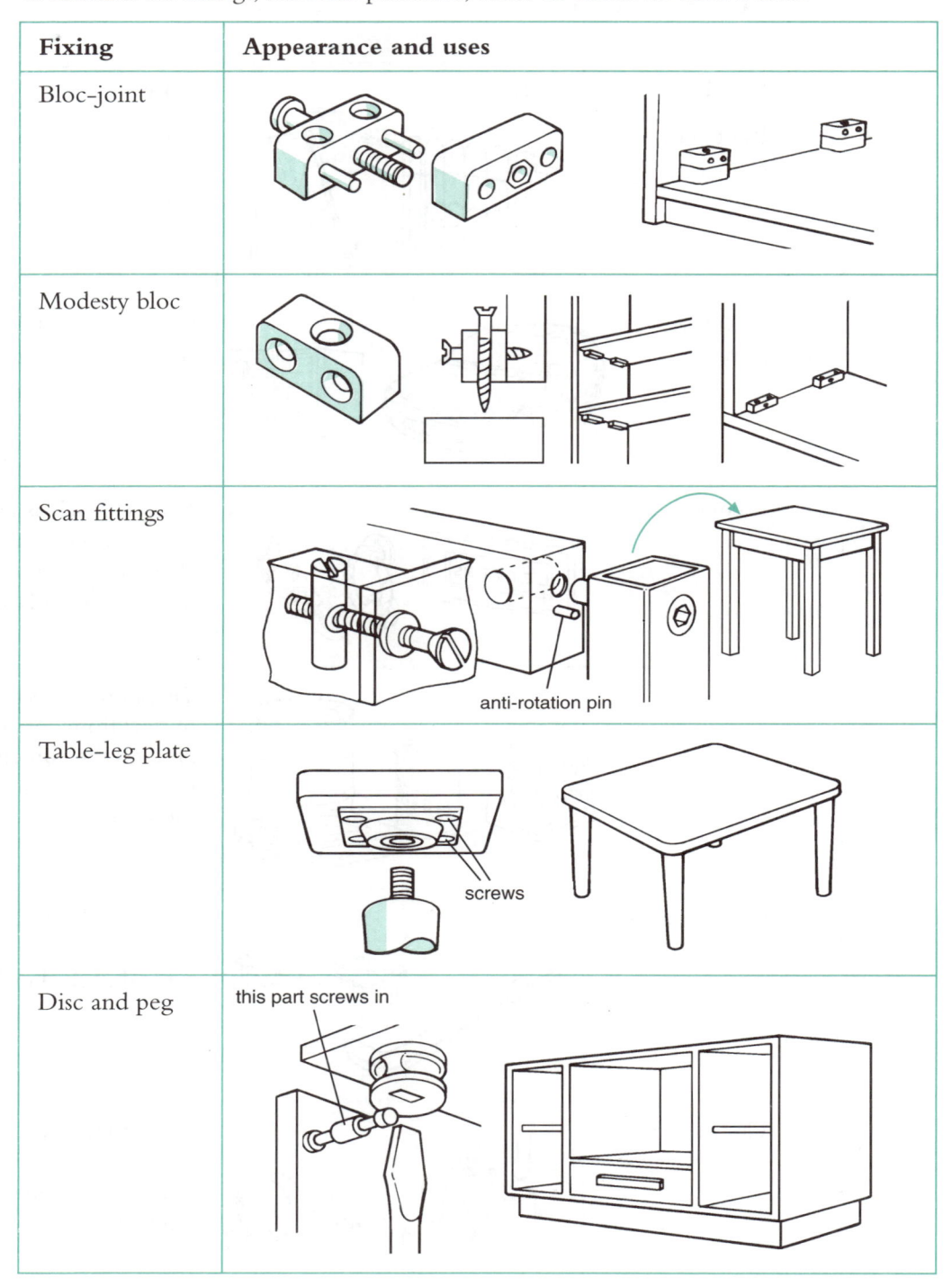

Fixing	Appearance and uses
Bloc-joint	
Modesty bloc	
Scan fittings	anti-rotation pin
Table-leg plate	screws
Disc and peg	this part screws in

Fig. 7.14 Knockdown fittings

Surface finishes

Whatever you have designed, the surface finish will be significant. It is important, therefore, to select a surface finish that will:

- improve the appearance of the product;
- protect the materials from physical damage;
- protect the surface from weathering;
- make the product easier to handle.

Core knowledge

Your choice of a suitable finish will depend upon:
- the material;
- the function of the finish;
- the method of application;
- the skill of the person applying it;
- what is available.

Finish	Uses	Notes
Paint and primer	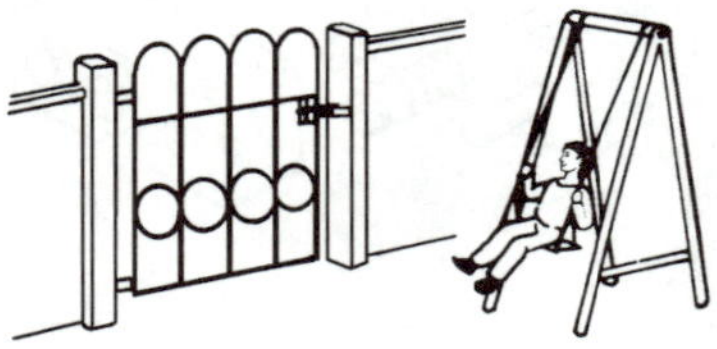	Take care to prepare surface. Remove rust or old paint before applying primer.
Cellulose paint		Usually sprayed with specialist equipment. Care must be taken to avoid breathing fumes.
Lacquer		Material, such as brass or copper, which will discolour after a time can be protected by a coating of lacquer.
Tin plating		Tin plating protects the surface of steel from corrosion and protects the contents, e.g., food, from contamination by the steel.
Chrome plating		Chrome plating gives a hard, shiny attractive finish. It can be applied to steel or brass.
Plastics coating	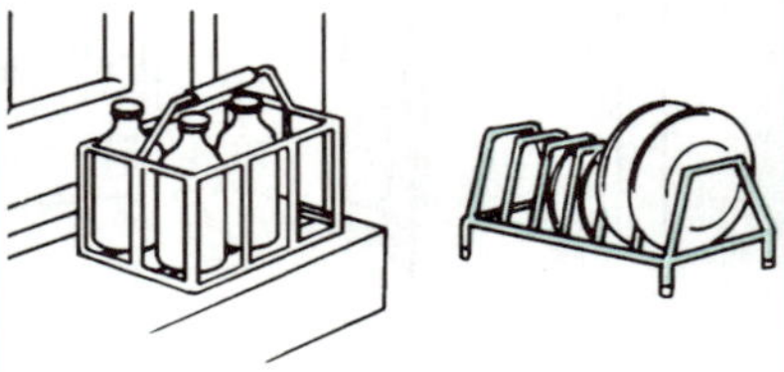	Commonly PVC and polythene are used to 'dip' steel. This is done in a fluidizing tank.
Enamelling		Enamels are applied to copper surfaces, which 'fuse' to the surface after heating.

Fig. 7.15 Finishes

Finish	Uses	Notes
Varnish	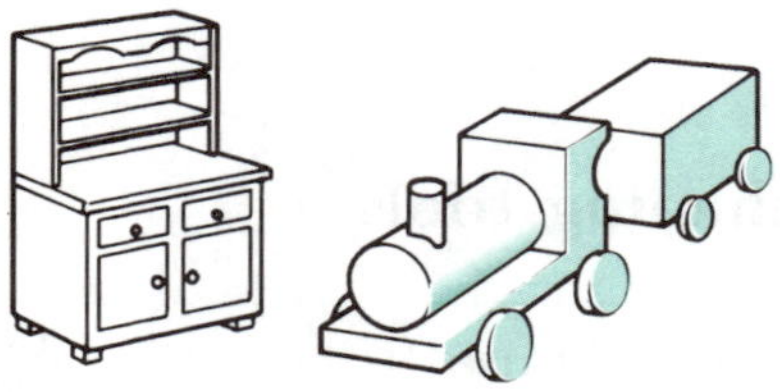	Prepare surface thoroughly. Apply two *thin* coats. Rub down between coats. Clean brushes with white spirit.
Primer, undercoat and paint	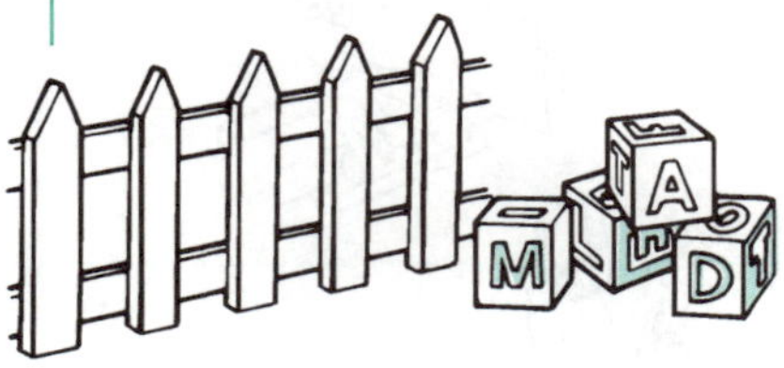	Top coat will only stick properly to an undercoat. The primer is designed to fill the grain of the timber.
Cellulose paint	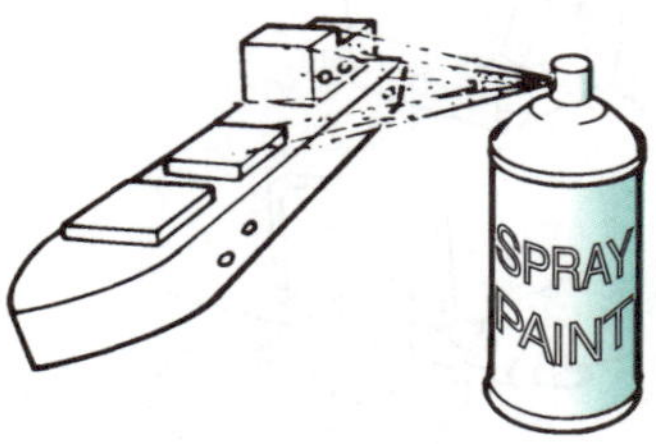	Aerosols containing CFCs should be avoided. Cellulose vapour is harmful. You must ensure good ventilation and wear a face mask.
French polish	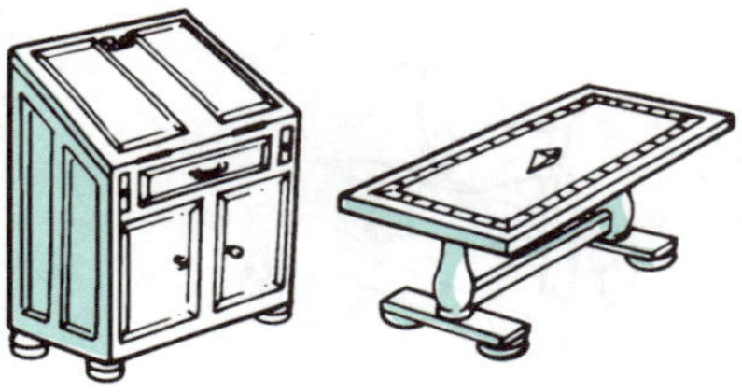	A difficult process best left to the experts. The finished surface is of a high gloss but is easily damaged by heat.
Oil	 Teak oil, Linseed oil, Olive oil	Oils provide good resistance to water. They are quick and easy to apply.

Fig. 7.15 Finishes (continued)

Core knowledge

7.2 Tools and equipment

Cutting and shaping tools

Tool	Tool in use	Use on	Notes
Tenon saw		W	Used to cut relatively small pieces of wood and for sawing joints, such as tenons and halvings.
Hand saw	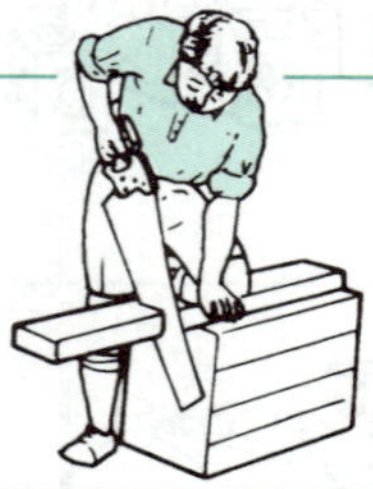	W	Available in different lengths and with different numbers of teeth per cm. Use to saw larger sections of wood.
Coping saw	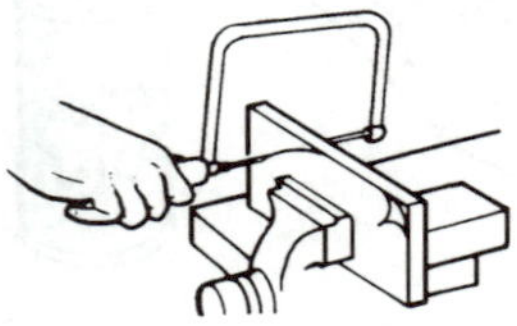	W P	Not ideal for straight cuts but good for curves and removing awkward shapes in wood and some plastics.
Firmer chisel	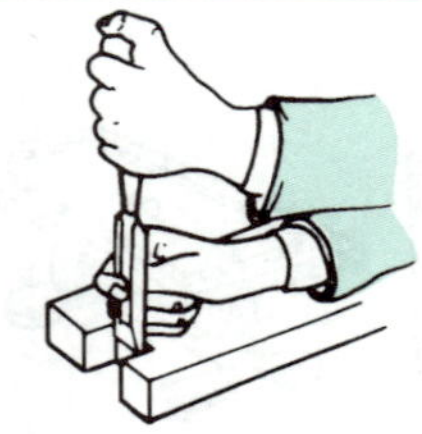	W	Generally used horizontally or vertically (as shown) for removing small amounts of timber accurately.
Jack/smoothing plane		W P	Used to prepare wood accurately to size and for final cleaning, prior to using glasspaper.
Taps and dies	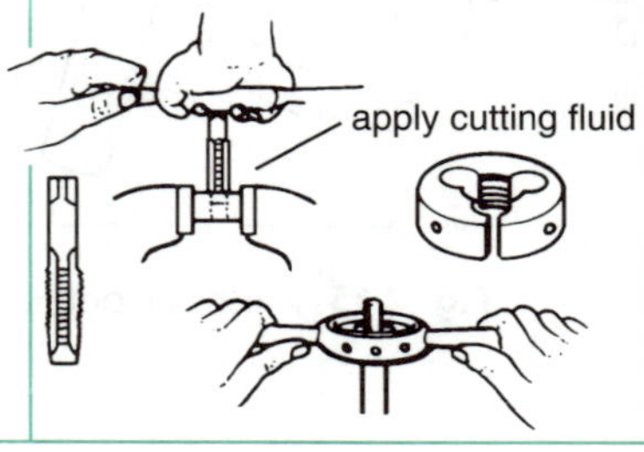	W P	For cutting screw threads. Sizes range from 3 mm up to 15 mm and larger.

Key:
W = wood
P = plastics
M = metals

Fig. 7.16 Cutting and shaping tools

7.2 Tools and equipment

Tool	Tool in use	Use on	Notes
Files	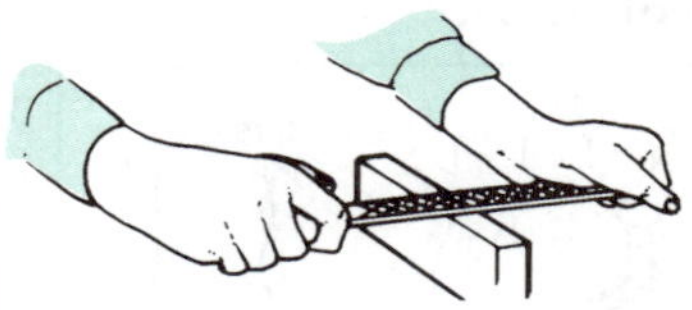	W M P	Available in a huge range of lengths, shapes and 'cuts'. Use on metals and plastics. If used on wood they tend to clog. Always make sure a handle is fitted.
Tin snips	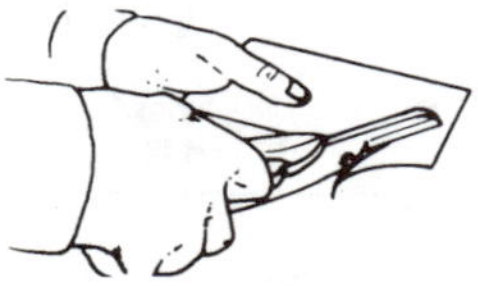	M P	Originally intended for cutting tin plate, but equally useful for sheet aluminium, copper, etc., as well as sheet PVC and polystyrene.
Side cutters	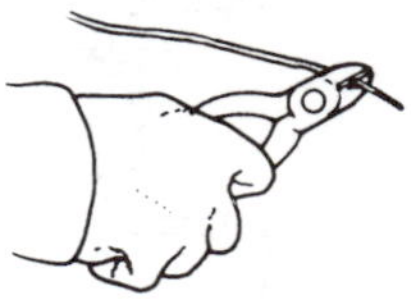	M	Used to snip off surplus wire after soldering electrical components. Can be used to cut electrical wire, but it should not be used to cut hard (piano) wire.
Acrylic cutter	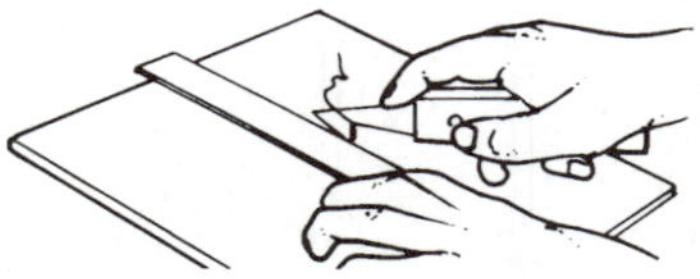	P	With this tool, the plastic (acrylic or polystyrene, for example) is scored and then broken along the line.
Trimming knife	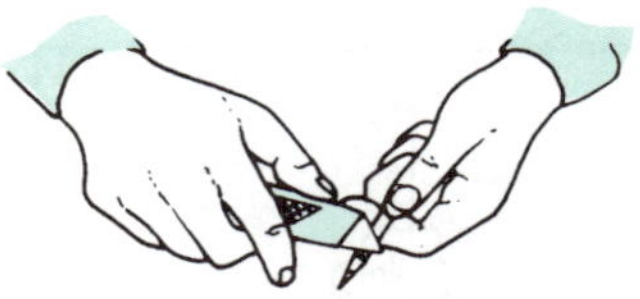	W P	Used for trimming paper, card, thin wood and plastics. It can also be used for accurate marking-out of wood.
Surform	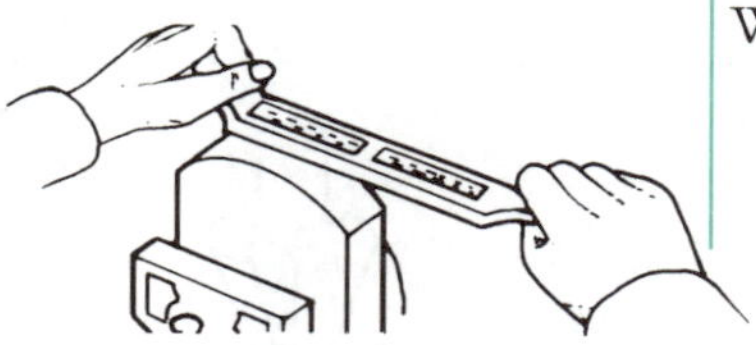	W	A very versatile tool for free shaping of wood, soft plastics, plaster, etc. Used with care, it can shape plastic foams, such as polyurethane.
Guillotine/ bench shear	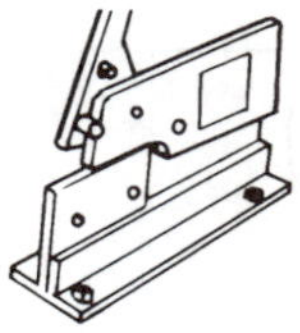	M P	For cutting sheet metal that cannot be cut with tin snips. It is usually locked closed when not in use, to avoid accidents.
Hacksaw	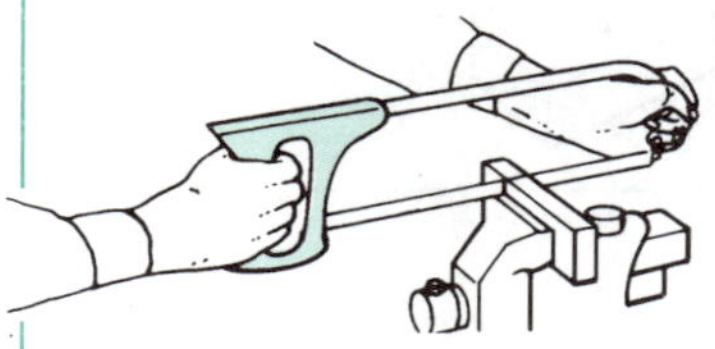	M P	For use on metals and plastics. The blade can be fitted sideways to allow cutting along the length of material without the frame getting in the way.

Key:
W = wood
P = plastics
M = metals

Fig. 7.16 Cutting and shaping tools (continued)

Core knowledge

Hole-making tools

Tool	Tool in use	Use on	Notes
Handrill/ twist drills	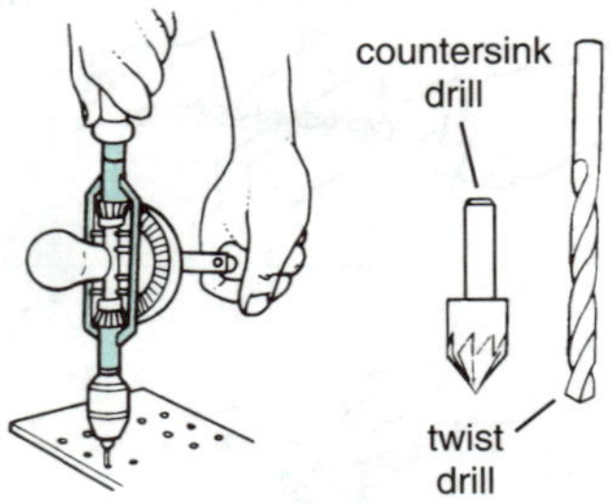 (countersink drill, twist drill)	W M	Difficult to use for large diameters.
Brace/bits	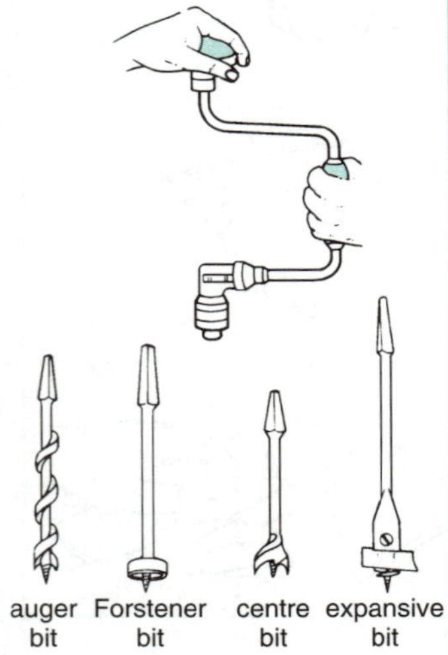 (auger bit, Forstener bit, centre bit, expansive bit)	W	A wide range of bits are available for boring holes from 6 mm up to 50 mm diameter. Expansive (adjustable) bits can be used for larger holes.
Hole saw		W M P	Use with a pillar drill at slow speed. Good for making wheels.
Cone cut	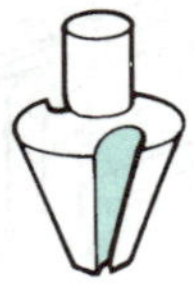	P	Useful for enlarging holes in sheet plastic and metal.
Bradawl	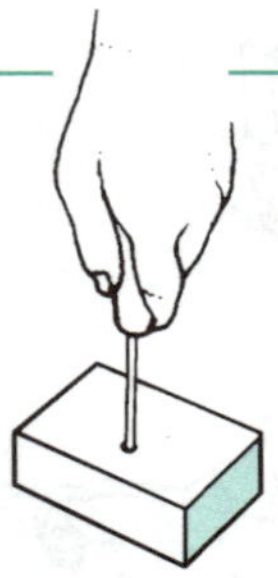	W P	For making small holes in timber and especially for 'starter' holes, prior to inserting woodscrews.

Key:
W = wood
P = plastics
M = metals

Fig. 7.17 Hole-making tools

7.2 Tools and equipment

Holding tools

Tool	Tool in use	Use on	Notes
G-cramp	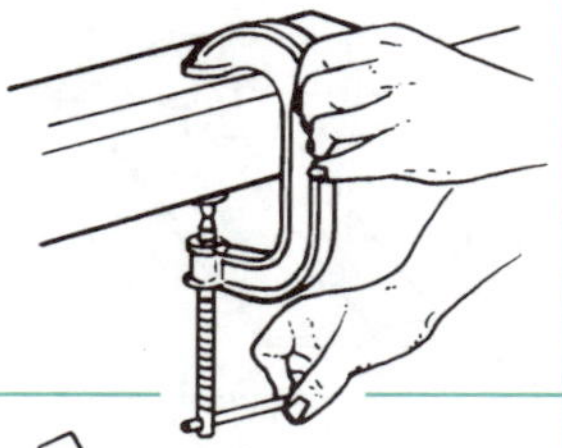	W M P	Used in almost all situations when two parts need to be held together for a short while, e.g., gluing up or drilling on the pillar drill.
Toolmaker's cramp	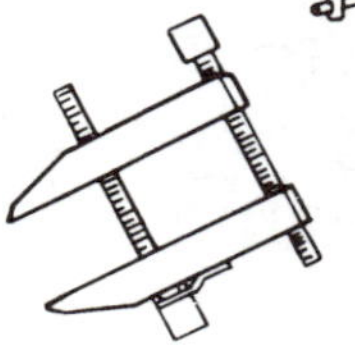	M P	For holding work together when a G-cramp is not appropriate. Usually used on small pieces of work and rarely with timber.
Engineer's/ carpenter's vice	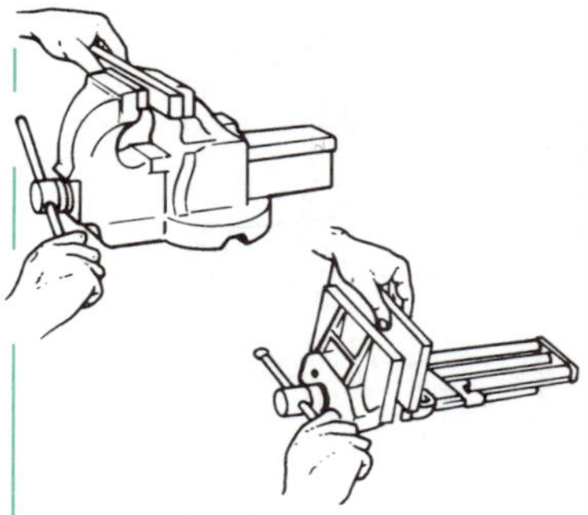	M P W P	Remember: the engineer's vice has jaws that may damage soft materials. The carpenter's vice is better for holding large pieces of work.
Machine vice	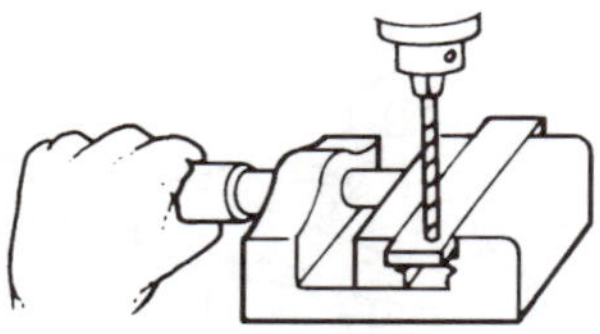	M P	Used to hold materials accurately and securely when drilling. The vice can either be hand held, bolted or cramped down.
Hand vice	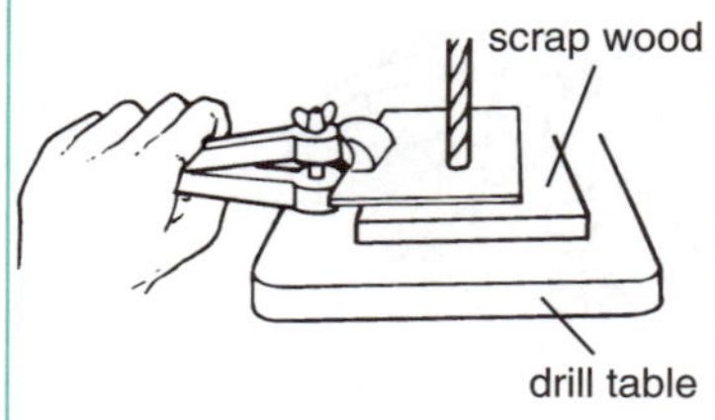	M P	Used to hold sheet materials when drilling. Make sure the wing nut is tight and hold securely in place.
Pliers	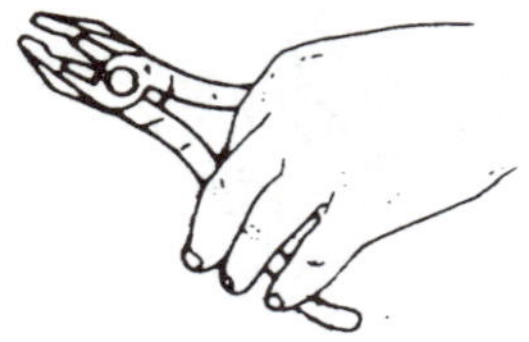	M P	Available in a variety of sizes. Used to hold small items when fingers would be too large or not strong enough. Do not use as a substitute for a spanner.

Key:
W = wood
P = plastics
M = metals

Fig. 7.18 Holding tools

Core knowledge

Marking-out tools

Tool	Tool in use	Use on	Notes
Scriber	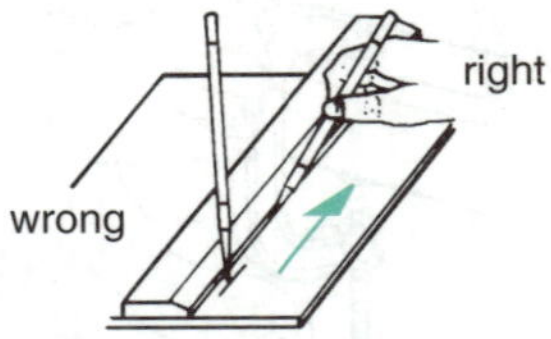	M P	Used to mark out on hard materials, such as metals.
Engineer's square/ tri-square	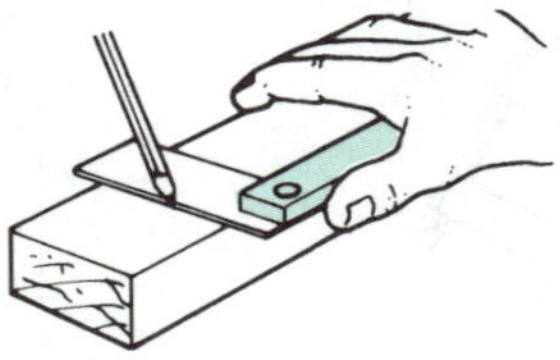	W M P	Marking line at right angles to the edge of metals, plastics and timber. Also used to check right angles.
Dividers		M P	For transferring measurements and marking out arcs and circles on metals and plastics.
Centre punch	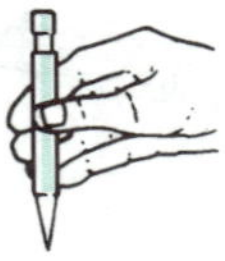	M P	Marking centres of holes before drilling or marking out with dividers.
Centre square		W M P	Used to find the centre of a round bar.
Micrometer	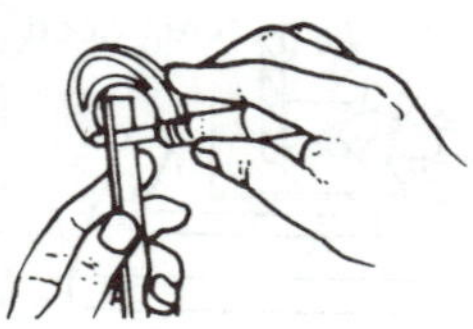	M P	Measuring and checking precise measurements. Cannot be used for internal measurements.
Sliding bevel		W M P	Marking out and copying of angles.
Marking gauge	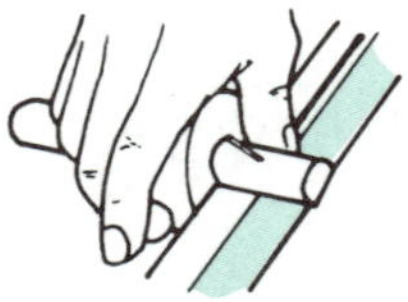	W P	Marking a line parallel to an edge.

Key:
W = wood
P = plastics
M = metals

Fig. 7.19 Marking-out tools

7.2 Tools and equipment

Machine tools

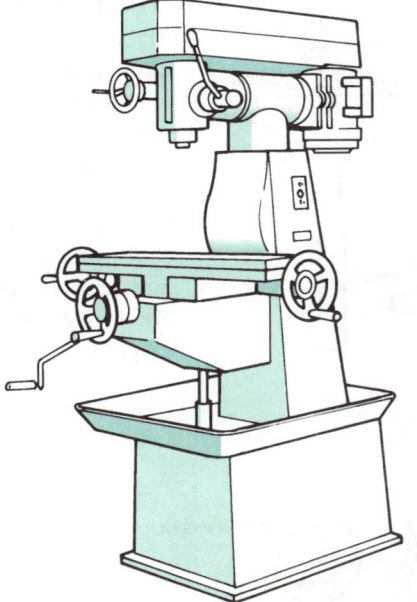

Fig. 7.20 Vertical milling machine

Milling machine. Many schools have a milling machine and it can be used either with the cutter vertical or horizontal. For safety reasons, schools frequently use a milling machine with the cutter vertical. It can be used to produce flat surfaces, rebates and slots. It is best used on metals and plastics, but if used on thermoplastics the heat produced can often cause melting, so it is useful to keep the job cool with soluble oil.

Band saw. This machine is used to cut curves in plastics, metal and timber. The blade is a continuous band and different blades are necessary to cut different materials. The width of the blades can vary; a bench-mounted machine may have a blade only 6 mm wide while a larger floor-mounted model may have a blade of 25 mm or more. Although this machine can be used for cutting curves, do bear in mind the width of the blade. As a guide, a machine with a blade width of 12 mm should not be used for curves having a radius of less than 75 mm.

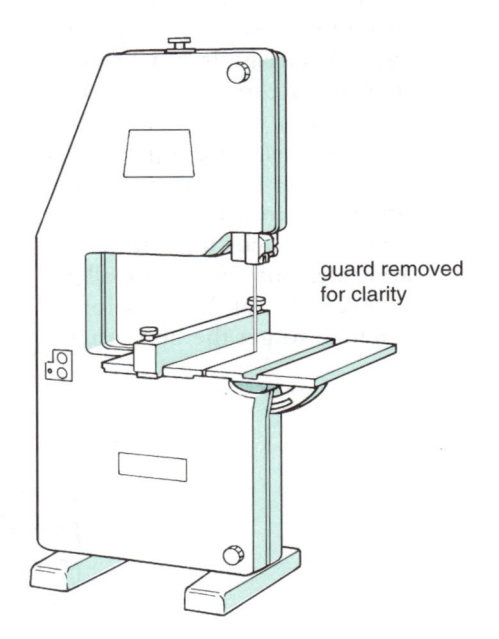

guard removed for clarity

Fig. 7.21 Band saw

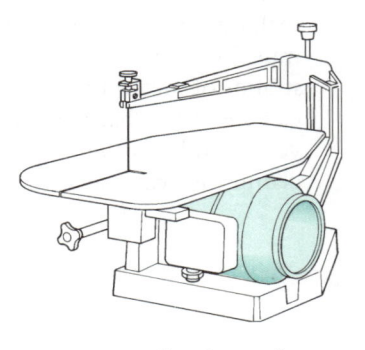

Fig. 7.22 Vibrating or jig saw

Vibrating (or jig) saw. This machine is used for cutting curves in timber, plastics and metals. You must be careful to select the correct blades for different materials, and be sure to wear safety goggles when using vibrating saws.

Core knowledge

Wood turning lathe. This machine is used to make circular objects, such as table legs and wooden bowls. The work is either held on a face plate or supported between centres. Small work can be held in a chuck. The turning tools are rather like gouges and chisels, but the handles are longer to allow a firmer grip.

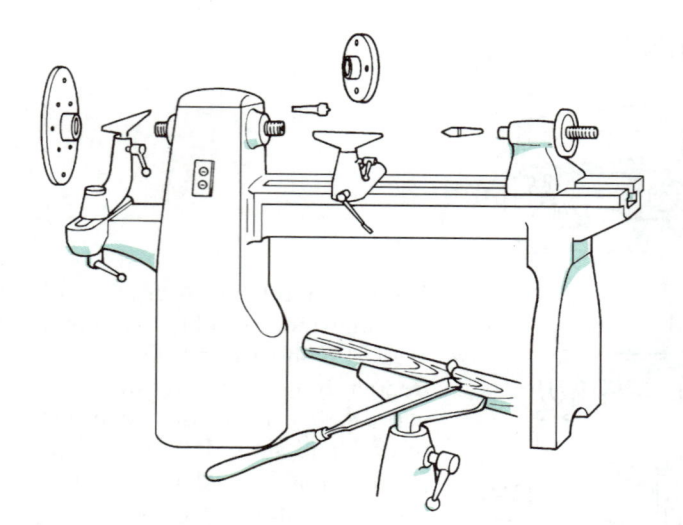

Fig. 7.23 Wood-turning lathe

Centre lathe. The centre lathe is the most versatile of all the machines used for working rigid materials. It can be used to manufacture a wide variety of shapes. The work is normally held in a chuck and if it is long, it is supported at the other end in a centre. A wide range of cutting tools is available, but they must all be sharpened and positioned carefully to get the best results.

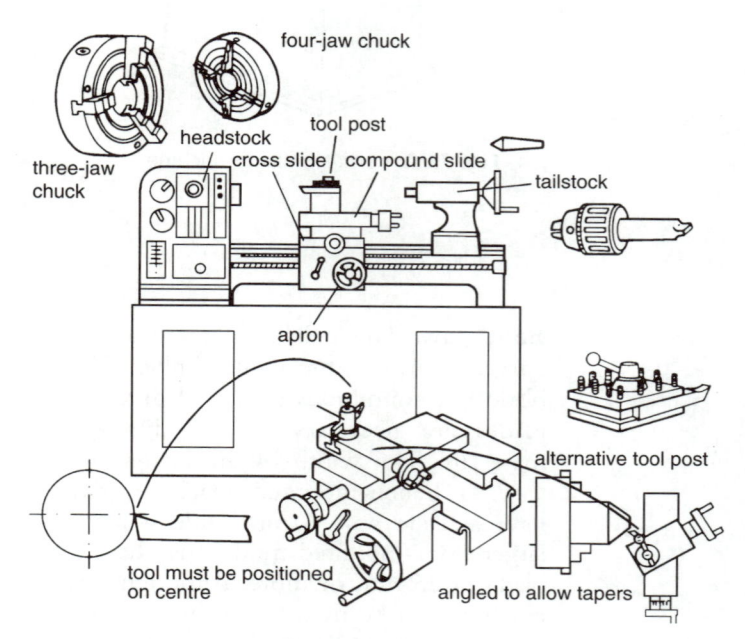

Fig. 7.24 Centre lathe

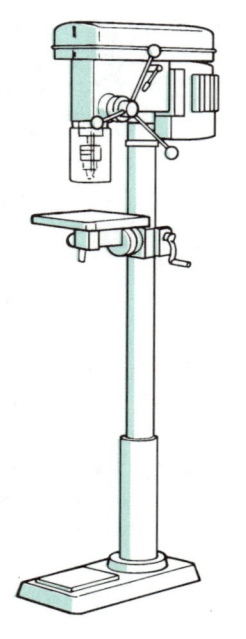

Pillar drilling machine. When using a pillar drilling machine for drilling holes in metals you must be careful to avoid the swarf (chippings or strands of metal) that come from the hole. These can be very sharp. One way of ensuring that your hands are kept away from the swarf is to clamp the work securely.

Fig. 7.25 Pillar drilling machine

7.3 Manufacturing processes

In the following examples of manufacturing processes some, e.g., from textiles and food, are shown for comparison. Such processes are not part of the core Technology curriculum.

Casting and moulding

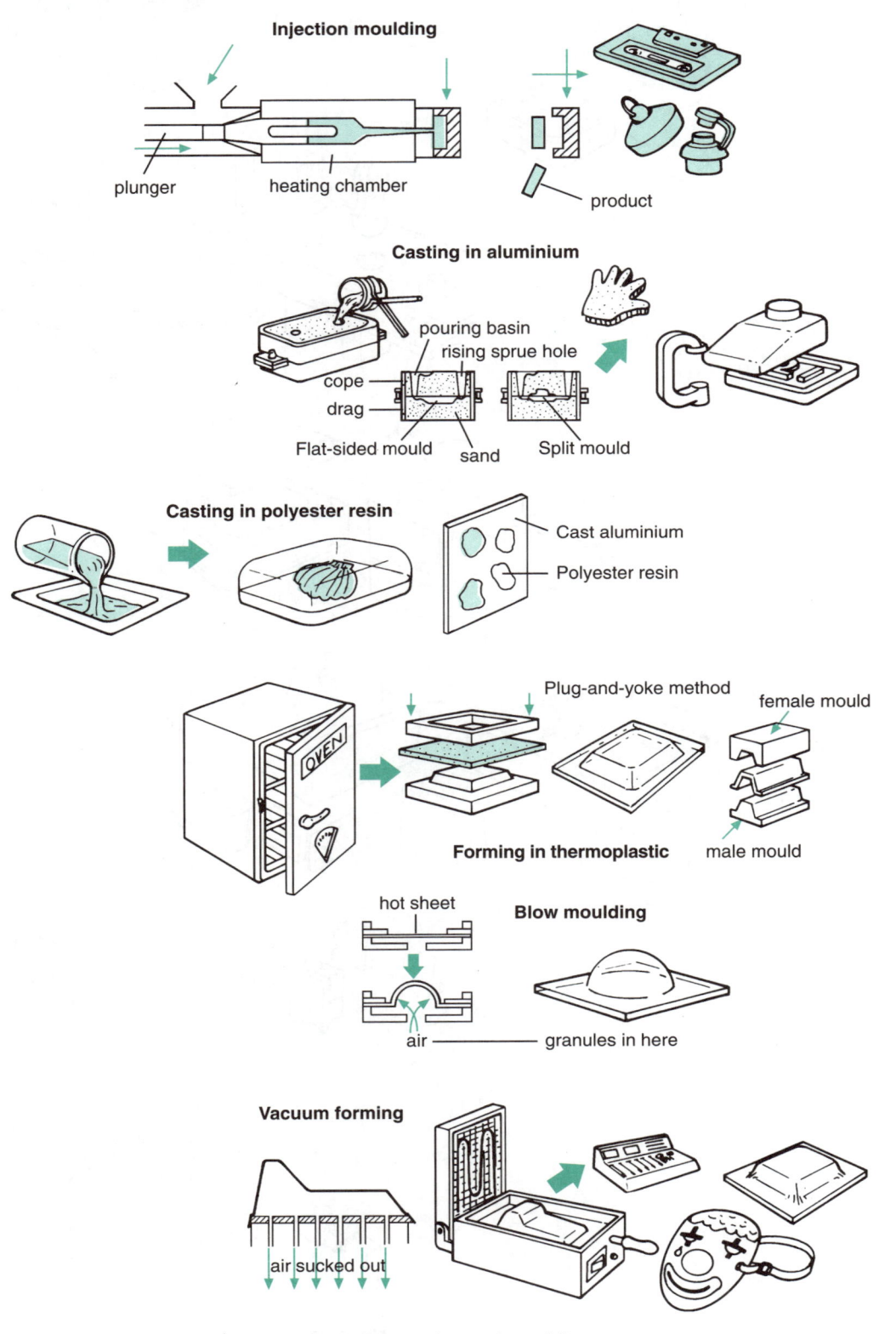

Fig. 7.26 Casting and moulding

Core knowledge

Fabrication – adding pieces together

masking tape

Fabricating acrylic, PVC, polystyrene and clay

Fabricating glass-reinforced polyester

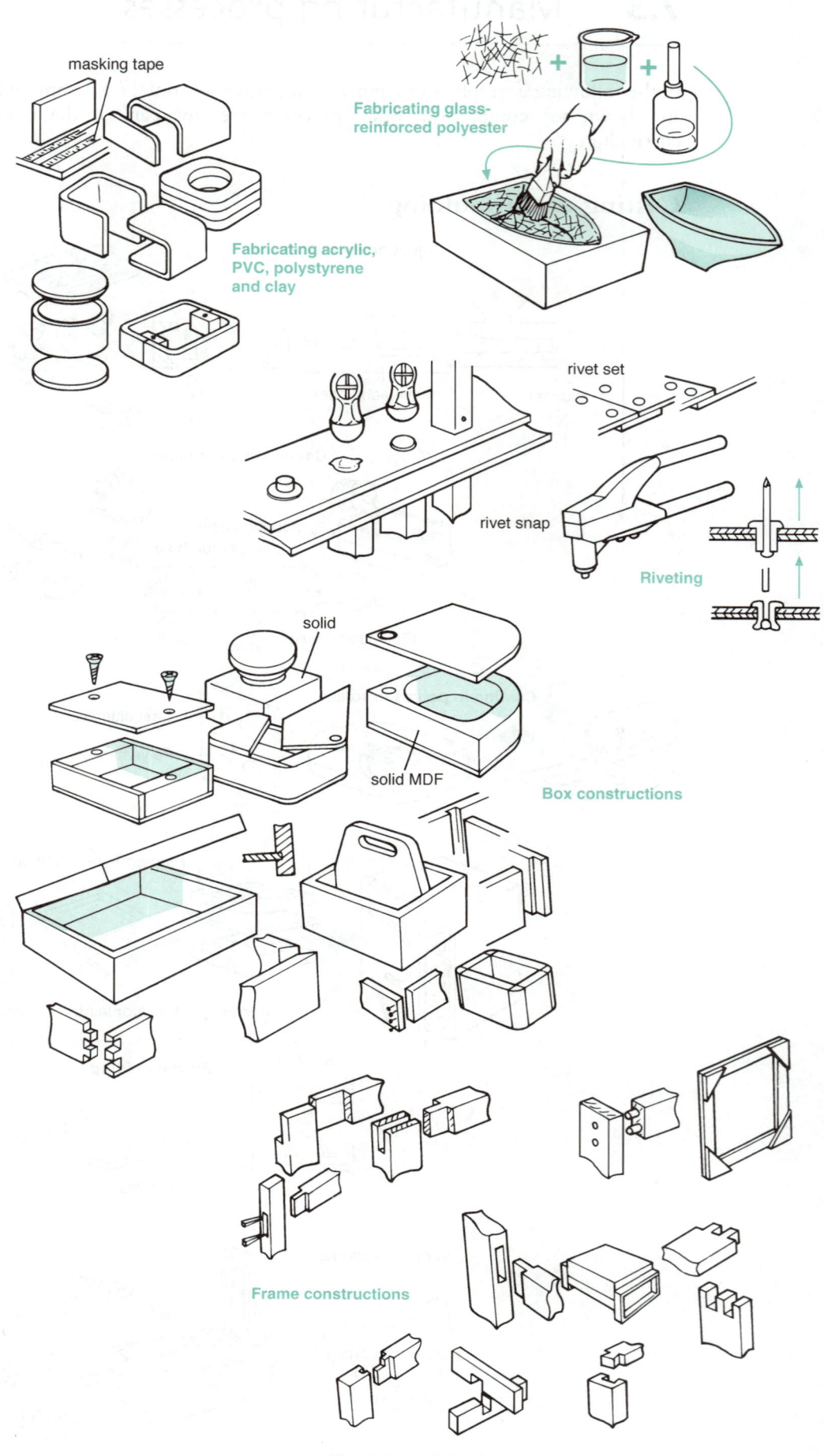

rivet set

rivet snap

Riveting

solid

solid MDF

Box constructions

Frame constructions

Fig. 7.27 Fabrication

116

7.3 Manufacturing processes

Deforming

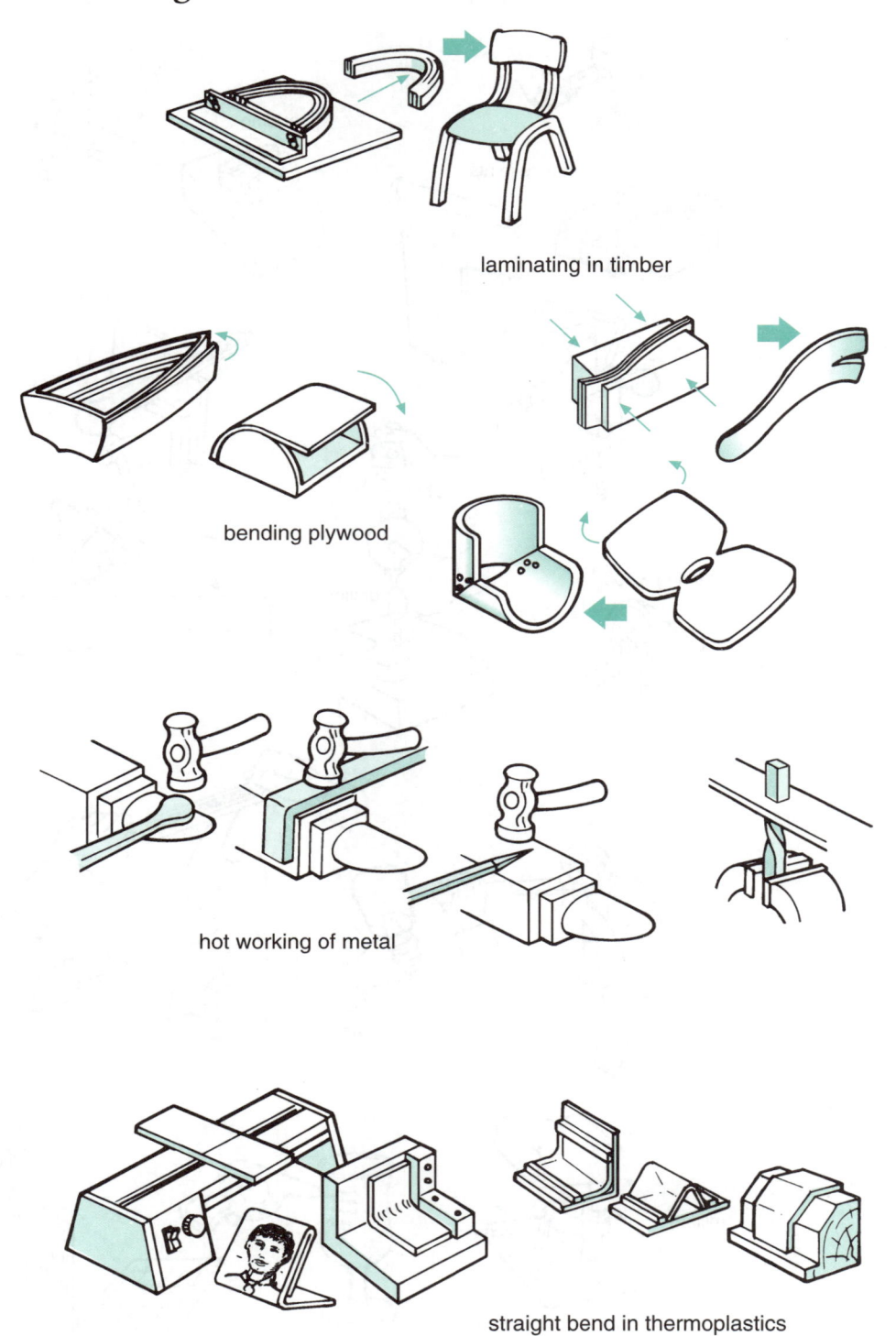

laminating in timber

bending plywood

hot working of metal

straight bend in thermoplastics

Fig. 7.28 Deforming

117

Core knowledge

Wasting – removing parts

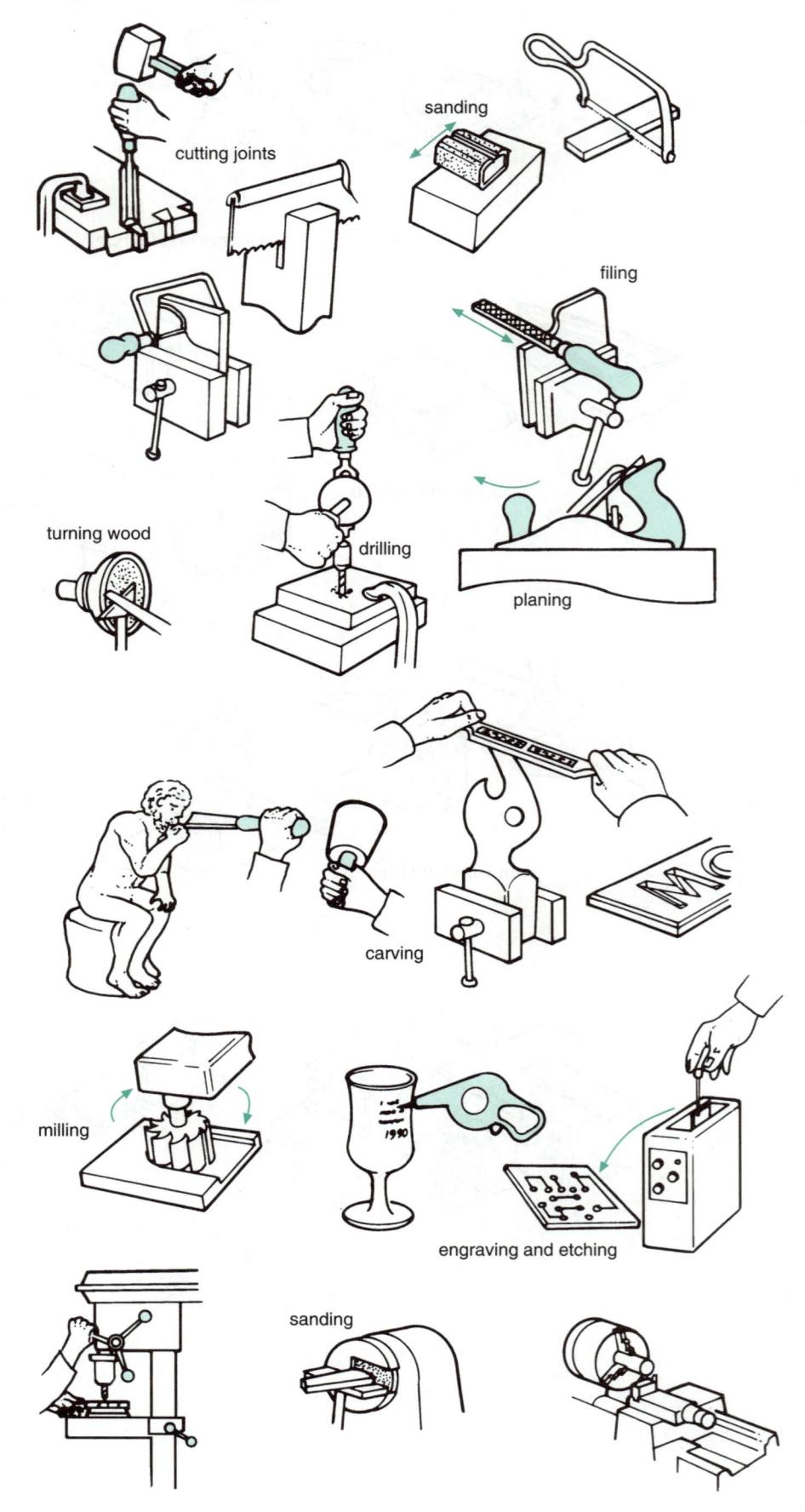

- cutting joints
- sanding
- filing
- turning wood
- drilling
- planing
- carving
- milling
- engraving and etching
- sanding

Fig. 7.29 Wasting

7.4 Mechanisms

Mechanisms are used in all machinery. There are five types of mechanism.
1. Levers enable forces to be applied at precise points.
2. Pulleys change the direction and speed of a movement, and allow the transmission of power.
3. Gears transmit rotary motion and force.
4. Cams and cranks convert uniform input motion to non-uniform output motion.
5. Screws allow rotary motion to transmit a linear force.

There are several mechanisms in this picture.

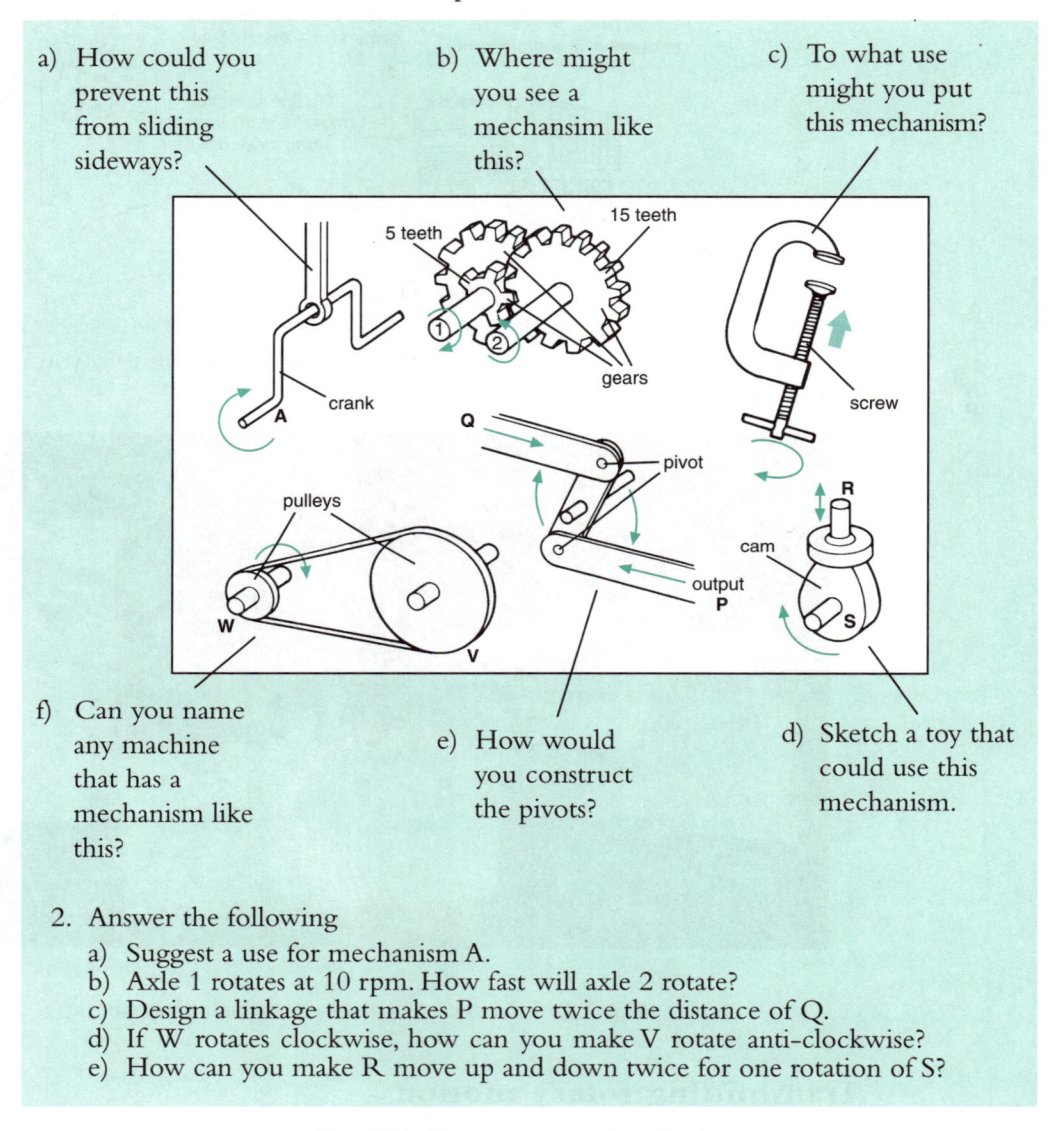

?

a) How could you prevent this from sliding sideways?

b) Where might you see a mechansim like this?

c) To what use might you put this mechanism?

f) Can you name any machine that has a mechanism like this?

e) How would you construct the pivots?

d) Sketch a toy that could use this mechanism.

2. Answer the following
   a) Suggest a use for mechanism A.
   b) Axle 1 rotates at 10 rpm. How fast will axle 2 rotate?
   c) Design a linkage that makes P move twice the distance of Q.
   d) If W rotates clockwise, how can you make V rotate anti-clockwise?
   e) How can you make R move up and down twice for one rotation of S?

Fig. 7.30 Common types of mechanism

Core knowledge

Mechanisms are used to change:
- the type of motion, e.g., rotary motion into linear;
- the direction of motion, e.g., by using spur gears;
- the speed of motion, e.g., by using pulleys;
- any combination of the above.

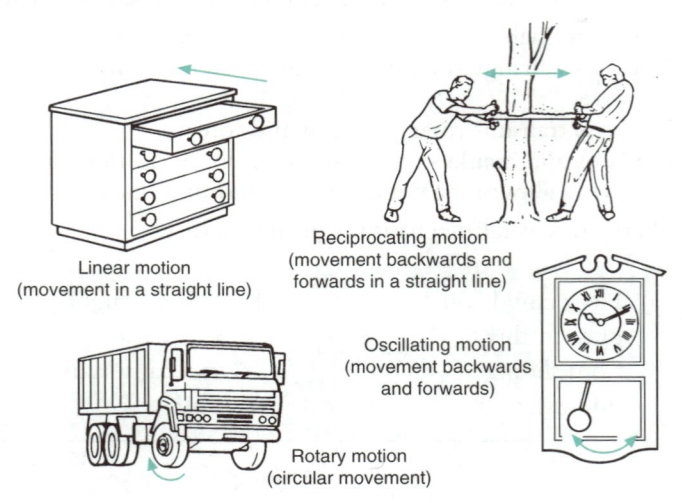

Fig. 7.31 Types of motion

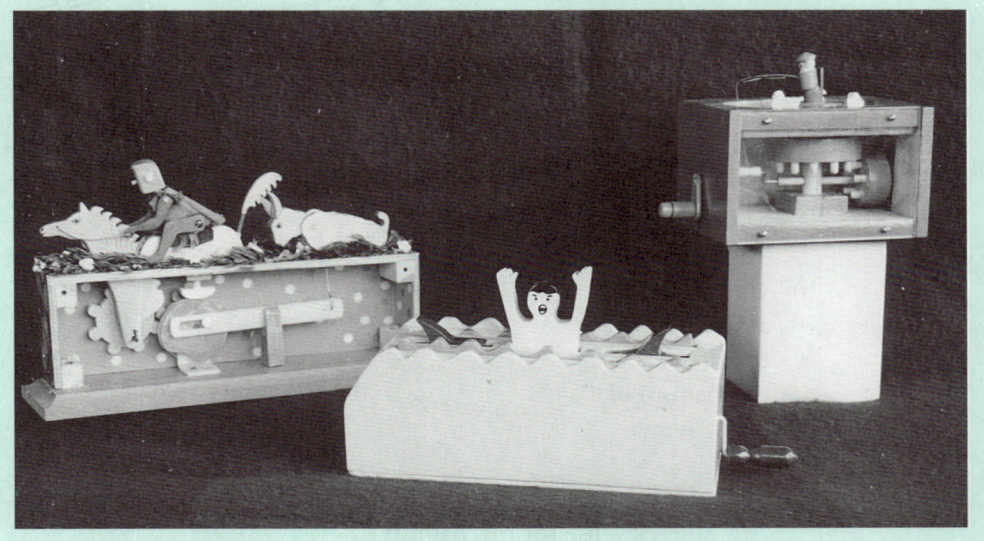

? Look at these toys designed by students. What mechanisms do you think operate inside these toys?

Fig. 7.32 Toys can be operated by different mechanisms

Transmitting rotary motion

Many pieces of equipment use belts and gears to transmit rotary movement, but when it is important to transmit large forces, and it is a disadvantage to have belts slip, then sprockets and chains are used.

Fig. 7.33 How many mechanisms can you find in a bicycle?

Advantages of sprockets and chains
1 Larger forces can be transmitted.
2 Chains do not slip.
3 Chains can be taken apart to allow removal.

Advantages of pulleys and belts
1 Belts are quiet.
2 Belts need no lubrication.
3 Belts can be stretched to get them on.
4 Crossed belts can change direction of rotation.

When it is unnecessary to transmit very large forces, but it is important that the belt does not slip, machines often have toothed belts:

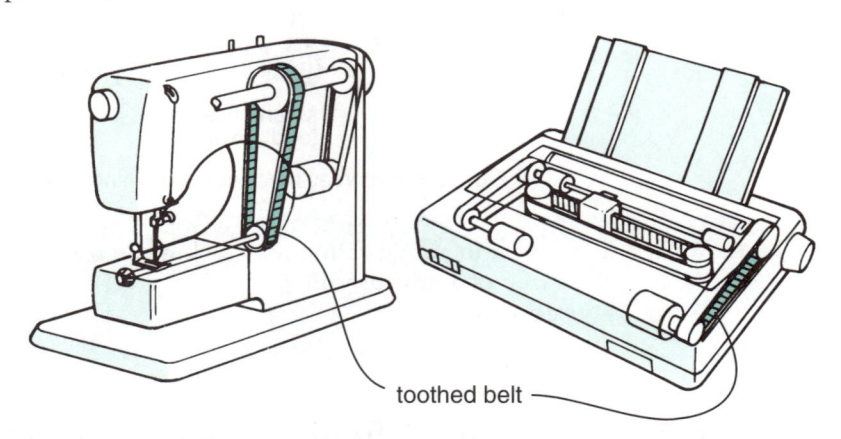

Fig. 7.34 Toothed belts are quiet and do not slip

1. How is movement transmitted in a food processor?
2. Why are some belts V-shaped?
3. Why does a drilling machine have several pulleys?
4. Ask your teacher if you can look at the drive belt on a metalwork lathe. Why is there more than one belt?

Gears

Gears are used in situations where it is necessary to transmit large forces. They are also used when it is important that the mechanism does not slip.

This diagram shows the most commonly used types of gears.

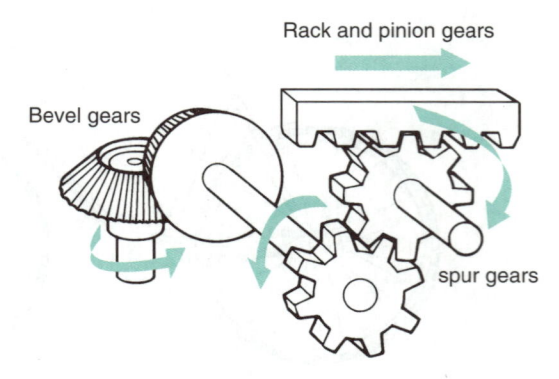

Fig. 7.35 Rack-and-pinion

The rack-and-pinion is a special two-geared mechanism in which one gear is straight. This mechanism allows rotary motion to be converted into straight-line motion.

Figure 7.36 shows gears commonly found at home.

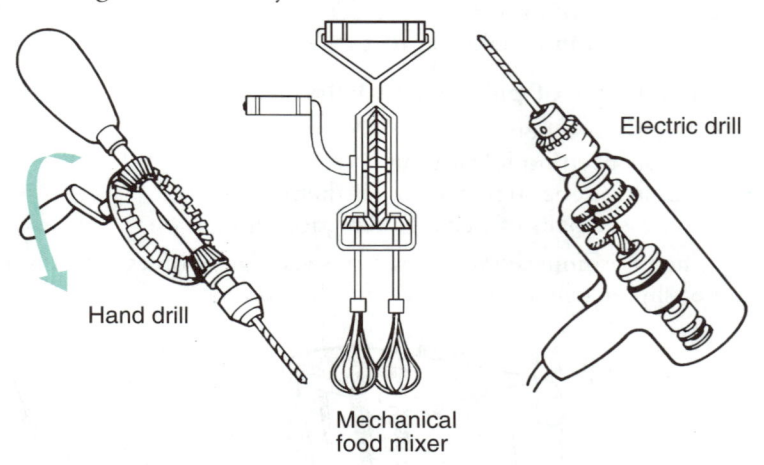

Fig. 7.36 Everyday machines containing gears

> 1 What are the gears in an old-fashioned clock made from?
> 2 What is the shape of a gear tooth?
> 3 What is a gearbox used for?

Mechanisms – some definitions and calculations

Work

The amount of work you get out of a system is calculated by multiplying the distance moved by the load (in metres) by the force applied to it (measured in newtons). You can never get more work out of a system than you put into it and, in practice, no system is completely efficient, so you will always get out less than you put in.

Velocity ratio (VR)

This is the distance that the effort moves divided by the distance that the load moves:

$$VR = \frac{\text{distance moved by effort}}{\text{distance moved by load}}$$

Mechanical advantage (MA)

This is the load divided by the effort:

$$MA = \frac{\text{load}}{\text{effort}}$$

If the velocity ratio is small then the mechanical advantage will also be small.

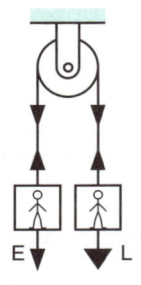

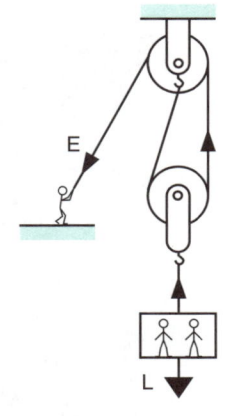

Fig. 7.37(a) Using a pulley as a lifting device

Fig. 7.37(b) Using two pulleys to increase efficiency

A single pulley can be used as a lifting device, but a more useful lifting device can be produced by arranging two pulleys as shown in Figure 7.37(b).

When an effort is applied at (E) for a distance of, say 10 m, the load will rise by a distance of 5 m. The system therefore has a velocity ratio of 2.

Providing there is no appreciable friction then the load can be twice the effort and the mechanical advantage is therefore also 2.

Efficiency

In all practical situations there is friction in a system, which will be inefficient, i.e., less than 100% efficient.

$$\text{Efficiency} = \frac{\text{work got out}}{\text{work put in}}$$

Consider the lifting system above. It was found that an effort of 50 N moving 8m could only lift a load of 80 N through a distance of 4 m.

Work put in (for a movement of 8 metres) = $50 \times 8 = 400$ Nm (newton-metres)

Work got out (for a movement of 4 metres) = $80 \times 4 = 320$ Nm

$$\text{Efficiency} = \frac{\text{work got out}}{\text{work put in}} = \frac{320}{400} = 0.8 \text{ or } 80\%.$$

The system is said to be 80% efficient.

7.5 Structures and forces

Structures are produced when a number of parts are joined together, e.g., a bridge, a spider's web, an aeroplane, an egg box, a skeleton. All structures must be designed to withstand forces, which have a tendency to change things. For example, stationary objects can be caused to move and moving things can be made to move faster.

Five types of force can exist in structures.

1. **Compression** – a force tending to reduce the length of a structure.
2. **Tension** – a force tending to stretch a structure.
3. **Bending** – a force acting across a structure, tending to bend it.
4. **Twisting** – when one force tries to turn a structure, while another force tries to resist the turning.
5. **Shear** – when two forces act opposite to each other, but not directly in line. Shear forces tend to make one part of a structure slide over another.

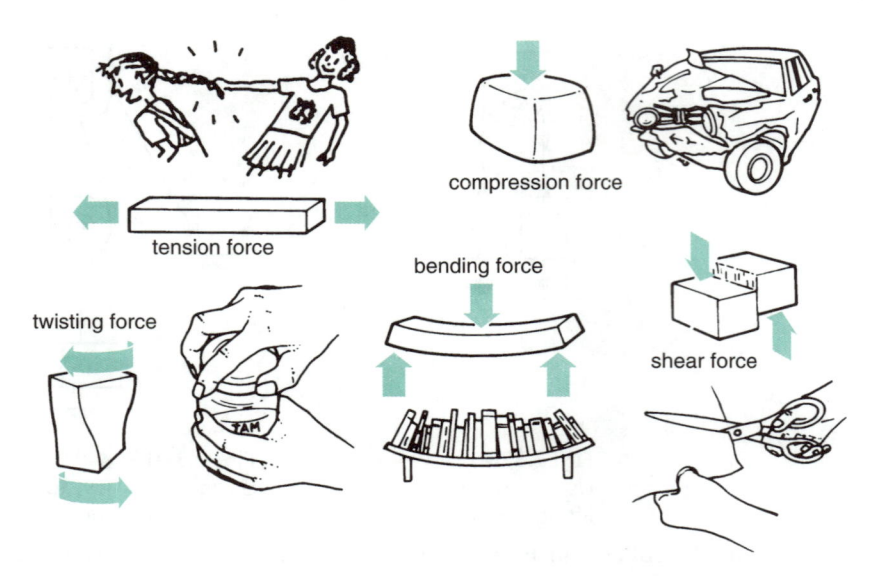

Fig. 7.38 The five types of force

Forces in framed structures

Many structures are made from frames, e.g., an apex roof, a girder bridge and a motor car chassis. The principle behind making a framed structure rigid is called triangulation.

For example, in the structure shown in Fig. 7.39(a), if a force was applied at the point of the arrow, the structure would tend to collapse. If, however, the structure was modified as in Fig. 7.39(b) then any applied force would be resisted by the diagonal BC. Adding such a diagonal is an example of triangulation.

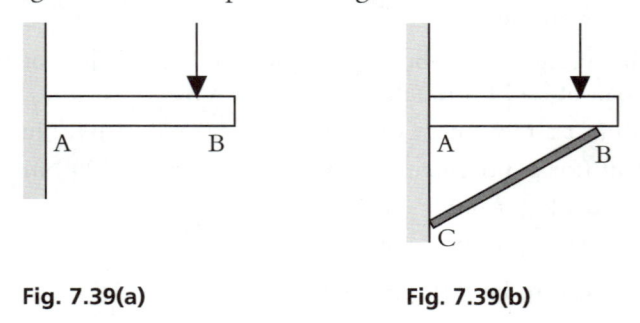

Fig. 7.39(a) **Fig. 7.39(b)**

Ties and struts

In framed structures, the parts are either being stretched or they are being compressed. In the step ladder shown in figure 7.40, the rope holding together the legs is being stretched, and it is known as a tie. In the case of the gate (figure 7.41), the diagonal is being compressed, and is known as a strut.

Fig. 7.40
Framed structure containing a tie

Fig. 7.41
Framed structure containing a strut

7.5 Structures and forces

Structures and forces – some definitions and calculations

The principle of moments

This says that for any system in equilibrium, the sum of the moments clockwise equals the sum of the moments anti-clockwise. To put it another way, the tendency for a system to rotate in one direction is balanced by a tendency for it to rotate in the opposite direction.

Consider this see-saw.

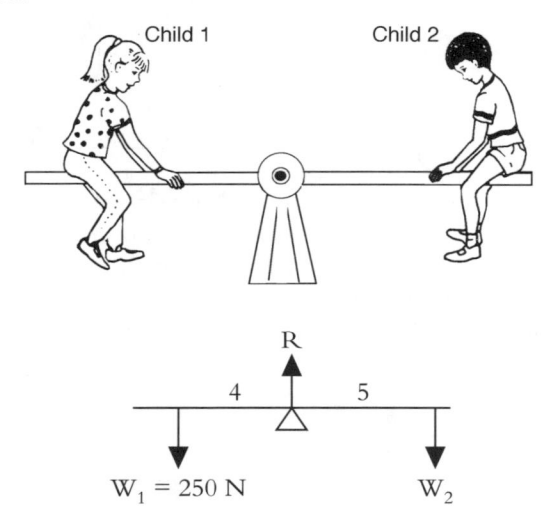

Fig. 7.42 Forces acting on a see-saw

A simple way to represent the situation is as follows, where W_1 and W_2 are equal to the weights of the children, measured in newtons. The middle point of the see-saw is known as the fulcrum and it pushes up with a force R, to balance the downward forces (weights) of the children.

The force $R = W_1 + W_2$

From the principle of moments: $W_1 \times 4 = W_2 \times 5$

If child 1 weighs 250 N, then $250 \times 4 = W_2 \times 5$

In other words $W_2 = \dfrac{250 \times 4}{5} = 200$ newtons.

So the force (R) with which the see-saw's fulcrum pushes up = $W_1 + W_2$
= 250 + 200
= 450 newtons

The triangle of forces

When three forces act on a body they appear to act at a single point. These three forces can be represented by a triangle.

Consider a decorator on a ladder leaning against a wall.

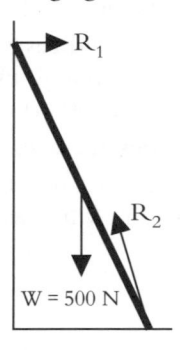

Fig. 7.43 Forces acting on a ladder

W is the weight of the decorator on the ladder. R_1 and R_2 are the forces exerted by the wall and the ground. Since we know that the decorator's weight must act vertically and the force from the wall will be horizontal, it follows that the forces will act like this:

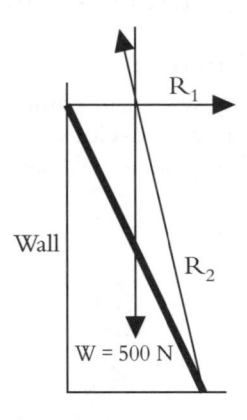

Fig. 7.44 Force diagram

By representing each force as a line drawn in the same direction as each force shown on the diagram, you will get a triangle of those forces. Providing the triangle of forces is drawn to scale, then the lengths of the sides will represent the magnitudes of the forces. The directions of the sides will also represent the directions of the forces.

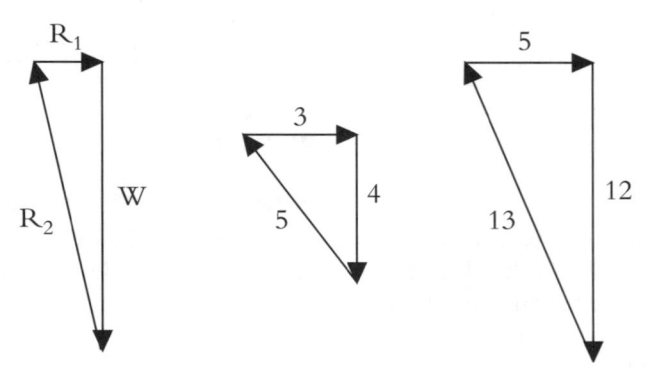

Fig. 7.45 Triangles of forces

7.6 Energy

Energy is the ability to do work. You cannot destroy energy but simply change it into different forms.

Sources of energy

Capital energy sources include:
- fossil fuels (coal, oil and gas);
- nuclear energy (fission and fusion);
- the Earth's energy (geothermal).

Income energy sources include:
- direct conversion (solar panels and solar cells);
- indirect conversion (wind, waves and water).

Fig. 7.46 Sources of energy

Energy conversion

Ultimately all energy comes from the Sun. In technology projects you may use solar energy to heat something directly or you may convert it first into electricity in a solar cell and then into movement (kinetic energy) by the use of an electric motor. The energy of the wind can be changed to noise or it can produce movement. This movement can drive a dynamo and so produce electricity. Chemical energy can produce electricity, as in batteries, or heat, when it is burned as a fuel

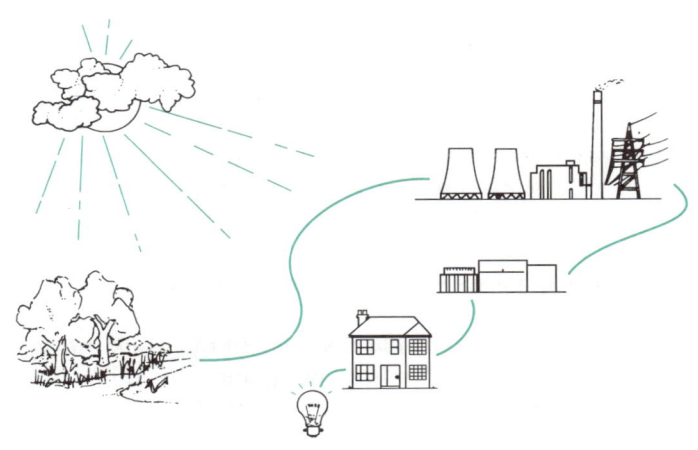

Fig. 7.47 Energy conversions

The following are examples of common energy conversions.
1 Mechanical energy → electrical energy, e.g., a bicycle dynamo producing electricity to light a headlamp.
2 Chemical energy → heat energy, e.g., a coal fire burning in a hearth.
3 Heat energy → potential energy, e.g., a hot air balloon.
4 Electrical energy → potential energy, e.g., an electric motor driving a lift in an office block.
5 Chemical energy → electrical energy, e.g., batteries in a torch.

Making the most of energy

All energy conversions can produce two kinds of output:

useful energy: used for heating, cooking or as rotary motion to drive a car;

non-useful energy (wasted energy): such as the light and sound of a gas cooker and the heat produced in a car engine. The most efficient systems produce a minimum of wasted energy. Wasting heat energy can be avoided by, for example, the use of good insulation. Losses from mechanical systems can be reduced by the use of efficient bearings and good lubrication.

Core knowledge

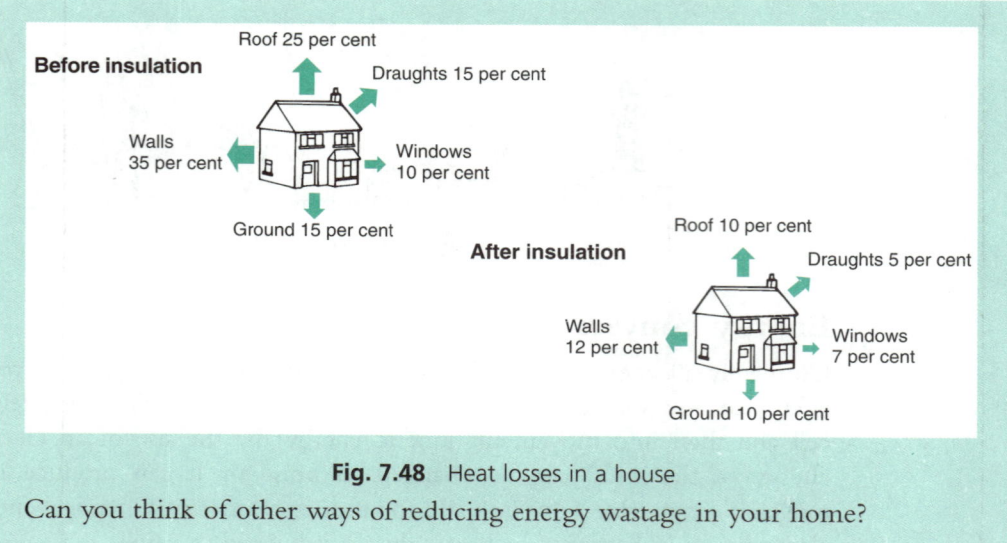

Fig. 7.48 Heat losses in a house

Before insulation: Roof 25 per cent, Draughts 15 per cent, Walls 35 per cent, Windows 10 per cent, Ground 15 per cent.

After insulation: Roof 10 per cent, Draughts 5 per cent, Walls 12 per cent, Windows 7 per cent, Ground 10 per cent.

Can you think of other ways of reducing energy wastage in your home?

Storing energy

Energy can be stored in a variety of ways, including the following.
1. **Hydroelectric dams** – energy is stored by the water in a dam. When the water level drops it releases potential energy, which is converted to electricity.
2. **Batteries** – electricity produced by a dynamo or alternator can be chemically stored in a battery.
3. **Rubber bands** – some toys are powered by the potential energy stored in a wound-up rubber band.
4. **Clockwork alarm clocks** – when the clock spring is wound up the energy needed to wind it is stored in the spring and is used later to move the clock hands.
5. **Air-brushes** – the energy used to operate the paint spray is stored in the form of compressed air.
6. **Flywheels or gyroscopes** – kinetic energy is stored in a spinning flywheel or gyroscope.

Calculating energy costs

If the 'rating plate' on the back of an electric cooker gives its power as 4kW (kilowatts), this means that in each second 4000 joules of electrical energy are converted into another form of energy (mostly heat).

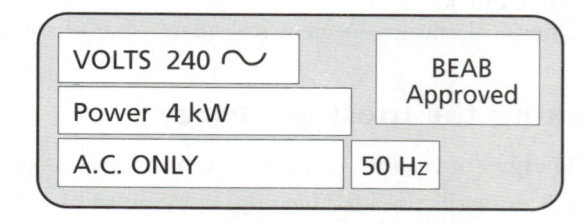

Fig. 7.49 Rating plate from cooker

VOLTS 240 ~
Power 4 kW
A.C. ONLY
BEAB Approved
50 Hz

Electrical energy is measured and charged for by the Electricity Companies in **kilowatt hours (kWh)** rather than joules, because one joule is a very small amount:

1 kWh = 1 kW for 1 hour
= 1000 W for 3600 seconds = 3 600 000 joules.

Imagine the cooker is switched on for 2 hours to cook a meal.
Total number of kWh (units) = 2 × 4 = 8 kWh
Cost of one unit (look at an electricity bill) = 7.42p
So cost of cooking for 2 hours = 8 × 7.42 = 59.36p or almost 30p per hour.

In practice, the temperature of the oven is controlled by a thermostat, which means the oven will be switching on and off, so that the temperature remains more or less constant. The total amount of electricity (and therefore cost) will be about one third less.

Some useful equations in energy calculations

Potential energy (joules) = mass (kg) × gravitational force (10 N/kg) × height (m)

Kinetic energy (joules) = mass (kg) × velocity (m/sec)^2 × $\frac{1}{2}$

Power (watts) = rate of doing work
$$= \frac{\text{total work done (joules)}}{\text{time taken to do the work (secs)}}$$

7.7 Systems and control

Systems

Almost any organisation of organised set of parts can be described as a system.
Every system has three components:

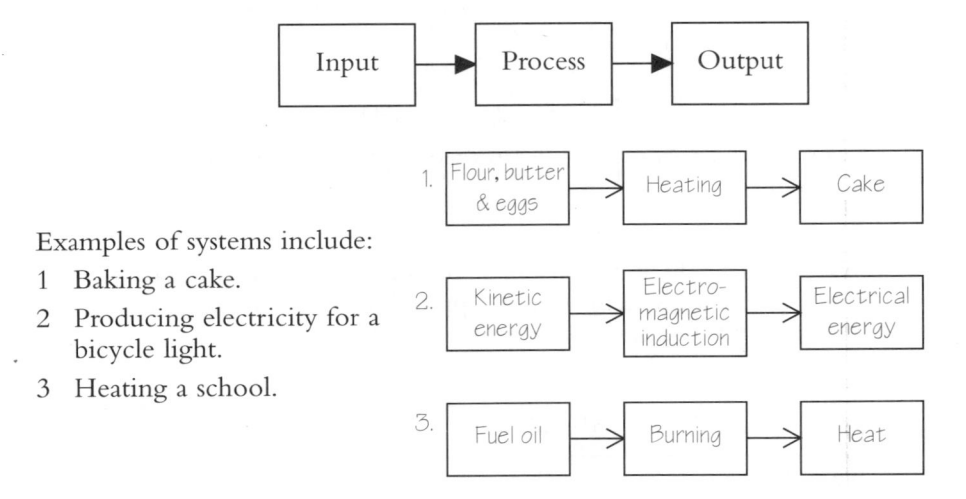

Input → Process → Output

Examples of systems include:
1. Baking a cake.
2. Producing electricity for a bicycle light.
3. Heating a school.

1. Flour, butter & eggs → Heating → Cake

2. Kinetic energy → Electro-magnetic induction → Electrical energy

3. Fuel oil → Burning → Heat

Control

Open-loop systems

In all systems, control is important. Simple systems of control consist of an input that causes something to happen, and this in turn produces an output. This is known as an open-loop system. Most systems operated by humans are open-loop systems.

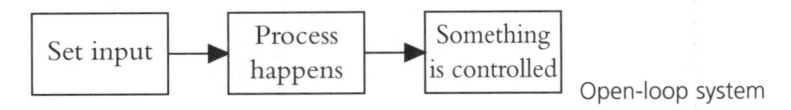

Set input → Process happens → Something is controlled

Open-loop system

Closed-loop systems

If we want a system that compares the output with what we expected to happen and then adjusts the input automatically, this is called a closed-loop system.

Examples of closed-loop systems

1. Regulating the amount of money in the economy.
2. Steering a car with the eyes, brain and muscles as parts of the feedback process.
3. An automatic ventilation system for a greenhouse.

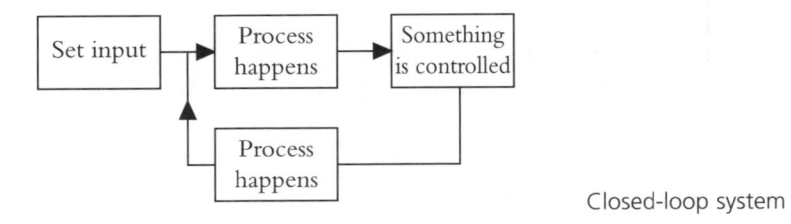

Set input → Process happens → Something is controlled
↑_____ Process happens _____|

Closed-loop system

Core knowledge

> **?**
>
> **The central heating thermostat**
>
> The required temperature is set on the thermostat. When the temperature reaches the required level the bi-metallic strip expands, bends and breaks the electrical circuit. The central-heating circulation pump stops and the radiators do not receive more hot water. The radiators cool until the thermostat detects that the temperature has fallen to its set point. The bi-metallic strip then makes a connection and the circuit is made. The pump starts again and the radiators begin to heat once more.
>
> **Fig. 7.50** Central-heating thermostat
>
> Is a central heating temperature control an open-loop system or a closed-loop system?

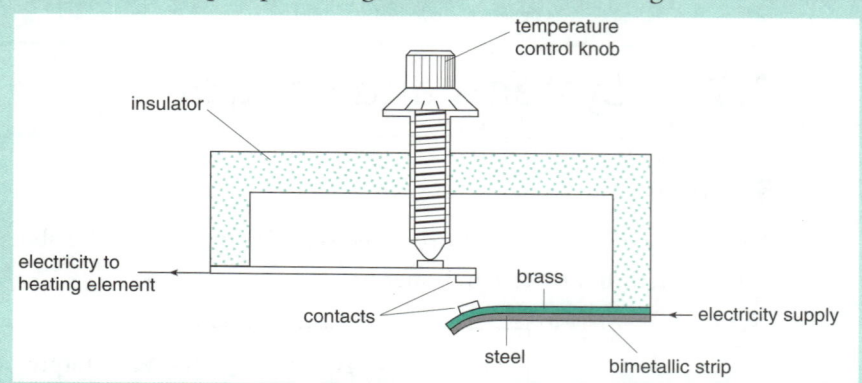

You may need to use controlling devices. The following chart will help you decide which device or system is most appropriate. It will also help you to understand the different kinds of control that exist.

	On/off	Variable	One way	Delay	Interchange
Electrical	Switch	Variable resistor	Diode	Time circuit (See circuits in Chapter 11)	Electronic to electrical: transistor/ relay
Mechanical	Clutch	Car brakes	Ratchet worm/ wheel	Pendulum escapement for a clock	Electronic to mechanical: solenoid
Pneumatic	2 and 3-port valve	Throttle or restrictor	Non-return valve containing a ball	Reservoir	Mechanical/ pneumatic to electrical: microswitch

Table 7.2 Types of controlling device

7.8 Business matters

Good ideas are of no value if no-one wants them and no-one is willing to buy them. Businesses must make a profit and the profit must be sufficient to finance the business and pay the bills.

Establishing the market

All ideas and products must be matched to the market. You must determine where or if your idea is needed. An idea has to be market researched. This can be achieved by:
- questionnaires;
- interviews;
- surveys of existing products.

You will need to do the following.
1. Decide who will buy your product.
2. Decide who your competitors are.
3. Decide if your product can be sold in sufficient numbers.
4. Decide what is the best price for your product (high price – low volume? or low price – high volume?)
5. Decide where you will sell your product.

Marketing

There are two parts to marketing: promotion and delivery of products to customers.

Promotion

The function of promotion is to:
- attract attention;
- generate interest;
- create desire;
- cause action.

Promotion consists of the following:
- advertising;
- sales promotions;
- exhibitions;
- press coverage (interviews, etc.).

Product delivery

Delivering your products involves:
- retail selling;
- wholesale selling;
- telephone sales;
- van selling;
- party planning;
- trade fairs;
- car boot sales;
- school fêtes.

Making a profit

If the money in a business cannot be managed properly then a business will not be successful. You will want to make some profit, and so you need to decide:
- the price of your products or services;
- the quantity you expect to sell;
- when you expect to sell your goods;
- what expenses you are likely to have.

To calculate the profits subtract your total expenses from the total amount you receive from selling the goods:

$$\boxed{\text{Income}} - \boxed{\text{Expenses}} = \boxed{\text{Profit}}$$

For example, if you sell 500 sets of candlesticks at £6 for each set, then your income will be £3000. If the materials and other expenses come to £1200, then the profit will be £3000 – £1200, that is, £1800.

What would happen if you increase the price of a set of candlesticks to £7?

Your expenses will be the same for 500 sets but your income will be £3500 – an increase in profit of £500. But is £7 too expensive? Use your market research to find out. One small company discovered that by increasing the price of the goods it was able to sell more. When the products were cheaper, the customers thought there was something wrong with them and wouldn't buy them!

Cashflow

When you are running a business, it is important that you always have enough money to pay your bills. All businesses should know how much money is moving into and out of the business at any time. This movement is called cashflow.

Consider, for example, a business supplying sandwiches to office workers. In order to make the sandwiches more attractive, the company decided to give the customers credit, i.e., they could pay for their sandwiches at the end of the month. The bills for ingredients and some other expenses would, of course, have to be paid first.

The people running the business must never allow the amount of cash to get below zero. This is achieved by having a starting capital of £400. By taking out wages of only £200 per month the business might not recover the initial expenditure until after several months of trading. Sometimes it takes much longer; wages of only £200 per month are very small unless this is a part-time business.

Production methods

The method by which a product is made depends upon a number of factors:
- quantity required;
- speed of manufacture;
- equipment available;
- amount of capital investment available.

There are three ways by which goods can be manufactured.

1. **One-off (job) production**

    This is specialist or individual production, such as a racing car or a space shuttle. Your own technology projects are probably also 'one-off'.

2. **Batch production**

    Where it is known how many are to be produced, a book for example, this will done by a process known as batch production. The cost per item is much lower than one-off production.

3. **Mass (flow) production**

    This is where a manufacturing process is created to continuously produce an item, such as a new motor car. Although the precise number of items is unknown it is expected that production will continue for some time. The cost of one item is low but the cost of setting up the process (capital cost) is high.

7.9 Technology and society

What benefits one part of society may not benefit another. In Chapter 4, page 60, you read that for all designs some people gain and others lose. Designers and technologists should be sensitive to this balance.

7.9 Technology and society

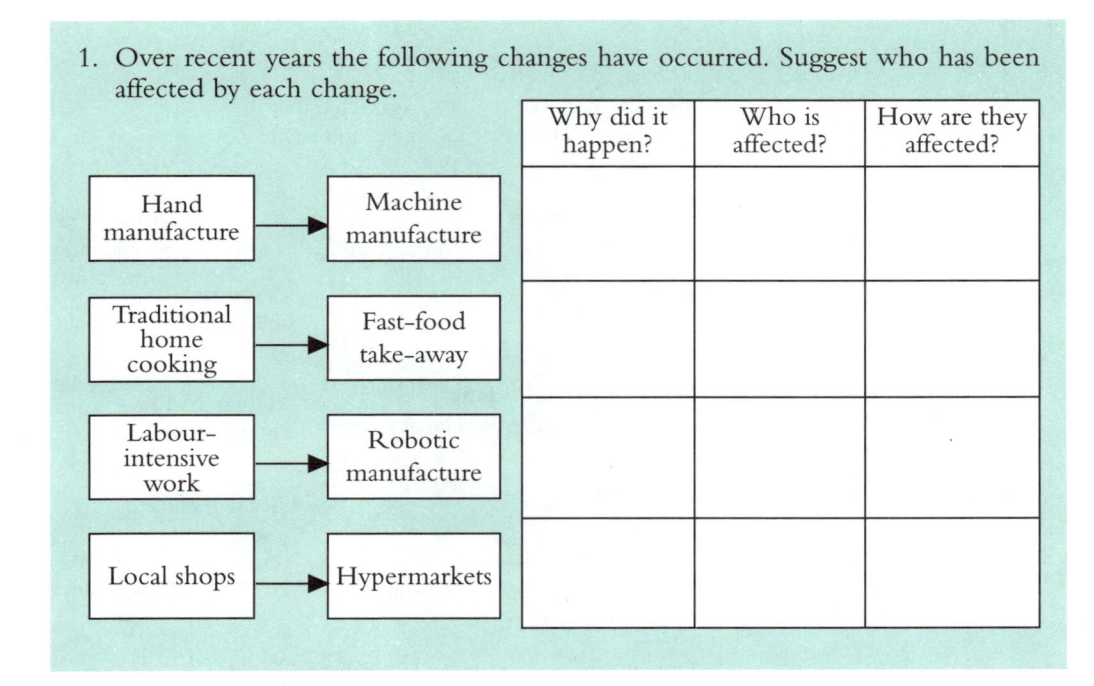

?

1. Over recent years the following changes have occurred. Suggest who has been affected by each change.

Change	Why did it happen?	Who is affected?	How are they affected?
Hand manufacture → Machine manufacture			
Traditional home cooking → Fast-food take-away			
Labour-intensive work → Robotic manufacture			
Local shops → Hypermarkets			

?

2. Think about the following features of modern life. Have they benefited society in general or have they benefited individuals?

Features	Benefits to society in general	Benefits to individuals
Improved medicine		
Longer leisure periods		
Unemployment		
Credit card		

Technology for society

It is important that the way you do things or the designs you propose are appropriate for the situation. For example, it is very easy to think that solutions (especially examination projects) have to be complicated. Some even think that if it is complicated it will gain more marks. The truth is that however you do something it must be appropriate to the situation, the resources available and the likely effect it will have on people.

For example, the technology appropriate for producing electricity in the United Kingdom will be very different from that, for example, in Central India. What you may need to store your information in your bedroom will be nothing like the needs of a multi-national electronics company in Tokyo. The meal you produce when you entertain your family to a special celebration will differ very much from the celebration meal you make when you reach the end of a long hike.

The following chart, based on an idea first published by the organisation Intermediate Technology, describes some of the considerations that should be made when assessing whether a design or an idea is appropriate.

Core knowledge

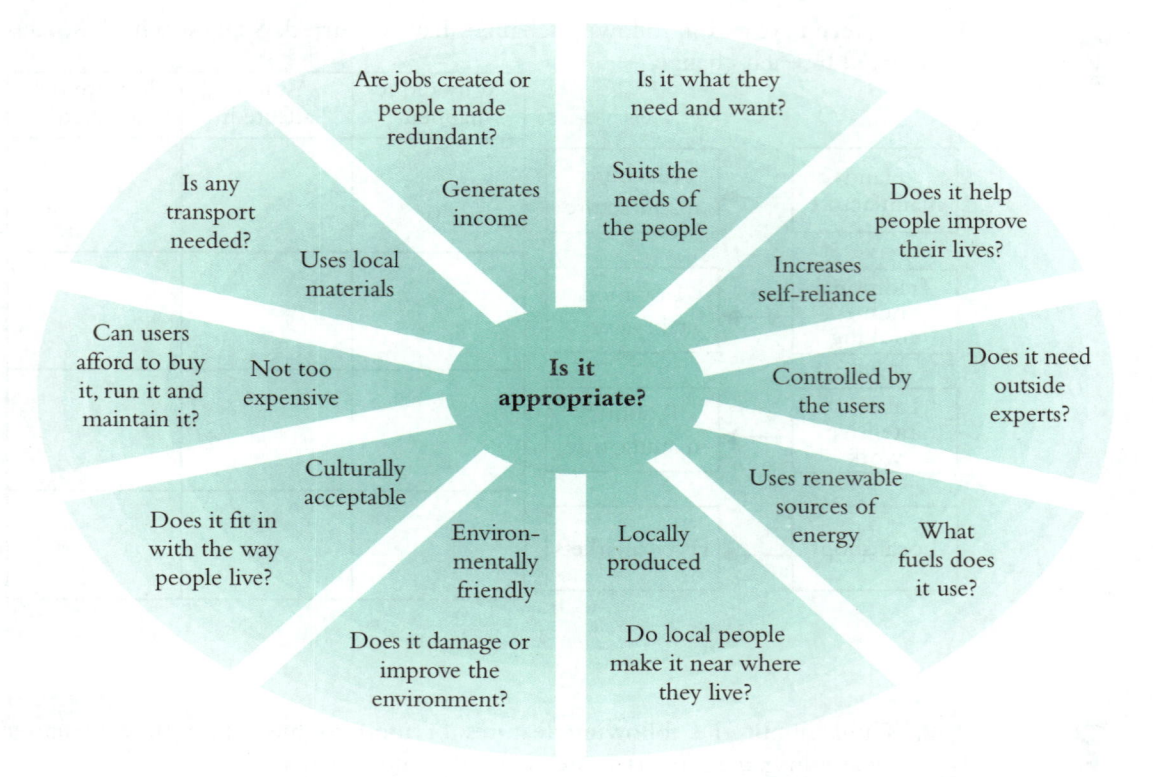

Is it appropriate?

- Are jobs created or people made redundant?
- Is it what they need and want?
- Is any transport needed?
- Generates income
- Suits the needs of the people
- Does it help people improve their lives?
- Uses local materials
- Increases self-reliance
- Can users afford to buy it, run it and maintain it?
- Not too expensive
- Controlled by the users
- Does it need outside experts?
- Culturally acceptable
- Uses renewable sources of energy
- Does it fit in with the way people live?
- Environmentally friendly
- Locally produced
- What fuels does it use?
- Does it damage or improve the environment?
- Do local people make it near where they live?

Fig. 7.52 Evaluating the appropriateness of a design

Chapter 8　　　　　　　　　　　　　　　　　Graphic media option

8.1　Opportunities for graphic media

Each technology syllabus allows you to work in different areas of graphic media. In the time available you will need to concentrate your work within a limited range of activities. The possible areas in which you may work are as follows.

1 **Environmental design**, e.g.,
   - architecture;
   - exhibitions;
   - interiors;
   - museums.

   Here is the design for a stand at an exhibition.

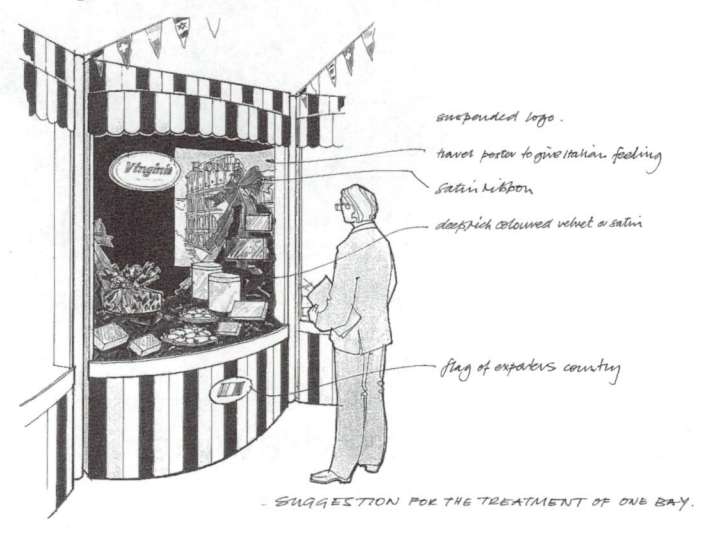

   Fig. 8.1 An exhibition stand should create an environment in which products can be displayed

2 **Information design**, e.g.,
   - illustrations;
   - typography;
   - graphic design.

   These illustrations come from an instruction leaflet produced for a student's project on contact lens holders..

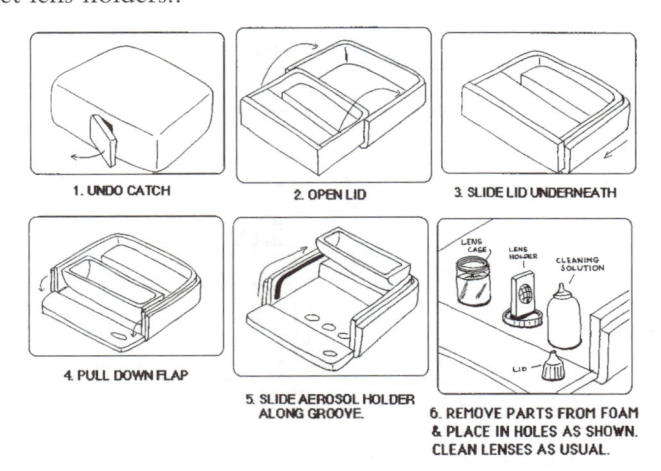

   Fig. 8.2 Graphics are ideal for presenting a step-by-step process

3 **Engineering design**, e.g.,
   - mechanical engineering;
   - electronic engineering;
   - civil engineering.

   You may need, for example, to produce detailed drawings of engineering components.

4 **Industrial design** e.g.,
- consumer products;
- furniture;
- packaging.

You may want to produce models, such as this model of an instrument to measure distances on maps.

Fig. 8.3 A model can convey more details of the design than a drawing

8.2 Technical drawing

You should try to become proficient in aspects of drawing that communicate the precise detail and form of a product, environment and system, so that they may be manufactured by others. Ensure that you can use the appropriate drawing conventions in order for everyone to understand your drawings.

The following are examples of what you might do.

1 A third-angle projection of the design for a model train.

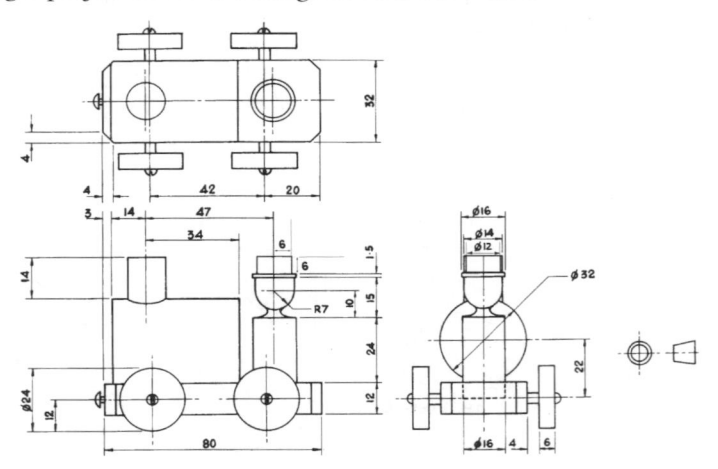

Fig. 8.4 Third-angle projection illustrates many of the construction details

8.2 Technical drawing

2 A circuit diagram for an electronic product. The components must be drawn by using the correct symbols.

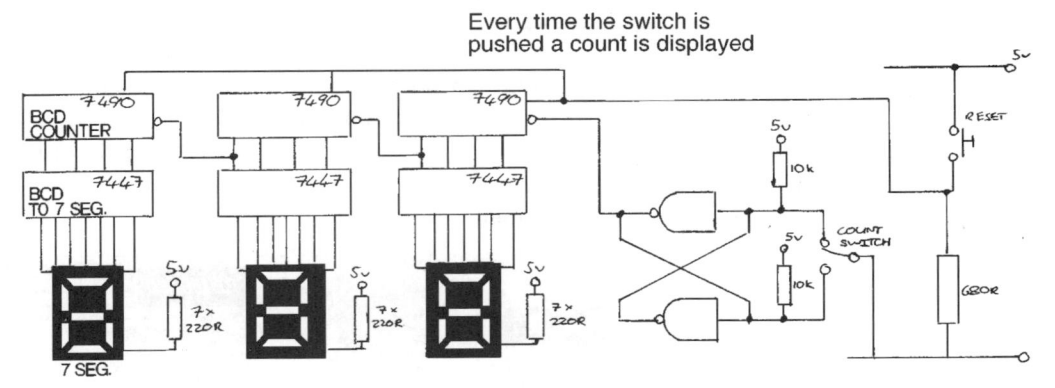

Fig. 8.5 Pulse-counting circuit

3 Designs for environments. You may need to adopt conventions normally used by an architect.

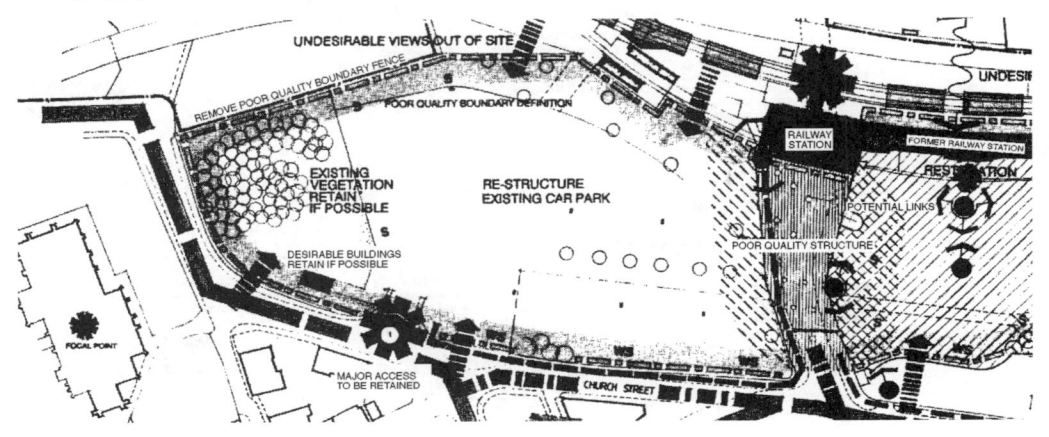

Fig. 8.6 Take into account local conditions when designing environments

4 Method of construction. Here the student has shown exactly how his design will be assembled.

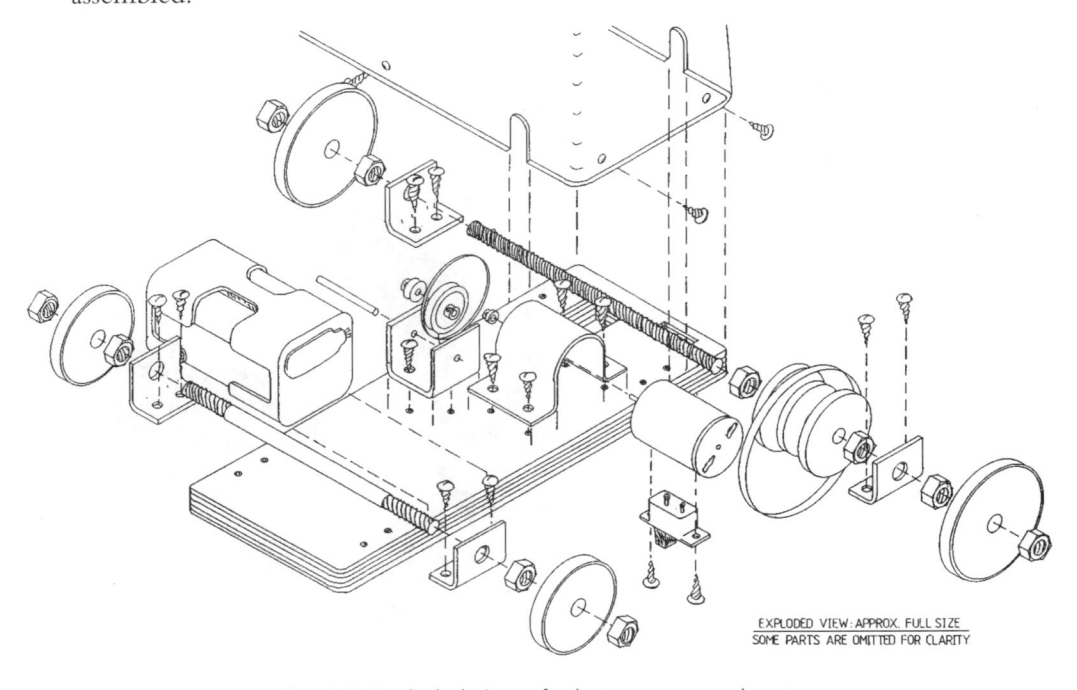

Fig. 8.7 Exploded view of a battery-powered motor

Graphic media option

8.3 Drawing systems

It is often important to illustrate products, environments and systems in such a way that clearly shows them in 'form', or in three dimensions. In this way, their appearance can readily be understood by others. You should be able to illustrate either how a product or a system should be assembled or how it works.

1 Here are examples of a student's isometric drawings.

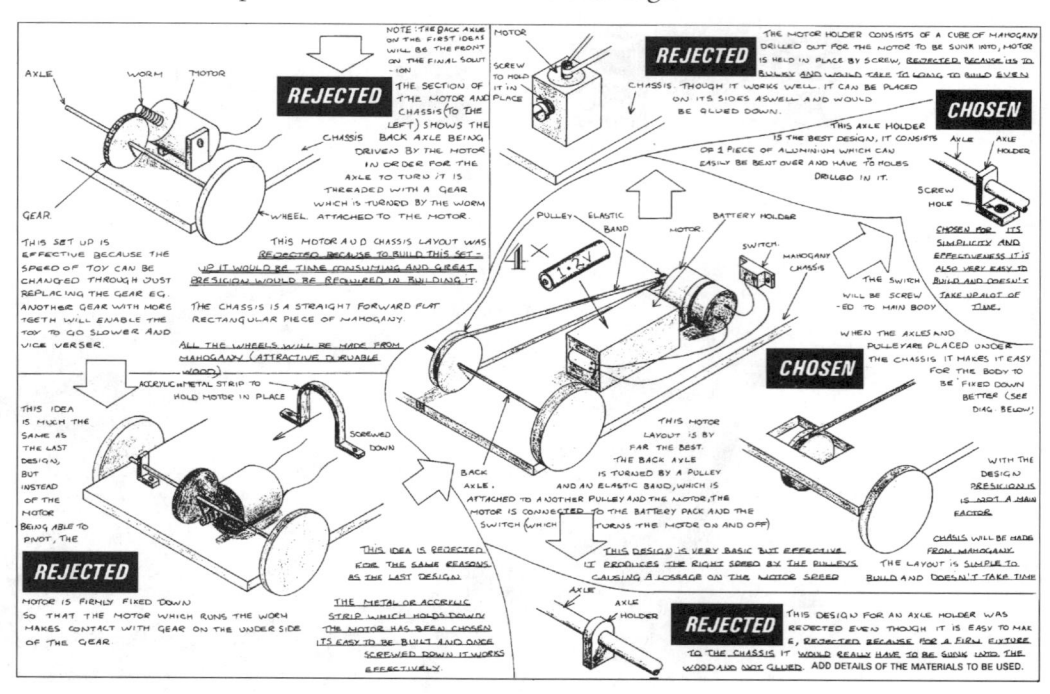

Fig. 8.8 Initial designs for a powered vehicle

2 In this design for an airport stopover unit, planometric projection has been used.

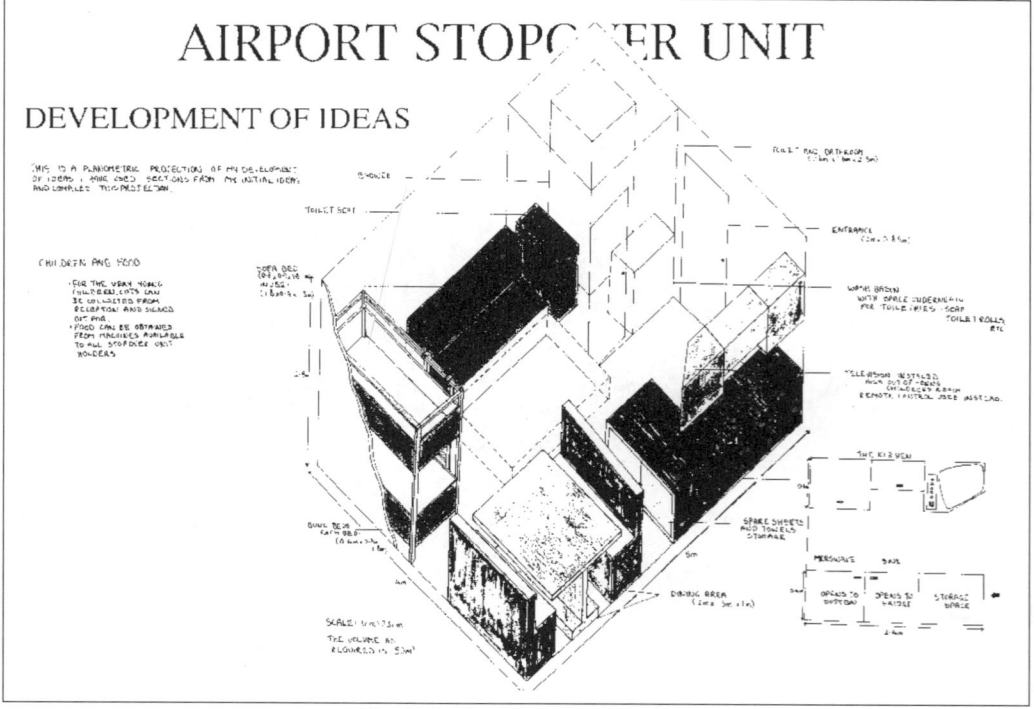

Fig. 8.9 Planometric projection

138

3 One-point perspective of an office block.

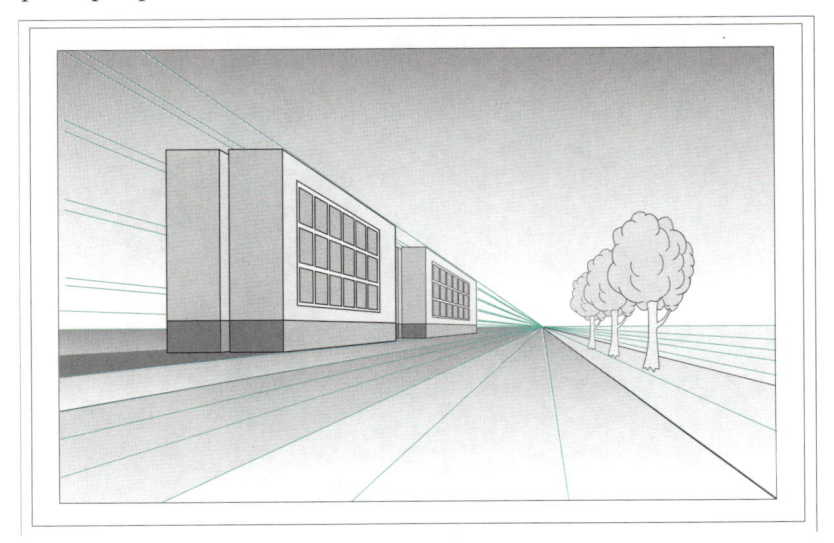

Fig. 8.10 One-point perspective

4 This two-point perspective drawing shows the proposals for a future railway station.

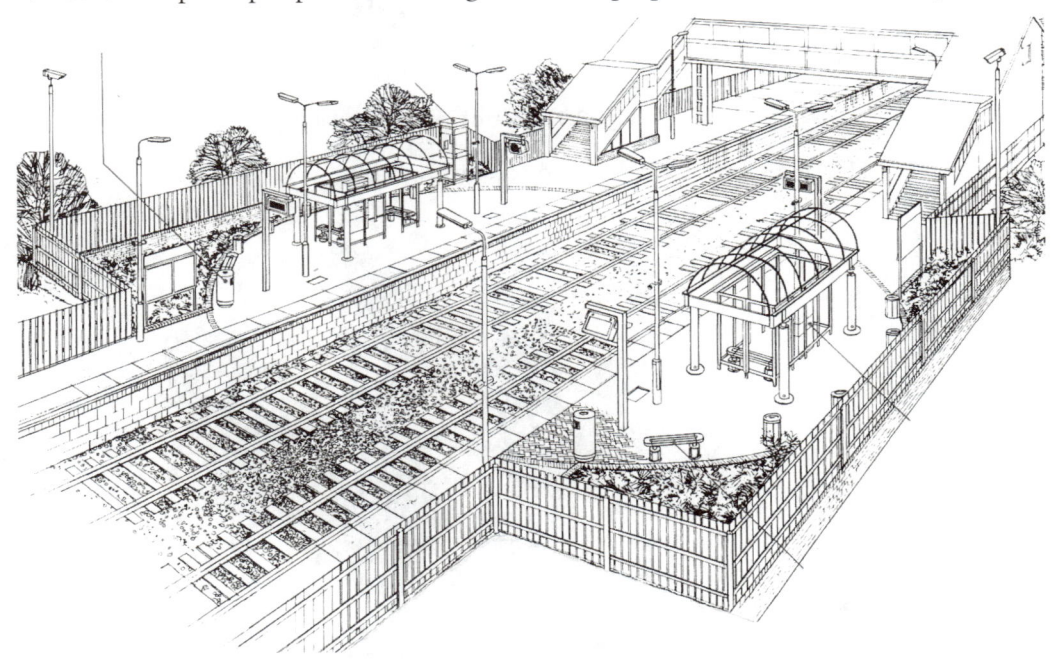

Fig. 8.11 Two-point perspective

8.4 Pictorial and presentational techniques

You should understand when and how to apply tone and colour to a drawing in order to enhance the communication of its form. You should experience rendering, using coloured pencils, felt-tip pens, colour wash and an air-brush. Try to ensure that the material from which the object is made is apparent to the viewer.

Here are some examples of what you might do.

Graphic media option

1 Ink and colour illustration of casual clothing. The highlights are achieved by the use of white crayon.

Fig. 8.12 Use of ink and highlighting in textile design

2 An air-brush can be used to convey form.

Fig. 8.13 Air-brushed graphics to emphasise perspective

3 Pencil rendering of a child's toy.

Fig. 8.14 Pencil sketch design for wooden toy

4 Felt markers are used to produce a 'rough' for an advert. Notice how, at this stage, there is no attempt to put in much of the text. It is simply indicated by light brown felt marker lines.

Fig. 8.15 Use of felt markers to produce a 'rough' design

8.5 Semiology and information graphics

You should understand and use graphics in such areas as corporate images, signs and symbols, and statistical information.

1 Maps need to be clear and must communicate information unambiguously.

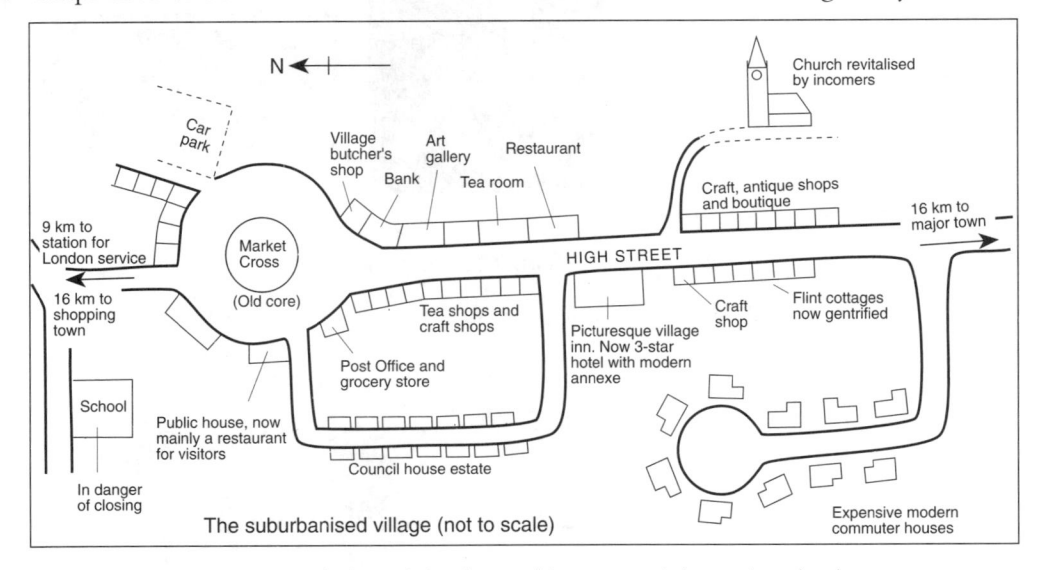

Fig. 8.16 Symbols and simple graphics convey information clearly

2 You may decide to produce the graphics for a corporate identity.

Fig. 8.17 A logo helps to create product identity

3 Remember that not everyone speaks English.

Fig. 8.18 Some universally-recognised signs

4 Look at the way information is conveyed graphically.

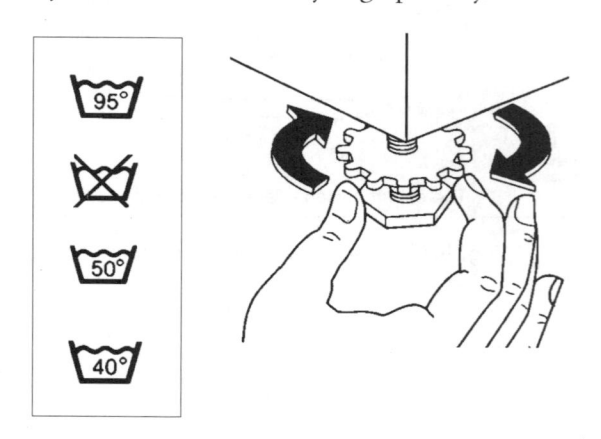

Fig. 8.19 Conveying information graphically

8.6 Modelling

Modelling is an important way of communicating ideas.

1. Models show how things work or how they are assembled. Computers are also useful for trying out different designs, especially if they have a 3-D drawing facility.

Fig. 8.20 A model shows how different elements interact

2. Exact models of products will enable you to demonstrate your making skills as well as communicate your ideas.

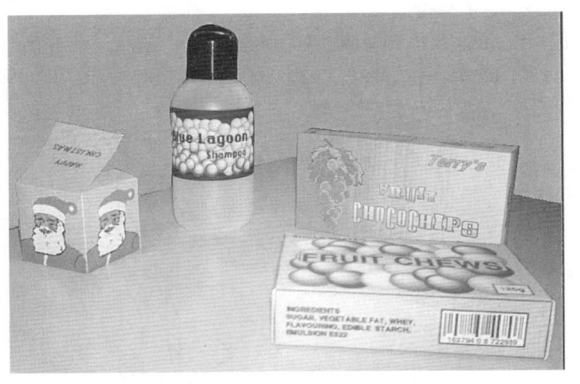

Fig. 8.21 Modelling helps you to consider product packaging

3. When designing environments, such as an exhibition stand, you will need to produce accurate models.

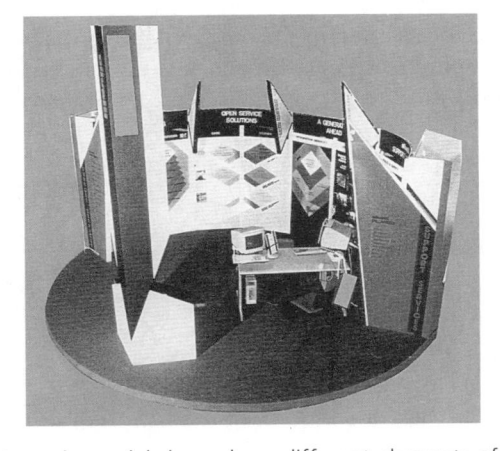

Fig. 8.22 An accurate scale model shows how different elements of a design fit together

Chapter 9   Food technology option

9.1 Food groups

The human body needs food regularly. Carbohydrates are needed for energy, proteins for growth, and vitamins and minerals are needed for good maintenance of tissues and body processes. The body also needs some fat and dietary fibre. A well balanced meal will contain something from each of the five food groups shown below.

1 Starchy foods

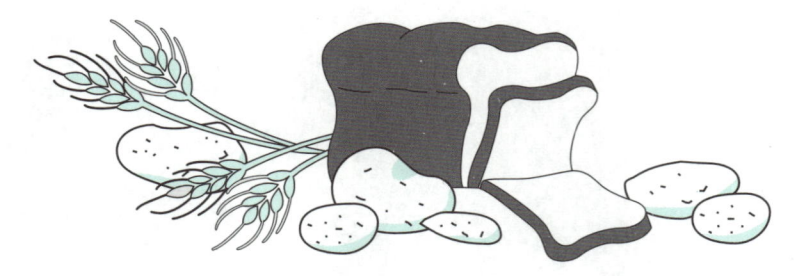

Fig. 9.1 Cereals, bread and potatoes are starchy foods

All meals need a good supply of starch. Starches are carbohydrates and are changed by the body into sugar, to supply energy. Each part of the world has its own basic (staple) carbohydrate food and this food forms the basis of the diet, e.g., rice in Asia, potatoes in Europe and corn in South America.

2 Fats and oils

These are only needed in small quantities. Fats and oils come from milk, oily fish, meat, seeds and nuts. Unsaturated fats should be eaten in preference to saturated fats.

Fig. 9.2 Margarine, butter, cheese and cooking oil contain fats

3 Meat, fish, eggs and milk

These foods contain proteins, vitamins A and D, and the minerals iron and calcium. If you prefer not to eat meat, it is essential that you eat the other items from this food group.

Fig. 9.3 Fish, meat and eggs contain proteins, vitamins and minerals

4 Fruits and vegetables

Fruits and vegetables are a rich source of nutrients. They also help to improve the texture, colour and flavour of a meal. Some, e.g., lentils and peas, are good sources of protein. In addition, fruits and vegetables contain vitamins B and C. They also contain roughage to help improve digestion.

Fig. 9.4 Fruits and vegetables contain many vital nutrients

5 Water

Water is essential for life and humans can only survive for a few days without it. We consume most of the water we need in fruit, fruit juice and milk. Drinks containing alcohol or sugar should be taken in moderation.

9.2 Dietary preferences and needs

For personal, health or religious reasons, you made need to take account of food preferences.

1 Diabetics
- need low fat, high-fibre foods;
- must control carbohydrate intake.

2 Pregnant women
- need foods containing calcium and iron;
- should consume plenty of fresh fruit and vegetables;
- need protein-rich foods;
- should have a limited intake of alcohol.

3 Vegetarians
- eat only food that does not involve killing animals;
- can eat milk, cheese and eggs.

4 Vegans
- must avoid all animal products.

5 Moslems
- must not eat pork or shellfish;
- must avoid alcohol;
- eat meat prepared in a special way;
- have regular periods of fasting.

6 Rastafarians
- consume no animal products except milk;
- should avoid canned or processed food;
- must not consume salt, coffee or alcohol;
- can eat only food that is organically grown.

7 Hindus
- must not eat beef;
- should eat mostly vegetables;
- must avoid alcohol.

8 Jews
- should not consume pork;
- can only eat fish with scales and fins;
- must have food prepared in a special way under supervision;
- cannot eat milk and meat together;
- insist on specially prepared food for the festival of Passover.

9.3 Characteristics and properties of food

Characteristics

These include the colour, taste, texture, and smell of food. All of them are important since each will effect the attractiveness of food to a consumer. It is often important in food design to consider the relationship between each characteristic. For example, people often associate certain flavours with particular colours and if food of a different colour is flavoured differently this may not be readily accepted. When planning meals you should try to ensure a balance of these characteristics.

Properties

The properties of a food or an ingredient describe what it can do.

Such properties are important in:
- cooking;
- serving;
- storage;
- processing;
- preserving.

Examples of properties are:
- thickens;
- aerates;
- sets;
- prevents discolouration;
- flavours;
- preserves.

When designing food you should consider both its characteristics and its properties.

9.4 Factors affecting food properties

The following chart describes the beneficial and negative properties of some of the factors that affect the properties of food.

Factor	Useful effect	Bad effect
Heat	Cooking	Premature rotting
Cold	Preserving	Can cause drying out (freezer burn)
Removal of moisture	Preserving	General deterioration
Acid	Pickling	Reacts with alcohol
Oxidation	Kills certain bacteria	Fats and oils become rancid
Enzymes	Used in soft-centred chocs	Soft fruits go brown when exposed to air
Yeasts	Make bread rise	Can cause infections
Moulds	Flavour cheese	Cause decay
Bacteria	Change milk sugar into acid to make yoghurt	Change flavour
Additives	Improving flavour	Cause illness
Preservatives	Keeping food longer	Can change flavour

Table 9.1 Factors affecting food properties

9.5 Food materials in cooking

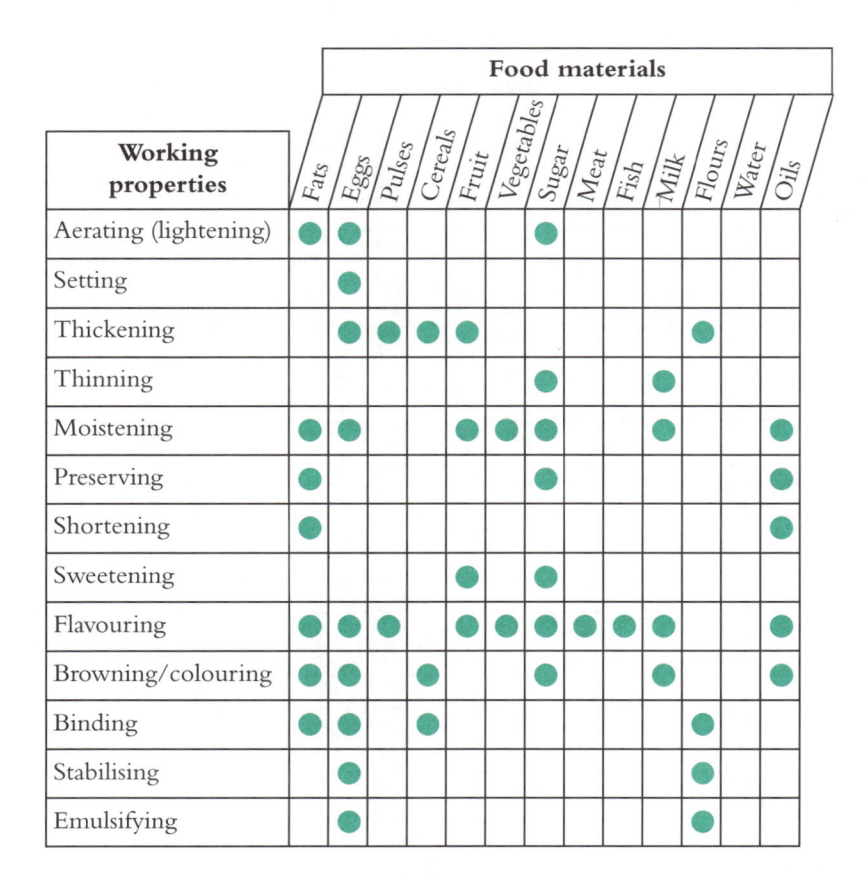

Working properties	Fats	Eggs	Pulses	Cereals	Fruit	Vegetables	Sugar	Meat	Fish	Milk	Flours	Water	Oils
Aerating (lightening)	●	●					●						
Setting		●											
Thickening		●	●	●							●		
Thinning							●			●			
Moistening	●	●			●	●	●			●			●
Preserving	●						●						●
Shortening	●												●
Sweetening					●		●						
Flavouring	●	●	●		●	●	●	●	●	●			●
Browning/colouring	●	●		●			●			●			●
Binding	●	●		●							●		
Stabilising		●									●		
Emulsifying		●								●			

Table 9.2 Use of food materials to affect properties of cooked food

Food technology option

9.6 The nutrient content of food

The following chart describes the nutrient content of a range of common foods.

	Energy (kcal)	Energy (kJ)	Protein (g)	Fat (g)	Carbohydrate (g)	Water (g)	Sodium (mg)	Calcium (mg)	Iron (mg)	Vit A (µg)	Vit B1 (mg)	Vit B2 (mg)	Niacin (mg)	Vit C (mg)
Apples	35	150	0.2	0	9.0	65.0	0	0	0.2	0	0.03	0	0.1	2
Bacon, gammon joint, boiled	270	1130	25.0	19.0	0	53.0	1000	0	1.3	0	0.40	0.15	3.5	0
Bacon rashers, streaky, fried	500	2090	23.0	45.0	0	27.0	1800	0	1.2	0	0.40	0.20	4.5	0
Bananas	80	330	1.0	0.3	20.0	70.0	0	0	0.4	200	0.04	0.07	0.6	10
Bean sprouts, canned	10	40	1.6	0	0.8	95.0	80	0	1.0	0	0	0.03	0.2	0
Beans, baked, canned in tomato sauce	65	270	5.0	0.5	10.0	74.0	480	45	1.4	0	0.07	0.05	0.5	0
Beans, French, boiled	7	30	0.8	0	1.0	96.0	0	40	0.6	80	0.04	0.07	0.3	5
Beans, red kidney, raw	270	1130	22.0	1.7	45.0	11.0	40	140	6.7	0	0.50	0.20	2.0	0
Beans, runner, boiled	20	85	2.0	0.2	3.0	91.0	0	25	0.7	60	0.03	0.07	0.5	5
Beef corned (canned)	220	920	27.0	12.0	0	59.0	1000	0	3.0	0	0	0.20	2.5	0
Beef, minced, stewed	230	960	23.0	15.0	0	59.0	300	0	3.1	0	0.35	0.33	4.4	0
Beef, rump steak, raw	200	840	19.0	14.0	0	67.0	50	0	2.3	0	0.08	0.26	4.2	0
Beef, sirloin, roast	280	1170	24.0	21.0	0	54.0	50	0	2.0	0	0.06	0.25	4.8	0
Beer, bitter	30	130	0	0	2.0	–	0	0	0	0	0	0	0.3	0
Biscuits, chocolate-coated	520	2180	6.0	27.0	67.0	2.0	160	110	1.7	0	0.03	0.15	0.5	0
Biscuits, digestive, plain	470	1970	10.0	20.0	66.0	4.5	440	110	2.0	0	0.15	0.10	1.5	0
Biscuits, water	440	1840	11.0	12.5	76.0	4.5	470	120	1.6	0	0.10	0.03	1.0	0
Bounty bar	470	1970	5.0	26.0	58.0	8.0	180	100	1.3	0	0.04	0.10	0.3	0
Bread, white	230	960	7.8	1.7	50.0	39.0	540	100	1.7	0	0.20	0.03	1.4	0
Bread, wholemeal	220	920	8.8	2.7	42.0	40.0	540	25	2.5	0	0.30	0.08	4.0	0
Breadcrumbs, white	350	1470	12.0	2.0	77.0	10.0	750	130	3.0	0	0.20	0.04	2.0	0
Brussels sprouts, boiled	20	80	3.0	0	1.7	92.0	0	25	0.5	60	0.06	0.10	0.4	40
Buns, currant	300	1260	7.0	8.0	55.0	29.0	100	90	2.5	0	0.20	0.03	1.5	0
Butter	750	3140	0.5	82.0	0	15.4	870	15	0.2	1000	0	0	0	0
Cabbage, white, boiled	20	80	2.0	0	3.5	9.0	0	45	0.4	0	0.06	0.05	0.3	40
Cabbage, winter, raw	20	80	3.0	0	3.0	88.0	0	60	0.6	50	0.06	0.05	0.3	60
Cake, sponge, with fat	460	1920	6.5	27.0	53.0	15.0	350	140	1.4	300	0	0.10	0.5	0
Cauliflower cheese	100	420	6.0	8.0	5.0	78.0	250	160	0.4	100	0.06	0.15	0.4	5
Cheese, cottage	100	420	14.0	0.5	1.5	79.0	450	60	0.1	30	0	0.20	0	0
Cheese, Stilton	460	1930	26.0	40.0	0	28.0	1200	350	0.5	450	0.07	0.30	0.2	0
Chicken, boiled, boned	180	750	29.0	7.0	0	63.0	80	0	1.2	0	0.06	0.20	7.0	0
Chicken, roast, boned	150	630	25.0	5.0	0	68.0	80	0	0.8	0	0.10	0.20	8.0	0
Christmas pudding	300	1260	5.0	12.0	48.0	39.0	240	90	2.0	20	0.10	0.40	0.7	0
Cod fillet, poached	90	380	21.0	1.0	0	78.0	110	30	0.3	0	0.10	0.40	2.0	0
Cornflour	350	1470	0.6	0.7	92.0	12.0	50	15	1.4	0	0	0	0	0
Cream, double	450	1880	1.5	48.0	2.0	48.0	30	50	0.2	400	0	0.40	0	0
Cucumber	10	40	0.6	0	2.0	96.0	0	25	0.3	0	0.04	0.04	0	8
Egg, whole, raw	150	630	12.3	10.9	0	74.8	140	50	2.0	140	0.10	0.50	0	0
Fish fingers, fried	230	960	13.5	13.0	17.0	56.0	350	45	0.7	0	0.10	0.10	1.4	0
Flour, white	340	1420	11.0	1.2	75.0	14.5	0	40	2.0	0	0.30	0.03	2.0	0
Fruit salad, canned	90	380	0.3	0	25.0	70.0	0	0	1.0	0	0	0	0.3	0
Ham	120	500	18.0	5.0	0	73.0	1200	0	1.2	0	0.50	030	4.0	0
Hamburgers, fried	260	1090	20.0	17.0	7.0	53.0	900	35	3.1	0	0	0.20	4.0	0
Ice cream, dairy	170	710	4.0	7.0	25.0	64.0	80	140	0.2	0	0.04	0.20	0	0
Jams	260	1090	0	0	69.0	30.0	0	0	1.5	0	0	0	0	10
Lard	900	3770	0	100.0	0	0	0	0	0	0	0	0	0	0
Lettuce	10	40	1.0	0	1.0	96.0	0	25	0.9	200	0.07	0.08	0.3	15
Liver, fried	250	1050	27.0	13.0	7.0	53.0	170	0	7.5	1700	0.30	4.20	16.0	10
Margarine, low-fat spread	370	1550	0	40.0	0	57.0	700	0	0	1000	0	0	0	0
Mars bar	440	1840	5.0	19.0	67.0	7.0	150	160	1.0	0	0.05	0.20	0.3	0

Table 9.3 Nutrient content of various foods

	Energy (kcal)	Energy (kJ)	Protein (g)	Fat (g)	Carbohydrate (g)	Water (g)	Sodium (mg)	Calcium (mg)	Iron (mg)	Vit A (µg)	Vit B₁ (mg)	Vit B₂ (mg)	Niacin (mg)	Vit C (mg)
Milk	65	270	3.3	3.8	4.7	87.6	50	120	0	50	0.05	0.20	0.1	1
Mushrooms, fried	210	880	2.2	22.0	0	64.0	0	0	1.3	0	0.07	0.40	3.5	0
Oil, vegetable	900	3770	0	100.0	0	0	0	0	0	0	0	0	0	0
Onions, raw	25	100	1.0	0	5.0	93.0	0	30	0.3	0	0.03	0.05	0	10
Orange juice	40	170	0.6	0	9.0	87.0	0	0	0.3	50	0.08	0	0.2	50
Pineapple, fresh	50	210	0.5	0	12.0	84.0	0	0	0.4	0	0.08	0	0.2	25
Potatoes, baked with skin	85	360	2.0	0	20.0	58.0	0	0	0.6	0	0.10	0.03	1.0	10
Rice, white, boiled	120	500	2.0	0.3	30.0	70.0	0	0	0	0	0	0	0.3	0
Sardines canned in oil	220	920	24.0	14.0	0	58.0	650	550	2.9	0	0.04	0.40	8.0	0
Sausages, pork, fried	320	1340	14.0	25.0	11.0	45.0	1000	60	1.5	0	0	0.20	4.4	0
Spaghetti, boiled	120	500	4.0	0.3	26.0	72.0	0	0	0.4	0	0	0	0.3	0
Steak, stewed, canned	180	750	15.0	13.0	1.0	70.0	400	0	2.1	0	0	0.10	2.4	0
Sugar	390	1630	0	0	100.0	0	0	0	0	0	0	0	0	0
Sweetcorn, canned	80	330	3.0	0.5	16.0	73.0	300	0	0.6	40	0.05	0.08	1.2	5
Toffees	430	1800	2.0	17.0	71.0	5.0	300	100	1.5	0	0	0	0	0
Tomato juice	15	60	0	0	3.0	93.0	230	0	0.5	80	0.06	0.03	0.7	20
Tuna, canned in oil	290	1210	23.0	22.0	0	55.0	400	0	1.1	0	0.04	0.10	13.0	0
Watercress	14	60	3.0	0	0.7	91.0	60	220	1.6	500	0.10	0.10	0.6	60
Wine, red	70	290	0	0	0	–	0	0	1.0	0	0	0	0	0
Wine, white, dry	65	270	0	0	0.6	–	0	0	0.5	0	0	0	0	0
Wine, white, sweet	100	420	0	0	6.0	–	0	0	0.6	0	0	0	0	0
Yoghurt, natural	50	210	5.0	1.0	6.0	86.0	80	180	0	0	0.05	0.30	0	0
Yorkshire pudding	200	840	7.0	10.0	26.0	56.0	600	130	1.0	40	0.10	0.20	0.6	0

Table 9.3 Nutrient content of various foods (continued)

9.7 Food hygiene and legislation

Throughout your course your teacher will insist that you prepare food hygienically. Food hygiene means the following four things.

1 **Personal hygiene**
- Wash hands, scrub nails and tie back hair.
- Wash hands after visiting the lavatory.
- Never cough or smoke near food.
- Cover up skin infections.
- Wear a clean apron or overall.
- Do not lick fingers.

2 **Food purchase**
- Buy from reputable shops.
- Check there are no animals in the shop.
- Check date stamps on food.
- Be wary of fresh food that is not covered to protect it from insects.

3 **Food storage**
- Store fresh foods in a cool place.
- Use up old stocks before starting new ones.
- Cool left-overs rapidly and eat soon.
- Protect food from pests, animals, etc.

4 **Kitchen hygiene**
- Wash regularly.
- Keep utensils clean.
- Wipe up mess as it occurs.

- Do not use a dishcloth for the floor.
- Wash dishes in hot water with detergent.
- Make sure frozen foods, such as chicken, are thoroughly thawed before use.

Legislation

The hygienic handling of food is of great importance in the prevention of food contamination and food poisoning. In establishments that prepare food for public consumption the food hygiene regulations must be obeyed and regular checks are made by the Environmental Health officers of each local authority.

Regulations exist for each of the following:
- manufacture and packaging of food;
- transport and storage of food;
- food preparation;
- sanitary facilities;
- waste disposal;
- food retail premises.

When designing food products you should consider the rules and regulations that would affect your product if it was to be produced commercially.

In addition to food hygiene regulations, there are regulations for the following:
- allowed additives;
- preferred packaging quantities.
- food labelling;
- food packaging;
- food names.

9.8 Preserving food

Food needs to be preserved to keep it safe and to increase the time for which it can be stored. If it is not preserved it will deteriorate because either enzymes in the foods will cause discolouration and change the texture and taste of the food, or micro-organisms, such as moulds, yeasts and bacteria, will cause the food to deteriorate.

Food preservation involves one or more of the following processes:
- destroying the enzymes or micro-organisms;
- preventing the enzymes or micro-organisms causing deterioration;
- preventing further access of micro-organisms into the food.

The following methods are used.

1 Drying
Removing water prevents enzymes and micro-organisms from becoming active.

Fig. 9.5 Some foods are preserved by drying

2 Temperature reduction
Fridges may be used for short periods. A freezer stops enzyme activity by lowering the temperature to about -18 degrees Celsius. Quick freezing is needed.

9.8 Preserving food

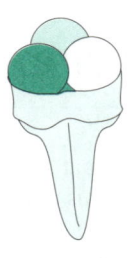

Fig. 9.6 Vegetables and ice cream are preserved by freezing

3 Heating
Heat is used especially for bottling and canning. Heating kills the micro-organisms that cause food spoilage.

Fig. 9.7 Fruit can be preserved by heating

4 Vacuum packing
Vacuum packing excludes air and so bacterial growth cannot take place.

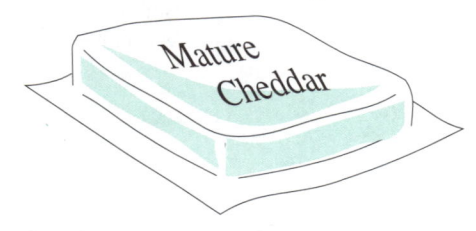

Fig. 9.8 Cheese can be preserved by vacuum packing

5 Chemicals
Sugar (jams) and acids (pickles) reduce micro-organism activity. The use of a chemical preservative, such as sulphur dioxide, destroys micro-organisms.

Fig. 9.9 Jams and pickles contain sugar and acid to kill microbes

6 Irradiation
Certain types of radiation destroy micro-organisms. Food can be irradiated to prevent deterioration of fruit, to kill insects and to render food sterile for use in hospitals.

Fig. 9.10 Fruit can be preserved by irradiation

9.9 Measuring food

Some cooks will tell you that it isn't necessary to measure food quantities accurately. All you need is experience. This is certainly true, but what you don't have is experience, so it is better to be careful in the measurement of food. Food can be measured in the following ways.

- Dry measure
- Liquid measure
- Weight

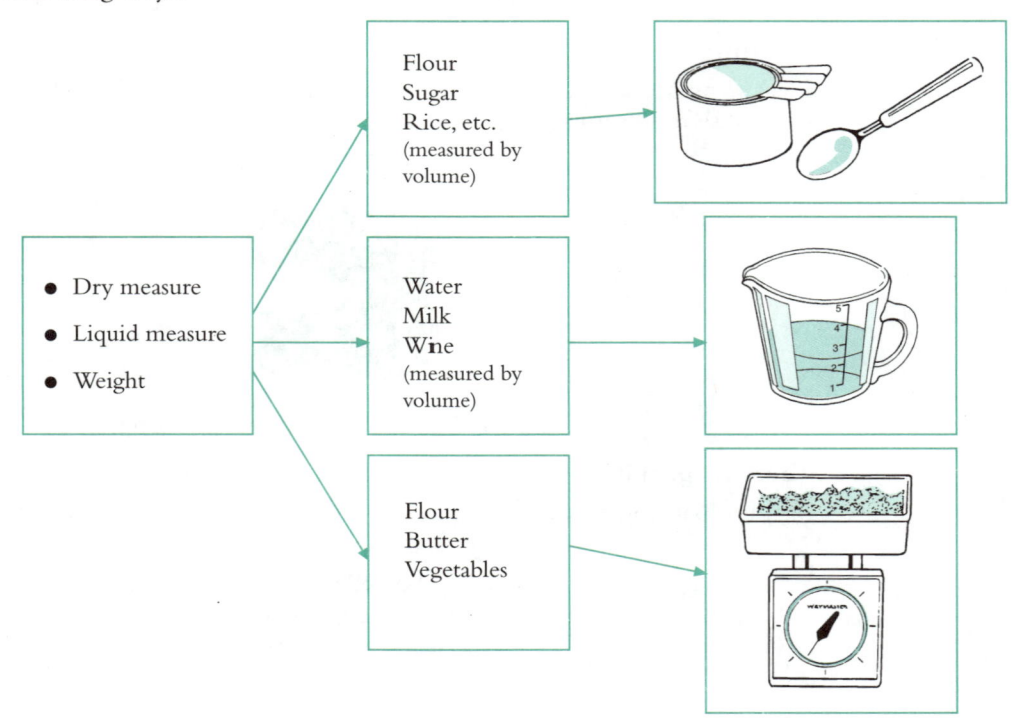

Flour, Sugar, Rice, etc. (measured by volume)

Water, Milk, Wine (measured by volume)

Flour, Butter, Vegetables

Fig. 9.11 Equipment for measuring food

Sometimes it is necessary to convert from dry measures, which may be in grams (g) or in cups, to liquid measure, which will be in millilitres (ml). Use this chart to help convert from weight to volume measurements.

Food	Weight (g)	Dry measure (cups)	Volume (ml)
flour and similar dry goods	125	1	275
sugar	125	$\frac{1}{2}$	150
butter and similar fats	125	$\frac{1}{2}$	150
cereals (rice, pearl barley, etc)	125	1	275

Table 9.4 Conversion chart for food measurements

9.10 Food preparation equipment

As you prepare your food products, you will use a variety of equipment. You should ensure that you have some experience of each of the following.

9.10 Food preparation equipment

Equipment	Appearance	Uses
Kitchen knives	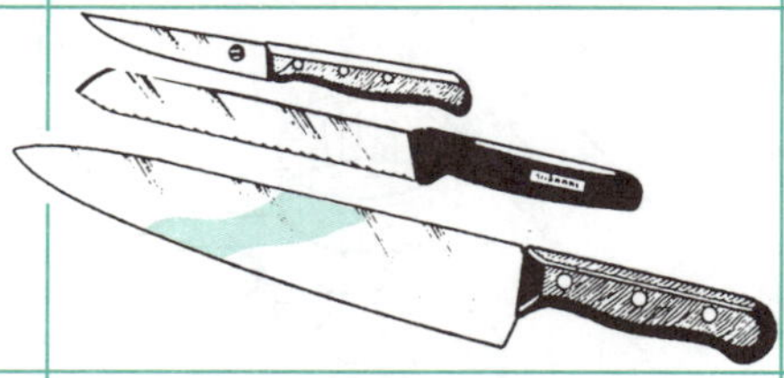	Those made from stainless steel are the most hygienic. They are safest when sharp.
Vegetable peelers	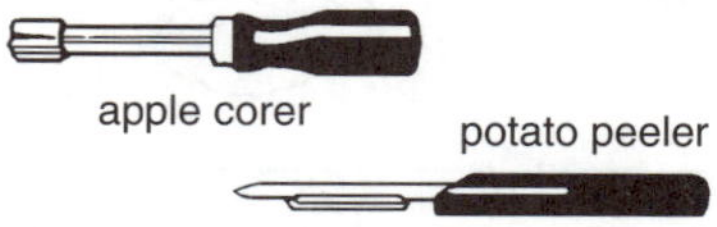 apple corer potato peeler	Usually better for the inexperienced than knives.
Auto chop	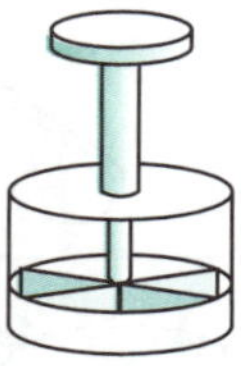	Useful for chopping vegetables, nuts, etc., but can be difficult to clean.
Graters		Used for cheese, vegetables, etc. Can also be used for slicing.
Hand whisk	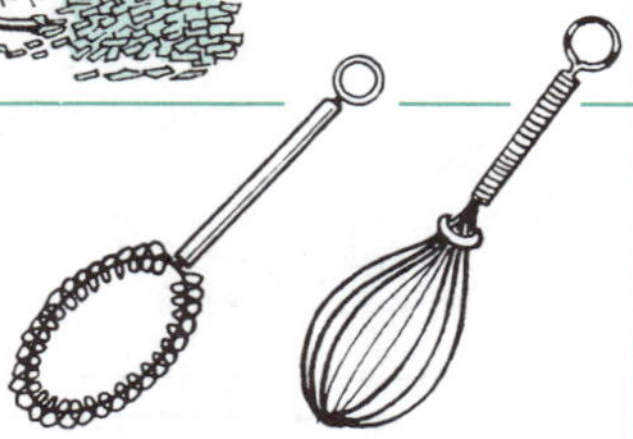	Nothing like as difficult to use as you might think and less trouble for small jobs.
Rotary whisk		Used for prolonged whisking when an electric whisk is not available. Take care to clean thoroughly.
Electric food mixer		Essential for larger quantities. Do not leave mixer unattended.
Food processor	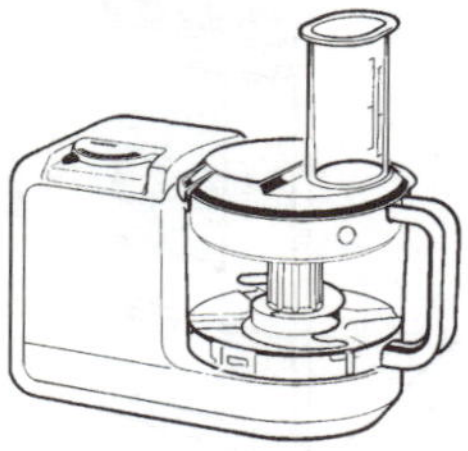	Takes the hard work out of tasks such as slicing food and kneading dough. You must ensure that the parts of a food processor are cleaned thoroughly.

Fig. 9.12 Food preparation equipment

Food technology option

Equipment	Appearance	Uses
Rolling pin Pastry cutters Cutting board	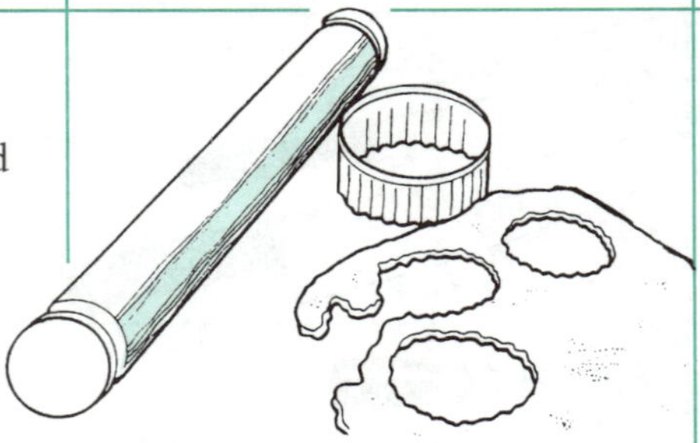	Basic equipment for all pastry and biscuit making. Best results are obtained when cool. A glass rolling pin filled with water is ideal. Plastic cutters are easily broken. Old 'tinplate' cutters can oxidise and are unhygienic.
Spatulas and palette knives	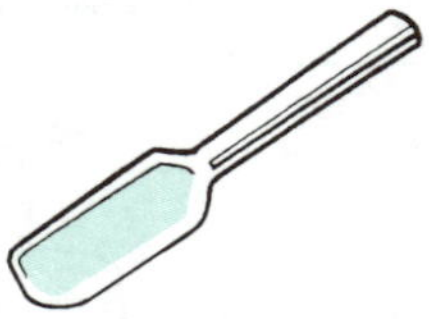	Used for scraping out bowls, spreading sauces, etc.
Saucepans		Available in a range of sizes. Used for sauces and boiling food. Make sure the handles are secure and insulated.
Frying pan		Used for shallow frying, but remember too much fat should be avoided.
Casserole dish	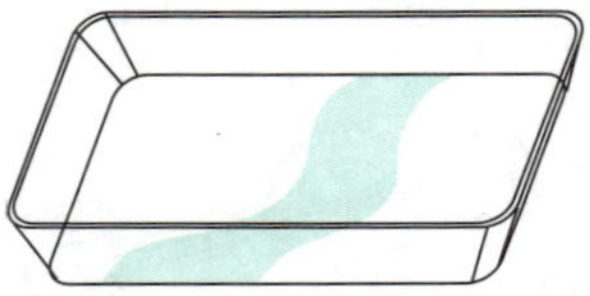	For cooking in the oven. Can be metal, glass or ceramic. Do not use metal in microwave oven.
Microwave oven	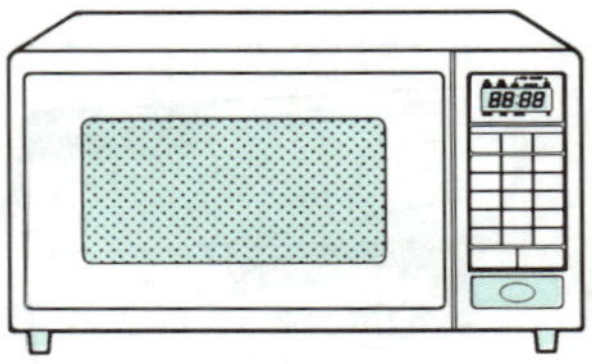	A quick and convenient piece of equipment. Food often is not 'browned' although it is possible to get microwaves with grills. Check that it is in good condition. Service regularly.
Conventional oven		The workhorse of any kitchen. Most these days have a fan to assist uniform heating. Otherwise remember the hottest part is at the top. Take great care when taking food out. Can be gas or electric. In many countries, ovens are fuelled by parafin.

Fig. 9.12 Food preparation equipment (continued)

9.11 Preparation of balanced meals

Here are some important things to consider when designing with food. You may be able to think of others.

Nutritional content
Try to get the balance right by including a range of food groups. You may also find it helpful to consult the nutrient content chart (Table 9.3). A single meal does not need to be completely balanced or contain the full range of nutrients.

Flavour
Try to provide a balance of flavours. Ensure that strong flavours follow delicate ones and not the other way round. If it is the first time you are preparing food for a different person, try to be sensitive. People do not always like to eat foods that are 'different'.

Texture
Try to achieve a mixture of textures within a meal.

Presentation
Think about the dishes and plates you will use. Make it look appetising.

Rules and regulations
Make sure your food is prepared, packaged, stored and served according to the appropriate rules and regulations.

Appearance
Take care with the appearance. Consider what it will look like on the plate. Don't forget that a little decoration can make all the difference.

Colour
Try to make the food bright and colourful. If it is attractive, people are more likely to want to eat it. Use colours that occur naturally with food. In other words: green, red, yellow, orange and brown.

Chapter 10 Textile technology option

10.1 Natural fibres

Name	Origin	Properties	Uses
Wool	A natural short fibre from sheep, alpaca, etc. 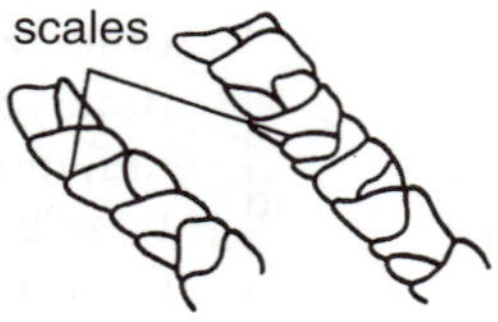 (scales)	A natural crimp. It absorbs water and shrinks badly. The scales help the fibres to become matted. Good wear resistance.	Clothing, carpets, etc.
Cotton	The fibres surrounding the seed head of the cotton plant. 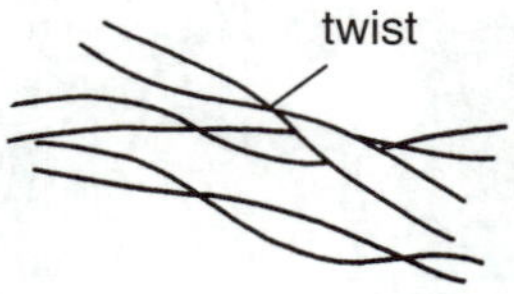 (twist)	Very absorbent. Washes well.	Lightweight clothing; bed linen. Often combined with polyester to reduce creasing.
Linen	The fibres come from the stem of the flax plant. 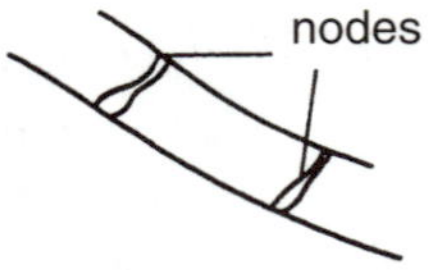 (nodes)	Expensive to produce and creases badly.	Tea towels, table cloths, napkins.
Silk	A protein filament fibre. Spun as a cocoon by the silkworm. 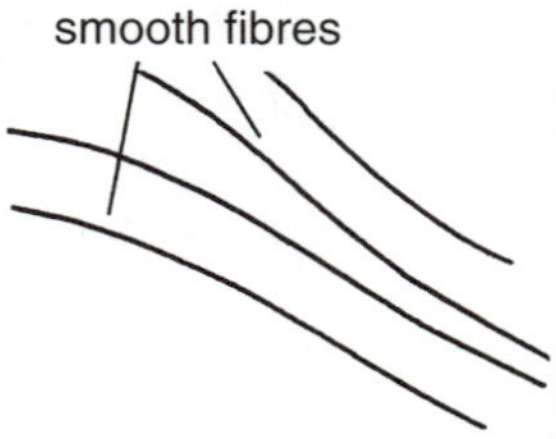 (smooth fibres)	Soft and shiny. It drapes well. Difficult to wash and iron. Expensive.	Clothing, bed linen. Expensive wall coverings.

Fig. 10.1 Natural fibres

10.2 Synthetic fibres

Name	Origin	Properties	Uses
Viscose	Cellulose from wood pulp steeped in carbon disulphide dissolved in caustic soda. It is spun wet.	Inexpensive. Shiny, does not 'breathe' well.	Linings for clothing. Sometimes mixed with other fibres, such as cotton, for kitted items.
Acetate	Made from wood pulp. It is spun dry.	Slippery and shiny. Available in a range of colours.	Used for lining materials, such as linings of suits and skirts.
Polyamide (nylon)	Made out of chemicals derived from oil and coal.	Strong, easily washed and drip-dried. Hard wearing.	Tights, stockings, shirts, waterproof clothing. Carpets.
Polyester	Synthesised from ethylene glycol and terephthalic acid.	Resists creasing. Easy to wash.	Mixed with cotton for shirts and blouses. Sometimes woven into a heavier fabric for other clothing, such as suits.
Polyproylene	Synthesised from chemicals.	Non-absorbent. Very strong and hard wearing. Somewhat slippery.	Carpets, furnishings and ropes. Specialist knots are needed for rope otherwise they will slip.
Acrylic	A kind of synthetic wool made from oil.	Soft, strong and hard wearing. Not a good insulator of heat when compared with natural fibres, such as wool.	Frequently used as a knitted yarn for inexpensive 'woollens'.
Eastene (lycra)	A type of polyurethane.	Very strong. Stretches well. Good support qualities.	Interlinings. Swimwear, underwear.

Fig. 10.2 Synthetic fibres

10.3 From fibres to yarns

Fibres need to be spun to make them into yarns. Before spinning a natural yarn, such as wool, it needs to be carded. Carding consists of pulling the fibres apart, using a pair of stiff wire brushes (carders). Machine carding is similar but, of course, it is a much faster process.

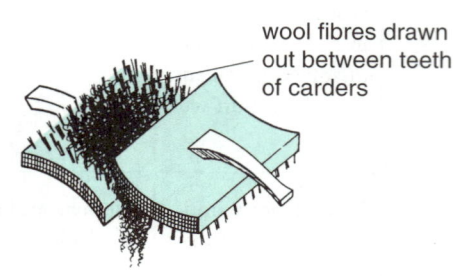

wool fibres drawn out between teeth of carders

Fig. 10.3 Carding raw wool

Spinning can be achieved by hand or by machine. Hand spinning is a slow process and the yarn produced is a little irregular in texture. Machine spinning can be done using hand or foot-operated spinning machines, while factory spinning is fast and produces a very uniform yarn.

Different uses require different yarns. For example, hand knitted jumpers need a bulky yarn with a long twist, but for clothing, woven fabric needs a yarn that is thinner with a lot of twist.

? What advantages can you think of for hand spinning?

Hand spinning

Fig. 10.4 Comparison of hand spinning with machine spinning

Machine spinning

10.4 Fabric construction

Fabrics can be constructed in a variety of ways.

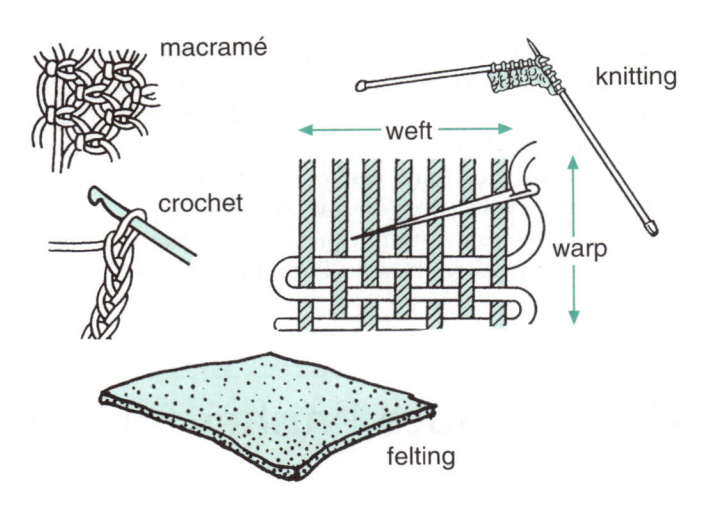

Fig. 10.5 Types of fabric construction

1. **Weaving**

   Weaving involves crossing threads under and over each other on a machine known as a loom. The horizontal threads are known as the warp and the up and down threads are known as as the weft. By arranging the crossing of the threads in different ways, different patterns or textures can be created The simplest form of weave is known as plain weave. To identify which are the warp threads and which are the weft threads try stretching the fabric. The warp threads usually stretch more than the weft threads.

2. **Knitting**

   Hand knitting is a slow process and now most knitted fabric is made by machine. The fabric is made by forming single strands of yarn into loops, which interlock with each other. Fabrics for T-shirts and jumpers are made in this way. There are two basic stitches, known as plain (knit) and purl. By combining these a large variety of patterns can be achieved.

3. **Felting and bonding**

   These are quick and cheap ways to make fabrics. Felt is suitable for carpet underlay and hats. Bonded fabrics are used for interfacings (frequently iron-on) and disposable cloths. Each sort of fabric is made by a combination of heat, moisture and pressure.

4. **Macramé**

   Macramé is a hand craft technique in which yarns, strings, ropes or cords are knotted together to produce fabric products with holes in them, such as bags, plant-pot hangers, wall hangings, rugs and hammocks. The basic knots used are the square knot and the clove hitch.

5. **Crocheting**

   This is similar in some respects to macramé, but is usually done with a thinner yarn. The yarn is looped together with a crochet hook and the loops are not knotted together. It can be used for clothing items, decorating the edges of handkerchiefs and decorative table mats. Like macramé it often produces fabric with 'holes'.

10.5 The properties of fabrics

When you are designing, consider the properties of fabrics, e.g.,
- washability (can it be hand or machine-washed?);
- absorbency (will it absorb liquids?);
- heat insulation (will it keep someone warm?);
- stain resistance (can it be wiped clean if a liquid is spilled on it?);
- elasticity (how well does it stretch and return to its original shape?);
- crease resistance (will creases drop out after it has been folded?);
- fire resistance (how easily does it catch alight?);
- abrasion resistance (does it scratch easily?);
- water resistance (will it prevent water soaking through?);
- wind resistance (how well does it prevent air moving through?).

10.6 Surface finishes for fabrics

The performance and hence the usefulness of fabrics can be improved by adding certain surface finishes.

Finish	Description	Effect and use
Anti-static	Chemicals can make synthetic fabrics better able to attract water and hence improve their ability to conduct electricity.	Used for clothing fabrics.
Water repellent	A coating of silicone makes the water run off the surface more easily.	Used for umbrellas and raincoats.
Shower/waterproof	Used mainly on cotton, polyurethane or PVC, it is used to coat the fabric.	Used for raincoats, tents and boat covers.
Moth-proof	Used on protein fibres. It makes the fibre taste unpleasant to the mouth.	Mainly used for carpets and upholstery.
Trubenised	Chemical process to stiffen fabric.	Used for shirt collars and cuffs.
Stain and soil resistant	Fabric finished using a mixture of silicone and fluorine.	Used for carpets and upholstery. Can be done at home by using a spray.

Table 10.1 Surface finishes for fabrics

10.7 Tools and equipment

You should become familiar with the following basic tools and equipment.

Name	Appearance	Uses and notes
Scissors and shears	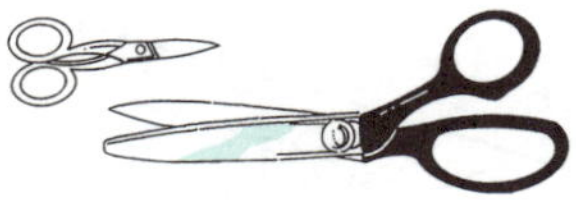	Shears are used for cutting out fabrics. Smaller scissors are for trimming and cutting thread.
Tape measure/ metre rule	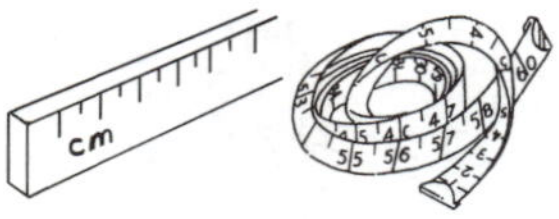	For transferring measurements from, say, a person. The rule is for measuring fabrics.
Tailor's chalk	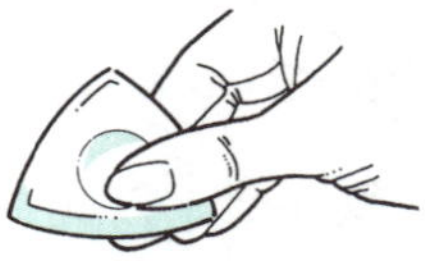	For marking out on 'dark' fabrics. Its shape ensures a thin accurate line.
Pins	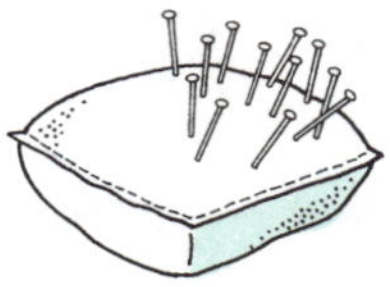	Used to hold fabrics together and mark positions, such as for buttons. Place pin at right angles to machining line.
Thimbles	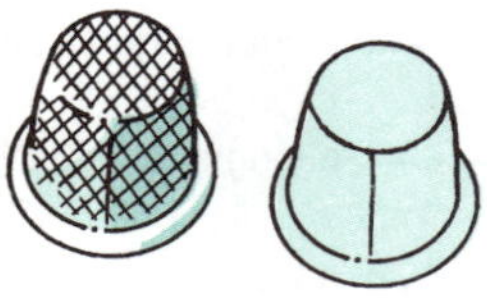	Used to protect the finger when hand sewing. They can be awkward to use if you haven't used them before, but they do protect your fingers.
Needles	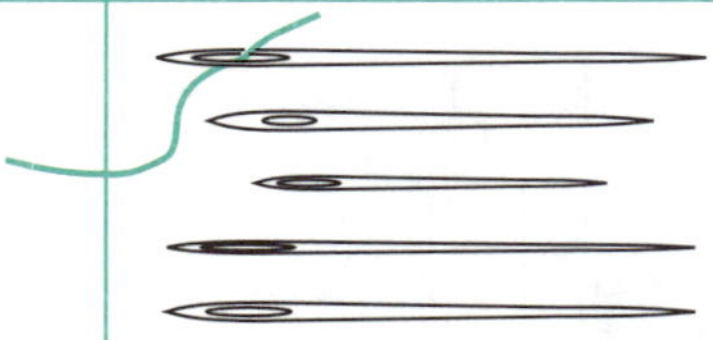	Use short, thin needles for thin fabrics. Special **crewel**-needles are used for embroidery, since they have a large eye.
Machine needles		One side has a 'flat' on it. Do not try to put it in the wrong way round. Use the correct needles for the fabric or thread.
Paper patterns	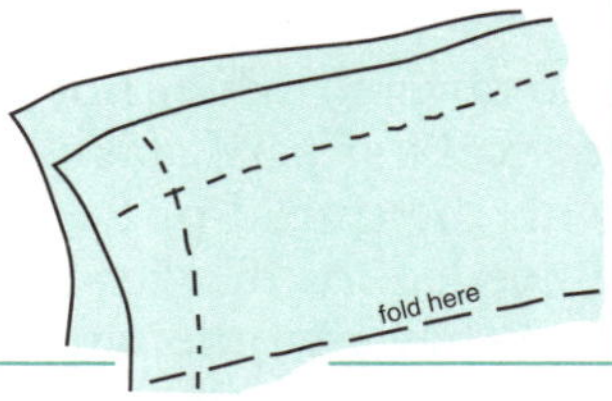	Can be cut from thin (tissue) paper or you may prefer to modify a commercially produced pattern.

Fig. 10.6 Textile tools and equipment

Textile technology option

10.8 The sewing machine

The sewing machine is the 'workhorse' of textile technology. You should become very familiar with it.

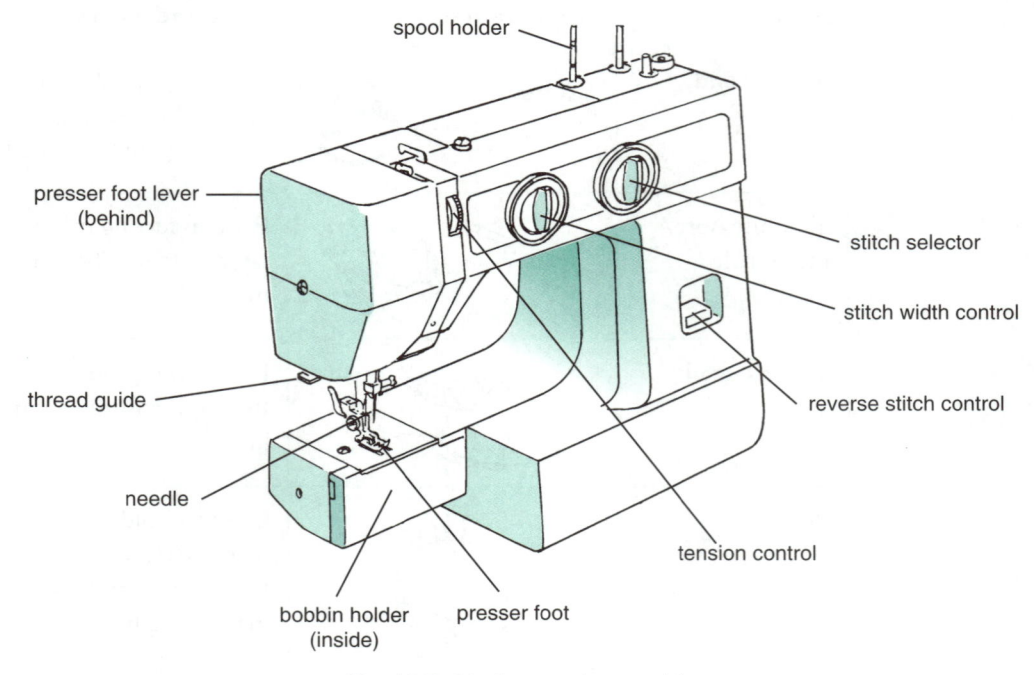

Fig. 10.7 Modern sewing machine

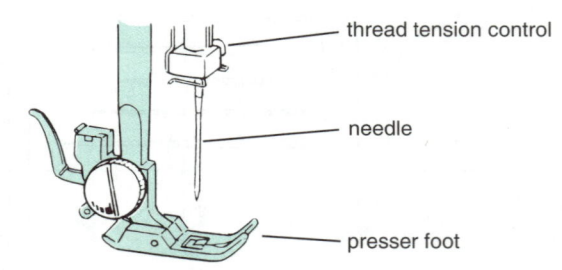

- - - - - - - - a small straight stitch

——— ——— a long straight stitch

∧∧∧∧∧ a zig-zag stitch

Fig. 10.8 Details of sewing machine foot and common stitches

Hints

1. Keep sewing machine covered when not in use.
2. Occasionally oil the working parts, taking care to avoid oiling any parts that will be in contact with the thread or the fabric.
3. Thicker needles are needed for heavier fabrics.
4. Replace needles when they become blunt.
5. Do not attempt to sew materials that are too thick for the machine.
6. The thread will break if the tension is too tight or the machine is wrongly threaded.
7. Stitches should look the same on the back of the fabric.
8. The fabric will ruck if the tension is too tight, or if a blunt or incorrect needle is being used.

10.9 Seams

Name	Appearance	Use
Plain seam		A simple row of stitches used to join two pieces of fabric together. The fabric should be placed right side to right side.
French seam		A kind of double seam. Stitched with fabrics wrong sides together. Used for fabrics that fray easily.
Double-stitched seam		Used as a decoration on, for example, the outside of jeans.
Top-stitched seam		A way of strengthening or decorating a plain seam.
Fusible web		A method of joining fabrics without the use of thread. The fabric is 'glued' by means of a fabric impregnated with a special glue. The glue is melted by the use of a hot iron. Used for hems of skirts and trousers.
Slip hemming		This is not really a seam. It is used to hold up hems where an invisible stitch is needed.

Fig. 10.9 Types of seam

10.10 Openings and fastenings

1 Buttons and buttonholes

These can be sewn by hand or by machine. Metal buttons can be bought that can be covered with fabric. Buttonholes can be made by hand or they can be made either using a buttonhole machine or a sewing machine with the appropriate attachment.

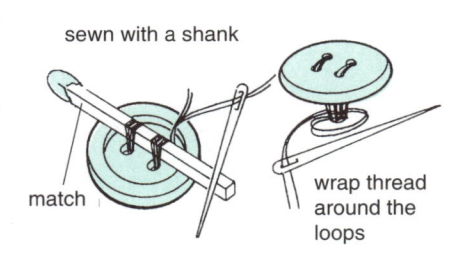

Fig. 10.10 Sewing buttons

Textile technology option

2. **Press studs**

   These give a quick and easy fastening, but must be hand sewn. They are seldom seen on commercial goods, because of the difficulty of sewing on by machine.

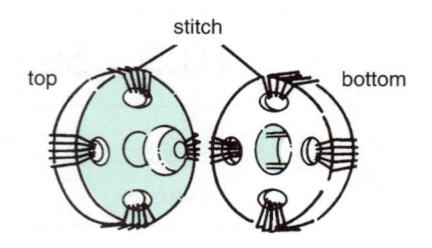

   Fig. 10.11 Sewing press studs

3. **Hooks and eyes**

   Hooks and eyes are also rarely used on commercial garments because they are difficult to sew by machine.

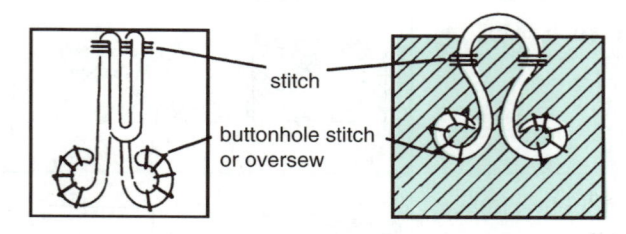

   Fig. 10.12 Sewing hooks and eyes

4. **Velcro**

   This is a convenient material with which to close articles. Velcro can be used for loose-fitting items as well as attaching things to notice boards, in which case one part of the velcro is replaced by a surface of the notice board, which should be made from loop nylon.

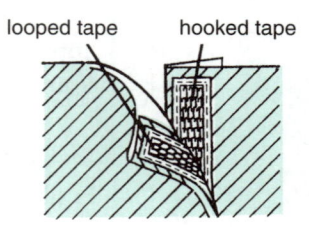

   Fig. 10.13 Velcro tape

5. **Zip fasteners**

   Zips can be visible or invisible and open or closed-ended. Zips are frequently used at the centre of an opening, such as a skirt or the back of a blouse. There are special ways to insert zips for fly fronts: faced openings, bound openings and continuous openings. Fig. 10.14 shows how to insert a centred zip. For best results, the opening should be tacked closed before inserting the zip. Make sure you choose the correct size, colour and type of zip for the material and for its position.

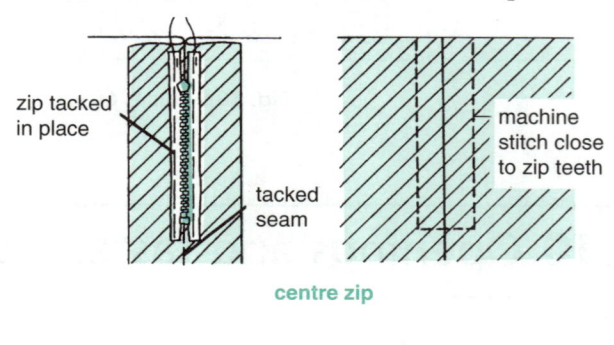

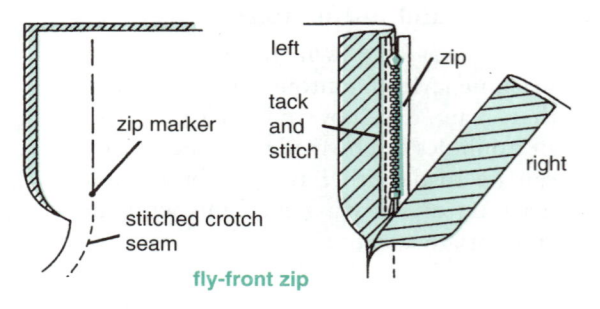

   Fig. 10.14 Sewing zip fasteners

10.11 Painting fabrics

1. **Fabric pens and crayons**

   By far the simplest way to apply colour to fabric is the use of waterproof fabric pens and crayons. These can be purchased in a wide range of colours and are ideal for 'one-offs' or mock-up ideas. You may also use transfer crayons. After drawing the design on paper use a hot iron to transfer it to the fabric.

2. **Spray painting**

   Fabric paints can be applied using a spray diffuser. The paint can be applied through a stencil. You can also block off areas with strips of paper. The paint is usually 'set' by first covering with paper and then passing a hot iron over the top.

3. **Brush painting**

   A simple way of applying paint is with a small soft brush. Painting in this way requires the paint to be very thin and therefore it does not work well on dark-coloured fabrics. Masking tape can help you to paint in the correct place. Brush painting is particularly suitable for use on silk.

4. **Marbling**

   Paint is floated on the surface of a base fluid consisting of water and wallpaper paste. The surface of the paint is mixed and swirled with a stick or comb. The fabric is drawn up through the paint and a marbled effect is deposited on the surface of the fabric. You can use oil-based or fabric paints.

10.12 Printing fabrics

1. **Handblock printing**

   Blocks can be cut from wood or made from cardboard and attached to a suitable block. You can also cut a shape into a potato or a carrot or use part of a cabbage to print an interesting texture.

2. **Stencils**

   Stencils can be cut from cardboard or it is possible to buy them made from plastic. A stencil is placed over the fabric and the ink 'pushed' through using a sponge. The ink can also be 'sprayed', using a stiff brush.

3. **Silkscreen printing**

   A piece of nylon fabric is stretched over a frame and either a paper mask is placed underneath or a design is formed onto the lower side by a photographic process. The fabric to be printed is laid flat and stretched out. The screen is placed over and ink is squeezed through.

4. **Commercial printing**

   When it is necessary to print large quantities of fabric it is done by a continuous process using inked rollers of different colours. You can achieve a similar effect by using a hand roller. You can either buy a roller or you can make one by using a card cylinder and gluing string or other pieces of card to it.

10.13 Dyeing fabrics

1 Batik

Batik consists of saturating the fabric in the places where you do do not want it to be dyed. This may be done by the use of either wax resist or starch.

Wax is used hot and can easily burn you. Starch tends to be less precise and care has to be taken to ensure it is of the correct consistency.

Fig. 10.15 Batik dyeing

2 Tritik

Tritik consists of pleating and sewing the fabric together to prevent certain areas being dyed.

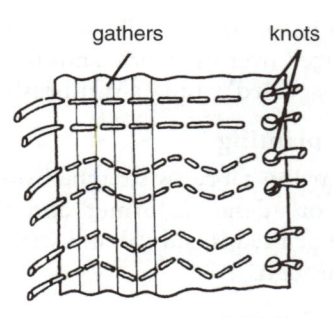

Fig. 10.16 Tritik dyeing

3 Tie-and-dye

Tie-and-dye is similar to tritik, however in this case areas are tied with strong thread. This causes a striking 'starburst' effect after the fabric is dyed.

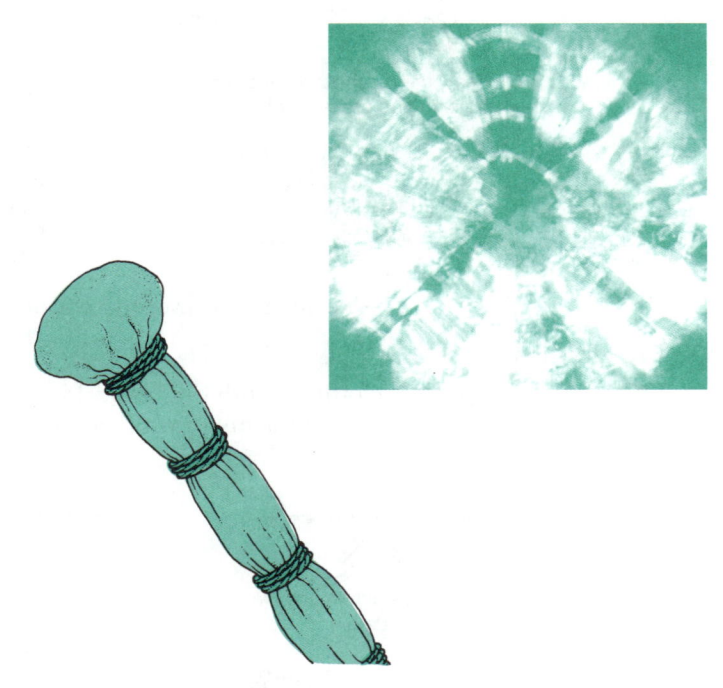

Fig. 10.17 Tie-and-dye dyeing

10.14 Adding decoration

1 Appliqué

Appliqué is a method of decorating fabrics by sewing on to the surface another piece of fabric, often in the form of a geometrical shape or motif. The applied fabrics should compliment in either colour, texture or pattern. Appliqué is frequently padded by placing wadding behind the applied piece of fabric.

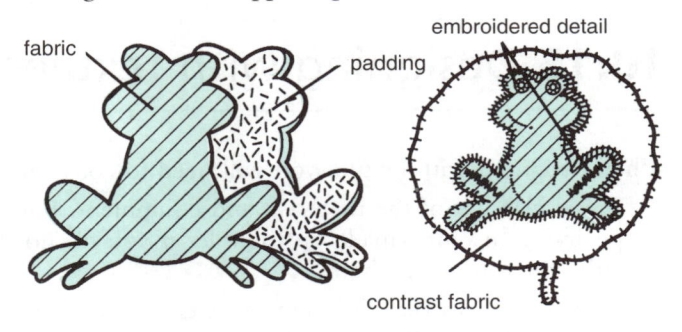

Fig. 10.18 Appliqué decoration

2 Patchwork

Fabric scraps are normally used in patchwork. Using templates, identically shaped pieces of fabric are cut out, with a seam allowance added. The seams are folded and pressed over and the corner flaps sewn together. The edges are then oversewn together. More-complicated designs can be produced by the use of more than one shape.

Textile technology option

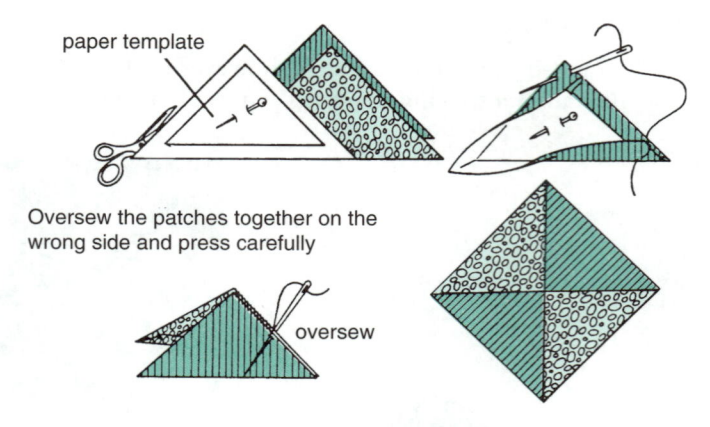

Fig. 10.19 Patchwork decoration

3 Embroidery

Embroidery is used on clothing, cushions, tablecloths and the like. There is a vast range of decorative stitches and a mixture of stitches can be used to achieve very creative patterns.

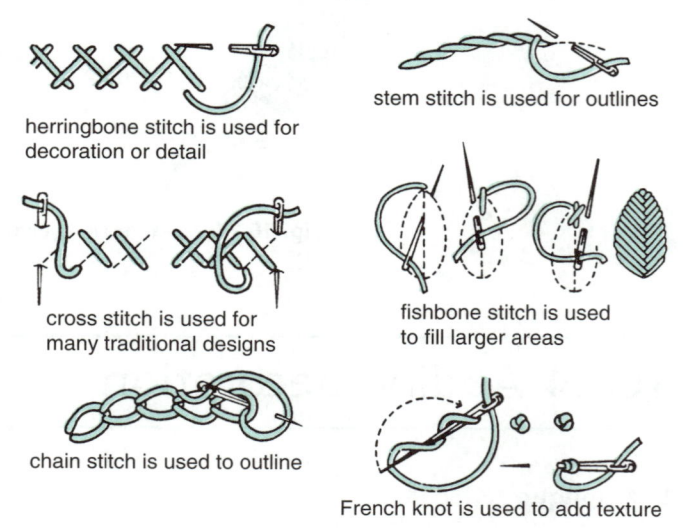

Fig. 10.20 Embroidered decoration

10.15 Designing with textiles

When designing with textiles you will need to consider the following factors.

1. The availability of the materials and equipment. For example, there is little point in specifying machine-made buttonholes if you do not have a machine or attachment with which to make them.
2. Your ability to make the item. As well as your own skill, you should consider any problems that might arise if the item was made on an industrial scale.
3. Keep a careful eye on fashion trends. Fashion can change quickly and you must make sure your ideas are not 'behind the times'.
4. What people want can be affected by social or cultural influences.
5. Consider the properties needed by the finished article, such as comfort, water resistance or good heat insulation.
6. Remember that not everyone has the same likes and dislikes. Consider carefully personal preferences.
7. Remember the consumer. They will need to look after the product. Consider such things as washability, need to iron, etc.

8 Consider the scale of production. Costs can be saved, but you may have to think of different ways of manufacturing. You may also have to use different fabrics if, for example, you intend to machine sew.

9 Consumers are very cost conscious. You must consider carefully whether you are providing value for money. Careful research may reveal, for example, that money can be saved by buying cheaper buttons or other trimming materials.

10.16 Information technology and textiles

Here are some ways in which you might use information technology to design textiles.

1 Information technology can be used to assist the creative design process.

Fig. 10.21 Using a computer to explore designs

2 Microprocessor-controlled sewing machines can be used to produce very interesting effects.

Fig. 10.22 Work produced on a computer-controlled sewing machine

3 Electronic knitting machines can reproduce patterns created electronically.

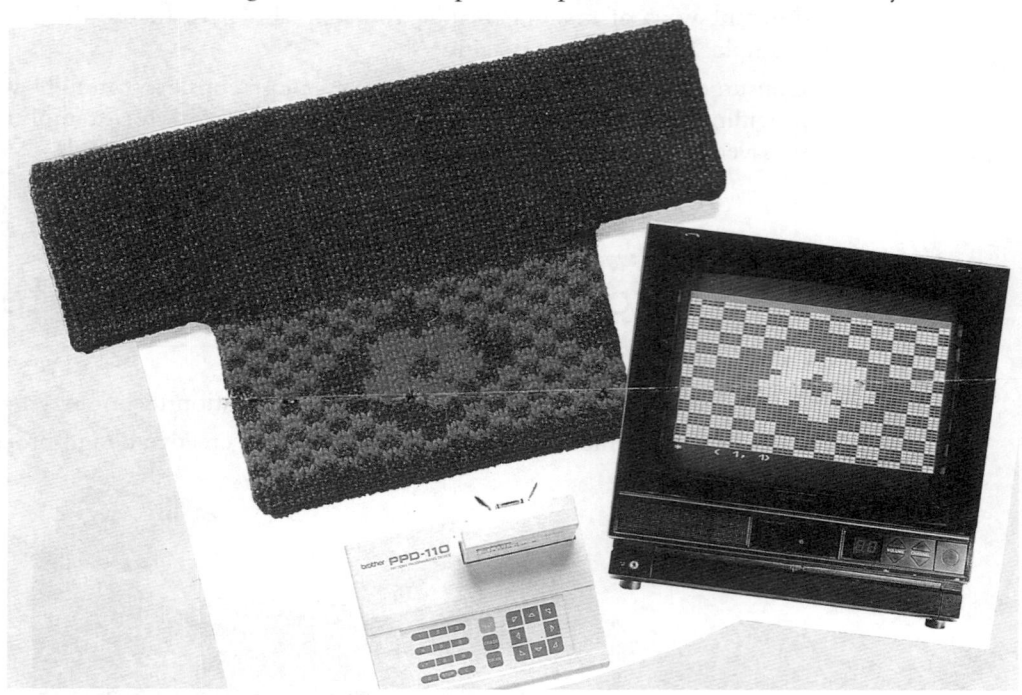

Fig. 10.23 Designed by an electronic knitting machine

Chapter 11   Data sheets

11.1 Measurements of everyday objects

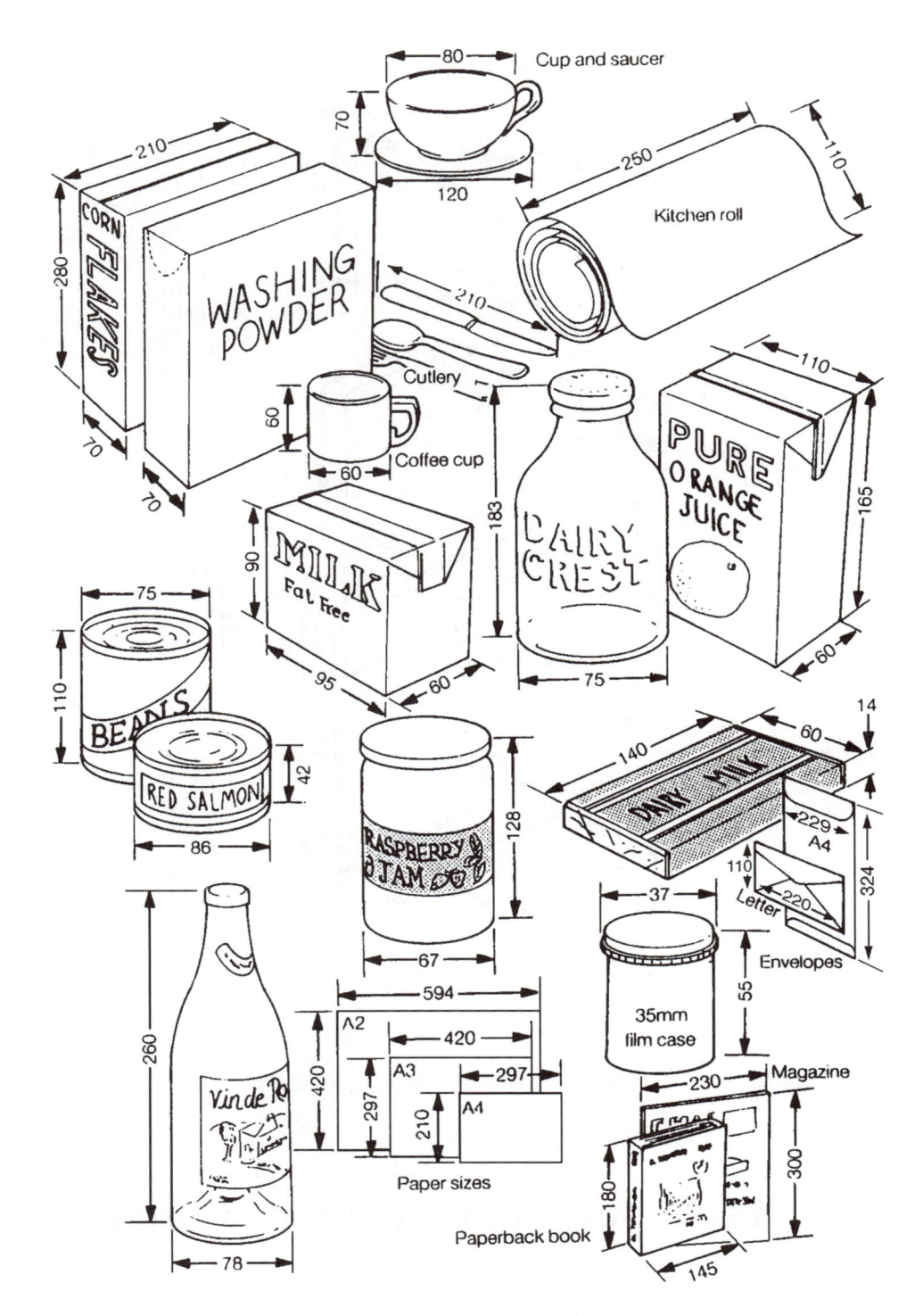

Fig. 11.1 Measurements of everyday objects (all dimensions in mm.)

11.2 Measurements of recreational items

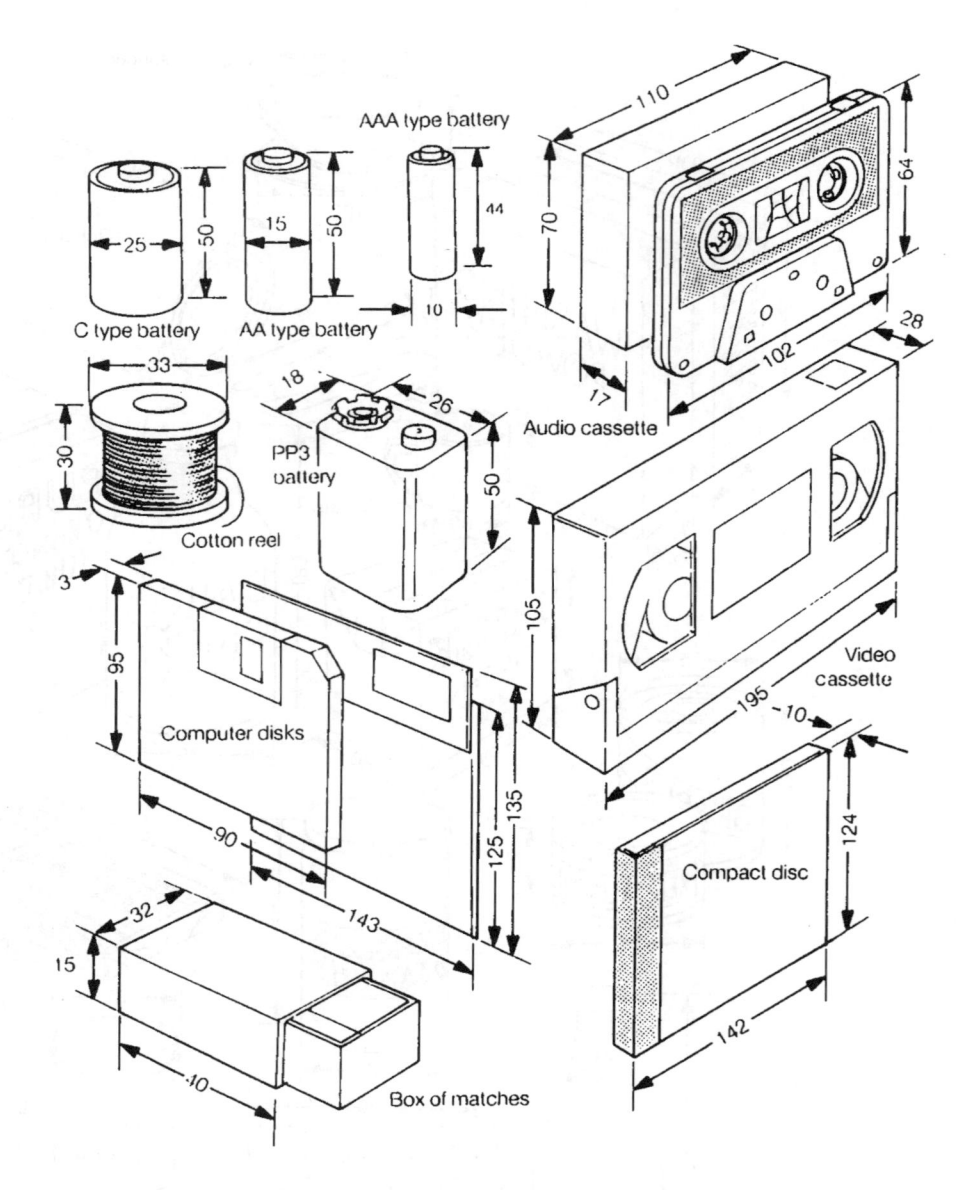

Fig. 11.2 Measurements of recreational items (all dimensions in mm.)

11.3 Anthropometric measurements

Much of your designing is for people. Fig. 11.3 gives you an idea of the measurements of the human body. If you are designing for a specific 'customer', a child for example, these precise measurements may not be of use. When designing for adults designers usually design for the ninety per cent of the population between the five per cent who are very small and the five per cent who are very large.

11.3 Anthropometric measurements

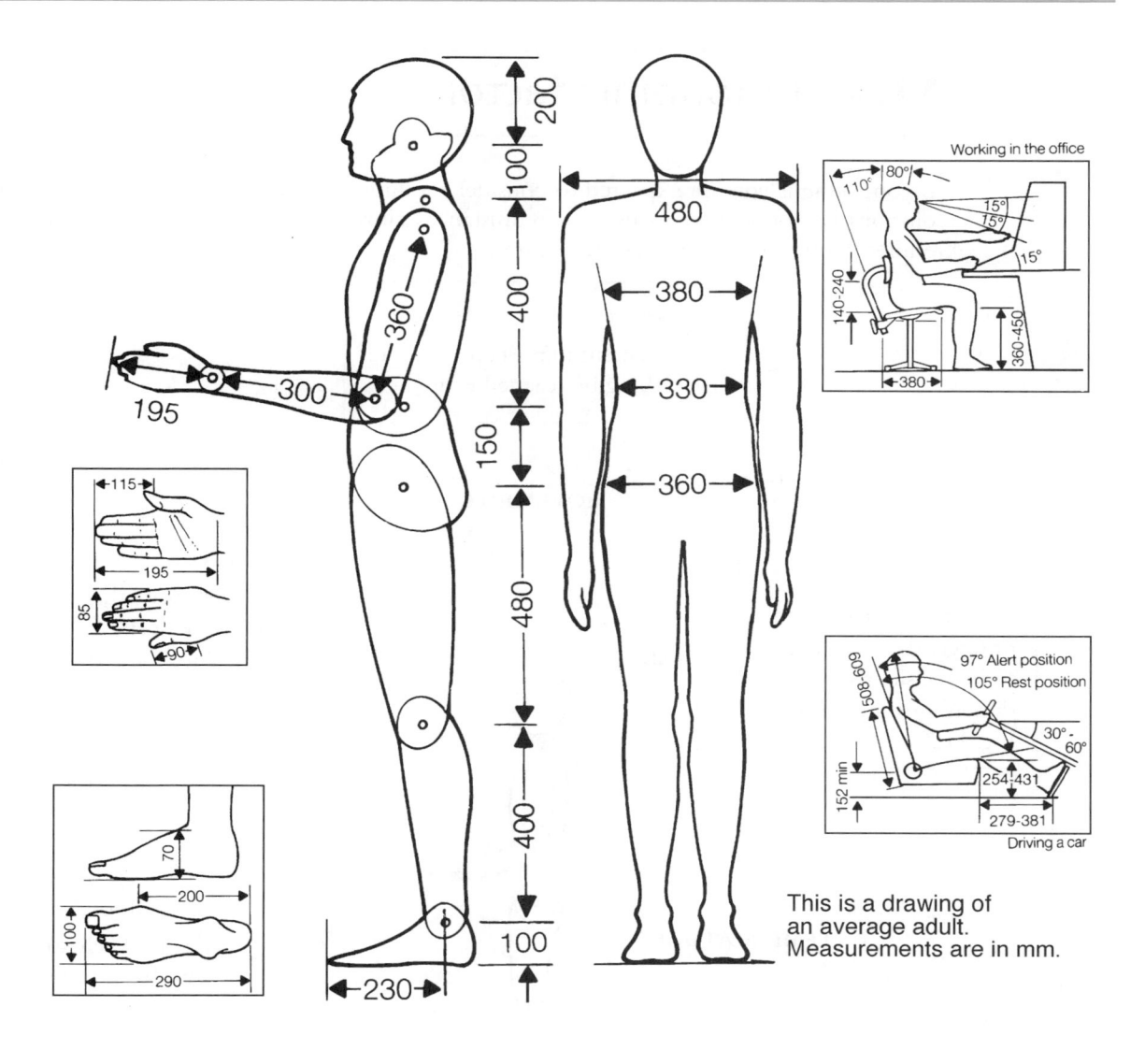

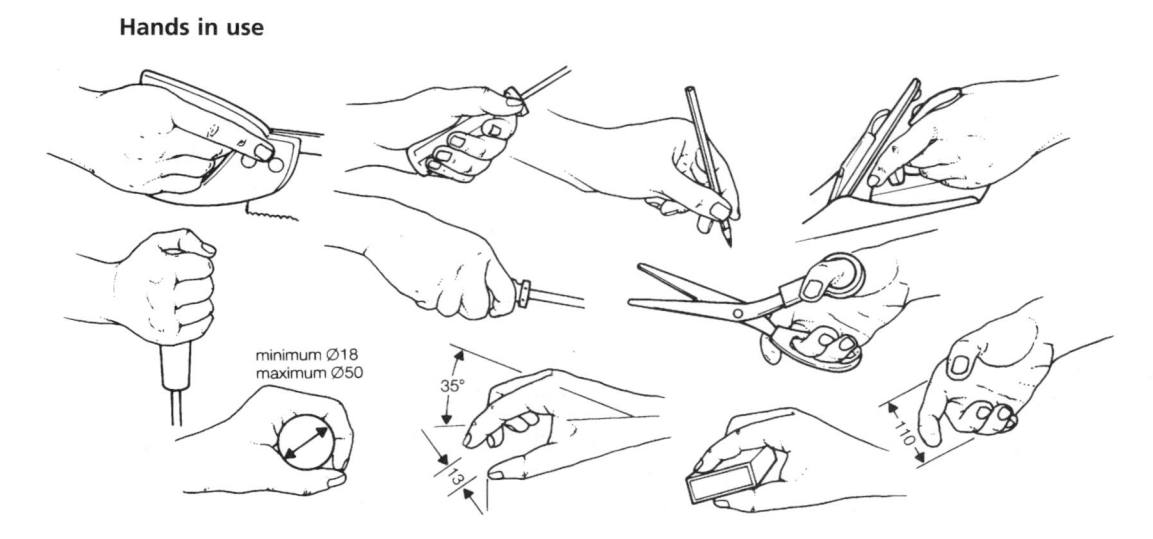

This is a drawing of an average adult. Measurements are in mm.

Working in the office

97° Alert position
105° Rest position
Driving a car

Hands in use

minimum Ø18
maximum Ø50

Fig. 11.3 Anthropometric measurements

11.4 Ergonomic factors

In your designs you are expected to consider the limits of the human body so that your solutions can be as easy to use as circumstances allow. Refer regularly to this sheet to remind yourself of the important features.

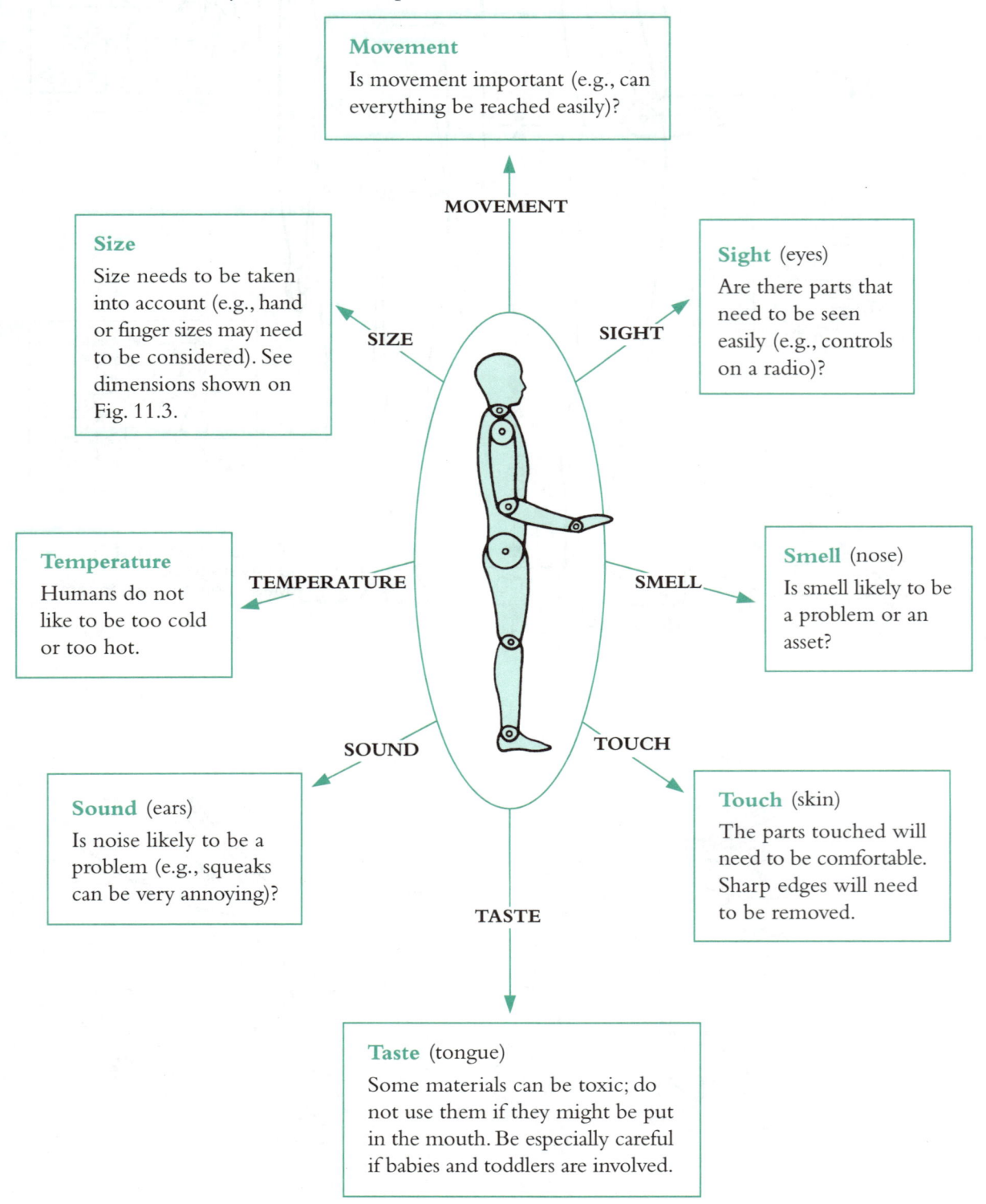

Movement
Is movement important (e.g., can everything be reached easily)?

Size
Size needs to be taken into account (e.g., hand or finger sizes may need to be considered). See dimensions shown on Fig. 11.3.

Sight (eyes)
Are there parts that need to be seen easily (e.g., controls on a radio)?

Temperature
Humans do not like to be too cold or too hot.

Smell (nose)
Is smell likely to be a problem or an asset?

Sound (ears)
Is noise likely to be a problem (e.g., squeaks can be very annoying)?

Touch (skin)
The parts touched will need to be comfortable. Sharp edges will need to be removed.

Taste (tongue)
Some materials can be toxic; do not use them if they might be put in the mouth. Be especially careful if babies and toddlers are involved.

Fig. 11.4 Ergonomic factors

11.5 Electrical and electronic symbols

These symbols are used in diagrams of electrical circuits. Although you are not expected to learn them, they will help you to understand electronics.

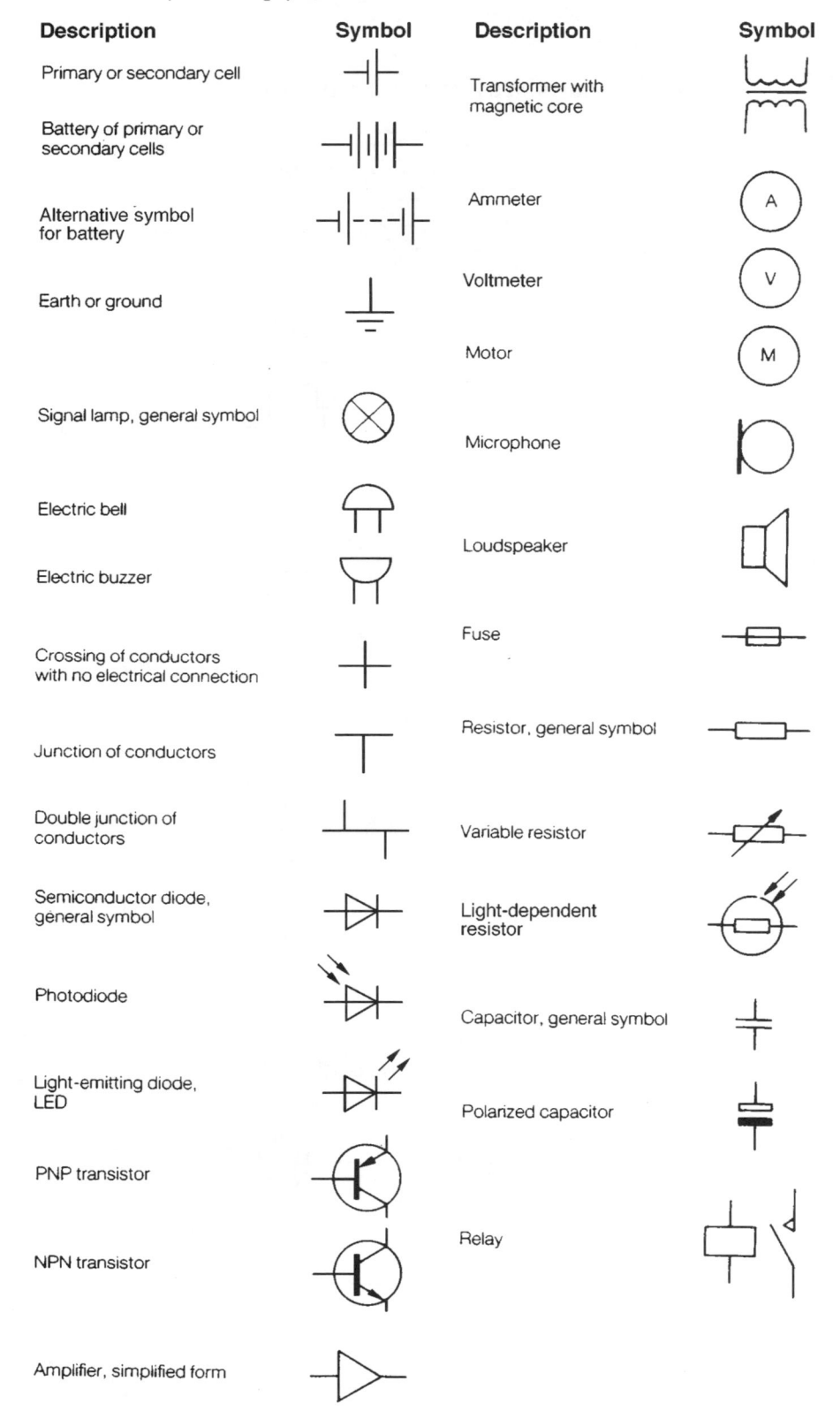

Description	Symbol	Description	Symbol
Primary or secondary cell		Transformer with magnetic core	
Battery of primary or secondary cells		Ammeter	(A)
Alternative symbol for battery		Voltmeter	(V)
Earth or ground		Motor	(M)
Signal lamp, general symbol		Microphone	
Electric bell		Loudspeaker	
Electric buzzer		Fuse	
Crossing of conductors with no electrical connection		Resistor, general symbol	
Junction of conductors		Variable resistor	
Double junction of conductors		Light-dependent resistor	
Semiconductor diode, general symbol		Capacitor, general symbol	
Photodiode		Polarized capacitor	
Light-emitting diode, LED		Relay	
PNP transistor			
NPN transistor			
Amplifier, simplified form			

Fig. 11.5 Electrical and electronic symbols

11.6 Electronic circuits

These circuits may be used within technology projects. If you are studying for GCSE Technology or Design and Technology with Electronics you will need to refer to textbooks on electronics.

Simple transistor switching circuits

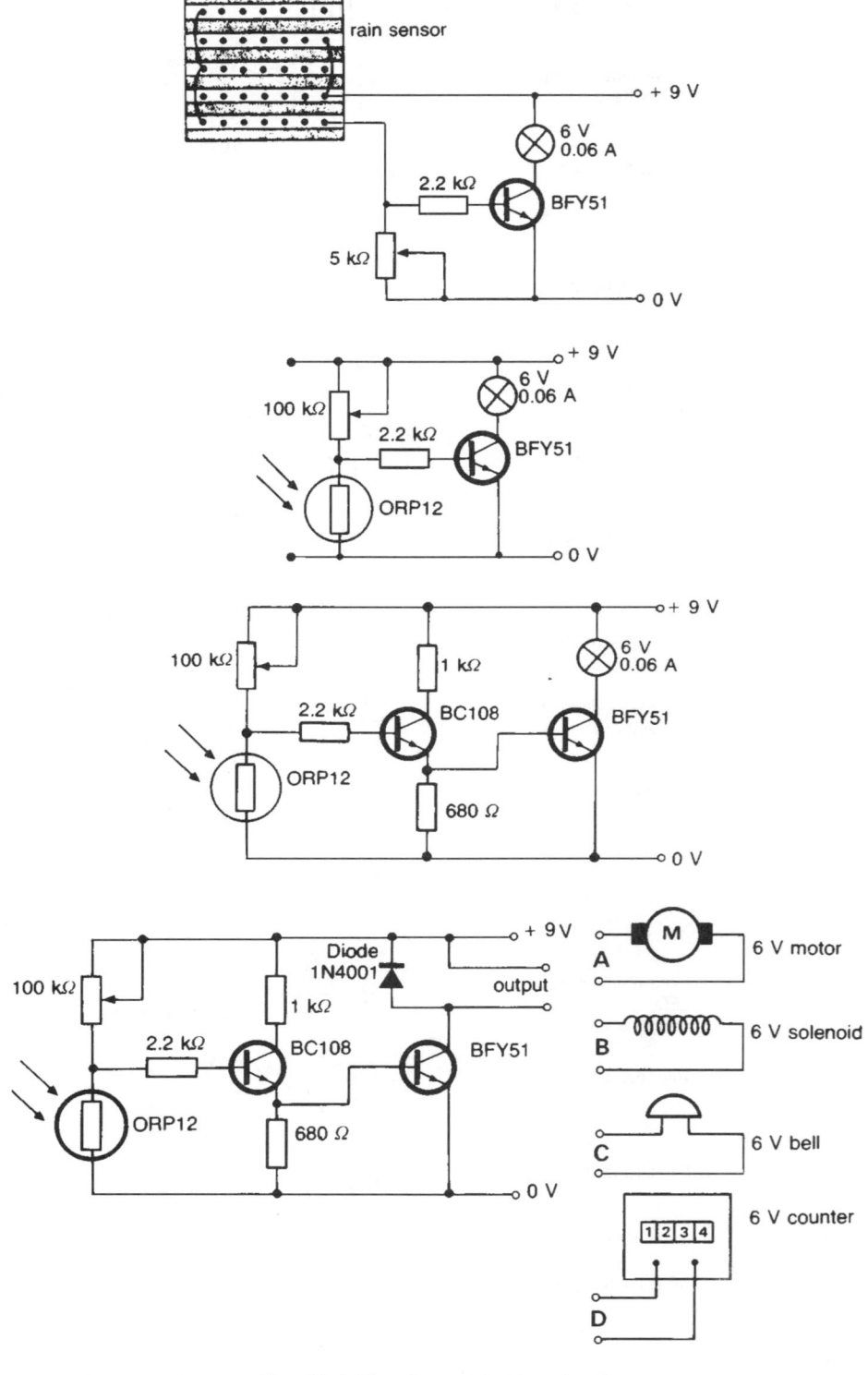

Fig. 11.6 Transistor switching circuits

11.6 Electronic circuits

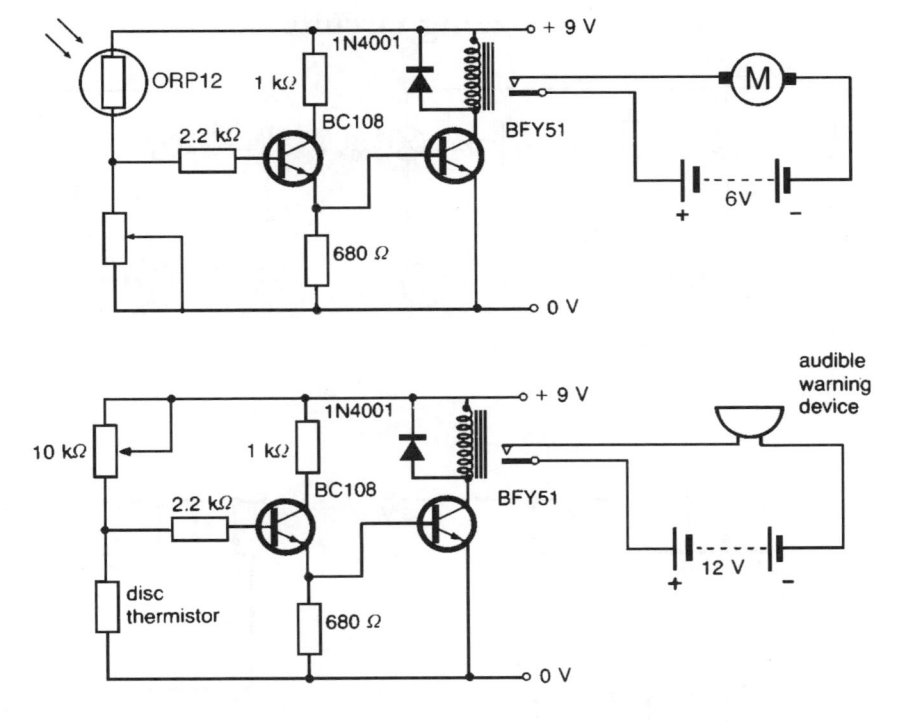

Fig. 11.6 Transistor switching circuits (continued)

Time-delay circuits

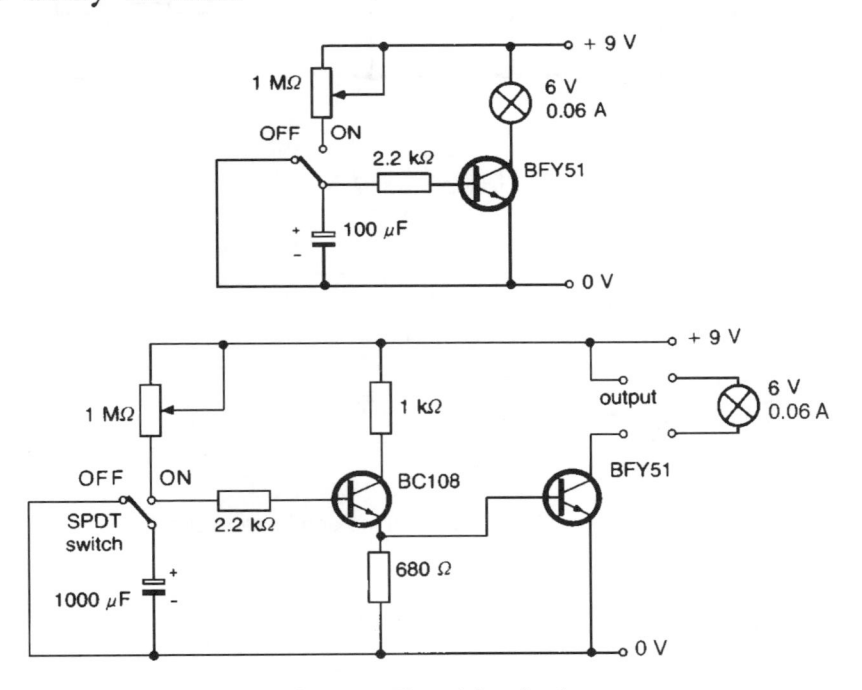

Fig. 11.7 Time-delay circuits

Data sheets

Flashing and buzzing circuits

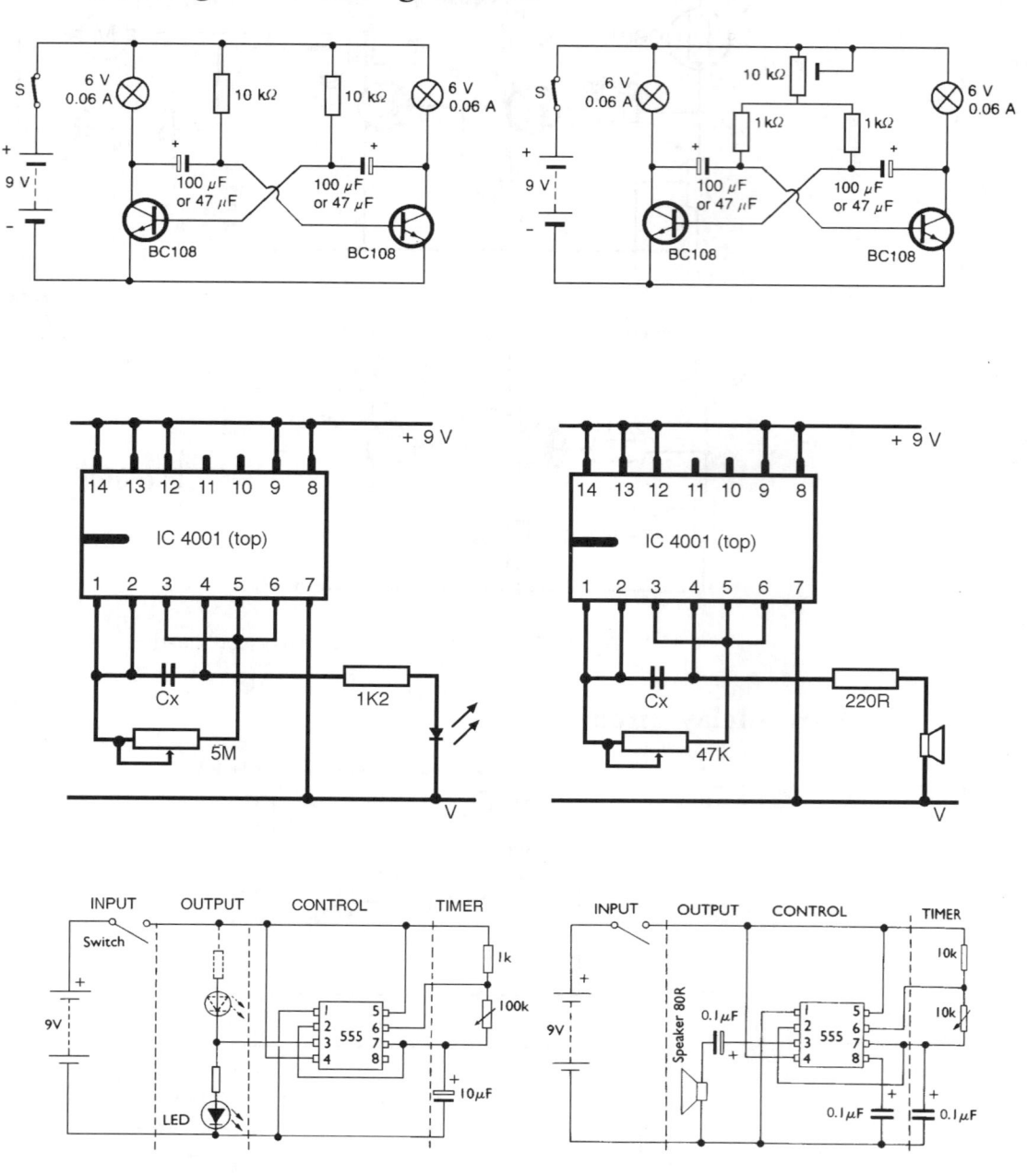

Fig. 11.8. Flashing and buzzing circuits

11.6 Electronic circuits

Circuits that use integrated circuits (ICs)

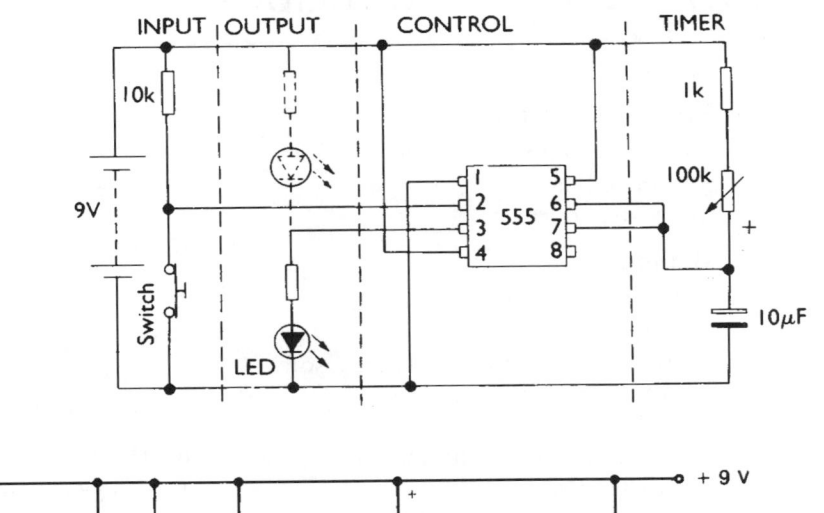

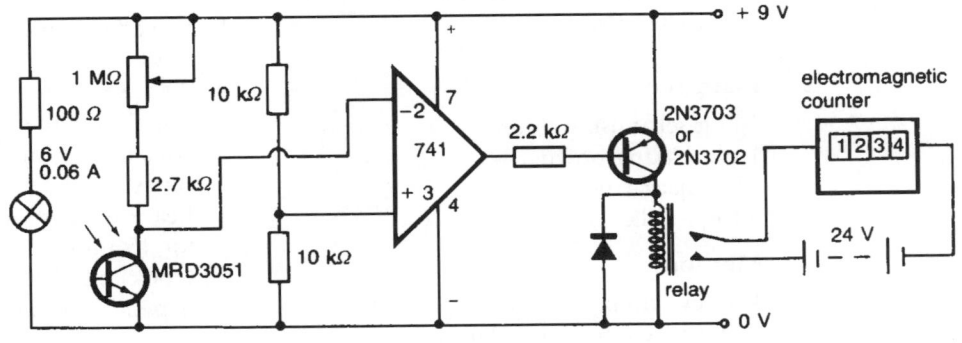

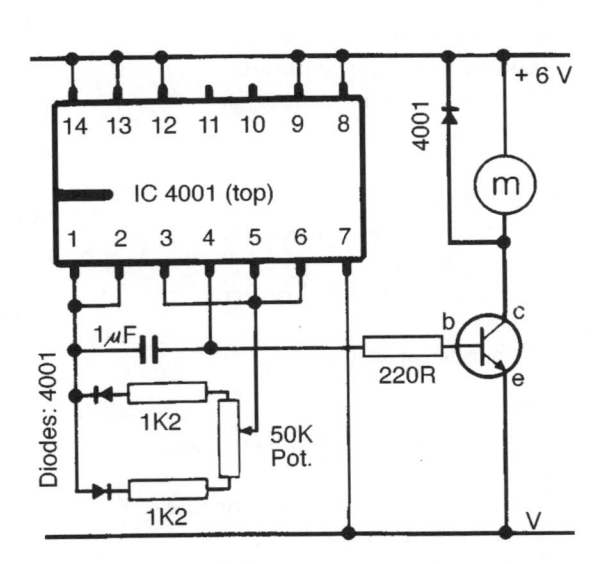

Fig. 11.9 Circuits that use ICs

11.7 Basic food recipes

1. **Shortcrust pastry**

    100 g plain flour
    50 g mixed fat
    cold water to mix

    Method
    1. Sieve flour. Cut fat into flour. Rub in.
    2. Add cold water to bind into a soft but not sticky dough.
    3. Roll to thickness required.
    4. Cook for 15 – 20 minutes at 210°C/ Gas 6.

2. **Plain scone**

    100 g self-raising flour
    1 tsp. baking powder
    25 g margarine
    3 tbsp. milk

    Method
    1. Sieve flour and baking powder. Cut fat into flour. Rub in.
    2. Add milk to bind to a soft but not wet and sticky dough.
    3. Knead gently for one minute.
    4. Roll to thickness required.
    5. Cook for 10 – 15 minutes at 220°/Gas 7.

3. **Pizza base**

    200 g brown or wholemeal flour
    7 g fast-acting yeast
    15 g polyunsaturated lard or firm margarine
    5 fl oz hand-hot water

    Method
    1. Set the oven to 220°C/Gas 7 and grease the baking tray.
    2. Place the flour, salt and yeast in a bowl and rub in the fat.
    3. Pour on the water and mix to a stiff dough. Turn out on to a floured surface and knead for 3 – 4 minutes.
    4. Place in an oiled polythene bag and leave in a warm place for 10 minutes.
    5. On a lightly floured surface, roll out the dough and use to line the prepared baking tray, making a lip around the edge.

    This recipe makes a large pizza that can be cut into squares. The pizza dough can be broken into pieces and rolled out to make four individual pizza bases.

4. **Bread dough**

    200 g plain white or wholemeal flour
    1 flat tsp salt
    $\frac{1}{2}$ sachet quick-dried yeast
    125 ml warm water

    Method
    1. Sieve flour and salt. Mix in dried yeast.
    2. Add warm water. Mix to bind dough together.
    3. Knead for 5 minutes. Roll to shape.
    4. Leave to stand in a warm place for 15 minutes.
    5. Cook at 220°C/Gas 7. Time depends on thickness.

5. **Savoury snack bar**

    50 g rice
    350 ml water
    $\frac{1}{2}$ stock cube
    2 tbsp dried vegetables
    25 g grated cheese
    $\frac{1}{2}$ tsp mixed herbs

    Method
    1. Boil the rice, water, vegetables, herbs and stock for 10 minutes. Stir regularly.
    2. When rice cooked (all water has gone) stir in cheese.
    3. Put mixture into a mould and chill.

    Coating

    $1\frac{1}{2}$ tbsp. breadcrumbs
    $1\frac{1}{2}$ tbsp. oil
    1 beaten egg

    Method
    1. Divide bar into portions.
    2. Brush with egg. Dip in breadcrumbs. Press firmly.
    3. Fry in heated oil until golden brown.

    Variations: add chilli, soy sauce or tomato puree.

6. **Basic sponge without fat**

   2 eggs
   50 g castor sugar
   50 g flour

   Method
   1. Break the eggs into a large mixing bowl and add sugar.
   2. Whisk until the mixture is stiff.
   3. Sift the flour into the mixture and fold in very gently with a metal spoon.
   4. Pour carefully into two greased and paper-lined sponge tins (18 cm diameter).
   5. Bake for 15 – 20 minutes at 180°C/Gas 4 until pale golden brown and springy to touch.

7. **Basic sponge with fat**

   100 g margarine
   100 g caster sugar
   2 beaten eggs
   100 g self-raising flour

   Method
   1. Beat the margarine and sugar in a large mixing bowl until soft and creamy.
   2. Beat in a little egg at a time. Take care that the mixture does not curdle.
   3. Stir in the flour gently until well mixed.
   4. Spoon the mixture into two greased and lined sponge tins (18 cm diameter). Spread evenly.
   5. Bake for 20 minutes, at 180°C/Gas 4 until golden brown and springy to touch.

8. **Uncooked chocolate biscuit cake**

   100 g margarine
   50 g caster sugar
   2 tbsp. golden syrup
   2 tbsp. milk
   2 tbsp. drinking chocolate
   1 tbsp. cocoa
   200 g crushed digestive biscuits
   50 g cake crumbs
   50 g glacé cherries
   50 g raisins

   Method
   1. Gently melt margarine, sugar and syrup together in a pan.
   2. Add drinking chocolate, cocoa and half the biscuits. Mix well.
   3. Add remaining ingredients. Stir well.
   4. Press into mould. Chill in refrigerator.

9. **Biscuit base**

   100 g self-raising flour
   50 g hard margarine
   50 g caster or soft brown sugar
   $\frac{1}{2}$ beaten egg

   Method
   1. Sieve flour. Stir in sugar. Cut fat into flour. Rub in.
   2. Mix in egg. Knead on a floured surface.
   3. Roll to thickness required.
   4. Arrange on greased baking tray. Cook for 15 – 20 minutes at 180°C/Gas 4.

   NB Biscuits will not feel crisp until cooled.

10. **Chocolate bars**

    50 g margarine
    200 g plain chocolate
    3 tbsp. golden syrup
    200 g crushed digestive biscuits

    Method
    1. Melt margarine, chocolate and syrup gently.
    2. Stir in biscuits. Mix well.
    3. Press into moulds and chill in refrigerator.

Chapter 12 — Guidance sheets

12.1 Undertaking research

The purpose of research is to find out information to help with your project. It is not to make your project folder thicker. Fig. 12.1 will help you find information of a variety of types.

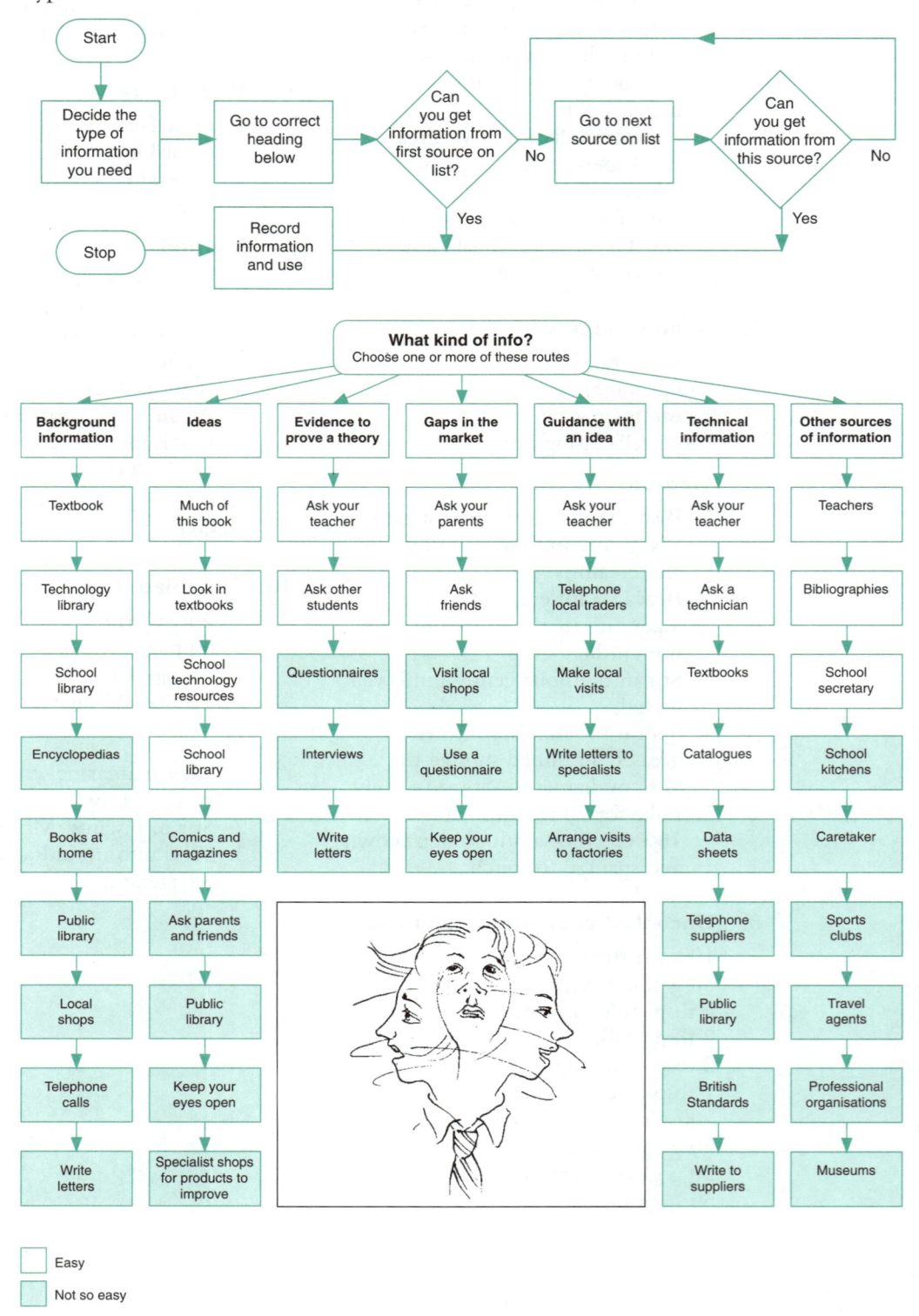

Flowchart (top):
Start → Decide the type of information you need → Go to correct heading below → Can you get information from first source on list? — Yes → Record information and use → Stop. No → Go to next source on list → Can you get information from this source? — Yes → Record information and use. No → Go to next source on list (loop).

What kind of info? Choose one or more of these routes

Background information	Ideas	Evidence to prove a theory	Gaps in the market	Guidance with an idea	Technical information	Other sources of information
Textbook	Much of this book	Ask your teacher	Ask your parents	Ask your teacher	Ask your teacher	Teachers
Technology library	Look in textbooks	Ask other students	Ask friends	Telephone local traders	Ask a technician	Bibliographies
School library	School technology resources	Questionnaires	Visit local shops	Make local visits	Textbooks	School secretary
Encyclopedias	School library	Interviews	Use a questionnaire	Write letters to specialists	Catalogues	School kitchens
Books at home	Comics and magazines	Write letters	Keep your eyes open	Arrange visits to factories	Data sheets	Caretaker
Public library	Ask parents and friends				Telephone suppliers	Sports clubs
Local shops	Public library				Public library	Travel agents
Telephone calls	Keep your eyes open				British Standards	Professional organisations
Write letters	Specialist shops for products to improve				Write to suppliers	Museums

Key: ☐ Easy ▨ Not so easy

Fig. 12.1 Routes to finding sources of information

12.2 Writing a questionnaire

Questionnaires can take some time to write and surveys can take a long time to do, but they do provide a valuable source of others peoples' opinions. Fig. 12.2 will guide you in the construction of a basic questionnaire.

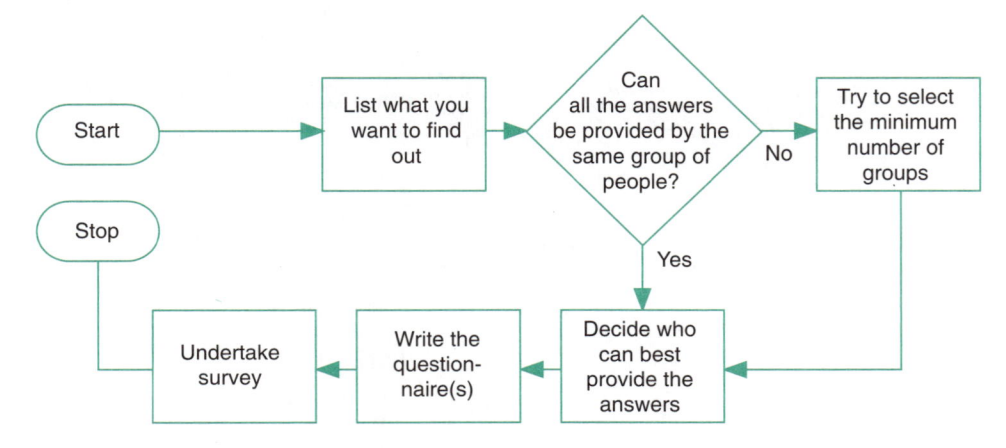

Fig. 12.2 Constructing a questionnaire

Hints

1. Decide what you want to find out.
2. Write a title for your questionnaire.
3. Decide how many people you will ask or interview.
4. Write the questions in rough and test them on others. You may need to change the questions if they don't make sense.
5. Arrange to ask easy questions first.
6. Begin with questions needing a 'yes' or 'no' answer.
7. Use multiple-choice questions where there are a number of possible answers. Include a question to find out opinions.
8. Check that your questions will tell you what you need to find out.
9. Plan the questionnaire carefully so that it is easy for both the interviewer and the interviewee.
10. Leave spaces or 'boxes' for the answers.
11. Add a space for comments.
12. Check to ensure the questionnaire isn't too long.
13. Make sure you thank the participant for his or her help.
14. Although you can write out your questionnaire by hand it is better to use a word processor.

Guidance sheets

12.3 Writing letters

Writing a letter can be a valuable way of obtaining information but you can waste a lot of time waiting for an answer. This sheet will help you decide if a letter is appropriate and help you to write one.

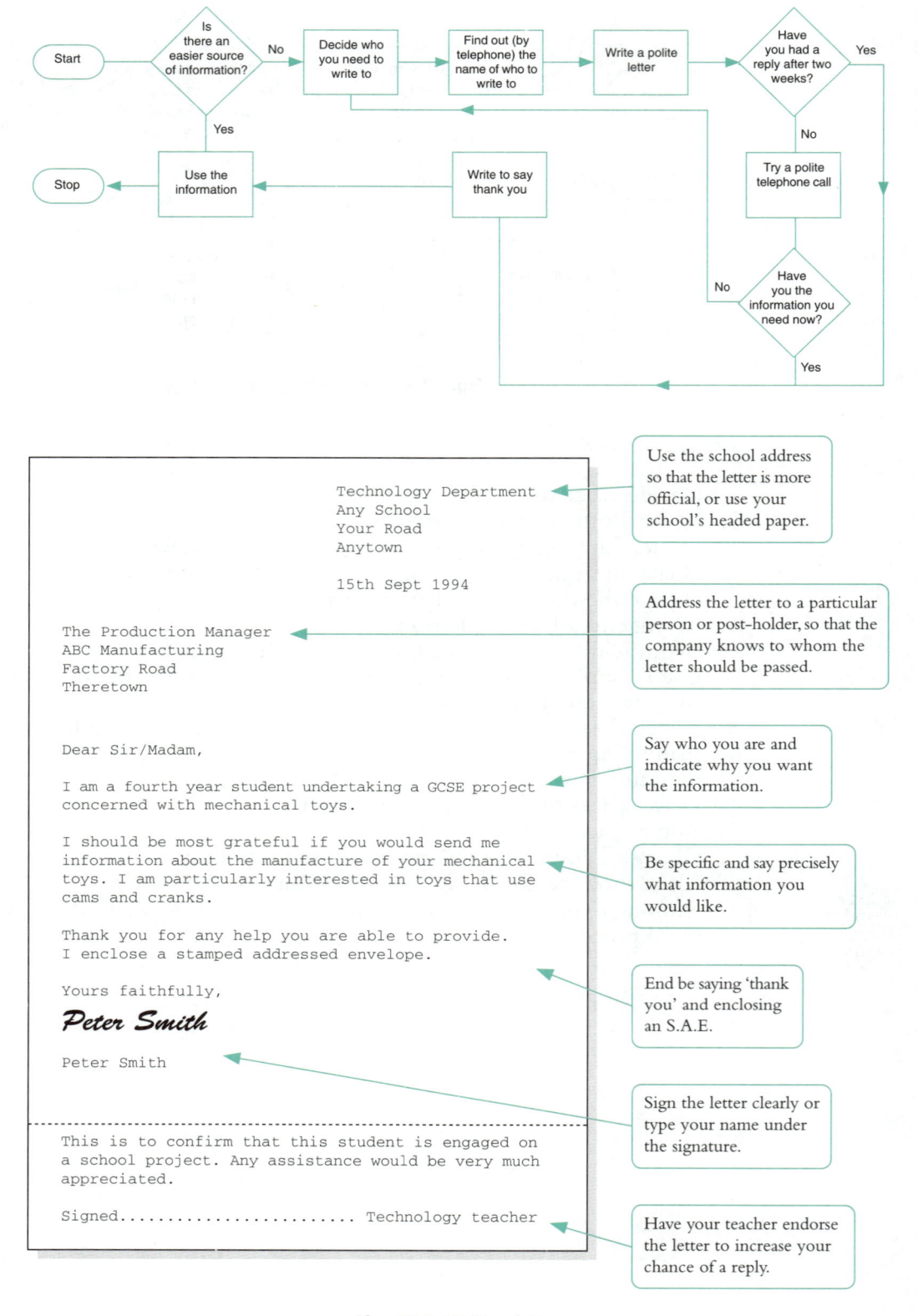

Flowchart:

Start → Is there an easier source of information?
- Yes → Use the information → Stop
- No → Decide who you need to write to → Find out (by telephone) the name of who to write to → Write a polite letter → Have you had a reply after two weeks?
  - Yes → Write to say thank you → Use the information → Stop
  - No → Try a polite telephone call → Have you the information you need now?
    - Yes → Write to say thank you
    - No → (loop back to Write a polite letter)

Sample letter:

```
                              Technology Department
                              Any School
                              Your Road
                              Anytown

                              15th Sept 1994

The Production Manager
ABC Manufacturing
Factory Road
Theretown


Dear Sir/Madam,

I am a fourth year student undertaking a GCSE project
concerned with mechanical toys.

I should be most grateful if you would send me
information about the manufacture of your mechanical
toys. I am particularly interested in toys that use
cams and cranks.

Thank you for any help you are able to provide.
I enclose a stamped addressed envelope.

Yours faithfully,

Peter Smith

Peter Smith
------------------------------------------------------
This is to confirm that this student is engaged on
a school project. Any assistance would be very much
appreciated.

Signed....................... Technology teacher
```

Annotations:
- Use the school address so that the letter is more official, or use your school's headed paper.
- Address the letter to a particular person or post-holder, so that the company knows to whom the letter should be passed.
- Say who you are and indicate why you want the information.
- Be specific and say precisely what information you would like.
- End be saying 'thank you' and enclosing an S.A.E.
- Sign the letter clearly or type your name under the signature.
- Have your teacher endorse the letter to increase your chance of a reply.

Fig. 12.4 Writing letters

Hints

1. Make sure the letter is polite.
2. Check your spelling.
3. Be careful with handwriting or use a word processor.

12.4 Producing working drawings

The purpose of a working drawing is to give you or others something from which your project can be made.

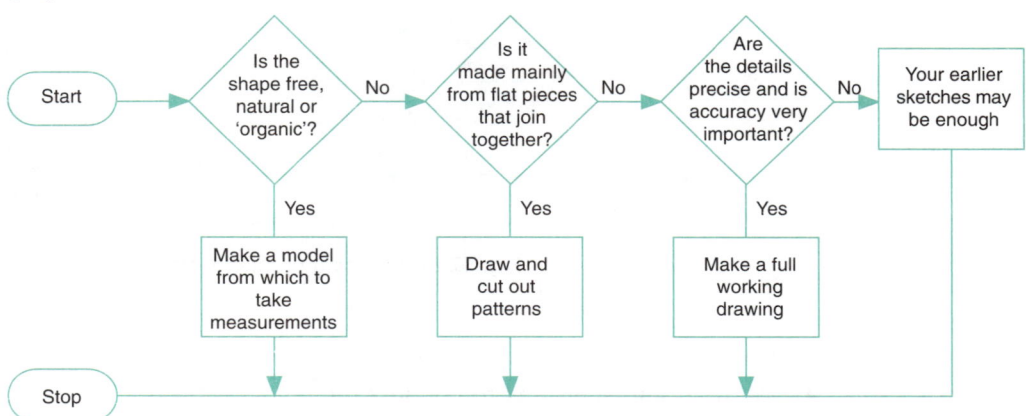

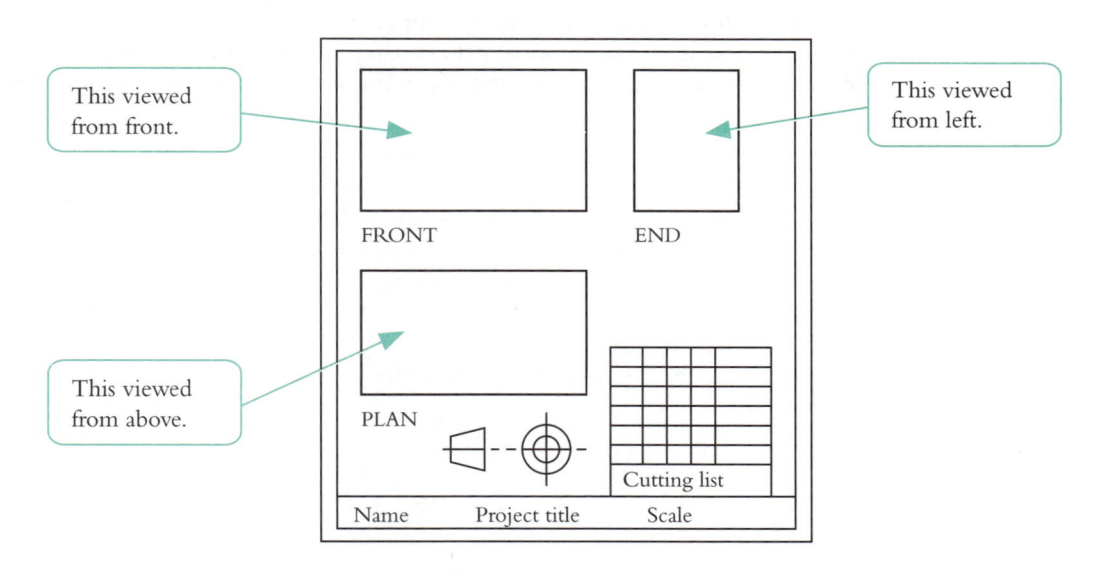

Fig. 12.5 Producing working drawings

Hints

1. Can someone else make your design from your drawings?
2. Have you included all dimensions?
3. Are all details of materials shown?
4. It is clear how all parts are fixed together?
5. Have you included a requirements list?
6. For some projects a traditional drawing is not appropriate. Freehand sketches or models may be more suitable.

12.5 Designing product tests

It is a requirement of the National Curriculum that you test your products and those of others. Testing your design is a way of finding out how good it is and if your ideas work.

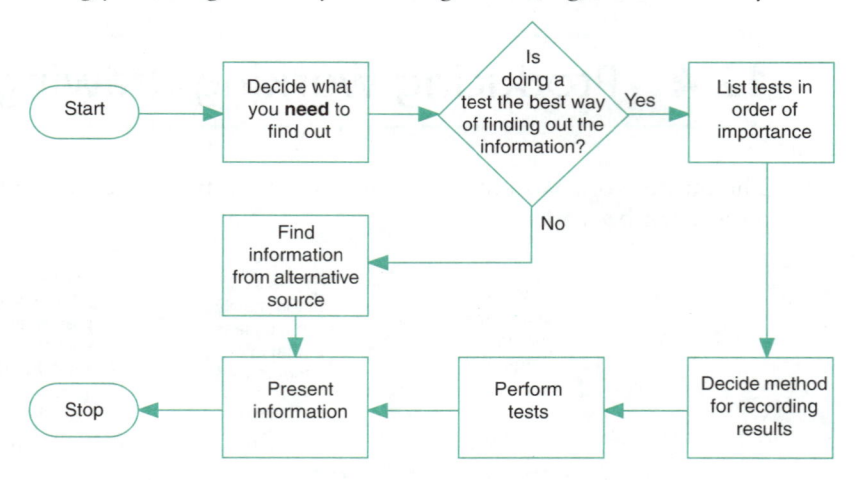

Fig. 12.6 Designing product tests

When planning a test try to ensure that:
- you have sufficient time to conduct the test;
- you are sure the test will answer the questions above;
- you are able to record your answers carefully and accurately;
- you perform each test more than once and take an average of the results;
- when asking the opinion of others, they give honest answers;
- you record your findings carefully and communicate them in an appropriate way.

Hints

When designing a test you should ask the following questions.
1. Does the design meet the brief and the specification?
2. Does it work? How well does it work?
3. Is it safe to use?
4. Is it attractive to look at?
5. Is it likely to be a commercial product?

Chapter 13 — Checklists

The following sheets provide valuable checklists to which you should refer at the appropriate stages of your coursework.

13.1 Specification checklist

Use this sheet to check that your haven't missed anything.

This checklist will ensure that you miss none of the important points.

Use this column to add your own explanations, comments, etc.

Tick this column when you are happy with everything.

	Comments	Done ✓
Does your specification state clearly what you intend your project to do?		
Have you stated relevant maximum and minimum sizes?		
Have you stated exactly what your project must contain?		
Are there any specific environmental considerations?		
Have you considered if the appearance is important?		
Do any specific safety requirements or regulations affect your project?		
Do you have a budget to work to?		
Have you considered how much time is available?		
Are there any restrictions on the use of materials or other resources?		
Are there any specific legal requirements with which your must comply?		

13.2 Costings checklist

Use this sheet when working out the cost of each project.

This checklist will ensure that you miss none of the important points.

Use this column to add your own explanations, comments, etc.

Tick this column when you are happy with everything.

	Comments	Done ✓
Have you considered the cost of all the materials?		
Have you included the cost of all wasted materials?		
Have you included any postage or packaging charges?		
Have you included any minimum order charges?		
Have you included the cost of trimmings, finishes and fittings?		
Have you included a figure to cover additional costs, such as glasspaper, needles, spices, etc?		
Have you included overheads, such as gas or electricity?		
Have you considered any VAT that you may need to pay?		
Will you be trying to make a profit?		

13.3 Problems checklist

Check these items before making your project.

This checklist will ensure that you miss none of the important points.

Use this column to add your own explanations, comments, etc.

Tick this column when you are happy with everything.

	Comments	Done ✓
Will all the materials you have selected be available?		
Will there be any difficulty putting the parts together?		
Have you worked out all the details either on paper or with the aid of a model?		
Have you had your proposal checked by someone else to make sure everything you are planning is possible?		
Have you planned everything in a logical sequence?		
Have you made some allowance for the things that may go wrong?		
Do you have the necessary skills to execute your proposal?		
If you need help, have you decided where you will go to get it?		
Does your idea satisfy the specification?		

13.4 Details checklist

Use this sheet when trying to develop and improve your ideas.

This checklist will ensure that you miss none of the important points.

Use this column to add your own explanations, comments, etc.

Tick this column when you are happy with everything.

	Comments	Done ✓
Can anything be done in a simpler way?		
Can anything be done with less materials?		
Can anything be done with cheaper materials?		
Do all the materials you have specified have the correct properties for their tasks?		
Have you specified the exact materials you want to use?		
Are all the materials you want to use readily available?		
Have you shown how the parts of your idea will be fixed together?		
Will you final idea be safe?		
Have you checked the opinion of others?		
Does your idea satisfy the specification?		

13.5 Planning checklist

Use this sheet to check that your planning has been done.

> This checklist will ensure that you miss none of the important points.

> Use this column to add your own explanations, comments, etc.

> Tick this column when you are happy with everything.

	Comments	Done ✓
Are the processes listed in a logical order?		
Have you consulted others on how long each task will take?		
Have you written a planning schedule, slip chart or created some kind of project diary?		
Are you thinking well ahead?		
Have you shown possible alternative tasks?		
Have you planned to make the best use of your time?		
Will you be able to keep an accurate record of all you do?		
Have you planned to order materials well in advance of when they will be needed?		
Have you checked if there may be times when you will not be allowed to use the school facilities?		

Checklists

13.6 Evaluation checklist

Use this sheet to check that you have done everything.

This checklist will ensure that you miss none of the important points.

Use this column to add your own explanations, comments, etc.

Tick this column when you are happy with everything.

	Comments	Done ✓
Throughout the project have you compared your ideas with the specification?		
Throughout the project have you recorded any observations?		
Did you do any testing during the project?		
Have you described any tests you did and have you shown the results of these tests?		
Have you tested the finished project?		
Have you compared the finished project with the original specification?		
Have you consulted others about your finished project?		
Have you carefully recorded all your findings?		
Have you made suggestions for improvements?		
Have you made sketches of any ideas for further improvement?		

13.7 Pre-assessment checklist

Use this sheet before submitting your work for assessment.

This checklist will ensure that you miss none of the important points.

Use this column to add your own explanations, comments, etc.

Tick this column when you are happy with everything.

	Comments	Done ✓
Have you checked that you are submitting what the examination group wants?		
Have you compared your work with the AT descriptions and made improvements?		
Are you sure you have submitted your best work?		
Have you arranged your work in a logical order?		
Are your design folders held together securely?		
Is your work suitably labelled so that the examiner can easily understand what you have done?		
Have you exhibited your work in a tidy well-organised way?		
Will the examiner get an immediate good impression? Try asking others.		
Is your work labelled with your name and candidate number?		
Are you prepared to talk about your work?		

Glossary

A

Absorbent The ability to absorb water.

Acid rain Industrial waste gases, such as sulphur dioxide, are absorbed into the atmosphere and then fall in the rain, damaging wildlife, countryside and buildings.

Acrylic A plastics material, commercially known as Perspex. Sometimes referred to as PMMA.

Adhesives Another word for glues. Used to bond materials together.

Advertising A way of communicating to the market. Used to promote a product or communicate product information.

Aerate To incorporate air into a mixture.

Alloying Fusing together a metal, usually with another metal or metals, to produce a material with different properties.

Ampere Unit of electrical current, often abbreviated to amp.

Analysis A breakdown into smaller parts. Often associated with the early stages of the design process.

Anneal To soften a material such as steel, copper or aluminium by heating and then allowing to cool.

Anodising Using an electrolytic process to produce a surface of oxide film on aluminium.

Anthropometrics Literally the 'measurements of man'. A knowledge of these is essential when designing objects for people to use.

Artefact An object designed and made by people.

Au gratin A food with a browned surface, usually obtained by covering with sauce, which may contain cheese, sprinkling with bread crumbs and then grilling.

B

Bake blind To bake a pastry case without a filling. The pastry is usually weighted down with foil or greaseproof paper, and baking beans.

Barbecue To cook food in the open on a spit or grill over charcoal.

Baste To spoon fat and juices from the roasting tin over a joint of meat while it is being cooked.

Batch production The production of a number of identical products in limited numbers.

BDMS Bright Drawn Mild Steel.

Bearings Objects designed to reduce friction between moving parts.

Bechamel A basic white sauce.

Bias A line across the grain of a fabric.

Binca A cotton fabric with even holes. Used for embroidery.

Bind To thicken a sauce or soup with eggs and cream. To combine ingredients, such as rissoles or burgers.

Blanch To scald with boiling water or bring to the boil and drain immediately.

Blend To combine starch, e.g., cornflour, with a little water or stock to make a smooth paste before adding to the rest of a mixture.

Blender Often called a liquidiser. A vessel with sharp blades, inside which ingredients can be puréed or blended.

Bondaweb An iron-on interfacing.

Bonne femme A dish cooked with a garnish of fresh vegetables or herbs.

Bouquet garni A mixture of fresh herbs tied up in muslin and added to the cooking of stews and soups.

Brainstorming A rapid method of developing ideas. Everyone suggests ideas, which are written down and discussed at the end of the brainstorming session.

Break-even point The point where the amount of money a company receives from the sale of a product is equal to the cost of production.

Brief A set of instructions describing what you have to do or what you are intending to design.

Brine A solution of salt in water.

BSI British Standards Institution. Organisation responsible for codes of practice, such as drawing standards PP 7308.

Buffet A table on which a selection of hot or cold dishes are set for people to help themselves.

C

CAD Computer-Aided Design.

Calico A plain weave cotton fabric. It can be used bleached or unbleached.

CAM Computer-Aided Manufacturing.

Case hardening Mild steel can have its surface hardened by 'soaking' red hot steel in a carbon-rich powder. It is reheated and then quenched in cold water.

Casserole Ovenproof dish with a lid.

Ceramic Made from clay and fused at high temperature in a kiln.

CFC Chloro-fluoro-carbons are chemicals associated with aerosol sprays. CFCs are thought to contribute to breaking down the protective ozone layer in the atmosphere.

Clarify To make clear, e.g., by straining through muslin.

CNC Computer Numerical Control.

Component An individual part, of which many may combine to make a complete object.

Concrete Sand, gravel and cement mixed dry and then water added. A chemical reaction causes it to set hard. Very good compression strength.

Conservation To save from destruction. Various organisations, such as Greenpeace and the Worldwide Fund for Nature, are dedicated to environmental conservation.

Constraints Limits that affect design, such as money, time and skill.

Glossary

Construction An arrangement of parts or components.

Consumer (customer) A person who buys a product or uses a service.

Corrosion Usually associated with the 'rotting' of metals due to the action of the air.

Cotton gaberdine A twill weave cotton fabric.

Counterbalance A weight used to compensate for the weight of a load, e.g., a crane is prevented from toppling over by the use of a heavy weight that balances the load.

Coursework That part of your technology course, consisting mostly of design-and-make projects, that is assessed by your teacher and may be moderated by an external assessor.

Cream To beat fat and air together in order to incorporate air as a raising agent.

Creole A dish with a rice, pepper and tomato garnish.

Croutons Cubes or triangles of fried bread used as a garnish for soups.

Customer See Consumer.

D

Data Facts and figures.

Database A collection of information or data, usually stored on a computer.

Degassing Removing trapped gas from molten metal immediately before it is poured into a mould.

Demand The number of products required by people over a period of time.

Denim A strong, twill weave cotton fabric with a white warp and a coloured weft.

Design An activity that uses a wide range of experiences, knowledge and skills to find the best solution to a problem, within certain constraints. It is more than just problem solving: design involves the whole process of producing a solution from conception of an idea to production.

Design brief A simple statement to explain your intentions.

Design Council Formed in 1972, it offers an advisory and information service to designers and manufacturers. Products judged to be 'good' design are displayed in London, Cardiff, Glasgow and Belfast.

Design proposal The idea for a design, arising from a need or an opportunity.

Design specification A list of targets that a designer tries to achieve.

Dice Small cubes of vegetable or meat.

Direct marketing Making direct contact with a customer, such as by mail order.

Dough Uncooked bread or pastry mixture. Should be smooth and soft but not sticky.

Draft When making a pattern for sand casting or vacuum forming it is essential that there is a taper or 'draft' so that the pattern can be removed.

Ductile Property of a material in which it can be stretched without easily breaking.

Dynamic force A moving force.

E

Economies of scale As more products are made the cost of one (unit cost) reduces. It is often cheaper to produce large numbers of an item than to produce a few.

Efficiency Working with the minimum of lost effort. Machines can be made efficient by the use of smooth bearings and lubrication.

Emulsion A mixture of fat and liquid, which is prevented from separating by the addition of another ingredient, such as lecithin in egg yolk.

Environment Our surroundings or the surroundings of others.

Ergonomics The study of finding ways to help humans work more efficiently.

Evaluation Making judgements about the suitability of a design and the way it is produced. Such judgements can be made during the design stages and at the conclusion of the project.

Examination group Two or more of the former GCE or CSE examination boards combined together to administer GCSE examinations. There are six such groups.

Exploded views Three-dimensional drawings in which the individual components are shown separately.

F

Fabric A material made from textile yarns.

Face marks Accurate and true surfaces from which measurements are taken are marked with 'face side' and 'face edge' marks.

Felt A non-woven fabric having no warp or weft, but produced using heat, moisture and pressure.

Fibonacci series A series of numbers in which each number is found by adding the two previous ones, e.g., 1, 1, 2, 3, 5, 8, 13, 21, etc.

Fibreglass The common term used for GRP (Glass-Reinforced Polyester).

Finish The treatment of the surface of a material.

Fixed costs The costs a company has to pay, for example, rent, fuel and wages. Fixed costs are not linked to the number of products made.

Flow chart a way of showing the stages of doing something.

Food processor A machine used for chopping, mixing and blending.

Former A shaped block around which a material, acrylic for example, is bent or formed.

Function What you expect your design solution to do. The function may be practical or it may be aesthetic (concerned only with appearance).

Fuse An electrical item that 'blows' to protect an electrical circuit from becoming overloaded.

Glossary

G

Garnish A coloured edible decoration to a savoury dish.

Generic A name meaning members of the same group or family, e.g., metal is the generic name for steel, copper and aluminium.

Glacé A type of icing made by dipping fruit into boiled syrup.

Glaze A thin coating of egg or milk brushed onto pastry prior to baking. Used to give a good colour or shine.

Gluten An elastic protein substance produced in bread dough by the effect of kneading the flour. Gluten gives bread a springy texture.

Golden mean Proportions based on successive numbers in the Fibonacci series. Such proportions are generally regarded as attractive, e.g., a rectangle of 5 × 8 or 13 × 21.

Grain The direction of cells in timber, crystals in metals and threads in a fabric.

Green design Products and services that are designed to cause least harm to the environment.

Gross profit The amount of money remaining when total purchases are subtracted from total sales.

H

Hardening and tempering The process of heating carbon steel to red heat and cooling quickly in oil is called hardening. Brittleness is removed by further gentle heating and cooling in water.

Hessian A strong, plain weave open fabric of jute or cotton used for sacking, oilcloths and tarpaulins.

Hors d'oeuvres Small items of food, usually cold, served to stimulate the appetite before a meal.

I

Injection moulding Injecting a molten material under pressure into a mould known as a die.

Insulation The prevention of the passage of heat from one area to another.

Interfacing A material used between the facing and the main body of a garment, such as in a lapel. It is used to give stiffness and line.

Isometric A method of drawing in three dimensions. Horizontal lines are drawn at 30° to the horizontal and vertical lines remain vertical.

J

Jacquard A decorative weave used for silk and cotton.

Jersey A knitted fabric made from wool, cotton, silk or artificial fibres.

Joining The fastening together of two or more parts.

Joule The unit in which energy is usually measured. It has replace the calorie.

Jute A strong brown fibre used in cord, carpet, canvas and hessian.

K

Kilo– One thousand. Used in front of other words, e.g., one kilometre is one thousand metres.

Knead To thoroughly mix dough and evenly distribute the yeast. It can be done by hand or by using a mixer.

L

Laminating Making something by building up thin layers, such as GRP or 'bent' timber, as used in some school furniture.

Liason A binding or thickening agent, e.g., cornflour or cream, for sauces or stews.

Limited company A company owned by shareholders and identified by either 'Ltd' or 'PLC' after its name.

Logo (logogram) A symbol used to identify a person, company or organisation.

M

Malleable Property of a material to be easily distorted under pressure without breaking. Malleability often improves with heating.

Marinade To cover raw meat or fish with a liquid containing wine, oil, vinegar, vegetables, herbs and spices, etc., for several hours prior to cooking. The purpose is to tenderise the meat or fish.

Marketing The process by which a product is 'sold' to the public. It includes such areas as market research and advertising.

Market research Investigating needs and requirements, often by means of questionnaires.

Market segment A market can be divided into different groups, or segments, by age, gender, religion, income, etc. This makes it possible to identify a group of people for whom you can develop a product.

Mass production Term used to describe the process of manufacturing a product in very large numbers.

MEG Midland Examining Group.

Mitre An angle of 45°. Picture frames commonly have their corners mitred.

Mocha Coffee flavouring.

Mull A lightweight or plain open cotton fabric.

Multimeter Device used to test electrical circuits. It usually measures voltage, current and resistance.

Muslin A plain weave cotton fabric, which can be coarse or fine, bleached or unbleached.

N

Nap A raised pile on a fabric.

National criteria A set of rules laid down for all GCSE subjects.

NEAB Northern Examinations and Assessment Board.

Needs The essentials of life, e.g., water, shelter and warmth.

Net profit The amount of money left over after subtracting overheads from the gross profit.

O

Oblique At an angle. Oblique projection is a form of drawing where the front view is drawn parallel to the vertical plane and the top and sides are drawn at 45° to the horizontal plane.

Orthographic projection A type of drawing often consisting of three views, drawn to scale, each taken at 90° to the others.

Overheads The costs of making a product, which are not part of making the product itself, including wages, electricity and rent.

Oxidation The surface of a material may react with oxygen in the atmosphere to oxidise, e.g., rusting of ferrous metals. Oxides on metal can make soldering and brazing difficult.

Ozone layer A condensed form of oxygen (O_3) forming a layer above the surface of the Earth and protecting us from harmful ultraviolet rays.

P

PAR Planed All Round (refers to timber).

Par boil To boil until partly cooked.

Partnership A company owned by between two and twenty people, but not financed by shareholders.

Perspective The appearance that objects have in which they look smaller when they are further away.

Petits fours Small fancy pastries, cakes and biscuits.

Plastic memory The ability of some materials to return to their original moulded shape after reheating.

Polyester An artificial fabric often use to imitate silk. Also available as a resin for producing GRP.

Polymer Long-chain molecules. The main structure of plastics.

Potential difference Often referred to as voltage. The 'pressure' that pushes electrical current around a circuit.

Preservative Chemical with which other materials are treated to prevent them from reacting with the atmosphere. Preservatives are also used in food to prevent deterioration.

Primary research Original research, that done by you, such as discussion, interview, survey or experiment.

Profit The difference between the selling price and the total cost of a product.

Project A design task, usually in the form of a design-and-make activity, beginning with a need.

Promotion A process used to increase consumer awareness of a product.

Proportion The relationship of one part to another. Sizes are often said to be 'in proportion' when they appeal to one's visual sense of balance.

Prototype A trial version of a product.

Purée Cooked fruit or vegetables either sieved or mixed in a blender to produce a thick, smooth consistency.

Q

Questionnaire A series of carefully designed questions forming part of a survey.

R

Ramekin A small straight-sided ovenproof dish used for individual portions of savoury dishes.

Ratatouille A dish of tomatoes, courgettes and aubergines cooked to a soft consistency in oil.

Reduce To evaporate water from a liquid and hence reduce its volume.

Research The gathering of information to assist in the production of a solution to a need.

Resistance The ability to prevent the flow of electrical current.

Resources The equipment, materials, skills and surroundings you have available to you.

Retail The selling of products, usually in a shop.

Revenue The money received from the sale of goods or services.

Roux A sauce made by cooking equal quantities of fat and flour together, then adding a liquid (usually milk), and heating until thickened.

S

Sample A group of people selected for a survey, who represent the views of many others. Also used to mean a typical example.

Sauté To toss food in a small amount of fat, over a low heat, until the fat is absorbed.

Scale Drawing to scale means drawing so that all parts are in the same proportion, i.e., if the width is one-half real size, then other dimensions must be one-half real size also.

Seam allowance The amount of material that extends beyond the fitting line.

Seasoning Careful drying of 'green' timber to make it usable in the manufacture of, say, furniture. Also used to mean the adding of salt and pepper to foodstuffs.

Secondary data Information collected by secondary research.

Secondary research Research done by other people, e.g., in books, magazines, etc.

SEG Southern Examining Group.

Shake A natural split in timber often caused by fast seasoning.

Glossary

Shareholders People who own shares in a company and, as such, are the owners. Shares are sold by a company to raise finance.

Shortening Any fat used to make cakes, pastries or biscuits.

Silver solder Solder that melts at a higher temperature than soft (tin/lead) solder. It is an alloy of silver, copper, zinc and cadmium.

Silver steel Precision ground carbon steel. (It does not contain silver.)

Simmer To maintain a pan of liquid at a slow boil with the bubbles just breaking the surface.

Soft solder A group of low-temperature solders made from tin and lead.

Solenoid A device in which an iron core is pulled into a coil of wire, which causes an electrical current to flow in the coil.

Solution A way of satisfying a need or providing an answer to a problem.

Souflée dish A straight-sided ovenproof dish.

Specification A set of targets to be achieved by a design solution.

Spider diagram A quick way of presenting ideas from a brainstorming session. Sometimes called a bubble diagram.

Supply The number of goods available at any one time.

Survey A way of finding out things by asking questions.

Stable Not easily moved, changed or destroyed.

Starch Edible insoluble material found in cereals and many vegetables, e.g., potatoes, sweet corn, beans and peas.

Starch resist paste A mixture of flour and water, used for batik.

Stock A well flavoured liquid used in soups and stews. It is made by simmering meat bones and vegetables in a large pan of water. You may also use prepared stock cubes.

Structure An arrangement of parts designed to withstand a load.

Swarf The waste material associated with drilling, milling and turning on the lathe.

Synthesis The bringing together of the various parts of a project.

System A set of connected parts organised to perform a function or functions.

T

Tasting panel A group of people who taste different foodstuffs and decide which they prefer.

Technology The application of knowledge and understanding to satisfy the needs of society. An active process employing analysis and synthesis.

Thermo-forming Material that becomes soft at high temperature and can then be shaped, e.g., by vacuum forming.

Toggle mechanism A mechanism often used in holding devices, such as a 'mole' wrench and the clamps on vacuum forming machines. It has a quick locking and release action. An umbrella is locked in position by a toggle mechanism.

Toile A dressmaker's muslin copy of a design, before making up the garment in the real fabric.

Total cost The sum of fixed costs and variable costs.

Tricot A knitted fabric with vertical lines.

U

Unique selling point An unusual or unique feature of a product or service, which makes that product or service different from others of a similar nature.

Unit cost The cost of producing an individual product. It is calculated by dividing the total overall cost of making the product by the number of products made.

V

Vacuum forming A process in which a heat-softened thermoplastic material is formed over a shaped former by the application of a vacuum.

Variable costs Costs, such as the cost of materials, that vary according to the number of products made.

Velcro A nylon tape with two interlocking surfaces, used for easy fastening. Can be used with looped nylon for mounting display materials on notice boards.

Vilene A form of stiffening material used for collars and cuffs, etc.

Vinaigrette A salad dressing made with oil, vinegar and spices.

W

Warp The threads arranged up and down a fabric.

Weave A method of fabric construction that uses only two threads.

Weft The threads going across a fabric.

Weld Joining components by allowing the parts to become melted together. This can be achieved by heating or, in the case of some plastics, by the use of chemicals.

Whip To beat or whisk cream until it has a thick consistency.

Wholesale The buying and selling of products from manufacturer to wholesaler. The products are usually bought in large quantities (bulk), which the wholesaler then sells (at a profit), usually in smaller quantities.

WJEC Welsh Joint Education Committee (Cyd-Bwyllgor Addysg Cymru).

XY

Yarn A thread made from spinning fibres.

Z

Zest The thin, outer skin of citrus fruits, containing flavoured oils.

Index

adhesives 101
advertising 86
air brush 87–91, 140
alloys 94
analysis, needs 14
anthropometrics 20, 172–3
appearance 20, 92, 155
appliqué 167
appropriate technology 133–4

batch production 132
belts 121
bending 123–4
brainstorming 10–11, 88
brief 14
bubblecharts 5, 11–12
business matters 130–2
buttons 163

cams 119
capital energy sources 126
carding 158
case studies
    air brush 87–91
    bird table 63–5
    local history guide 79–82
    map holder 75–8
    soya food 83–7
cashflow 132
casting 115
catalogue illustrations 37
ceramics 10
chains 121
charts 36, 45–6
checklists 187–93
chemical preservatives 151
circuit diagrams 137
circuits, electronic 176–9
closed-loop system 129
co-operative projects 3, 52
colour 30, 139–40, 155
comfort 20
communicating ideas 27–35, 143
community groups 3–4
competitions, design 4
compression 123–4
Computer Numerical Control 73–4
computers
    computer-aided drawing 32
    control systems 73–4
    databases 66–8
    desktop publishing 72
    graphics 71
    models/simulations 72, 143
    software packages 70
    spreadsheets 68–70, 71
    textile design 169–70
construction 137, 159
control systems 73–4, 129–30
cooking 147
copyright laws 37

corrosion resistance 92
costs 20
    checklist 188
    energy 128–9
    estimation 24, 26, 62
    problems 52
    spreadsheets 69
cramps 111
cranks 119
crochet 159
cutting tools 108–9

data sheets 171–81
databases 66–8
decoration, fabrics 167–8
deforming 117
density 92
design
    brief 14, 63, 83
    competitions 4
    folio 14, 38–40
    specification 18–19, 58
    textiles 168–9
desktop publishing 72
details checklist 190
diaries 43
diet 145–6, 155
drawing
    aids 35
    computer-aided 32
    exploded 33, 137
    freehand 27–8
    highlighting 29–31, 140
    systems 138–9
    working 185
drills 110, 114
drying, food 150
dyeing, fabrics 166–7

efficiency 123
electrical properties 92
electrical symbols 175
electronic
    circuits 137, 176–9
    symbols 175
embroidery 167
enamelling 106
energy 126–9
    conversion 127
    costs 128–9
    sources 134
    storing 128
engineering design 135, 137
enterprise projects 3
environment 20
    design 135, 137
    impact 134
equipment 108–14
    computer-controlled 73–4
    food preparation 152–4
    textiles 161

ergonomics 20, 88, 174
evaluating work 54–65, 75, 91
    checklist 192
exhibition stand 135–6, 143
exploded drawings 33, 137

fabrication 116
fabrics
    construction 159
    decoration 167–8
    dyeing 166–7
    finishes 160
    joining 162–3
    painting 165
    printing 165
    properties 160
fasteners, textiles 163–4
fats 144
felting 159
ferrous metals 93
fibres 156–7
finishes 105–7, 160
fixed costs 69
flow charts 45–6
food 10
    balanced meals 155
    basic recipes 180–1
    characteristics 146
    dietary preferences/needs 145–6
    groups 144–5
    hygiene 149–50
    legislation 150, 155
    measuring 152
    nutrient content 148–9, 155
    planning projects 47
    preparation equipment 152–4
    preserving 147, 150–1
    properties 146–7
    soya 83–7
    testing products 56–7
forces 123–6
framed structures 124
freehand drawing 27–8
freezing food 150–1

gears 119, 121–2, 122
glues 101
graphic media 10, 135–43
graphics 71, 80, 87, 141–2
group projects 2, 52
guidance sheets 182–6

hardness 92
hardwoods 95
heating, preserving food 151
hinges 104
holding tools 111
hole-making tools 110
hooks and eyes 164
hygiene, food 149–50

Index

ideas 21–7
    communicating 27–35, 143
    developing 26, 29, 75–7, 90
    recording 10–13
    selecting 24–6
income energy sources 126
index cards 13
individual projects 1–2
industrial design 136
information
    design 135
    graphics 141–2
    presentation 36–7
    requirements 15
    sources 182
information technology 66–74, 169–70
integrated circuits 179
iron 93
irradiation 151
isometric drawings 33, 138

knitting 159, 170
knockdown fittings 105

lacquering 106
lathes 114
legislation, food 150, 155
letter writing 184–5
lettering 31–2
levers 119
local history guide 79–82
logo 142

machine tools 113–14
macramé 159
manufactured boards 97, 105
manufacturing processes 23–4, 47–8, 50–1, 75, 115–18
map holder 75–8
maps 141
market, establishing 131
market forms 100
marketing 86, 131
marking-out tools 112
mass production 132
materials 9–10, 92–107
    availability 52
    choosing 23–4, 26, 49
    food 147
    properties 92
    selection chart 92
measurement
    anthropometric 172–3
    everyday objects 171
    food 152
    recreational items 172
mechanical advantage 122
mechanical fixings 103–4
mechanisms 119–23
metals 9–10, 93–4, 100
minerals 144
mistakes 39–40
mock-ups 34
modelling 143
models 34–5, 72, 77, 81, 136
moment 125
motion 120–2
moulding 115

nails 103
natural fibres 156
needs 134
    analysing 14–15
    food 145–6
    identifying 1–17, 75
non-ferrous metals 94
notes 31–2
nutrients 144–5, 148–9, 155
nuts and bolts 104

oils 144
one-off production 132
open-loop systems 129
opportunities, identifying 1–17
optical properties 92
outlines 29, 30

paint 106–7, 165
patchwork 167–8
performance 19–20
personalisation 39
perspective 28–9, 139
photocopiers 37
photographs 34–5
pictorial techniques 139–41
planning 39, 41–51, 75
    checklist 191
    schedules 43–4
planometric projection 138
plastics 9, 98–9, 100, 106
plating 106
pre-assessment checklist 193
presentation
    first ideas 23
    food 155
    information 36–7, 62–3
    techniques 139–41
preserving food 147, 150–1
press studs 164
primary research 15, 36
printed circuits 176–9
printing, fabrics 165
priorities, identification 19–21
problems 52–3, 89, 189
product
    analysis 61–2
    evaluation 54–65, 78
    identity 142
    testing 59–60, 75, 85, 90, 186–7
production drawings 26–7
production methods 132
profits, calculation 131–2
programming, control language 74
projects
    choice 1, 3–8
    starting 14–17, 51–3
    types 1–8
properties
    fabrics 160
    fibres 156–7
    food 146
    materials 92
protein 144
prototype 77–8
pulleys 119, 121

questionnaires 36, 183

recipes 180–1
recording ideas 10–13
reliability 19
religion, diet 145–6
research 15, 36–7, 75, 88, 182
rivets 104
rotary motion 120–1
rough designs 141

safety 19, 26
saws 108–9, 113
scale models 143
schedules, planning 43–4
school-focused projects 8
screw mechanism 119
screws 103–4
seams 163
secondary research 15, 36
semiology 141–2
sewing machines 162, 169
shading 30

shaping tools 108–9
shear 123–4
simulations 72
skills 8
slippage chart 45
society 74, 132–4
software packages 70
softwoods 96
soldering 102
soya food 83–7
specification 18–19, 58, 75–6
    checklist 187
spidergrams 11–12
spinning 158
spreadsheets 68–70, 71
sprockets 121
starch 144
steel 93
stiffness 92
storing energy 128
story boards 46
strength 92
structures 123–6
struts 124
survey findings 62–3, 84
symbols 142
    electrical 175
    maps 141
synthetic fibres 157
systems
    computer-controlled 74–5
    control 129–30
    drawing 138–9

technical drawing 136–7
temperature, food 150–1
tension 123–4
testing 55–7, 59, 75, 85, 186–7
textiles 10, 156–70
    information technology 169–70
    tools 161
texture, food 155
thermal properties 92
thermoplastics 98
thermosets 99
third-angle projection 136
ties 124
timber 9, 95–7, 100
time, organising 41, 52
time-delay circuits 177
tone 139–40
tools 108–14, 161
toughness 92
transistor switching circuits 176–7
triangle of forces 125–6
twisting 123–4

vacuum packing 151
variable costs 69
varnishing 107
velcro 164
velocity ratio 122
vices 111
vitamins 144–5

wants 134
wasting 118
water 145
weaving 159
welding 102
word processing 66
work 122, 126, 129
working drawings 26–7, 185
writing 31–2

yarn 158

zip fasteners 164